EMERGENCY POWERS IN THEORY AND PRACTICE

Emergency Powers in Theory and Practice

The Long Shadow of Carl Schmitt

MICHAEL HEAD
Western Sydney University, Australia

Routledge
Taylor & Francis Group
LONDON AND NEW YORK

First published 2016 by Ashgate Publishing

2 Park Square, Milton Park, Abingdon, Oxfordshire OX14 4RN
711 Third Avenue, New York, NY 10017

Routledge is an imprint of the Taylor & Francis Group, an informa business

First issued in paperback 2017

British Library Cataloguing in Publication Data
A catalogue record for this book is available from the British Library.

Library of Congress Cataloging-in-Publication Data
Head, Michael, 1952– author.
Emergency powers in theory and practice : the long shadow of Carl Schmitt / by Michael Head.
pages cm
Includes bibliographical references and index.
ISBN 978-1-4094-4610-1 (hardback)
1. War and emergency powers. 2. Schmitt, Carl, 1888–1985—Influence. I. Title.
K3344.H43 2015
342'.062–dc23

2015025287

ISBN 978-1-4094-4610-1 (hbk)
ISBN 978-0-8153-9344-3 (pbk)

Contents

Preface

This book probes the following question: Why have the early years of the twenty-first century seen increasing use of emergency-type powers or claims of supra-legal executive authority, particularly by the Western countries regarded as the world's leading democracies, notably the United States?

It also examines in some detail the extraordinary range of executive and prerogative powers, emergency legislation, martial law provisos, indemnities and exceptional modifications to criminal law processes in several comparable countries with English-derived legal systems, primarily the United Kingdom, the United States and Australia.

This volume challenges efforts by various legal and academic theorists to relativise, rationalise, legitimise or propose supposedly safe limits for the use of, emergency powers, especially following the September 2001 terrorist attacks and subsequent terrorist-linked incidents.

The book's focus shifted somewhat in writing. From the original title, *Emergency Powers: Theory and Reality*, the title became *Emergency Powers in Theory and Practice: The Long Shadow of Carl Schmitt*. While the volume still provides a survey of emergency law and the expanding resort to exceptional powers, and a critique of the politico-legal theories that have sought to address the issue, it became increasingly clear that a central question had to be tackled: the promotion and even rehabilitation of Carl Schmitt.

Why is Schmitt, the best-known champion of 'exceptional' dictatorial powers during the post-1919 Weimar Republic in Germany – and who later enthusiastically served and sanctified the Nazi dictatorship – being elevated to centre stage? Why are arguments being made that his totalitarian doctrines have much to offer modern society? Why are his views reverberating within the political and judicial establishment?

Another factor that arose during the writing of the book was a new series of declarations of states of emergency, notably within the United States. Eruptions of social unrest, featuring protests against police killings, triggered emergency decrees in Ferguson, Missouri, in 2014, and Baltimore, Maryland, in 2015. President Barack Obama, also in 2015, declared a 'national emergency' to deal with what he termed 'the unusual and extraordinary threat to the national security and foreign policy of the United States' posed by the Venezuelan government. Clearly, the analysis developed in this volume had to take account of these remarkable and portentous developments.

Hopefully, this book will form part of a four-part contribution. It augments my *Crimes Against the State* (2011), which reviewed in detail the range of criminal offences that governments use to protect themselves against perceived political or existential threats – subversion, rebellion, treason, mutiny, espionage, sedition, terrorism, riot and unlawful assembly.

The present volume also helps complete the picture, presented in my previous writings, such as *Calling Out the Troops* (2009), of military call-out measures, some of which rely on emergency powers.

One major pressing issue remains to be addressed – the powers to declare war, both in domestic and international law. With an escalating series of wars, predominantly led by the United States, especially since 2001, and war preparations being made by the US and its allies against China and Russia, these powers require critical attention.

My thanks, as always, go to my darling wife Mary and our four remaining children – Clayton, Tom, Daniel and Kathleen – for their understanding and forbearance during the researching and writing of the book. I am grateful to my wonderful colleagues and students at the University of Western Sydney for their encouragement and intellectual insights, and to Alison Kirk, the wise and helpful law and legal studies publisher at Ashgate Publishing, for her support and assistance.

This volume is dedicated to the memory of Lincoln Wimbus, my stepson, who regrettably passed away on 19 July 2012. He was too good for this world.

Michael Head
Western Sydney University

Introduction
Emergency Powers and the Shadow of Carl Schmitt

This book challenges prevailing views in legal, political and academic circles about both the practice and theory of emergency powers. It does so in the context of rising use of emergency and other executive powers, particularly, but not only, under the banner of the endless 'war on terrorism'.

This volume also examines the lengthening shadow of Carl Schmitt, the best-known legal scholar of the Weimar Republic in Germany, who later sanctified the Nazi dictatorship. It poses the question: Why are Schmitt's views being echoed in the corridors of power, including within the judiciary? Why are efforts underway to rehabilitate Schmitt and argue that his totalitarian doctrines have much to offer contemporary society? After all, Schmitt's service to Hitler flowed logically from his endeavours to bolster the Weimar order against the developing threat of working-class discontent amid the worsening impact of the Great Depression of the 1930s.

The early years of the twenty-first century have seen increasing resort to emergency-type powers or claims of supra-legal executive authority, including by the Western countries regarded as the world's leading democracies, notably the United States. These powers have been invoked for a range of purposes, including: to conduct military interventions; combat alleged terrorist activities; control social and industrial unrest; and counteract financial breakdowns and bankruptcies. These trends point to an underlying shift to more totalitarian methods of rule, which this book argues are bound up with preparations for war, further economic crises, deepening austerity programmes and political disaffection.

One prominent aspect of this creeping authoritarianism is that, both globally and domestically, the indefinite supposed 'war on terrorism' declared by the US government in 2001 has set far-reaching precedents which have already been used to justify practices such as overturning legal and constitutional proscriptions against torture, detention without trial and extrajudicial executions.

The abrogation of legal norms traditionally associated with the 'rule of law' has not stopped there. On the broader pretext of protecting 'national security', core principles such as freedom from warrantless searches and eavesdropping by government have also been cast aside. Largely also on the pretence of protecting ordinary people against terrorism, mass electronic surveillance – directed against millions of ordinary people – has been instituted, notably by the US National Security Agency (NSA) and its global 'Five Eyes' partners in the UK, Canada, Australia and New Zealand.

'Counter-terrorism' and 'national security' are not the only justifications. Eruptions of social unrest, including protests against police killings and violence, have triggered declarations of states of emergency in the name of protecting public safety and welfare, such as those imposed on the city of Ferguson in St Louis County, Missouri, in 2014, and the city of Baltimore in 2015.

Amid the ongoing impact of the global economic breakdown that began in 2008, governments have also used emergency powers to suppress strikes and protests against the cutting of wages, the destruction of jobs and other severe austerity measures being dictated by the finance houses and international financial institutions. Three examples during 2012 and 2013 occurred in Greece, Egypt and Canada.

Emergency financial powers have also been asserted in various countries to justify exceptional measures to rescue the economic system from financial breakdown, inflict social spending cuts or demand the elimination of previous entitlements, such as public sector job security or retirement benefits. Two notable examples, discussed below, occurred in Australia and in the United States city of Detroit. These instances point to another dimension in emergency powers: the use of purported emergency measures to prop up businesses, as with the Australian stimulus packages of 2008–09, or impose social and economic cuts, such as the decimation of city workers' pensions in Detroit in 2013–14.

Far from providing any protection against the expansion of arbitrary executive power, the judiciary has been complicit in it. In repeated instances, courts have dismissed applications by victims, or their families, to challenge these practices or seek redress. Many case studies in this book illustrate the extent to which judges have shielded governments from legal accountability. Despite paying lip service to the 'rule of law', the judiciary has substantially facilitated, and blocked scrutiny of, the adoption of arguably unlawful or lawless measures – such as secret 'renditions' of detainees to be tortured and assassinations by remote control, via drones, without any trial or due process.

Nevertheless, resort to emergency powers has become a major political and legal issue since 2001, generating intense public debate and opposition as well as academic attention. New terms such as 'legal black holes', 'grey holes' and 'rendition' have entered the legal and political lexicon. While this debate initially focused on the implications of the 'war on terrorism', it has since extended to other contexts, including financial breakdown; environmental and natural disasters; and political, social and industrial convulsions.

This volume examines in some detail the range of executive and prerogative powers, emergency legislation, martial law provisos and modifications to criminal law processes in several comparable countries with English-derived legal systems, primarily the United Kingdom, the United States and Australia.

It refutes claims by some legal theorists that resort to arbitrary, potentially dictatorial powers, invoked on the pretext of responding to dire and existential emergencies, has steadily been eliminated over the past century in the countries regarded as advanced democracies. In the three such countries examined in most detail – the US, the UK and Australia – in addition to far-reaching emergency legislation of various kinds, great care has been taken within the political and judicial establishment to preserve potential recourse to authoritarian forms of rule from earlier periods, such as executive orders, royal prerogative powers and martial law. Moreover, emergency powers have been invoked with wide implications in these countries since the turn of the century.

This volume calls into question efforts by legal and academic theorists to relativise, rationalise, legitimise or propose supposedly safe limits to the use of emergency powers, particularly in the wake of the September 2001 terrorist attacks and subsequent terrorist-linked incidents. None of these jurisprudential exercises acknowledge the depth and vast implications of the powers invoked, such as, for example, to incarcerate people indefinitely without trial, torture detainees, or arbitrarily execute citizens via drone assassinations. At the same time, they all have great difficulty in differentiating the resort to emergency powers in the first years of the twenty-first century from the doctrines enunciated last century by Schmitt.

Governments are adopting extraordinary provisions, arguably of a legal, semi-legal, extra-legal or non-legal character – often suspending or overriding the traditional legal framework – as well as basic or constitutional protections of legal and democratic rights. In many cases, the measures are justified by, or associated with, alleged threats to 'national security'. That concept has proven to be ill-defined and susceptible to political exploitation.

Lessons of History

The significance of these trends can be assessed only by placing them in an historical context. Despite arguments that 'everything changed' on 9/11, history demands a highly sceptical approach to such claims. These considerations explain the structure of the book, which begins with an examination of the historical record – from the Roman Republic to the installation of Hitler and beyond.

One lesson of history is that emergency powers are often associated with war. Both World War I and II produced broad-ranging instances, including large-scale internments of foreign-born residents and bans on anti-war activities and dissident political parties. Already, the twenty-first century has generated a series of wars, such as those in Afghanistan, Iraq, Libya, Syria, Gaza and Ukraine, and another global war is a distinct possibility.

This volume does not seek to examine the related, but substantial, issue of domestic powers to declare or conduct war. Declarations of war, or commitments of troops without formal declarations, can be regarded themselves as expressions of emergency powers. They also have many implications for the domestic assertion of exceptional powers. Yet, they fall beyond the scope of this book. Nor does it examine the international law of war, which may also have consequences for emergency measures adopted during military conflicts. The focus of this work is on domestic emergency measures, although it examines, in Chapter 10, the manifest failure of international human rights law to constrain emergency powers.

The connection between war and totalitarianism was depicted graphically last century in dystopian form by George Orwell. Three decades on from 1984, the year immortalised by Orwell (Orwell 2003), many features that he anticipated – thought crimes, guilt by association, arbitrary detentions and Big Brother is watching – seem to be present. Essential protections against tyranny are being subverted in the name of human security.

Life in Orwell's imaginary Oceania was dominated by posters featuring the moustachioed face of a dictator: 'It was one of those pictures which are so contrived that the eyes follow you about when you move. BIG BROTHER IS WATCHING YOU, the caption beneath it ran' (Orwell 2003: 3). Regular police patrols, snooping into people's windows, were not the primary threat to freedom of political thought: 'Only the Thought Police mattered', because every whispered conversation could be detected by a telescreen (Orwell 2003: 4–5). Winston Smith wrote: 'Thoughtcrime does not entail death: thoughtcrime IS death' (Orwell 2003: 33). Those suspected of harbouring opposing thoughts routinely disappeared without any official explanation.

At first light, it may seem an exaggeration to assert that similar processes are under way in today's political and legal climate. We do not have ubiquitous posters of government leaders, figuratively watching our every move. But, thanks to the courageous efforts of whistleblowers like Julian Assange, Bradley (Chelsea) Manning and Edward Snowden, broad masses of people know that their every electronic communication is monitored and are now aware of some of the crimes and abuses being conducted by governments behind the scenes.

In summary, this work examines, and places in historical context, the resurgence of emergency measures during the opening years of the twenty-first century in response to 9/11; the wars in Afghanistan, Iraq, Libya, Syria and Ukraine; the global financial crisis; climate change; recurring natural disasters; social and political unrest; and revolutionary upheavals. In particular, it will ask whether emergency powers adopted in the name of the 'war on terrorism' provide precedents to be extended to cover a broader range of nominated threats to society.

To some extent, this book augments my *Crimes Against the State* (Head 2011), which reviews in detail the range of what are generally classified as crimes against the state or against the nation – subversion, rebellion, treason, mutiny, espionage, sedition, terrorism, riot and unlawful assembly. Whereas *Crimes Against the State* examines 'offences', this volume examines 'powers' – and also the complementarities between the two.

This volume is necessary to complete the picture drawn in *Crimes Against the State* of the powers of last resort in the hands of the political establishment and the authorities to defend the existing legal and political order against perceived serious security and political threats. The book also adds an essential dimension to my previous writings, such as *Calling Out the Troops* (Head 2009), on military call-out powers, some of which rely on emergency powers.

Flawed Theoretical Frameworks

Even before the turn of the century, there was evidence of a global trend toward the adoption and implementation of emergency powers. By 1996, at least 147 countries had constitutional provisions allowing for states of emergency. In 1978, an estimated 30 countries were in some form of state of emergency; in 1986 the number was 70. That trend intensified after 2001.

This book critically examines recent scholarly attempts to develop theoretical frameworks to justify, while sometimes calling into question, the turn to emergency powers. In particular, it reviews and debates Gross and Ní Aoláin, *Law in Times of Crisis*; the essays in Ramraj, *Emergencies and the Limits of Legality*; and Agamben, *State of Exception*; and their efforts to deal with the assertions of Schmitt, whose Weimar Republic period writings on a theory of exception helped pave the way for Nazism.

A common problem with these works is that they take as their starting point the continuation or re-establishment of the existing political and legal order, and discuss how to accommodate the resort to emergency rule. There is also little examination of the actual, often violent, measures adopted to restore order; why these extraordinary practices were employed; or the underlying implications for democracy. In particular, they lack an examination of the socio-economic foundations and class character of the relevant ruling elites.

In general, these works make a number of underlying assumptions:

- That the recourse to emergency or extra-legal powers is a temporary response to a particular perceived threat to the established order, rather than a more long-term and systemic tendency to turn to more authoritarian forms of rule.
- That the existing Western states are democratic, and ultimately subject to the will of ordinary people, rather than increasingly plutocratic states, scarred by a widening gulf between the rich and poor, and ultimately dominated by the interests and power of a wealthy corporate elite.
- That the state itself, and its apparatus of enforcement – police, intelligence, military and judicial agencies – is a neutral institution, dedicated to serving the needs of society as a whole, rather than an instrument of rule serving the interests of the most powerful class: the capitalist class.
- That the judiciary, in particular, functions as an independent arbiter, bound by law, even if it does not always acquit itself steadfastly or courageously, rather than being part of the mechanism of governing society in the interests of the ruling elite.
- That the executive too is a distinct legal entity, such as a president, prime minister or cabinet, with its own inherently institutional composition and interests; and that, while it may be susceptible to aggregation and abuse of power, it is not also a vehicle for the financial and corporate interests that dominate the economic life of the planet.
- That 'national security' is a concept that, although subject to misuse, is likewise an expression of the needs and interests of society as a whole, rather than those of the prevailing economic powers that be.
- That the 'rule of law' is similarly a neutral phenomenon, rather than one that can not only accommodate and legitimise dictatorial measures, but also mask and magnify social inequality and the imbalance in power between those at the top and bottom of society.

The Embrace of the 9/11 Paradigm

As a rule, these works also accept the 9/11 framework: that is, the claim that the terrorist attacks in New York and Washington on September 11, 2001 represented a genuinely new political and security paradigm that required an adjustment, perhaps even a fundamental adjustment, to the legal system. In the first place, the events of 9/11 themselves are accepted uncritically, both as to their historic origins and antecedents and, more immediately, how they were able to be carried out. Secondly, the executive responses to 9/11 are stripped out of their political context. No reference is made to the deeper factors involved.

Under the doctrine first enunciated by President George W. Bush's administration, the 'war on terror' is an endless state of war. By definition, it has no time limits or boundaries. 'Terrorism' is not a tangible enemy, or even an ideological or political cause. It is, at most, a set of tactics to which resort can be had by a multitude of disaffected political currents. Whoever is perceived, or depicted, as a threat to the political and economic system can be branded as terrorist. First it was Al Qaeda, then the Islamic State of Iraq and Syria (ISIS), both of which had murky connections to Western and Western-backed intelligence agencies. In the coming period, opponents of the predatory wars being conducted on the pretext of fighting terrorism may be labelled as terrorist supporters or sympathisers. Next, those opposing social spending cuts, job losses and other austerity measures may be tarred with that brush.

Moreover, the collapse of the reasons used to justify the United States-led invasion of Iraq – 'weapons of mass destruction' and Saddam Hussein's supposed links to Al Qaeda-backed terrorism – suggest that lies were told to divert attention away from the real motives of the 'war on terror', both domestically and internationally. The Middle East and Central Asia, as is well known, contain the largest proven concentrations of oil and natural gas reserves in the world. The outrages in New York and Washington provided the pretext for the implementation of plans prepared much earlier – during the 1990s – for the conquest of Afghanistan and Iraq (Bacevich 2002).

The report of the US national commission investigating the terrorist attacks of September 11 was filled with criticisms of the Bush and Clinton administrations and the performance of the government agencies responsible for intelligence, and national security emergency response. But the commission attributed all of these failures to incompetence, mismanagement or 'failure of imagination'. The fundamental premise of its investigation was that the CIA, the FBI, the US military and the Bush White House acted in good faith (The 9/11 Commission 2004). The report thus excluded, *a priori*, the most important question raised by the events of 9/11: did US government agencies permit – or even assist – the carrying out of this terrorist atrocity in order to provide the Bush administration with the necessary justification to carry out its programme of war in Central Asia and the Middle East and a huge build-up of forces of state repression at home?

For all their claims to be introducing democracy to the Middle East by removing governments in Afghanistan and Iraq, Washington and its allies have for decades financially, diplomatically and militarily propped up dictatorships like the Saudi monarchy and Gulf kingdoms in the interests of controlling access to the region's oil wealth (Shalom 1993: 63–88). Equally, the claims of exporting democracy are belied by the erosions of legal and democratic rights at home.

All the various definitions of terrorism adopted since 2001 are so broad and vague, and politically loaded, that they have given governments and their security agencies considerable scope to persecute and criminalise political dissenters and government opponents. Legitimate protests, acts of civil disobedience and industrial action could be targeted under these provisions. Although the measures were initially used against alleged Islamic fundamentalists, supporters of other causes not favoured by the Western powers have found themselves accused of terrorism, including Kurdish and Sri Lankan Tamil separatists.

In 2010, some leading US politicians called for WikiLeaks founder Julian Assange to be treated as a 'terrorist' for disseminating leaked diplomatic cables that revealed US involvement in illegal spying, wars of aggression, coup plots, assassinations and other crimes. A wider range of groups could be subjected to prosecutions in the future, particularly in the event of intense unrest and protests over austerity measures imposed because of the global financial crisis that began in 2008.

In most Western states – notably the three leading participants in the United States-led 'coalition of the willing' that invaded Iraq in 2003 – the alleged threat of terrorism has been used, particularly since September 2001, as a pretext to make far-reaching inroads into basic democratic rights, including free speech; freedom of political association protections against arbitrary detention; and the right to open and public trial for any serious offence.

Despite criticisms by civil liberties groups, both the British and American governments introduced an array of measures, including detention without trial and proscription of organisations (Hancock 2002: 2–8). Amnesty International condemned the Bush administration for breaching the International Covenant on Civil and Political Rights and other international protocols against arbitrary detention and inhuman treatment of prisoners. In Australia, legislation has been introduced to substantially increase the surveillance, detention and proscription powers of the government and its security and intelligence agencies. Like its US and UK counterparts, the Australian legislation has four fundamental features. It (1) defines terrorism in vague terms; (2) permits the banning of political groups; (3) allows for detention without trial; and (4) shrouds the operations of the intelligence and police agencies in secrecy and provides for semi-secret trials (Head 2002b, 2004, 2012).

The inroads into basic rights include the creation of extensive surveillance over citizens, as laid partially bare by the revelations of US National Security Agency (NSA) whistleblower Edward Snowden. His continuing flow of leaked documents demonstrates that the NSA and its 'Five Eyes' partners – the intelligence agencies of Britain, Canada, Australia and New Zealand – are compiling ever-growing databases on the social, political and cultural affiliations of millions of people. The 'security agencies' are collecting virtually every type of data in existence, and analysing and disseminating it throughout the state apparatus, where it can be used for politically repressive purposes (Greenwald 2014).

Even before Snowden's revelations, it was clear that ominous changes were being made to the state apparatus. In 2010, the *Washington Post* conducted an investigation into the scale of the US domestic intelligence apparatus built up since the 9/11 terrorist attacks. The project concluded that the federal government was carrying out the collection and integration of personal information on hundreds of thousands, and potentially millions, of Americans, most of whom had committed no criminal offence and were not engaged in anything that could reasonably be considered 'terrorism'. A total of 4,058 federal, state and local organisations had 'counterterrorism' functions, with one-quarter of these either newly created since 9/11 or involved in counter-terrorist activities for the first time since then.

US police agencies were deploying technologies tested on the battlefields of Iraq and Afghanistan and using them to monitor and target American citizens. State and local police agencies were monitoring legal political activities, including protests over environmental, immigration and other issues, and filing reports with counterterrorism 'fusion centres' in the 50 states. The *Washington Post* report drew attention to an aspect of the connection between the foreign and domestic features of the 'war on terrorism'. It noted: 'The special operations units deployed overseas to kill the al-Qaeda leadership drove technological advances that are now expanding in use across the United States' (Priest and Arkin 2010).

Posing the Wrong Questions

One of the most extensive works on emergency powers, Gross and Ní Aoláin's *Law in Times of Crisis*, set out to examine 'the quandaries posed by defining and structuring responsible responses to crises', whether arising from 'wars against external enemies' or 'violent movements within their own borders' (Gross and Ní Aoláin 2006: 1). From the outset of the work, therefore, the phenomenon of emergency rule was presented from the standpoint of finding the most credible means of justifying or rationalising the resort to authoritarian methods, not from that of opposing or overthrowing the ruling elites that have imposed the measures. According to this approach, the crucial questions are:

> How to allow government sufficient discretion, flexibility, and powers to meet crises while maintaining limitations and control over governmental actions so as to prevent or at least minimize the danger that such powers would be abused? How to allow government to act responsibly, i.e., 'with sufficient vigor to meet the nation's challenges, but without intruding on protected liberties' ([Tushnet 2005: 2673]? How to balance security and liberty? These questions are as ancient as the Roman republic and as new as the realities wrought by the terrorist attacks on London's public transportation system on July 7 and July 21, 2005. (Gross and Ní Aoláin 2006: 1–2)

Emergencies were depicted ahistorically and abstractly, without raising the question of the socio-economic and class character of the regimes involved, or the underlying historical contexts in which they arose and fell. The sources and agendas of the 'wars against external enemies' and the causes and aims of the allegedly 'violent movements within their own borders' were not identified as vital issues to be considered. False dichotomies, such as 'how to balance security and liberty', imply that 'liberty' must be curtailed or subordinated, to some extent or other, to 'security', however that is defined or interpreted by ruling establishments.

Further, Gross and Ní Aoláin drew an arbitrary distinction between 'democratic' and 'authoritarian' regimes. They focused their book on 'democracies', as 'authoritarian regimes are not faced with the tragic choices that violent emergencies present to democracies' because for them 'security is everything and liberty does not count for much' (Gross and Ní Aoláin 2006: 3). This dichotomy leaves a myriad questions unanswered. The most obvious is: how is democracy defined?

The authors assumed, as if it were axiomatic, that contemporary capitalist nation-states like the United States, the United Kingdom and the Western European countries are democracies with 'liberal democratic values' with 'democratic, constitutional orders'. They cited, with seeming approval, the Cold War-era assertion of Carl Friedrich, a Harvard University political science professor, that the tension between national security and civil rights and liberties arises 'wherever a constitutional order of the libertarian kind has been confronted with the Communist challenge, and with the Fascist response to that challenge' (Gross and Ní Aoláin 2006: 3, citing Friedrich 1957: 13).

This stance raises serious political issues. *First*, are these countries, exemplified by the United States, which emerged from World War II and the Cold War as the world's dominant economic and military power, democracies in any meaningful sense? Is democracy compatible with a system in which handfuls of billionaires monopolise society's wealth, giving them an extraordinary grip over both the economic and political levers of power?

In 2015, the international charity Oxfam issued a report on social inequality showing that the gap between the super-rich and the majority of society was not only not shrinking – it was growing at an ever-faster pace. In 2013, the 92 richest multi-billionaires had as much wealth as the bottom 50 per cent of society. In 2014, this figure dropped to 80 billionaires. In other words, a group of people who could fit into a single train carriage controlled more wealth than 3.5 billion people, equivalent to the combined populations of China, India, the United States and the European Union. Inequality was growing at such a rapid pace that the richest 1 per cent would control more wealth than the bottom 99 per cent of society by 2016 (Oxfam 2015).

To take another indicator, the combined net worth of the world's billionaires reached a new high in 2015 of $7.05 trillion, according to *Forbes* magazine. There were a record 1,826 billionaires, each with an average wealth of $3.8 billion (Forbes 2015). Not surprisingly, the United States, the home of Wall Street and centre of global financial capital, had easily the highest number of billionaires – 536. Billionaires made up an estimated 0.000033 per cent of the world's population. Yet this tiny social layer possessed about 4.5 times the total wealth of the bottom half of the population, or 3.5 billion people. It is quite possible that, on a global scale, society has never been so unequal through thousands of years of human history, including in Roman slave society.

Whatever the pretence of 'one person, one vote', the wealthiest 0.1 per cent dictates policy, assisted by a slightly broader, but still highly privileged and small, section of the population – the top 5 or 10 per cent. Is this not plutocracy? The right to vote means little in political processes dominated by heavily funded corporate-backed political parties. Likewise, freedom of the press means little when the major media outlets are controlled by powerful corporate interests. Moreover, genuine democracy would require mass democratic participation in economic decision-making itself, including control over the transnational finance houses and corporations.

Might not the extreme concentration of wealth require, and go hand in hand with, increasingly repressive forms of rule designed to prevent or suppress the social unrest and political discontent generated by this ever more blatant inequality? Might not this explain the tendency, identified and documented by Gross and Ní Aoláin, for 'exceptional' and 'temporary' emergency measures to become 'normal'?

Second, the world's leading 'democracies' have a record of supporting, and helping to impose, dictatorships in less developed countries in order to further their own geo-strategic and economic interests. This makes it doubly artificial to separate the 'democratic' regimes from the 'authoritarian' ones, ignoring the connections between them. In 2013–14, for example, the United States government quickly established cordial relations with, and resumed multi-billion dollar aid and arms supplies to, the military regime in Egypt in the wake of its coup, even as its courts sentenced hundreds of political opponents to be executed (BBC 2014). This must be added to a long list of countries in which Washington has backed despotic and violent regimes, from the Shah of Iran to General Suharto in Indonesia, General Pinochet in Chile, Presidents Sadat and Mubarak in Egypt and the Saudi royal dynasty (DeConde et al. 2001).

Third, what is the 'communist challenge' invoked by the quote from Friedrich? Despite the ultimate degeneration of the 1917 Russian Revolution into a dictatorship headed by Stalin, a process that reflected the tremendous economic and military pressures on the first isolated workers' state (Trotsky 1991), the stark and worsening inequality of global capitalism means that socialist uprisings are bound to continue among the working people and the poor. Significantly, Friedrich insinuated that the 'Fascist response to that challenge' was only a secondary threat to 'libertarian' constitutional orders. This relativises the barbaric crimes of fascism as a reaction to communism. As a matter of historical record, Hitler was called into office by the German capitalist establishment, and was able to utilise the despotic features of the 1919 Weimar Constitution to cement his totalitarian rule, as examined in Chapter 2.

Types and Typologies of Emergencies

Gross and Ní Aoláin also excluded from their study emergencies that arise from economic crises as well as natural disasters, confining their attention to 'violent crises' such as wars, international armed conflicts, rebellions and terrorist attacks. These are artificial demarcations.

Natural disasters do not necessarily trigger political emergencies; but powers and resources mobilised for catastrophic events such as earthquakes, hurricanes, tsunamis and fires can establish precedents, and acclimatise public opinion, for political exploitation of emergency powers. Moreover, arguments have emerged that climate change, which can intensify natural disasters, is an existential threat that justifies extraordinary measures of an emergency kind.

Economic breakdowns and crises are even more closely related to political disturbances, both because their causes will be attributable, to a greater or lesser extent, to the character of the regime in power. The impact of economic meltdowns will also be felt by entire populations, and may well spark convulsive political struggles that come to threaten the prevailing socio-economic order.

Gross and Ní Aoláin acknowledged that economic crises may lead to governmental demands for broad emergency-style powers to fight off the alleged threat to the nation, and those measures may pave the way for the routine and deleterious use of emergency powers. They referred to President Roosevelt's New Deal measures during the Great Depression of the 1930s, as well as to Article 48 of the Weimar Constitution, which enabled rule by decree amid the fallout from the 1929 Wall Street crash (Gross and Ní Aoláin 2006: 4–5). The authors argued that economic failures may not require the same kind of immediate response as a violent political crisis. Yet catastrophic meltdowns can occur quickly, as happened in 1929 and 2008. Furthermore, their distinction between urgent, temporary crises and more protracted ones cuts across one of their own central theses, that allegedly short-term emergencies have often become transformed into prolonged use of authoritarian measures.

In the wake of the 2008 global economic crisis, 'financial emergencies' have again been advanced as equivalents to wartime threats, or to justify the suspension of democratic processes in order to implement the debt-repayment and austerity requirements of the financial markets.

Several, ostensibly distinct, models have been postulated by academic writers to categorise different approaches to the theory and practice of governmental responses to acute crises. Each of them, however, is premised on similar assumptions about the alleged need to legitimise emergency action, in some way or another, so as to preserve the maximum degree of legality. The typology suggested by Gross and Ní Aoláin consists of four broad classes: (1) models of accommodation; (2) business as usual; (3) the realist school and (4) extra-legal measures. While varying, the descriptors for these four schemas set as their remit the task of best justifying supposedly temporary resort to emergency rule.

Models of accommodation were said to 'countenance a certain degree of accommodation for the pressures exerted on the state in times of emergency, while, at the same time, maintaining normal legal principles and rules as far as possible'. On this view, 'when a nation is faced with emergencies, its legal, and even constitutional, structure must be somewhat relaxed (and perhaps even suspended in parts)'. Such a 'balance', it was claimed, 'enables continued adherence to the principle of the rule of law and faithfulness to fundamental democratic values, while providing the state with adequate measures to withstand the storm wrought by the crisis' (Gross and Ní Aoláin 2006: 9). In other words, the preoccupation is with defending, upholding and legitimising the existing (supposedly democratic) state, even after resort to dictatorial measures.

Business as usual models maintain, somewhat differently, that 'ordinary legal rules and norms continue to be followed strictly with no substantive change even in times of emergency and crisis'. As Gross and Ní Aoláin noted, such models are often criticised 'as being either naive or hypocritical' for disregarding 'the reality of governmental exercise of extraordinary measures and powers in response to emergencies'. Further, Gross and Ní Aoláin acknowledged that both the business as usual models and the models of accommodation are constitutional models. That is, these models rely on 'an assumption of constitutionality that tells us that whatever responses are made to the challenges of a particular exigency, such responses are to be found and limited within the confines of the constitution' (Gross and Ní Aoláin 2006: 10). Such assumptions are also based on bolstering the stability and politico-legal reputation of the existing socio-economic order, by interpreting constitutions as permitting 'necessary' recourse to emergency powers when confronted by supposedly existential threats.

Realist and extra-legal measures models are both said to challenge the assumption of constitutionality. The realist school insists that 'legal rules and norms are too inflexible and rigid to accommodate the security needs of states' and 'democracies have no real conundrum in dealing with emergencies' because the only constraints on government emanate from 'efficiency and limited resources'. Gross and Ní Aoláin dismissed this view as unacceptable 'to those who believe that law matters' (Gross and Ní Aoláin 2006: 11).

Even that school, while more blunt about the underlying political calculations and machinations involved in suppressing threats to the state, is predicated on purportedly restoring a legal and democratic framework once a crisis has been dealt with.

The extra-legal measures model 'suggests that under extreme circumstances, public officials may act extra-legally when they believe that such action is necessary for protecting the nation and the public in the face of calamity, provided that they openly and publicly acknowledge the nature of their actions'. According to this view, the public can subsequently either accept or reject the emergency action. 'Once an extra-legal action is taken, it is then up to the people to decide, either directly or indirectly (e.g., through their elected representatives in the legislature), how to respond to such actions.' This is based on the unrealistic notion that, having cast legality aside, those in power will abide by 'ethical concepts of political and popular responsibility, political morality and candor' (Gross and Ní Aoláin 2006: 11). Moreover, it presumes that 'the people' will still be in a position, unaffected by the authoritarian measures imposed on them, to state and assert their judgement on those holding the economic, political and police-military power.

Each of these models is also based on the assumption that emergency or exceptional powers, including anti-terrorism measures, are exercised temporarily or are temporary departures from the norm. Supposedly, the public can be expected to tolerate extraordinary or dictatorial provisions because these will facilitate a return to normalcy, or at least they will ultimately be replaced by a return to ordinary legal rules and norms.

This premise is false, on numerous levels. In the first place, as the endless 'war on terror' has illustrated, once police-state powers that eviscerate basic legal and democratic rights are imposed, they become permanently institutionalised and, in fact, their features establish precedents for wider use throughout the legal system. Secondly, emergency provisions accumulate and become entrenched, ready for implementation whenever those in power regard their use as politically necessary and feasible, as has happened in the United States since World War II. In the words of a US Senate commission working paper: 'Emergency government has become the norm' (Relyea 1974: v). Thirdly, this creeping authoritarianism can help lay the basis for dictatorial regimes to seize power indefinitely, as happened in Germany during the 1920s and 1930s. Finally, there is a considerable list of countries where emergency rule became the norm for decades during the twentieth and twenty-first centuries, including Iran under the Shah; Indonesia under General Suharto; Chile under General Pinochet; Saudi Arabia under the House of Saud; and Egypt under Presidents Sadat and Mubarak. In each of these instances, the dictatorship was installed or maintained with the backing of Washington and its allies (DeConde et al. 2001).

What is an Emergency?

The short-sightedness of drawing clear lines between 'violent' emergencies and those of a natural or economic kind, points to some of the issues involved in seeking to define a state of emergency. An examination of the academic literature and the relevant legislation in numerous countries underscores two conclusions: the term 'emergency' is said to be, by its very nature, an 'elastic concept' (Lee 1984: 4); and ruling authorities, legislatures and courts prefer to leave it either undefined or as loosely defined as possible. The language employed is 'inherently open-ended and manipulable' (Gross and Ní Aoláin 2006: 6). According to a 1984 report by the International Law Association:

> It is neither desirable nor possible to stipulate *in abstracto* what particular type or types of events will automatically constitute a public emergency within the meaning of the term; each case has to be judged on its merits, taking into account the overriding concern for the continuance of a democratic society. (Gross and Ní Aoláin 2006: 5–6)

The leeway thus afforded to executive governments to define emergencies for themselves is compounded by the prevalence of definitional references to threats to the safety or existence of the 'nation'. This concept asserts a social order unified by common interests, regardless of class or wealth, when, in reality, the 'nation' may consist of diametrically opposed socio-economic forces, one of which is seeking to maintain its grip over society. The American aphorism that the constitution must not be turned into a 'suicide pact' (*Haig v Agee* 453 US 280 at 309–10 (1981)) is redolent with nostrums of surviving, and holding on to power, at all costs.

As will be examined in Chapter 10, international law reserves to the national state the power to override fundamental legal and democratic rights in alleged 'public emergencies' that challenge the stability of the state. These emergency circumstances are often not defined, however, or defined only in open-ended and politically subjective terms. In the Universal Declaration of Human Rights (UDHR), the International Covenant on Civil and Political Rights (ICCPR) and other related instruments – such as the European Convention on Human Rights and Fundamental Freedoms and the UK Human Rights Act – the listed civil and legal rights are mostly subject to far-reaching 'emergency' exemptions.

Article 4 of the ICCPR states that governments may take measures derogating from their obligations under the Covenant 'in time of public emergency which threatens the life of the nation and the existence of which is officially proclaimed', provided that measures are 'strictly required by the exigencies of the situation'. Neither requirement has any meaningful definitional limit. Likewise, governments can derogate from most obligations under the European Convention 'in time of war or other public emergency threatening the life of the nation' (Article 15). Under the European Convention on Human Rights and Fundamental Freedoms even the right to life is carefully circumscribed to permit killing by state forces in order to make arrests, prevent escapes from detention and quell 'riots and insurrections' (Article 2).

The toothless United Nations Human Rights Committee (HRC) has considered few cases challenging derogation under Article 4 of the ICCPR. Its decisions have no binding legal status in any case. Its record has been summed up as follows:

> The HRC has traditionally failed to assess the existence of emergency in certain states and has frequently declined to endorse the principle of proportionality in its examination of state practice … problem emergencies, and specifically permanent emergencies, have always managed to escape the net of thorough examination. (Gross and Ní Aoláin 2006: 302)

The Revival of Carl Schmitt

A striking feature of the opening years of the twenty-first century has been the revival of references, in academic literature, governmental documents and judicial utterances, to conceptions of 'exception' that mirror those of Carl Schmitt (1888–1985). Under doctrines developed by Schmitt, a legal academic who ultimately served the Nazi regime in Germany, urgency can justify a 'state of exception' under which basic legal and democratic rights can be abrogated, the rule of law suspended and the executive branch granted exceptional powers. Schmitt insisted that this facility was not merely a temporary or peripheral feature of a political order, but an inherent and indeed essential characteristic of a viable society.

Schmitt is often cited for his association with Nazism, as the 'crown jurist of the Third Reich' (Frye 1996: 818). However, his doctrine developed more than a decade before the fascist seizure of power in 1933. Moreover, Schmitt's conceptions, fashioned during the formally democratic period of Germany's Weimar Republic, helped clear the path for Hitler, both theoretically and practically.

In a 2011 article, Georgetown law professor David J. Luban noted the growing popularity of the theories of Schmitt in legal academic circles, citing 'five law review references to Schmitt between 1980 and 1990; 114 between 1990 and 2000; and 420 since 2000, with almost twice as many in the last five years as the previous five' (Luban 2011). Other authors have noted a resurgence of interest in Schmitt's concepts in intellectual and political realms (Meier 1988; Muller 2003; Caldwell 2005). One scholar expressed surprise at the fact that so much of the post-9/11 academic debate on the 'war on terrorism' had 'tried to tackle the tasks at hand by relying on the work of Carl Schmitt, twentieth-century Germany's most impressive authoritarian right-wing political thinker' (Scheuerman 2006a: 61).

Within the academic realm, efforts have been made to rehabilitate Schmitt. There have been attempts to either justify his views, or at least relativise them – that is, suggest that they deserve reconsideration as a legitimate response to the political instability of the Weimar Republic and the allegedly twin dangers of fascism and communism. Moreover, it has been claimed that Schmitt has considerable positive 'contemporary relevance' (Salter 2012: 24). In one view: 'It is our claim that Schmitt's legacy cannot be disregarded and that his insights into the nature of law and politics are absolutely worthwhile' (Croce and Salvatore 2013: 9).

Arguments have been made that Schmitt's legal theories must be studied and appreciated in isolation from his 'deplorable' (Salter 2012: 1) or 'appalling' (Croce and Salvatore 2013: 9) 'political choices'. Such references are typically confined to Schmitt's collaboration with the Nazi regime from its inception in 1933. His complicity in the fascist mass murder and barbarism, it has been suggested, was simply an aberration, divorced both from his earlier support for the highly repressive but crisis-wracked Weimar regime and from the authoritarian logic of his legal theorising.

This supposed dichotomy between Schmitt's political views and his jurisprudence flies in the face of the historical record. An earlier study of Schmitt's prolific and enthusiastic Nazi-period writings concluded that 'Schmitt's marriage to Nazism stems immanently from core elements of his jurisprudence' (Scheuerman 1997: 1744). This issue will be examined in Chapter 5.

For now, it is necessary to note that Schmitt's record is an undeniably unsavoury one. Against the backdrop of the instability of the Weimar years, which saw frequent resort to emergency decrees under Article 48 of the Weimar Constitution, which entitled the president to issue such decrees without prior parliamentary consent (see Chapter 2), Schmitt developed increasingly dictatorial conceptions of state rule, based on 'exceptions' and 'emergencies' that justified deviations from the political 'norm'.

Writing in the wake of the German revolution that overthrew the monarchy in 1918 and the bloody suppression of the further socialist revolution in 1919, Schmitt was obsessed with what he viewed as the inherent weakness of liberal democracy. He considered liberalism, particularly as manifested in the Weimar Constitution, to be inadequate to the task of protecting state and society menaced by the great threat of another communist-led revolution by the working class.

Schmitt was not, initially, a fascist. He represented a conservative Catholic wing of the German ruling elite that sought an accommodation with Hitler, or others in the fascist movement, in the hope of averting an absolute handover of power to the Nazis, at least until 1933. Schmitt became a close supporter of a key military figure, General Kurt von Schleicher, who ultimately served as the last German chancellor before Hitler. Like his immediate predecessors, Heinrich Brüning and Franz von Papen, Schleicher conducted a series of authoritarian efforts by the traditional German big business and military establishment to stabilise the capitalist order through repressive means, above all in order to block the communists, while also seeking, if possible, to co-opt or forestall the Nazis (McCormick 1997: 266; Kershaw 1998: 366–423).

In the end, Schleicher's machinations with sections of the Nazis led by Gregor Strasser collapsed in the face of Hitler's intransigence, whereupon President Hindenburg installed Hitler as chancellor to replace him (Kershaw 1998: 366–423). Almost immediately, Schmitt seamlessly became an adviser to the new National Socialist-led coalition, which sought his assistance to help cloak its rapidly developing dictatorship in flimsy legal clothing (McCormick 1997: 266).

Many treatments of Schmitt's doctrines tear them out of this historical context. Schmitt first formulated his theories in the aftermath of the brutal suppression of the January 1919 workers' uprising in Germany. His ideas dovetailed with the ruthless and cynical exploitation of presidential emergency powers, starting in 1919 with the Social Democrat Friedrich Ebert, the first Weimar president (from 1919 to his death in 1925). This background is explored in Chapter 2, and Schmitt's despotic views and political connections are reviewed further in Chapter 5. But at this point a brief summary is necessary.

Schmitt's Politico-Legal Evolution

In 1921, Schmitt became a professor at the University of Greifswald, where he published his essay *Die Diktatur* (On Dictatorship), in which he discussed the foundations of the newly established Weimar Republic. He emphasised the office of the president, which he categorised as a comparatively effective element within the constitution, because of the power granted to the president to declare a state of emergency under Article 48. Schmitt saw this potentially dictatorial power as more in keeping with the underlying mentality of political power than the comparatively slow and ineffective legislative processes. He sought to remove the taboo surrounding the concept of dictatorship by showing that the concept is implicit whenever power is wielded outside the cumbersome channels of parliamentary politics. He insisted that every government capable of decisive action must include a dictatorial element within its constitution. Crises and states of emergency were not exceptional, but the predominant form of the life of modern nations (Scheuerman 2006a).

Die Diktatur was followed by another essay in 1922, titled *Politische Theologie* (Political Theology), which began with Schmitt's notorious definition: 'Sovereign is he who decides on the exception.' Schmitt, then a professor at the University of Bonn, further elaborated his authoritarian theories, expounding the idea of the 'state of exception' (*Ausnahmezustand*). This theory was developed through a jurisprudential critique of 'normativism' in positivist legal thought, which held that law was the expression of general abstract norms applicable in all circumstances. In particular, Schmitt opposed the positivist legal theories of the Austrian legal scholar Hans Kelsen (Schmitt 1985a).

A year later, Schmitt supported the emergence of totalitarian power structures in his paper *Die geistesgeschichtliche Lage des heutigen Parlamentarismus* (roughly: The Intellectual-Historical Situation of Today's Parliamentarianism). He criticised liberal politics, arguing that its faith in rational discussion and openness was at odds with actual parliamentary politics, in which outcomes are hammered out by party leaders in back rooms (Scheuerman 2006a).

In 1926, Schmitt became a law professor at the Handelshochschule in Berlin, where he wrote *Der Begriff des Politischen* (The Concept of the Political), in which he based his concept of state sovereignty on the distinction between friend and enemy. The enemy was anyone who represented a serious threat to one's own interests 'in a specially intense way, existentially something different and alien, so that in the extreme case conflicts with him are possible' (Schmitt 1976: 26–7).

For Schmitt, the key to successful prosecution of warfare against such a foe is *demonisation*. The enemy must be seen as absolute. He must be stripped of all legal rights, of whatever nature. The executive must be free to use whatever tools it can find to fight and vanquish this foe. In Schmitt's classic formulation: 'a total war calls for a total enemy'.

Like many others in German ruling circles, Schmitt regarded the emergence of the United States after World War I as the pre-eminent global power as an unwelcome development, particularly from the standpoint of the aspirations of the German business elite itself to economically dominate Europe.

It was for this standpoint that Schmitt viewed American articulations of international law as fraught with hypocrisy. He saw in American foreign policy in the late nineteenth and early twentieth centuries a menacing new form of imperialism. '[T]his form of imperialism … presents a particular threat to a people forced in a defensive posture, like we Germans; it presents us with the greater threat of military occupation and economic exploitation', he wrote in 1932 in *Die USA und die völkerrechtlichen Formen des modernen Imperialismus* (Schmitt 2005: 365).

Schmitt became a professor at the University of Berlin in 1933, the same year he joined the Nazi Party. Hermann Göring appointed him Prussian State Counsellor, and Schmitt became president of the Union of National-Socialist Jurists in November 1933. He later became a Nazi 'Crown Jurist' (Salter 2012: 13). In October 1936 he publicly became a rabid anti-Semite, calling for German law to be cleansed of the 'Jewish spirit' and for all publications of Jewish scientists to be marked with a small symbol (Scheuerman 1997: 1743). He later had a falling out with sections of the Nazi movement, as a result of which he lost a number of his posts, but he retained his professorship (Scheuerman 1997: 1765).

Under fascism, the political logic of the conceptions advanced by Schmitt, a virulent anti-communist, became clearer. Having asserted that rapid changes in the political situation rendered any legal system built on fixed legal codes unstable, he justified permanently in-built emergency powers. Schmitt supported Hitler's continual suspension of the legal constitutional order during the Third Reich, first with the 28 February 1933 decree on the Reichstag fire, which was falsely attributed to communists, then the suspension being renewed every four years (see Chapter 2).

The Nazi-controlled Reichstag passed 'enabling' legislation declaring that the executive had the power to make laws. The Act, referred to as 'the Act to Relieve the Distress of the People and the Reich', cemented dictatorial power in Germany under Hitler. In line with his previously expressed legal opinions, Schmitt defended the enabling legislation in the *Deutsche Juristen Zeitung*, maintaining that the executive prerogative was unlimited at a time of national crisis (Neumann 1942).

Schmitt's doctrine also supported Hitler's claim of supreme personal authority, which was a logical extension of his assertion, in 1922, that the sovereign 'decides on the state of exception'. Schmitt maintained that 'like every other order the legal order rests on a decision and not a norm'. Sovereignty itself was based on decision and not legality. There could be no 'normative' regulation of exceptional situations.

As the Nazis consolidated power, Schmitt propounded theories in support of the *Führerprinzip* – the leader principle (Scheuerman 1997: 1753). He claimed that the Führer was the highest judge in the nation, from whom there lay no appeal. The leader was the embodiment of the people's will and therefore, Schmitt claimed, 'law is the plan and the will of the leader' ('Fuhrer Schutzt das Recht' in *Positionen und Begriffe*, Berlin 1934).

The practical implications of the theory of exception were demonstrated by Schmitt in the aftermath of the 'Night of the Long Knives' on 30 June 1934. Hitler carried out a bloody purge of suspected dissidents within his own movement, including Hitler's former comrade-in-arms, SA (paramilitary army) boss Ernst Röhm, who was murdered along with dozens of other politicians (including General Schleicher) on Hitler's orders. Schmitt sanctioned the event – involving the murder of several thousand people – as the highest form of administrative justice. Schmitt was quick to praise 'the Führer's deed' in an essay entitled 'The Führer Protects the Law' (Kershaw 1998: 521).

Following this massacre, Hitler and his cabinet promulgated the Law for the Emergency Defence of the State. In a single paragraph it stated: 'The measures taken on 30 June and 1 and 2 July for the suppression of high treasonable and state treasonable acts are, as emergency defence of the state, legal' (Kershaw 1998: 518). The decree could have been scripted from Schmitt's normless theory of exception. Indeed, Schmitt hailed Hitler's measures as expressions of 'genuine jurisdiction' and the 'highest judicial process'. Schmitt rejected any legal enquiry into this act of state terror, since it would be 'destructive of the law and the state' (Neumann 1942).

Significantly, Schmitt was not alone. His embrace of Nazism was emblematic of the response of German academics, many of whom placed themselves at the service of the regime. Notable among them was the well-known philosopher Martin Heidegger, who helped initiate a manifesto of German professors declaring their allegiance to 'Adolf Hitler and the National Socialist State' (Kershaw 1998: 481).

White House Parallels: From Bush to Obama

Contemporary linkages to Schmitt are not confined to academic writings. Appeals to similar conceptions of exception have been made by officials of the George W. Bush and Obama administrations in the United States and by members of the US Supreme Court. Vice President Richard Cheney forthrightly claimed extraordinary executive powers for the Bush administration after 9/11. In a speech several weeks after the terrorist attacks, he declared:

> Homeland security is not a temporary measure just to meet one crisis. Many of the steps we have now been forced to take will become permanent in American life. They represent an understanding of the world as it is, and dangers we must guard against perhaps for decades to come. I think of it as the new normalcy. (Cheney 2001)

In a secret declaration issued by President Bush to leading officials on 7 February 2002, he insisted that he could dispense with international and domestic law in order to detain people indefinitely: '[D]etainees had no inherent protections under the Geneva Convention – the condition of their imprisonment, good, bad, or otherwise, was solely at his discretion' (Scheuerman 2006b: 119).

Various political and legal commentators have pointed out that the practices of the Bush administration mirrored Schmitt's views. Most notably, the legal opinions offered by administration lawyers like John Yoo – sanctioning 'enemy combatant' detention without trial and 'enhanced interrogation techniques' in defiance of the Geneva Conventions and the US Constitution – echo Schmitt's writings (Levinson 2008; Abraham 2007; Kutz 2005; Horton 2005).

These legal memos interpreted the president's authority along the lines of a fundamentally normless legal black hole in which unfettered power holds sway. In a 2002 memorandum to White House Counsel Alberto Gonzales, Jay Bybee, Head of the Justice Department Office of Legal Counsel, declared that 'the President enjoys complete discretion in the exercise of his Commander-in-Chief authority and in conducting operations against hostile forces'. As a result, Bush could discard international and domestic prohibitions on torture during the 'current war against Al Qaeda' (Scheuerman 2006b: 118). Bybee also radically redefined torture as an act accompanied by 'serious physical injury such as death or organ failure', which comes close to murder (Scheuerman 2006b: 118), not 'severe pain or suffering, whether physical or mental' as specified by the international Convention against Torture.

Equally Schmittian was a 13 September 2003 report prepared by US Army Major General Geoffrey Miller, who extended the 'enhanced interrogation' techniques employed at Guantanamo Bay to the US-run Abu Ghraib prison in Iraq. He insisted that the United States needed to 'rapidly exploit internees for actionable intelligence' and 'improve the velocity and operational effectiveness of counterterrorism interrogation' (Scheuerman 2006b: 121). This resonates with Schmitt's view that outright political power can never be constrained by legal means.

Further documented evidence came to light in 2014, when two secret legal memoranda on the subject of National Security Agency (NSA) spying were publicly released as a result of a Freedom of Information Act lawsuit filed by the American Civil Liberties Union. The heavily redacted documents, dating from 2004, were signed by Assistant Attorney General Jack L. Goldsmith, then head of the Justice Department's Office of Legal Counsel, and addressed to the Attorney General, who at that time was John Ashcroft.

The first memorandum (Memorandum for the Attorney General 2004) addressed the NSA's practice of gathering the content of the communications of American citizens through its secret Stellar Wind programme, which was a special unit of the President's Surveillance Program (PSP). The Stellar Wind programme was later enlarged by the Obama administration, which divided it into four separate expanded programmes – one of which was PRISM revealed by NSA whistleblower Edward Snowden in 2013.

The Stellar Wind programme from the start was in violation of the American Bill of Rights, which prohibits searches without a warrant and without evidence of a crime, and which also guarantees the right of the people 'to be secure in their persons, houses, papers, and effects against unreasonable searches and seizures'. The basic argument that Goldsmith employed in favour of the legality of the Stellar Wind programme echoed Schmitt's 'state of exception' theory. Goldsmith argued that the September 11, 2001 attacks created a 'national emergency' that justified ignoring civil liberties.

'On September 14, 2001, the President declared a national emergency', Goldsmith wrote. 'As the President made explicit in his Military Order of November 13, 2001, authorizing the use of military commissions to try terrorists, the attacks of September 11 "created a state of armed conflict", thus activating the president's supposed wartime powers.'

The memorandum referred to the president's 'inherent authority as Commander in Chief and the sole organ of the nation in foreign affairs'. Goldsmith maintained that 'Congress does not have the power to restrict the President's exercise of that authority.'

Schmitt's echo did not cease with the Bush administration, but continued into the Obama administration. During 2012, in an address at Northwestern University Law School in Chicago, US Attorney General Eric Holder painted a picture in which military tribunals and extrajudicial assassinations were permanent, codified features of the American judicial landscape. His speech included an assertion of quasi-dictatorial presidential powers, such as the power of the president to secretly sign death warrants for any person, including US citizens, without any form of judicial review. Holder defended the power of the president to order the abduction and imprisonment of any person, anywhere in the world, and to try that person before a military tribunal (Holder 2012).

The speech was a response to pressure on the administration to provide a legal rationale for the killing of three US citizens by American drone missile strikes in Yemen. On 30 September 2011 the Obama administration assassinated US citizen and alleged Al Qaeda leader Anwar al-Aulaqi (or Awlaki) in Yemen after placing him on a secret 'kill list'. Other

US citizens killed by US missile strikes include Samir Khan and Abdulrahman al-Aulaqi, the 16-year-old son of Anwar al-Aulaqi.

On the subject of assassination, Holder declared that 'our government has the clear authority to defend the United States with lethal force'. He insisted that the president requires no 'judicial approval' to exercise that power. Arguing in favour of the constitutionality of assassination, the Attorney General made a distinction between 'due process' and 'judicial process', saying: 'The Constitution guarantees due process, not judicial process.'

This formulation effectively repudiated the Bill of Rights – the first 10 amendments to the US Constitution, ratified in 1791. The Bill of Rights contains numerous guarantees of judicial process, including the right to a speedy and public trial; the right to an impartial jury; the right to an attorney; the right to exclude evidence obtained through torture or other unlawful means; the right to confront one's accuser; and the right to be free from cruel and unusual punishment.

The Fifth Amendment's guarantee of due process itself – 'No person … shall be deprived of life, liberty, or property, without due process of law' – clearly prohibits extrajudicial assassination.

Holder's distinction between due process and judicial process was an attempt to formulate a pseudo-constitutional rationale for stripping the population of these fundamental legal and democratic rights. The Attorney General also defended the Guantanamo Bay military tribunals, where alleged 'enemy combatants' are detained indefinitely without trial, holding them up as a model. 'I have faith in the framework and promise of our military commissions', he proclaimed.

The implication is that the state can seize people and hold them indefinitely without trial, or kill them, without violating the constitutional requirement of due process. Holder's principal justification for this was the 'war on terror'. He asserted: 'We are a nation at war.' The United States was in an 'hour of danger'.

In reality, the 'war on terror' is a political, legal and propaganda device to justify an expansion of American militarism, starting with the invasions of Afghanistan and Iraq, and a frontal assault on legal and democratic rights. Never declared by Congress, it has no definite objective or end. It is a means of justifying a permanent siege on basic democratic rights in the name of 'national security'.

The 'war on terror' has witnessed not only assassinations, but also torture; rendition; detention without trial; military tribunals; widespread monitoring and surveillance of the population; warrantless and intrusive searches; the militarisation of the police; attacks on free speech; crackdowns on anti-war groups; and expansion of the operations of intelligence agencies.

Holder's pseudo-legal arguments in favour of military tribunals and assassinations bear more than a passing similarity to the Nazi jurisprudence facilitated by Schmitt, who also insisted that national security and military urgency can justify a 'state of exception' in which basic democratic rights can be abrogated, the rule of law suspended and the executive branch granted exceptional powers.

Schmittian Views on the US Supreme Court

Not just US government leaders, but judges have proven sympathetic to Schmitt-like conceptions. Such an outlook was expressed on the US Supreme Court, for example, in the 2006 case of *Hamdan v Rumsfeld* (548 US 557 (2006)). Following the 2001 invasion of Afghanistan, the Bush administration decided to detain at Guantanamo Bay alleged 'enemy combatants' in a legal vacuum. After two years of captivity without charge, the government convened military commissions. The procedure of the commissions, set down by the Defence Secretary and the president, departed in fundamental ways from normal military courts martial.

Hamdan challenged the legality of the military commissions. He argued that they violated the laws of the United States Congress, which required that he be tried in accordance with the established laws of war. The Supreme Court, by a 5–3 vote, agreed with him. The majority, following customary legal principles and reasoning, held that President Bush's military commissions did not comply with the laws of Congress because they did not provide procedural fairness as mandated under the Geneva Conventions' laws of war and as required by Congress. In particular, the military commissions failed to provide basic elements of fairness such as the right to be present, to see and hear evidence and witnesses, to exclude unreliable evidence and other important rights. The majority concluded that the commissions failed to provide for 'a regularly constituted Court affording all the judicial guarantees which are recognised as indispensable by civilised peoples'.

The majority judgments indicated that what was at stake was the continued existence of the liberal-democratic rule of law, and, in particular, legal control over the executive itself. Justice Stevens declared: '[I]n undertaking to try Hamdan and subject him to criminal punishment, the executive is bound to comply with the Rule of Law that prevails in this jurisdiction.'

The minority judgments, however, invoked the administration's claimed 'exceptional circumstances' arising from the 'war on terror' to sanction extraordinary action by the executive 'in the nation's interest' and to 'protect the people' without judicial scrutiny. Justice Thomas declared:

> The legitimate uses of the great power of war ... increase or diminish as the necessity of the case demands ... The jurisdiction of our common law war courts has been adapted in each instance to the need that called it forth ... The president has found that the war against terrorism ushers in a new paradigm ... Our nation recognizes that this new paradigm – requires new thinking in the laws of war.

Significantly, Justice Thomas, joined by Justices Scalia and Alito, sought to justify departures from the law with regard to military commissions by invoking the legal tradition of the development of the common law. Justice Thomas said:

> The plurality's newly minted clear-statement rule is also fundamentally inconsistent with the nature of the common law which, by definition, evolves and develops over time and does not, in all cases, 'say what may be done ... ' Similarly, it is inconsistent with the nature of

warfare, which also evolves and changes over time, and for which a flexible, evolutionary common-law system is uniquely appropriate.

As the majority view made clear, ordinary rules of long standing were applicable to determine the case. No innovations in the law, or 'evolution', were required. To refer to the trial of an accused by a Star Chamber-style military commission as an evolutionary development of the common law demonstrated the capacity of judicial reasoning to sanction a legal system that has much in common with the legal procedures and ideas of the Third Reich. This resembles the process whereby basic constitutional rights were suspended in 1933 in Germany following the Reichstag fire.

German Echoes

Significantly, Germany too has witnessed a resurgence of Schmitt's influence. Chancellor Angela Merkel for years courted the support of a professed admirer of Schmitt. Erich Vad, a Christian Democratic Union member and ex-federal army officer, was Merkel's security policy adviser. One 2003 essay, published (in German) in the right-wing magazine *Sezession*, bore the headline 'Friend or Foe: On the Relevance of Carl Schmitt' (Vad 2003).

Vad justified Schmitt's 'occasional collaboration with the Nazi regime' by claiming that this 'seemed to be the only way of preventing a complete collapse of the country'. Schmitt's 'epoch-making achievement' was said to have consisted primarily in the theory he drew in the sphere of politics, 'which he essentially understood in terms of the distinction between friend and foe'. Vad insisted that this conception holds true 'for today'. He quoted Schmitt to claim: 'As long as a people exists in the political sphere, it must determine for itself the distinction between friend and foe, if only in the most extreme case – the actuality of which, however, it must also decide for itself. Herein lies the essence of its political being.'

Schmitt himself had emphasised what he meant: 'The terms "friend", "foe" and "war" obtain their real meaning when they specifically make and retain reference to the real possibility of physically killing people' (Schmitt 1976: 33).

Chapter 1
Emergency Powers on the Rise: Case Studies

There has been a resurgence of emergency measures during the opening years of the twenty-first century, primarily in response to 9/11, but also to the wars in Afghanistan, Iraq, Libya, Syria and Yemen; the global financial crisis; climate change; recurring natural disasters; social and political unrest; and revolutionary upheavals. Not only has the frequency of such measures increased, but also the breadth of the situations in which they have been invoked. The following case studies provide a picture of the rise of emergency powers.

Social and Political Unrest: Emergency Powers Invoked in Greece, Egypt and Canada

During 2012 and 2013, governments in Greece, Egypt and Canada adopted or promulgated emergency provisions in response to strikes and protests by working-class people and students against austerity measures. This resort to authoritarian forms of rule highlighted the capacity of emergency measures, including those supposedly intended to deal with natural disasters or terrorist threats, to be used to suppress popular unrest, particularly under deteriorating economic and social conditions.

Greece

In January 2013, the Greek government placed striking Athens metro rail workers under martial law, forcing them back to work under pain of imprisonment. Hundreds of police stormed the central subway depot to break up a workers' occupation of the depot, arresting a number of workers. Solidarity strikes by other public transport employees were subsequently declared illegal as well.

The 'civil mobilisation' law used to attack the strike was supposedly intended for use only in case of a natural disaster, a massive danger to public health or the outbreak of war. Since the end of the Greek colonels' dictatorship in 1974, it had been invoked only nine times – including three times between 2010 and 2013. In 2010, it was utilised to force striking lorry drivers back to work, and in 2011 it was used against sanitation workers.

The strike by subway workers expressed the intense popular opposition to the sweeping attacks on Greek workers' living standards. The strike was directed against the fifth round of post-2008 austerity measures, passed by parliament on the orders of the 'troika' – the European Union (EU), the International Monetary Fund and the European Central Bank.

The new austerity package included a further 25 per cent public sector wage cut, on top of wage cuts of up to 60 per cent imposed over the previous three years.

After using emergency powers to break the nine-day strike by subway workers, the New Democracy-led coalition government extended its orders to 2,500 rail and tram workers who had struck to protest against the repression of the subway workers. Such 'civil mobilisation' orders conscript those targeted into the military and carry the threat of mass firings, arrests and jail sentences of up to five years.

The turn to emergency powers to crush workers' resistance was by no means confined to Greece. In 2010, as Europe-wide EU austerity programmes began, several major strikes – by Greek truckers, Spanish air traffic controllers and French oil refinery workers – had been ended by police and army interventions.

Egypt

In January 2013, Egyptian President Mohamed Mursi declared a 30-day state of emergency in three Suez Canal cities as protests begun on the second anniversary of the 2011 Egyptian revolution spread throughout the country. Police and army units fired live ammunition, killing dozens of people and injuring hundreds, while protesters attacked police stations and offices of Mursi's Muslim Brotherhood (MB) in cities across Egypt.

Mursi imposed a state of emergency on Port Saïd, Suez and Ismailia, as well as a 9 p.m. to 6 a.m. curfew. The state of emergency allowed the police and military to detain protesters indefinitely without charge and prosecute them in military courts, to suspend constitutional rights and to censor the press.

Before 2011, Hosni Mubarak had ruled throughout his 30-year presidency under a state of emergency. Mursi's decision to reimpose it to crush protests underscored how quickly the new regime had returned to similar methods, as it also sought to impose austerity measures required by the International Monetary Fund, in return for a $US4.8 billion loan.

Six months later, this repression helped pave the way for a new military coup in July 2013, installing a junta that later imposed an anti-protest law to effectively 'legalise' its violent crackdown on protests and strikes, and threatening participants with extensive jail time and heavy fines. In January 2014, having carried out mass arrests and outlawed the Muslim Brotherhood, the junta called a referendum to legitimise its coup and enshrine continued military dictatorship in a constitution (Stern 2013).

Ever since the British occupation of Egypt, the country has been under emergency rule of some kind almost continuously. The British first declared martial law in 1914 (see Chapter 4). Since then, its people have suffered a 'dizzying array of exceptional measures and courts', making it an example of 'endless emergency' (Reza 2006: 533).

Canada

The recourse to emergency powers was not limited to the most impoverished or marginalised countries. Similar measures were invoked in Canada during 2012 in a drive to halt a students' strike. Although adopted by legislation, the Canadian provisions exemplified the adoption of far-reaching powers to suppress basic democratic rights, including freedom of expression and assembly, and the right to strike.

In May 2012, the government of the province of Quebec introduced Bill 78, officially titled 'An Act to enable students to receive instruction from the postsecondary institutions they attend' (LQ, 2012, c. 12/Laws of Quebec, 2012, chapter 12), which was passed by the National Assembly of Quebec. The law restricted protest or picketing on or near university grounds, and required organisers of a protest consisting of 50 or more people in a public venue anywhere in Quebec to submit their proposed venue and/or route to the relevant police for approval.

Bill 78 suspended winter semester classes at 11 universities and 14 colleges where over 150,000 students were demonstrating or continued to demonstrate, and specified that classes for the autumn and winter semesters at those locations would be completed later in 2012. The Minister of Education, Recreation and Sports was granted the ability to deem as not applicable certain other regulations or laws or to '[prescribe] any other necessary modification to' Bill 78 so as to provide for any dispositions deemed necessary to ensure the continuation of classes throughout the duration specified by the act.

The law made it illegal to deny a person access to any place where that person had a right to be, and further restricted 'any form of gathering' that might cause such denial from assembling inside any educational building, on the grounds of such a building and within 50 metres of the limits of those grounds. The bill established a date after which all education employees had to return to work, and prohibited them from striking should this, 'by act or omission', prevent students from receiving instruction or indirectly impede services (Jones 2012).

The Obama Administration and Emergency Powers

As well as being closely involved in the states of emergency declared by state governors in Ferguson, Missouri, in 2014 and Baltimore, Maryland, in 2015, President Obama personally invoked emergency or extraordinary powers on numerous occasions. Three prominent instances indicated an ongoing trend.

1. The Military-Police Boston Lockdown of 2013

In April 2013, a major American city was placed under the equivalent of martial law. On 15 April, two bombs exploded near the finish line of the Boston Marathon in the city's centre. Three people were killed and over 170 were injured, some seriously. This was a criminal act with tragic consequences. But it became the pretext for a massive mobilisation of military, police and intelligence forces. Thousands of heavily armed police and National Guard troops occupied the streets, backed up by machine gun-mounted armoured vehicles, Humvees and Black Hawk helicopters in scenes that resembled the US occupation of Baghdad.

President Obama declared an emergency in Massachusetts and ordered the Department of Homeland Security Federal Emergency Management Agency (FEMA) to coordinate all disaster relief efforts and 'provide appropriate assistance for required emergency measures, authorised under Title V of the Stafford Act, to save lives and to protect property and public health and safety, and to lessen or avert the threat of a catastrophe' (Obama 2013a).

The people were told to remain indoors while police, with automatic weapons drawn, conducted warrantless house-to-house searches. Some of those who strayed out of doors were surrounded by police and ordered to go home. The mass transit system was shut down; passenger train service along the northeastern corridor was halted; businesses, universities and other public facilities were closed.

Boston – the cradle of the American Revolution, and the country's premier centre of higher education – was turned into an armed camp, all supposedly to track down a 19-year-old youth allegedly involved in the bomb attacks. Following the capture of the suspect, Dzhokhar Tsarnaev, President Obama issued a late-night statement from the White House in which he stressed the role of his administration in the police-state mobilisation, boasting that he had 'directed the full resources of the federal government … to increase security as needed'. Ignoring the presumption of innocence, he referred to the captured suspect and his dead brother as 'these terrorists' (Obama 2013b).

The Justice Department announced that it would not read the suspect his 'Miranda right' to remain silent and obtain legal counsel before speaking to police investigators. It would instead question the seriously injured youth 'extensively' not just on matters related directly to public safety, but more broadly on 'intelligence matters'. This sets a precedent for denying these rights to anyone arrested under anti-terrorism statutes, which has already included political dissidents such as Occupy Wall Street and anti-NATO protesters (Cockburn 2013).

2. President Obama's Drone Assassination Memorandum

A long-suppressed Justice Department memorandum released in 2014 established that President Obama, in the most calculated and criminal manner, authorised the murder of an American citizen, Anwar al-Aulaqi. The memo supported the targeting and drone killing of a man far from any battlefield, who was never charged with a crime (Miller 2014). Its tortured logic underscored the premeditated character of the act.

The drone attack that killed Aulaqi and three others in Yemen on 30 September 2011 – including a second US citizen, Samir Khan – was not carried out in the heat of battle. Neither was the drone attack one month later that obliterated Aulaqi's teenage son. The assassinations of selected US citizens was part of the White House's ongoing campaign of drone attacks, which have killed many thousands of people in Afghanistan, Pakistan, Yemen, Somalia and other countries.

Obama's secret decision to place Aulaqi on his 'kill list' was leaked to the press in April of 2010. The memo by the then head of the Justice Department's Office of Legal Counsel, David Barron, claiming that the Constitution and US laws gave the president the power to kill a US citizen without charge or trial, was sent to Attorney General Eric Holder in July 2010. Aulaqi's father filed a suit in federal court to remove his son from the kill list, but the case was thrown out in December 2010 (see Chapter 3).

Thus the extra-judicial killing of Aulaqi was organised over a protracted period of time. Aulaqi had not been indicted prior to his killing. In fact, it was not established that he had committed a criminal act. None of the assertions by the government of his role as an 'operational leader' of an Al Qaeda group or his alleged involvement in terror plots against the US were substantiated, although Barron's memo treated them all as indisputable fact.

Even if Aulaqi engaged in propaganda hostile to the policies of the US government, such behaviour is not necessarily criminal, let alone grounds for execution without trial. There has been no congressional investigation into the killing of Aulaqi. There have been no public hearings. There has been no move to impeach Obama or prosecute him.

It is notable that the memorandum deals only cursorily with the Fifth Amendment to the US Constitution, which states: '[N]or shall any person … be deprived of life, liberty, or property, without due process of law'. These words were not cited in the memo.

Instead, the memo restated the pseudo-legal argument that in prosecuting the 'war on terror' against Al Qaeda and 'associated forces', the president and his unelected military/intelligence aides have virtually unlimited powers, including the power to wage war and carry out killings, kidnappings and indefinite detention anywhere in the world, including within the US itself.

The memo repeatedly cited the congressional Authorization for Use of Military Force (AUMF), passed three days after the 9/11 attacks, as legal support for any and all actions taken in the name of fighting terrorists, including the assassination of US citizens and other repressive measures against Americans. At the time it was passed, the AUMF was presented as a narrowly defined sanction for retaliation against those responsible for the attacks.

Barron accepted uncritically all the assertions of the government about Aulaqi – his role as an 'operational leader' of Al Qaeda and involvement in previous terror plots against the US; the 'imminent' threat to Americans he supposedly represents; the 'infeasibility' of capturing him etc. – in order to declare that the government could kill him without any independent trial of the facts or any opportunity for the victim to defend himself in a court of law. The presumption of innocence was a dead letter.

On this basis, the memo concluded: '[W]e do not believe that al-Aulaqi's US citizenship imposes constitutional limitations that would preclude the contemplated lethal action under the facts represented to us by DoD [Department of Defense], the CIA and the Intelligence Community'.

The document was carefully worded so as not to limit the president's asserted power to order the murder of Americans to the specific circumstances surrounding Aulaqi. It stated, for example, that the use of lethal force is acceptable 'at least' where government officials have determined capture is not feasible. It also defined 'imminent' in such a way as to render the term meaningless, declaring that the government did not need to know 'precisely when such attacks will occur'.

In testimony during 2014 before the Senate Foreign Relations Committee, Defense Department and State Department lawyers argued that the president has unlimited war powers and does not even require congressional authorisation. The lawyers declared that the White House had the power to authorise the invasions of Afghanistan and Iraq, the air war against Libya, indefinite detention, drone assassinations and all the other military actions of the Bush and Obama administrations without reference to the Authorization for Use of Military Force.

'The US has the authority to target individuals, *including Americans*, who pose an imminent threat to attack our country', State Department Deputy Legal Adviser Mary McLeod told the committee (emphasis added).

3. The Venezuela 'Emergency'

In 2015, President Obama issued an executive order declaring a 'national emergency' to deal with what he termed 'the unusual and extraordinary threat to the national security and foreign policy of the United States' posed by the Venezuelan government.

The order, on its face, turned reality inside out. Far from Venezuela posing a threat to the US, successive US governments have repeatedly intervened in Venezuela's affairs, sponsoring coups like the failed attempt to overthrow the late President Hugo Chavez via a military coup in 2002 (Avilés 2009). In that context, the latest assertion of a 'national emergency' and threat to 'national security' suggests that more direct intervention is under contemplation, including by military means.

Obama's decree asserted that the supposed 'threat' was the result of the Venezuelan government's:

> erosion of human rights guarantees, persecution of political opponents, curtailment of press freedoms, use of violence and human rights violations and abuses in response to antigovernment protests, and arbitrary arrest and detention of antigovernment protesters, as well as the exacerbating presence of significant public corruption. (Obama 2015a)

The president stressed that his actions served to 'implement and expand upon' the Venezuelan Defense of Human Rights and Civil Society Act, passed by the US Congress and signed into law by Obama in December 2014. No such legislation, however, pertains to any of Washington's dictatorial allies, such as Egypt and Saudi Arabia.

The substance of the executive order was far less sweeping than the claim of an emergency. It imposed sanctions on seven Venezuelan military, intelligence, police and prosecutorial officials whom it claimed were involved in human rights violations. Nevertheless, the authority claimed by Obama was broad. His Executive Order stated:

> By the authority vested in me as President by the Constitution and the laws of the United States of America, including the International Emergency Economic Powers Act (50 U.S.C. 1701 *et seq.*) (IEEPA), the National Emergencies Act (50 U.S.C. 1601 *et seq.*) (NEA), the Venezuela Defense of Human Rights and Civil Society Act of 2014 (Public Law 113–278) (the 'Venezuela Defense of Human Rights Act') (the 'Act'), section 212(f) of the Immigration and Nationality Act of 1952 (8 U.S.C. 1182(f)) (INA), and section 301 of title 3, United States Code,
>
> I, BARACK OBAMA, President of the United States of America, find that the situation in Venezuela, including the Government of Venezuela's erosion of human rights guarantees, persecution of political opponents, curtailment of press freedoms, use of violence and

> human rights violations and abuses in response to antigovernment protests, and arbitrary arrest and detention of antigovernment protestors, as well as the exacerbating presence of significant public corruption, constitutes an unusual and extraordinary threat to the national security and foreign policy of the United States, and I hereby declare a national emergency to deal with that threat. (Obama 2015a)

In another example of the increasingly frequent invocation of emergency powers, President Obama also issued an executive order in 2015 declaring a state of emergency in the name of combating cyber attacks on US targets. The order authorised economic sanctions and the seizure of financial assets and other forms of property from any entity considered a risk to 'national security'.

The order, 'Blocking the Property of Certain Persons Engaging in Significant Malicious Cyber-Enabled Activities', stated that sweeping powers were needed to combat an 'unusual and extraordinary threat to national security' posed by 'the increasing prevalence and severity of malicious cyber-enabled activities' against US infrastructure (Obama 2015b).

Among other things, the order authorised the US Treasury Secretary to impose financial sanctions on foreign entities accused of hacking American computer systems. No specific targets were listed, but the US government had accused the Russian, Chinese and Iranian governments of sponsoring hacking operations against Western banks and corporations. The order also asserted new powers to impose travel restrictions against alleged security threats, which could be exercised against any 'partnership, association, trust, joint venture, corporation, group, subgroup, or other organisation'.

The order was broad, not only in terms of its powers but also the alleged threatening conduct. Sanctions and property seizures could be instituted against any person determined 'to be responsible for or complicit in, or to have engaged in, directly or indirectly, cyber-enabled activities' that were 'reasonably likely to result in, or have materially contributed to, a significant threat to the national security, foreign policy, or economic health or financial stability of the United States and that have the purpose or effect of:

> (A) harming, or otherwise significantly compromising the provision of services by, a computer or network of computers that support one or more entities in a critical infrastructure sector;
> (B) significantly compromising the provision of services by one or more entities in a critical infrastructure sector;
> (C) causing a significant disruption to the availability of a computer or network of computers; or
> (D) causing a significant misappropriation of funds or economic resources, trade secrets, personal identifiers, or financial information for commercial or competitive advantage or private financial gain. (Obama 2015b)

This language is wide enough to authorise sanctions or other retaliatory actions to pursue the interests of US corporations against allegedly nefarious commercial activities by international rival firms. What is a 'significant threat' to the 'economic health' of the US? What is 'a significant misappropriation' of 'financial information' for 'competitive advantage'?

Financial Emergencies

Another kind of emergency, one which goes to the heart of the prevailing economic system itself, is a fiscal one. The global financial crisis that erupted to the surface in 2008 and the ensuing international slump, deep austerity measures and social and industrial struggles raised further questions about the stability of the existing socio-economic order. Indeed, the threatened international economic breakdown posed a truly existential danger to the prevailing private profit system.

In numbers of countries, the potential meltdown of the financial system led to extraordinary and even unprecedented measures to bail out or prop up major corporations, at the expense of jobs, wage levels, social programmes and welfare entitlements. The protracted character of that turmoil, which still continued six years after the collapse of the giant American investment bank Lehman Brothers in September 2008, points to the likelihood of such measures, or other emergency provisions, being applied further in the future – and not necessarily on a temporary basis.

Significantly, the billions of dollars spent by the US government to bail out Wall Street's banks and finance houses were expressly designed as emergency measures, as in the Emergency Economic Stabilization Act 2008. Although it has been argued that the during the twentieth century invocations of an 'economic state of emergency' were 'increasingly separated from any evidence of military conflict or armed rebellion' (Scheuerman 2000: 1878), that does not mean that such measures will not be accompanied by police-military repression in the coming period in response to social discontent or rebellion. As others have noted, President Roosevelt's 'New Deal' measures during the 1930s Great Depression were initially instigated under wartime legislation that remained on the books after World War I, and may have been unconstitutional (Roots 2000).

Two examples, one from Australia and the other from the United States, illustrate the potential scope of the powers being asserted, and how they can be used to dismantle social rights as well as to deliver handouts for the benefit of big business. The logic employed in both instances, by the relevant governments, authorities and courts, also went beyond economic considerations, suggesting wider precedents for use in other types of emergencies.

Australia and the Global Financial Crisis

In Australia, the majority of the High Court evinced a readiness to expand the constitutional boundaries of executive power in response to the global financial crisis of 2008–09. The Labor government of Prime Minister Kevin Rudd, after discussions with the Governor of the Reserve Bank of Australia, instituted two economic stimulus packages, which included measures to promote retail and construction spending by granting additional temporary welfare payments and tax concessions.

In a joint judgment in *Pape v Commissioner of Taxation* (2009) 238 CLR 1, Gummow, Crennan and Bell JJ said that the challenged tax bonuses were within the power of the executive to defend the Australian body politic in the event of a 'crisis'. After noting that the parties to the litigation had agreed that there was a global financial and economic crisis, the three judges stated:

> It can hardly be doubted that the current financial and economic crisis concerns Australia as a nation. Determining that there is the need for an immediate fiscal stimulus to the national economy in the circumstances set out above is somewhat analogous to determining a state of emergency in circumstances of a natural disaster. The Executive Government is the arm of government capable of and empowered to respond to a crisis be it war, natural disaster or a financial crisis on the scale here. This power has its roots in the executive power exercised in the United Kingdom up to the time of the adoption of the Constitution but in form today in Australia it is a power to act on behalf of the federal polity. (at [233])

Notably, the judgment gave no consideration to whether a legislative power existed under the Australian Constitution to make laws regarding national emergencies. In other words, the case explicitly concerned an expansion of executive power, not legislative power. The other member of the majority in the case, French CJ, expressly withheld his support for the proposition that s 61 of the constitution confers power on the executive to respond to national emergencies. Nevertheless, even he favoured an expansive interpretation of the executive power, saying it extended to 'short-term fiscal measures to meet adverse economic conditions affecting the nation as a whole', where such measures were peculiarly within the capacity and resources of the federal government (at [133]).

Reflecting the Australian Constitution's continuing reliance on its British roots, including the murky powers of the English monarchy, s 61 states: 'The executive power of the Commonwealth is vested in the Queen and is exercisable by the Governor-General as the Queen's representative, and extends to the execution and maintenance of this Constitution, and of the laws of the Commonwealth.' The *Pape* decision has given an unprecedentedly broad peace-time interpretation to this executive power. In the words of one constitutional lawyer:

> [I]t has left an implied executive nationhood power floating untethered above the Constitution, to be used in the future as a justification for Commonwealth legislation on anything that the Commonwealth regards as an 'emergency' that it considers can best be addressed by the Commonwealth financial power. (Twomey2010, 343)

One must add, however, that this 'floating untethered' power is not confined to justifying Commonwealth legislation. The logic of the *Pape* ruling is to expand the 'implied executive nationhood power' to executive decisions made above and beyond legislative measures. The judges nominated 'the Executive Government' as 'the arm of government capable of and empowered to respond to a crisis', not the parliament.

United States: The Detroit Bankruptcy

In the United States, the city of Detroit was declared bankrupt in 2013, utilising an emergency manager law. The Constitution of the state of Michigan provided that public sector pensions could not be diminished or impaired. Yet, the bankruptcy was utilised to cut the pension entitlements of city workers, as well as to slash jobs and public services and sell off city assets, including the famous Detroit Institute of Arts.

A particularly anti-democratic law, Michigan Public Act 436 of 2012, titled the Local Financial Stability and Choice Act, essentially permits state officials to usurp local government and impose an unelected dictator on the city. Section 6 of the Act authorises the state governor to declare 'the existence of a financial emergency within a local unit of government or school district'. Section 9 empowers the state governor to 'appoint an emergency manager to address a financial emergency within that local government' and states that 'an emergency manager shall act for and in the place and stead of the governing body and the office of chief administrative officer of the local government'.

Section 9 specifies that an emergency manager has 'broad powers in receivership to rectify the financial emergency and to assure the fiscal accountability of the local government and the local government's capacity to provide or cause to be provided necessary governmental services essential to the public health, safety, and welfare'. Section 12 adds that an emergency manager may take a long list of additional actions 'with respect to a local government that is in receivership, notwithstanding any charter provision to the contrary'. These include:

- Notwithstanding any minimum staffing level requirement established by charter or contract, establish and implement staffing levels for the local government.
- Reject, modify, or terminate 1 or more terms and conditions of an existing contract.
- Reject, modify, or terminate 1 or more terms and conditions of an existing collective bargaining agreement.

In other words, the emergency manager can eliminate jobs, repudiate contracts and scrap existing working conditions.

The constitutional right to pensions in Michigan and several other US states was the result of major industrial and political struggles. Originally, under the law, pension funds were considered 'gratuitous allowances'. The pensioner had no vested right; the pension could be terminated at the will of the grantor. A 1948 Michigan Supreme Court case, *Brown v Highland Park* (320 Mich 108), found that municipal pensions were 'terminable at the will of the municipality'.

Workers then fought for their pensions to be recognised under the law as vested rights. Ultimately, seven states felt compelled to pass constitutional amendments that protected public employee pensions: New York in 1938; Alaska in 1956, Michigan in 1963, Illinois in 1970, Louisiana in 1974, Hawaii in 1978 and Arizona in 1998 (Secunda 2011). As a result, Article IX, section 24 of the Michigan Constitution of 1963 states:

> The accrued financial benefits of each pension plan and retirement system of the state and its political subdivisions shall be a contractual obligation thereof which shall not be diminished or impaired thereby. Financial benefits arising on account of service rendered in each fiscal year shall be funded during that year and such funding shall not be used for financing unfunded accrued liabilities.

In December 2013, however, in *In re: City of Detroit, Debtor* (Case No. 13-53846) a US Bankruptcy Court Judge, Steven W. Rhodes, decided that Detroit was eligible for bankruptcy, and that under federal bankruptcy law pensions could be impaired. To justify this ruling, Judge Rhodes invoked the phrase 'contractual obligation' in the Michigan Constitution, ruling that federal bankruptcy law permitted the impairment of contracts.

Michigan's emergency manager law had its origins in the state's Public Act 72 of 1990. The 1990 Act gave state officials the power to appoint an emergency financial manager in a given municipality who would assume certain powers ordinarily held by local elected officials. Significantly, this 1990 law did not authorise bankruptcy, presumably because it was understood that the state constitution prohibited a city bankruptcy that impaired pensions.

During 2011, however, the 1990 law was replaced with Public Act 4 of 2011, the 'Local Government and School District Fiscal Accountability Act'. It granted an emergency manager expanded powers – such as to remove elected officials, eliminate local governmental departments, enact school curricula and modify, terminate or reject contracts – and said an emergency manager could file for bankruptcy.

This law purported to give an emergency manager the power to override the entire system of democratically elected officials and representatives in a given local political entity. This unelected official was empowered to fire local politicians, administrators and workers; rip up employment contracts; and unilaterally take municipalities against their will into bankruptcy. Nevertheless, it still required any emergency manager to 'fully comply' with section 24 of Article IX of the Michigan Constitution, which guaranteed that workers' pensions could not be impaired.

The 2011 version of the law faced widespread opposition. In November 2012, it was struck down by a popular referendum, with over 2.3 million people in the state voting to repeal the law (Michigan 2012). Within weeks, however, a revised version of the law was passed by a post-election 'lame duck' session of the Michigan legislature. On the advice of lawyers, Michigan legislators tacked two minor appropriations provisions onto the bill in order to prevent it from being struck down by another popular referendum. Significantly, the 2011 version of the law required the emergency manager to comply with the Michigan Constitution. The revised law, Michigan Public Act 436 of 2012, did not.

Michigan state judge Rosemarie E. Aquilina heard challenges to the revised emergency manager law in 2013 in *Webster v Michigan* (Case No. 13-734-CZ, Ingham County Circuit). She struck down the law as unconstitutional, and also ordered that a bankruptcy petition could not be filed. She ordered that the law was 'unconstitutional and in violation of Article IX Section 24 of the Michigan Constitution to the extent that it permits the Governor to authorize an emergency manager to proceed under Chapter 9 [bankruptcy] in any manner which threatens to diminish or impair accrued pension benefits'. Judge Aquilina also ordered:

> The Governor is prohibited by Article IX Section 24 of the Michigan Constitution from authorizing an emergency manager under PA 436 to proceed under Chapter 9 in a manner which threatens to diminish or impair accrued pension benefits, and any such action by the Governor is without authority and in violation of Article IX Section 24 of the Michigan Constitution.

> … In order to rectify his unauthorized and unconstitutional actions described above, the Governor must (1) direct the Emergency Manager to immediately withdraw the Chapter 9 petition filed on July 18, and (2) not authorize any further Chapter 9 filing which threatens to diminish or impair accrued pension benefits.

However, to bypass this ruling, of which they had been advised in advance, Detroit's emergency manager, Kevin Orr, filed a bankruptcy petition ahead of schedule. The city of Detroit officially entered bankruptcy 9 minutes before Judge Aquilina's hearing to deliver her order. The emergency manager then argued in the federal bankruptcy court – and Judge Rhodes agreed – that this 9-minute difference meant that Judge Aquilina no longer had jurisdiction over the case when she issued her order. Judge Rhodes ruled that Judge Aquilina's order had no effect.

The outcome sets a precedent that can be sought to be applied across the United States, potentially giving state authorities the power, under financial emergency laws, to abrogate pension rights and abolish jobs and long-standing working conditions (White 2013).

From Financial to Climate Emergency?

Arguments have begun to appear in favour of emulating the emergency action to rescue the financial markets by taking similar actions to respond the 'climate emergency' produced by economically generated global warming and other environmental damage.

The term achieved some prominence in environmental movements in Australia through the publication of Spratt and Sutton's *Climate Code Red*. This book, which was shortlisted for the 2009 Premier's Literary Award for science writing in the Australian state of Victoria, calls for a wartime-style response in which government, industry and labour are supposedly redirected to meet a common threat: 'Because the last emergency mobilisation on this scale was during World War II, few people today have any direct experience of a situation like this; however, there is plenty of history from which to learn, and expertise available, to plan for such a scenario (Spratt and Sutton 2008: 158).

This war analogy, eulogising the militarist mobilisation employed in the war against Germany and Japan, was hardly original. It was advanced two years earlier in the US:

> As we contemplate mobilizing to rescue a planet under stress and a civilization in trouble, we see both similarities and contrasts with the mobilization for World War II. In this earlier mobilization, there was an economic restructuring, but it was temporary. Mobilizing to save civilization, in contrast, requires a permanent economic restructuring … The year 1942 witnessed the greatest expansion of industrial output in the nation's history – all for military use. (Brown 2006: 253–4)

As the review of wartime powers in Chapter 2 indicates, such calls have distinctly anti-democratic implications, indicating a readiness to violate basic legal and democratic rights. Spratt and Sutton dismissively declare that during the last wartime regime, '[t]he economy, real wages, and profits all grew, although many civil rights were significantly curtailed'

(Spratt and Sutton 2008: 219). While Spratt and Sutton suggest that such an emergency could help make 'democracy work more effectively' (Spratt and Sutton 2008: 235–6), their views have spawned a febrile discussion in certain quarters about embracing the concepts of 'necessity' and 'emergency' to overcome the perceived failures of democracy. One Australian Greens leader sprang to defend Spratt and Sutton against a warning by a Canadian activist that climate change could 'become the next excuse for authoritarianism' (Bandt 2009: 27–32).

Not surprisingly, these writings have actually invoked Schmitt's doctrines in support of their proposals. Without referring to how Schmitt's theories served as an antechamber for Nazism, Bandt enthusiastically explains that for Schmitt the key issue was 'unmediated control over labour' as the only real source of authority, rather than formal proclamations (Bandt 2009: 25–6). Likewise, Honig uncritically canvassed Schmitt's 'still influential' ideas before postulating means of 'democratizing emergency and … de-exceptionlizing it' (Honig 2014: 46, 48–9).

Bandt was cited favourably by Lindsay, who sought to relativise and legitimise resort to emergency powers as part of a continuum of necessary reactions to challenges facing a society (Lindsay 2010: 263–8). According to this argument, 'public power is generally purposive (serving interests, goals, social and economic forces, and particular political projects) and that emergency government is similarly conditioned' (Lindsay 2010: 266). This uncritical view of the state as a 'purposive' power also drew upon Lazar's contention that 'emergency or "crisis" government is an indissoluble part of the legal and constitutional landscape, and that the preferable (and safest) approach is to construct emergency institutions adhering, at least generally, to desired norms rather than solely relying on positive rules to control and enable limits' (Lindsay 2010: 264, citing Lazar 2009: 5).

From these musings, Lindsay drew a conclusion that is capable of justifying authoritarian forms of rule, including martial law, in the name of averting environmental catastrophe:

> This strategic conception of the state of emergency renders more explicable the wide range of variability in scale, intensity, urgency and form in the operation of emergency measures or emergency government. Such measures are deployed to given ends, including, at the extreme, to martial law or revolution. Much more limited instances of emergency government obviously exist, such as response to localized natural disasters, and there are a broad range of other manifestations in between. The forms and permutations of emergency government represent adapted, contingent, strategic and, at times, political and/or partisan responses to circumstances of crisis. (Lindsay 2010: 267)

Having uncritically embraced the use of emergency provisions to bail out the financial markets in 2008–09, Lindsay ended up arguing:

> Employment of emergency laws by governments is not in fact especially peculiar. 'Climate emergency' laws would arguably represent an evolution in the model of emergency powers, as well as an evolution in government strategy in combating climate change. (Lindsay 2010: 280)

Chapter 2
Critical Lessons of History

History can be used or abused. Attempts to draw simple analogies from history, such as proposing models of emergency rule based on the Roman Republic's dictatorship provisions, can be ahistorical. That is, they ignore the many critical divergences between different periods of history and the class structures and political dynamics of the societies being compared, whether they be founded on slavery, feudalism or capitalism. Moreover, what is presented as history can amount to a distortion or falsification of history to serve contemporary pseudo-legal or political agendas.

Three oft-cited historical episodes of emergency provisions – the Roman dictatorship, the French 'state of siege' and Article 48 of the German Weimar Republic – offer some very instructive lessons, if approached with these considerations in mind. Also of great relevance is an examination of the historical experiences associated with the rise and evolution of the capitalist democracies that arose out of the English and American revolutions of the seventeenth and eighteenth centuries. The records of three other former British colonies – Australia, New Zealand and Canada, are also revealing.

The Roman Republic's Dictatorship: Concept and Reality

Contemporary efforts to legitimise, rationalise or accommodate resort to emergency powers often hark back to the Roman Republic of 509 to 27 BC, and its appointment of temporary dictators in periods of crisis. These endeavours, however, tend to divorce the dictatorship provisions from their historical and socio-economic contexts, thus presenting an idealised and therefore false picture. Little reference is usually made to the origins of the office of dictator, arising out of the revolution that overthrew the previous Roman monarchy, or to the degeneration of the institution in the face of mounting economic, social and class tensions, not least the struggles of the plebeians against the ruling patricians and the mighty slave uprisings of 135 to 71 BC.

In their study *Law in Times of Crisis*, Gross and Ní Aoláin conducted a survey of 'models of accommodation' – which countenance some accommodation for resort to emergency rule while maintaining normal legal principles and rules 'as much as possible'. They began by suggesting:

> The institution of the Roman dictatorship is the prototype for all modern forms of models of accommodation. The Romans introduced a system in which an emergency institution was a recognized and regular instrument of government built into a constitutional framework. (Gross and Ní Aoláin 2006: 17)

Paeans of praise have been written to the Roman system. According to Rossiter, writing in post-World War II America:

> The splendid political genius of the Roman people grasped and solved the difficult problem of emergency powers in a manner quite unparalleled in all history, indeed so uniquely and boldly that a study of modern crisis government could find no more propitious a starting point than a brief survey of the celebrated Roman dictatorship. (Rossiter 1948: 15)

Ackerman, a more contemporary, post-9/11 American scholar, also lauded the Roman institution, while rejecting it as impractical in the modern world. It 'represents the first great experiment with states of emergency' and served as 'an inspiration for my heavy reliance on a political system of checks and balances' (Ackerman 2004: 1046).

The American Revolution itself drew upon references to the supposedly heroic example of the Roman Republic. What was depicted as the almost ideal working of the temporary dictatorship – the rapid relinquishment of supreme power by the dictator Lucius Quinctius Cincinnatus after defeating enemy forces – was cited as the exemplar for the conduct of America's first president. Upon the victory of the American Revolution in 1783, George Washington surrendered his military powers as commander-in-chief and returned to private life, at least until re-entering political life and being elected as the United States' inaugural president in 1789. He was also the first president general of the Society of the Cincinnati, a military society that in turn gave its name to the city of Cincinnati, Ohio (Wills 1984: 23).

The actual record of the Roman dictatorship was not as 'splendid' as often claimed. Following the overthrow of the monarchy in 509 BC, the Roman patricians sought to curtail the future usurpation of political power by establishing an executive headed by two powerful, but limited-term, chief magistrates, the consuls. Each consul was elected for a period of one year, without the possibility of consecutive re-election (Cary and Scullard 1975: 56–63).

Because a co-equal partnership between the two consuls might be problematic in times of extreme peril, another institution, the dictatorship, was created to exercise absolute power during emergencies (Rossiter 1948: 19). However, the dictator's term of office was limited to six months or to the end of the term of the consuls who appointed him, whichever came first. Throughout the dictatorship, moreover, the regular institutions of the state – the consuls, tribunes, Senate and other office holders – continued to function and retained their full authority, providing a check on the dictator's conduct (Gross and Ní Aoláin 2006: 23).

Most depictions of this system leave aside its socio-economic context and ultimate degeneration. Gross and Ní Aoláin do caution against an uncritical glorification of the Roman model and provide a brief outline of its demise (Gross and Ní Aoláin 2006: 82–3, 239–42). They suggest that once Rome acquired unparalleled military might and was safe from invasion and attacks, it no longer needed the dictatorship (Gross and Ní Aoláin 2006: 239). At the same time, they refer to the 'socio-political crises – the struggle of the Orders and the continued conflicts between the aristocracy and the Popular party' that led to the patricians eschewing the appointment of dictators in favour of strengthening the position of the Senate, from which the plebeians were excluded, and resorting to conferring dictatorial powers on the consuls (Gross and Ní Aoláin 2006: 239–40).

Thus, 'the decline of the dictatorship did not signal the disappearance of emergency powers form the life of the republic. Rather, such powers came to be institutionalized and normalized' (Gross and Ní Aoláin 2006: 241). This 'normalization of emergency' was augmented by the retention of the office of dictator, the shell of which was revived in a distorted form during the final period of the republic, most infamously by Julius Caesar, who was eventually anointed a perpetual dictator. 'Caesar's dictatorship did not comport with any of the constitutional limitations and requirements under the constitution of the republic' (Gross and Ní Aoláin 2006: 83).

The conflicts between the patricians and the plebeians were not the only class struggles that ultimately tore the republic apart and led to the imposition of rule by emperors from 27 BC onward. Between 135 BC and 71 BC, in the final period of the republic, Rome was seriously affected by several slave uprisings, which reflected the underlying contradictions of a slave economy and society. Vast tracts of land were devoted to slave farming, in which the slaves greatly outnumbered their Roman masters. During this period, there were at least 12 civil wars and rebellions, including three 'servile wars' involving slave revolts. The third and final uprising was the most serious, with the gladiator Spartacus ultimately commanding between 120,000 and 150,000 slaves (Santosuosso 2003: 43).

Rather than providing a model for a constrained and delineated recourse to emergency powers, the Roman Republic's descent into dictatorial rule points more to the increasing resort to authoritarian forms of rule to suppress the upheavals produced by the creation and threatening rise of an exploited class.

The Repressive Face of the French 'State of Siege'

A similar conclusion can be drawn from another sometimes-cited classical model of constitutional accommodation of emergency powers – the civil law 'state of siege'. Derived from France, this device for invoking emergency rule has been adopted in many Latin American states (Gross and Ní Aoláin 2006: 26). Most depictions of this institution by legal scholars are also devoid of any examination of its historical role and repressive content.

In Rossiter's view: 'No instrument of crisis government conform[ed] so closely to the theory of constitutional dictatorship as the famed and widely-imitated state of siege' (Rossiter 1948: 129). Radin also presented a rosy picture of the state of siege as a constitutionally constrained mechanism:

> [T]he vital point is that the state of siege is not a condition in which law is temporarily abrogated, and the arbitrary fiat of a 'commander' takes its place. It is emphatically a legal institution, expressly authorized by the constitutions and the various bills of right that succeeded each other in France, and organized under this authority by a specific statute. (Radin 1942: 637)

In reality, the doctrine originated in the pre-French Revolution *ancien régime* of the absolutist monarchy. It was adapted for violently repressive purposes during the suppression of the 1848 revolution in France, which was part of a wave of popular revolutions in Europe in which, for the first time, leading roles were played by the emerging working class.

These democratic revolutions were betrayed by their leaders, after the working class rose up in Paris in June as an independent revolutionary force. Frightened by this new social force which threatened their property and privileges, the capitalist and middle-class leaders preferred to reconcile themselves with feudal reaction. The above-mentioned constitution of the short-lived Second Republic in France was in fact written on the back of a bloody military onslaught against the workers of Paris, which was followed by the deportation of thousands of insurgents without trial (Marx 1969a: 34–5).

General Cavaignac, the leader of the army, first withdrew his soldiers from Paris to allow the insurgents to deploy their barricades, and then returned with overwhelming force to crush the uprising; from 24 to 26 June, there were battles in the streets of the working-class districts of Paris. An estimated 5,000 insurgents were killed at the barricades; 15,000 were arrested and 4,000 deported (Séguin 1990: 108–9).

Even the somewhat critical view of the state of siege outlined by Gross and Ní Aoláin conveyed no idea of this brutal counter-revolution or the way it paved the way, despite the formal guarantees of legality enshrined in the constitution of the Second Republic, to the seizure of power by Louis Napoleon (Napoleon III), which culminated in his *coup d'état* of December 1851. In the words of Gross and Ní Aoláin:

> Following the imposition of a state of siege on Paris between June 24 and October 12, 1848, and the introduction of article 106 of the Constitution of the Second Republic – providing that a law would be promulgated for the regulation of the institution of state of siege – a law was passed on August 9, 1849, which sought to regulate such issue as the declaration, termination, and the effect of a state of siege. However, the law of 1849 was thereafter used to impose indiscriminately and arbitrarily a state of siege regime for extended periods of time and on a wide scale. (Gross and Ní Aoláin 2006: 27)

What actually happened during this period? Following the February 1848 mass overthrow of the Orleans monarchy of Louis Philippe, who abdicated and fled to Britain, there was an elected government that proclaimed the Second Republic. But, reflecting the interests of the most powerful business layers, the bourgeoisie, this government increasingly dismantled the social concessions, such as the employment workshops, that had initially been made to the workers and poor who mounted the revolution.

On 23 June 1848, the working class of Paris rose up in protest over the closure of the National Workshops. On that day, 170,000 people came out into the streets to erect barricades. The government appointed General Cavaignac to lead the military forces to cut down the uprising. Between 23 and 26 June 1848, the battle between the working class and Cavaignac came to be known as the 'June Days Uprising'. Cavaignac began a systematic assault, targeting the blockaded areas of the city. However, even with a force of 120,000 to 125,000 soldiers, Cavaignac still required two days to complete the suppression of the uprising. Fearful of a renewed rebellion, the government continued the state of siege until 12 October (Rudé 2005: 164–79).

By the time of his December 1851 coup, Louis Napoleon had dissolved the National Assembly without having the constitutional right to do so, and became the sole ruler of France. Cells of resistance surfaced but were put down, and the Second Republic was officially over. Louis Napoleon took the title Emperor Napoleon III, and the Second Empire began, which lasted until 1870, when it collapsed in the wake of France's defeat in the Franco-German War.

Then, in March 1871, the workers of Paris rose up to oppose preparations by the royalist-majority National Assembly to restore the monarchy, and the provisional government's decision to disarm the National Guard, which consisted largely of workers who had fought the German forces during the Siege of Paris. After municipal elections resulted in victory for representatives of the working-class resistance, they formed the Paris Commune government, which called for social measures such as the limiting of the workday to 10 hours.

The Paris Commune was subjected to furious repression. With active aid from German Chancellor Otto Bismarck, the aristocratic-, landlord- and business-dominated ruling class launched military operations against the Commune. After pitched battles, more than 20,000 Communards were killed and at least 38,000 arrested, many of whom were executed, and more than 7,000 deported (Lissagaray 2007).

Seven years later, once capitalist rule had been stabilised, a new law on state of siege was introduced in 1878. Formally, it stipulated that a state of siege could be only declared by law, and only 'in the event of imminent danger resulting from a foreign war or an armed insurrection' (Gross and Ní Aoláin 2006: 28). But in practice this limitation was swept aside when the first test of the law came in World War I. On 2 August 1914, a state of siege covering the whole of France was imposed by a presidential decree when parliament was in recess, in order to enforce a general mobilisation for the war against Germany. Three days later, a law declared that the state of siege would remain in place 'for the duration of the war' and could be lifted, and reimposed, by presidential decree. The declaration handed all police and security powers to the military (Gross and Ní Aoláin 2006: 29).

During World War I, the French cabinet also promulgated decrees that derogated from previous legislation or imposed sweeping measures without any constitutional or statutory basis. Proponents of the 'accommodation model' of emergency powers also embraced this type of 'wartime' regime as justified by the concept of 'war powers' or the doctrine of necessity (Rossiter 1948: 112–13). In 1918, the Conseil d'État upheld the inherent powers of the executive government to take such actions (Bell 1992: 84).

Likewise, during the economic breakdowns, political turmoil and class battles of the 1920s and 1930s, the formal limits of state of siege provisions were overturned by the adoption of enabling acts that provided for emergency powers.

First adopted by the Poincaré government in 1926 (the year of the British General Strike), this mechanism reached its epitome with the Daladier government. From 1938 until the collapse of the Third Republic and the formation of the pro-Nazi Vichy regime, Daladier's administration ruled through executive decrees facilitated by four enabling acts.

The Act of 8 December 1939 made executive decree a permanent emergency institution for the duration of the war (Gross and Ní Aoláin 2006: 29–30). In 1940, Marshal Pétain, having been appointed premier of France by President Lebrun, signed an armistice with the Nazis, dissolved the Third Republic and established an authoritarian regime by claiming full dictatorial powers (Lackerstein 2012).

Despite this record, advocates of a state of siege-style mechanism contrast it with Article 48 of the German Weimar Constitution, the prevalent use of which helped pave the way for Nazi rule (see below). Purportedly, the state of siege was an emergency institution to be applied only in the most acute and violent crises (Gross and Ní Aoláin 2006: 29). In reality, there are many parallels between the two emergency provisions, and the outcomes were similar – they helped lay the groundwork for despotic and dictatorial regimes.

Germany's Weimar Republic

The record of the post-World War I German Weimar Republic provides an object lesson in the worthlessness of any formal constitutional constraint on emergency powers under capitalism, and how such constitutions prove to be antechambers of authoritarianism whenever the ruling elite feels fundamentally threatened by discontent erupting from below.

In his historical study *The Rise and Fall of the Third Reich*, Shirer described the Weimar Constitution as 'on paper, the most liberal and democratic document of its kind the twentieth century had ever seen ... full of ingenious and admirable devices which seemed to guarantee the working of an almost flawless democracy' (Shirer 1960: 56). Yet this constitution, with its Article 48 providing for presidential emergency powers, both facilitated the spiral into fascist rule and provided the initial legal justifications for Hitler's dictatorial measures.

Between 1919, when the Weimar Republic was instituted, and 1932, on the eve of Hitler's appointment as German chancellor, Article 48 was invoked more than 250 times, most often in the context of economic upheavals (Gross and Ní Aoláin 2006: 84).

The Weimar Constitution also allowed the president to dismiss the chancellor, even if the chancellor retained the confidence of the Reichstag (parliament). Similarly, the president could appoint a chancellor who did not have the support of the Reichstag. In effect, the president acted as a 'replacement Kaiser', assuming powers the monarch would have wielded.

Formally, the constitution protected a list of civil liberties. The relevant articles included 114 (habeas corpus), 115 (inviolability of residence), 117 (correspondence privacy), 118 (freedom of expression/censorship), 123 (assembly), 124 (associations) and 153 (expropriation). Yet, these could be overridden by the exercise of emergency presidential powers.

Article 48 allowed the president, under certain circumstances, to take emergency measures without the prior consent of the Reichstag. The article did not precisely define the kind of emergency that would justify its use. The president had to inform the Reichstag immediately of the issuance of the emergency decree, and the Reichstag could nullify the decree by a simple majority.

This presidential power was understood to include the promulgation of 'emergency decrees' (*Notverordnungen*). Article 48 did not expressly give the president the power to enact, issue or otherwise promulgate legislation. However, such an inherent presidential legislative power is implied, since the article expressly gives the Reichstag the power to cancel the emergency decree by a simple majority vote; and this parliamentary power suggests that the issuance of the decree could, by its express terms or its operation, impinge on the Reichstag's constitutional function (Mommsen 1998: 57–8). Article 48 stated:

> In the event of a State not fulfilling the duties imposed upon it by the Reich Constitution or by the laws of the Reich, the President of the Reich may make use of the armed forces to compel it to do so.
>
> If public security and order are seriously disturbed or endangered within the German Reich, the President of the Reich may take measures necessary for their restoration, intervening if need be with the assistance of the armed forces. For this purpose he may suspend for a while, in whole or in part, the fundamental rights provided in Articles 114, 115, 117, 118, 123, 124 and 153.
>
> The President of the Reich must inform the Reichstag without delay of all measures taken in accordance with Paragraphs 1 or 2 of this Article. These measures are to be revoked on the demand of the Reichstag.
>
> If danger is imminent, a State government may, for its own territory, take temporary measures as provided in Paragraph 2. These measures are to be revoked on the demand of the President of the Reich or of the Reichstag.
>
> Details are to be determined by a law of the Reich.

From the very first years of the Weimar Republic, the extensive resort to Article 48 led to a broad interpretation of what was meant by 'public security and order are seriously disturbed or endangered'. The Reichsgericht (Imperial Court of Justice) ruled that it permitted the president to 'take any measure necessary to the restoration of the public safety and order … Absolutely everything that the circumstances demand is to be allowed him in warding off the dangers that imperil the Reich (Rossiter 1948: 64). Toward the end of the republic, Article 48 became practically the exclusive legal source for government action, with the legislative and administrative processes virtually suspended. The Reichstag became simply a rubber stamp of approval for presidential emergency measures, as did the courts (Gross and Ní Aoláin 2006: 85).

According to Gross and Ní Aoláin, 'Article 48 instituted a modern version of the ancient Roman dictatorship' (Gross and Ní Aoláin 2006: 83). Rossiter offered an apologetic view of its incorporation into the Weimar Constitution:

> The stress of the times had forced men to whom arbitrary government had been lifelong anathema, to put into their model charter a device of emergency government that was a relic

> of the past and a possible platform for despotism. It was their hope and somewhat over-confident expectation that only good democrats devoted to the cause of the Republic would ever be in a position to resort to this unusual fund of power. (Rossiter 1948: 35)

This charitable interpretation flies in the face of the historical record. The Weimar Republic was founded on the back of the suppression and defeat of the German revolution that initially overthrew the Kaiser and stopped World War I.

In an uprising that began in Kiel, workers' and soldiers' councils seized most of Germany, to put an end to the war and the monarchy. Upon the Kaiser's abdication, the Social Democratic Party (SPD) and the anti-war Independent Social Democratic Party (USPD) assumed power in November 1918. However, this government refused to work with those who supported any type of council–socialist democracy and opted for a national assembly, meaning a transition to a parliamentary system (Hoffrogge 2014: 93–100).

Headed by Friedrich Ebert, the SPD government leaders sought an alliance with the military Supreme Command, which allowed the army and the *Freikorps* (right-wing militias) to violently suppress a second revolutionary wave that swept Berlin in January 1919, led by the Spartacist League of Rosa Luxemburg and Karl Liebknecht. *Freikorps* troops captured Luxemburg, Liebknecht and some of their supporters. Luxemburg was shot and her body thrown in Berlin's Landwehr Canal. A new wave of repression then began in Berlin and across Germany. Thousands of Spartacist supporters and workers were killed, although strikes and other forms of resistance continued until May 1919 (Kershaw 1998: 110–12).

It was on this political foundation that a supposedly democratic constitution was adopted at Weimar in August 1919. It did not take long for the repressive purpose of Article 48 to be demonstrated. Ebert, the Weimar Republic's first president, used Article 48 on 136 occasions, including to remove legitimately elected governments in the states of Saxony and Thuringia.

Ebert's regime faced the constant danger of a resurgence of a working-class uprising, which was to erupt again in 1921 and 1923, as well as threatened coups by the military and the Nazis. During 1923, French and Belgian troops occupied the Ruhr and reignited the political and social crisis in Germany. The government's counter-measures led to hyper-inflation, which devastated the lives of millions of people and triggered both an abortive coup by Hitler and a botched revolution led by the Communist Party (Trotsky 1971). Ebert's regime relied on the military generals to survive and rested on a virtual military dictatorship for months in 1923–24, legitimised by the Weimar constitution (Broué 2006).

During the final period of the republic, from 1930 to 1933, Article 48 was invoked by President von Hindenburg repeatedly. Amid the economic breakdown of the Great Depression, it was used to override the Reichstag, on behalf of German big business, at the behest of successive chancellors – Brüning, Papen, Schleicher and ultimately Hitler (Kershaw 1998: 315–423).

On 30 January 1933, Hitler was named chancellor, even though he lacked a majority in the Reichstag. On his appointment by President Hindenburg, he duly pledged to uphold the Weimar Constitution and respect the rights of the president (Kershaw 1998: 423). Initially, Hitler formed a coalition with the Nationalists, and then called elections for 5 March. Six days before the election, on 27 February, the Reichstag fire damaged the parliament building in Berlin. Claiming that the fire was the first step in a communist revolution, the Nazis used the fire as a pretext to get President von Hindenburg to sign the Reichstag Fire Decree, officially the Presidential Decree for the Protection of People and State.

Under the decree, issued by von Hindenburg on the basis of Article 48, the government was given authority to curtail constitutional rights including habeas corpus, free expression of opinion, freedom of the press, rights of assembly, and the privacy of postal, telegraphic and telephonic communications. Constitutional restrictions on searches and confiscation of property were likewise suspended. In the historian Kershaw's words:

> With one brief paragraph, the personal liberties enshrined in the Weimar Constitution – including freedom of speech, of association and of the press, and privacy of postal and telephone communications – were suspended indefinitely … The hastily constructed emergency decree amounted to the charter of the Third Reich. (Kershaw 1998: 459)

The Reichstag Fire Decree was one of the pivotal steps the Nazis took toward the establishment of a single-party dictatorship. Within a month, about 25,000 social democrats, communists, trade unionists and left-wing intellectuals had been dragged into improvised prisons, often in the cellars of SA or SS local headquarters, and savagely beaten, tortured and in some cases murdered in Prussia alone (Kershaw 1998: 460). With several key government posts in the hands of Nazis and with the constitutional protections on civil liberties suspended by the decree, the Nazis were able to use police power, as well as militias, to suppress, intimidate and arrest their opposition, in particular the communists. Hitler's utilisation of Article 48 thus gave his regime the mark of legality.

The 5 March elections gave the Nazi–DNVP (German National People's Party) coalition a narrow majority in the Reichstag. Nonetheless, the Nazis were able to secure on 23 March 1933 the passage of the Enabling Act by the required two-thirds parliamentary majority, effectively abrogating the authority of the Reichstag and placing its authority in the hands of the cabinet (in effect, the chancellor).

Over the years, Hitler used Article 48 to give his dictatorship the stamp of legality. Thousands of his decrees were based explicitly on the Reichstag Fire Decree, and hence on Article 48. The Reichstag Fire Decree was never abolished during the Nazi period; thus, for the next 12 years Hitler ruled under what amounted to martial law, with the help of Article 48.

Moreover, the Enabling Act was effectively a constitutional amendment. It met the constitutional requirements (two-thirds of the Reichstag's members were present, and two-thirds of the members present voted in favour of the measure). That was because the Communist Party deputies were in detention (Kershaw 1998: 465–8). The Act did not explicitly amend the Weimar Constitution, but stated that the procedure sufficient for constitutional reform was followed. The constitution of 1919 was never formally repealed, but the Enabling Act meant that all its other provisions were a dead letter.

The final acts that Hitler took to consolidate his power in 1934 actually violated the Enabling Act. Article 2 of the Act stated: 'Laws enacted by the government of the Reich may deviate from the constitution as long as they do not affect the institutions of the Reichstag and the Reichsrat. The rights of the President remain undisturbed.'

Hindenburg died on 2 August 1933, and Hitler appropriated the president's powers for himself in accordance with a law passed the previous day. However, in 1932 the constitution had been amended to make the president of the High Court of Justice, not the chancellor, acting president pending new elections. Nonetheless, the Enabling Act did not specify any recourse that could be taken if the chancellor violated Article 2, and no legal challenge was ever mounted. Hitler secured a cabinet vote, a day before Hindenburg died, to transfer the presidential powers to the one supreme post, that of the 'Fuhrer and Reich Chancellor' (Kershaw 1998: 524–6).

The fascist dictatorship was 'brought about by a combination of pseudo-legal measures, terror, manipulation – and willing collaboration (Kershaw 1998: 435). At every step of the way, the Nazis were assisted by the willing complicity of leading legal scholars. As Kershaw noted: 'Some leading constitutional lawyers – most prominent among them Carl Schmitt, the renowned constitutional theorist who in 1933 would place himself at the service of the Third Reich – were ready with their legal arguments to back the introduction of an authoritarian state' (Kershaw 1998: 384).

Great Britain's Legacy

Britain has been portrayed as a bulwark of the 'rule of law', most notably by Dicey (Dicey 1962). But its history, including that of the twentieth and twenty-first centuries, has been characterised by the repeated adoption of emergency powers. These measures were implemented not only during both World War I and World War II but also in peacetime, particularly against industrial action by the working class and left-wing political activity, as well as in Ireland.

In the lead-up to the English revolution of the 1640s, the 1628 Petition of Right demanded that Charles I remove the 'great companies of soldiers and mariners [who] have been dispersed into diverse counties of the realm … against the laws and customs of this realm and to the great grievance and vexation of the people'. The petition is regarded as making it unconstitutional for the Crown to impose martial law on civilians (Holdsworth 1902.) Yet, as will be discussed in Chapter 3, martial law has remained firmly entrenched in the armoury of the British state, despite some doctrinal disputes over its precise legal foundations.

As a result of the 1688 settlement between the monarchy and the parliament, the Bill of Rights also declared it illegal for the Crown to raise or keep an army without parliamentary consent (Greer 1983: 580). More generally, after the 'Glorious Revolution' of 1688, military force was seen as a grave threat to civil government, and its subordination to civilian rule was established as a 'constitutional priority' (Greer 1983: 592).

However, during the late eighteenth and early nineteenth centuries, the emergence of mass protests fuelled by the conditions of the Industrial Revolution and the growth of the working class caused the British authorities to resort to the military as riot controllers with increasing frequency (Greer 1983: 581). During the late eighteenth century, the Secretary at War warned magistrates against too readily calling out troops:

> Frequent use of soldiers to suppress civil commotions has an evident tendency to introduce military government, than which there cannot be a more horrible Evil in a State. (Greer 1983: 592)

In effect, successive governments, with the eventual acquiescence of parliament, relaxed the principle that the Secretary at War should approve any troop call-out by a magistrate. As a result of the rising civil unrest, the courts elaborated a common law right and duty of magistrates to opt for military intervention. In a series of statements in his dual role as a judge and parliamentarian toward the end of the eighteenth century, Lord Mansfield resurrected the feudal *posse comitatus* doctrine, which had been effectively extinguished in the seventeenth century. *Posse comitatus* arose in the Middle Ages, when both law enforcement, including the suppression of riots, and the waging of war was conducted by the king or his local representative, the sheriff, conscripting able-bodied freemen into a posse (Greer 1983: 578–81).

Lord Mansfield insisted that this disused power could be resumed by local magistrates and Justices of the Peace. In 1781, the chief London magistrate, Brackley Kennett, was charged with criminal breach of duty for refusing to read the Riot Act and order military intervention to put down the Gordon Riots. He was convicted and fined 1,000 pounds. Lord Mansfield instructed the jury:

> The common law and several statutes have invested justices of the peace with great powers to quell riots, because, if not suppressed, they tend to endanger the constitution of the country; and as they may assemble all the King's subjects, it is clear they may call in the soldiers, who are subjects and may act as such; but this should be done with great caution. (Greer 1983: 582)

Probably the most notorious mobilisation of the military against civilian protesters was the Peterloo Massacre of 1819. Cavalry troops charged into a crowd of 60,000 to 80,000 people gathered at St Peter's Field, Manchester for a public meeting, which had been declared illegal, to demand parliamentary representation. Shortly after the meeting began, local magistrates called on the military to arrest the speakers on the platform and to disperse the crowd. Soldiers on horses charged in with sabres drawn, killing 15 people and injuring 400–700, including women and children (Reid 1989). Whereas the arrested speakers were charged with sedition, found guilty and jailed, a test case against four members of the armed forces ended in acquittal, because the court ruled that their actions had been justified to disperse an illegal gathering (Reid 1989: 203–4).

Citing a range of sources and authorities, one scholar noted that both the parliament and the judiciary were prepared to cast aside constitutional principle in the face of rising social unrest, which reached new heights during the Chartist movement for voting and other basic rights:

> [I]t is debatable whether the eventual acquiescence of Parliament in the 'Mansfield doctrine' constituted sufficient authorisation for the valid revival of the magistrates' common law duty.

> The judiciary, however, refused to consider the constitutional dimension and blithely built upon the *posse comitatus* principle without regard to its shaky foundations. Civil libertarian reservations about the increasing use of the army in riots seem to have been overwhelmed by the general establishment view that what was good for the maintenance of public order was desirable and, therefore, legal. The fear of disorder had by this stage largely replaced the spectre of military intervention in civil affairs as the *bête noir* of the status quo. (Greer 1983: 583)

The last English case in which calling out the troops was directly examined was the 1832 case of *R v Pinney* ((1832) 5 Car & P 254; 170 ER 962). The mayor of Bristol and nine aldermen were prosecuted by the Attorney General for breaching their common law duty to assemble a sufficient force to put down three days of riots during which thousands of people – some allegedly armed with 'iron bars, iron crows, pickaxes, hammers, pieces of wood, and bludgeons' – broke open a jail and forced the release of prisoners. A military major advised the mayor that it would be 'imprudent to put arms in the hands of young troops'. The jury found the defendants not guilty.

The law report of *R v Pinney* also records Tindal LCJ's *Charge to the Bristol Grand Jury* after the riots. Lord Tindal insisted that soldiers had a duty, as citizens, on their own authority to do their utmost to 'put down riot and tumult'. Two officers who had refused to order the troops to fire without a magistrate's sanction were found guilty of neglect of duty, causing one to commit suicide. The third officer, who had fatally shot a boy during an incident, was acquitted of manslaughter. Lord Tindal instructed the Grand Jury that if the shot was 'discharged in the fair and honest execution of his duty, in endeavouring to disperse the mob', the killing was justified and amounted to accidental death only (170 ER 962, 969).

During this period, social tensions were so acute that summoning military personnel could inflame rather than subdue disturbances:

> Commentators were aware that the appearance of uniforms could provoke the crowd to further violence, especially since certain military units, for example the yeomanry, were identified with the propertied classes against whom the riots in this era were generally directed. The opposite could also, ironically, be the case. Other army units often identified with, and on occasion even joined, the rioters. (Greer 1983: 585)

Nevertheless, the power of magistrates to call out the troops without reference to the Home Office remained in use throughout the nineteenth century, as can be seen from the 1893 English *Report of the Select Committee on the Featherstone Riots*. Two people were killed when an infantry captain ordered soldiers to fire on striking coal miners and their supporters after a local magistrate had read the proclamation from the Riot Act 1714. The Committee exonerated the captain and his troops, although it warned that 'officers and soldiers are under no special privileges and subject to no special responsibilities as regards this principle of the law'. The taking of life must be shown to be necessary, and resort to military assistance must be the 'last expedient' of the civil authorities; but when such a call was made, 'to refuse such assistance is in law a misdemeanour' (United Kingdom 1893–94: 381).

By the beginning of the twentieth century, the creation of larger police forces meant that troops were rarely deployed in Britain to control riots. Military units were mobilised against industrial disputes, most notably in the British General Strike of 1926 (Laybourn 1993), but the decisions were made by the British government through the Home Office (Greer 1983: 586–7). The turmoil from the late eighteenth century through to the early twentieth century demonstrated the propensity of the British authorities to call out the armed forces against civilians if the establishment felt seriously threatened, and the readiness of the courts to sanction such operations.

In addition, notwithstanding the 1628 Petition of Right, British law was also prepared to support recourse to the imposition of martial law, with far-reaching military powers, including the right to summarily try and execute individuals, to put down civil unrest. After the final defeat of the absolute monarchy in 1688 and up until the nineteenth century, martial law was regarded as an emergency suspension of the rule of law, strictly confined to cases of necessity in times of war, not in times of peace when ordinary courts were open (Capua 1977). Yet, this view shifted during the nineteenth century (see Chapter 3).

Britain's Twentieth-Century Record

The Defence of the Realm Acts 1914–15, which initially authorised the making by the executive of regulations of the most far-reaching kind, were passed in wartime and conferred powers for the duration of the war only. But these powers were invoked for broader purposes than the war effort, in particular to suppress industrial action and political opposition, including to the war itself. The measures were applied to socialist opponents of the so-called 'Great War' who indicted the war as an essentially capitalist conflict over markets, trade, profits and colonial possessions, and suggested that workers should reject nationalism, fraternise and unite with their fellow workers in a common struggle against the nation-based wealthy elites.

Moreover, many of the powers were retained after the war. Thus, the Emergency Powers Act 1920 gave the United Kingdom government power to declare an emergency by proclamation in certain peacetime circumstances. These provisions were invoked 12 times during industrial and political unrest, notably during the 1926 General Strike and the 1970–74 period of discontent that eventually led to the defeat of the Heath government (Walker and Broderick 2006: 39).

During the 1920s, the usual practice was to have draft regulations prepared to be promulgated whenever necessary. These regulations were largely based on the Defence of the Realm Regulations 1914 ('DORA Regulations') (Young 1976: 32). There is no reason to believe that this practice has been discontinued. Sweeping emergency powers, including to make regulations that override Acts of Parliament, were re-adopted in the Civil Contingencies Act 2004 (see below).

By Regulation 42 of the 1914 DORA Regulations, it became an offence to cause mutiny, sedition or disaffection among the civilian population. This provision was used to suppress political and industrial unrest on Clydeside. A particular victim was the British Socialist Party leader John MacLean, who was jailed in 1916, and again in 1918, for anti-war speeches (Ewing and Gearty 2000: 57). MacLean was initially sentenced to three years' penal servitude for allegedly making inflammatory statements against conscription and encouraging the Clyde workers to strike. At one meeting, police reported that he said: 'Workers are being made slaves to suit the bloody British capitalists, which was pure Kaiserism and Prussianism' (Ewing and Gearty 2000: 77–8).

Maclean was released after 14 months, only to be arrested again in 1918, accused of 'making statements likely to prejudice recruiting and cause mutiny and sedition among the people'. The essence of his crime was to urge workers to follow the example of the October 1917 Russian Revolution by taking control of the Glasgow city chambers, the post office and the banks. Addressing the jury, the Lord Advocate said there was nothing in the law, as then framed, to prevent people talking about socialism, 'however inappropriate it might be, but there came a time when such discussion of social questions became seditious' (Ewing and Gearty 2000: 79–80). MacLean was sentenced to five years' jail, but released several months later, then imprisoned again before his death in 1923 (Ewing and Gearty 2000: 80).

Taken as a whole, the regulations gave the civilian and military authorities vast powers to restrict civil liberties. These included freedom of assembly and association (either by banning meetings or authorising a police presence at them); freedom of the press (by censoring or suppressing newspapers); and personal liberty (by internment or deportation for behaving 'in a manner prejudicial to the public safety or the defence of the Realm') (Ewing and Gearty 2000: 61–2). The courts proved to be reliable enforcers of the measures, regardless of the impact on rights and liberties traditionally regarded as enjoying the protection of the common law. A study of the emergency measures adopted in Britain found that 'there is not a single case of significance in the Law Reports of legislation passed between 1914 and 1945 to restrict personal and political liberties being restrained in its scope by the judicial power of interpretation' (Ewing and Gearty 2000: 29).

How these powers were perpetuated under the Emergency Powers Act 1920 was demonstrated by widespread arrests of members of the newly formed Communist Party in 1921. Emergency Regulations 1921, initially made after the declaration of a state of emergency in response to the national lockout of coal miners, closely resembled the wartime regulations (Ewing and Gearty 2000: 106). Regulation 19 dealt with incitement to sedition or mutiny (of the armed forces, police forces, fire brigades or civilian population), as well as actions designed to impede essential services. Regulation 20 authorised the Home Secretary and – if authorised by the Home Secretary – magistrates and police chiefs to ban public meetings and processions on the grounds that a meeting would give rise to 'public disorder' or a procession would lead to a breach of the peace or promote disaffection. Other regulations gave police wide powers of arrest, search, entry and seizure, including to arrest without warrant anyone who 'acts to endanger the public safety' or is suspected of any offence against the regulations (Ewing and Gearty 2000: 106–7).

More than 50 communists were arrested while the regulations were in force, many for sedition. One was arrested for suggesting at a public meeting that the king be put to work in the mines 'with his shirt off' and 'do the same work as the miners'. Another was arrested for discouraging trade unionists from signing up as reservists because 'You workers have nothing to lose. Now is the time to throw over the rotten Government system and the capitalist class' (Ewing and Gearty 2000: 107–8). The culmination was the arrest of the Communist Party's general secretary, Albert Inkpin, under Regulation 19 in connection with the publication of the *Theses and Statutes of the Communist International*. This prosecution challenged the very programmatic basis upon which the party had been established. Inkpin was found guilty and sentenced to six months' hard labour, and his conviction was upheld on appeal (Ewing and Gearty 2000: 109–12).

The 1926 General Strike saw the longest declaration of a state of emergency under the Emergency Powers Act, lasting some six months (Ewing and Gearty 2000: 155–213). Again, the regulations closely resembled the wartime provisions. Between the nine-day General Strike and the end of the miners' lockout in December 1926, hundreds of miners were jailed. Altogether, 3,304 people were charged under the regulations, with the bulk of the cases relating to 'damage to property', 'seditious speeches and literature' and 'disrupting supplies' (Ewing and Gearty 2000: 197–8).

Examples of the punishments handed out by magistrates included a man sentenced to three months' hard labour for pulling a government notice off a wall. A miner was jailed for three months for advising workers not to enlist as special constables. A trade unionist was sentenced to three months' hard labour and a 50 pound fine for telling workers 'what he conceived to be their duty to their trade union'. Teenage pickets were jailed for a month (Ewing and Gearty 2000: 198). Many people were arrested for producing or distributing Communist Party publications containing 'seditious matters' or 'false rumours' (Ewing and Gearty 2000: 202–4). Marxist books were confiscated, and one leader of the Young Communist League was jailed for three months for distributing a leaflet in a mining area calling for mass pickets to stop scabs (Ewing and Gearty 2000: 207–8). Public meetings and marches were banned on a widespread basis. At one point, the Home Secretary informed parliament he had invoked a ban on communist meetings, while acknowledging that he had no legal authority to do so (Ewing and Gearty 2000: 204–5).

Alongside the use of the emergency powers came some extraordinary uses of ordinary criminal law offences and judicial powers. Among the estimated 1,000 Communist Party members arrested was Shipurji (or Shapurji) Saklatvala, a Communist Party MP. He was arrested on a warrant charging him with inciting the public to commit a breach of the peace during a 1926 May Day speech in London's Hyde Park, in which he called upon the army to 'revolt and refuse to fight'. Saklatvala refused to be bound over, and was jailed for two months (and the Speaker of the House of Commons dismissed a subsequent appeal by a fellow MP for parliamentary privilege to protect Saklatvala) (Ewing and Gearty 2000: 201).

World War II again saw resort to emergency powers. Provisions included 'corruption of public morale', 'foment opposition' to the war and 'caus[ing] alarm or despondency', as well as wide-ranging internment powers (Ewing and Gearty 2000: 401). This regime gave rise to the House of Lords ruling in *Liversidge v Anderson* [1942] AC 206, which demonstrated the judiciary's willingness to accept wide-ranging use of the powers, including for mass detentions without trial. The issue arose from the internment of people suspected of being of 'hostile origin or association' under regulation 1B of the 1939 Defence Regulations, made under the Emergency Powers (Defence) Act 1939. After parliamentary objections to the initial form of the regulation, it was redrafted to require the Secretary of State to have a 'reasonable cause to believe' certain facts before exercising the power. This formulation was thought to impose an objective test but, after a series of legal challenges, the Home Office declined to file affidavits to justify internments. By a majority of four to one, the House of Lords upheld this practice, effectively interpreting 'reasonable cause' as merely requiring a belief in such a cause.

Lord Atkin dissented on the basis that some evidence was essential if the proper, objective meaning was to be given to the regulation. He commented that on the majority's interpretation, the Secretary of State enjoyed 'an absolute power which, so far as I know, has never been given before to the executive' (*Liversidge v Anderson* [1942] AC 206, 226). Atkin commented that in the case he had heard arguments that 'might have been addressed acceptably to the Court of King's Bench in the time of Charles I' and that his colleagues had responded in a manner that was 'more executive minded than the executive' *Liversidge v Anderson* [1942] AC 206, 244). Atkin's dissent was a narrow one, however. All he sought was the filing of a pro forma Home Office affidavit, of the kind he had accepted in the previous case of *Greene v Secretary of State for Home Affairs* [1942] AC 284. Ewing and Gearty concluded that Atkin's observations pointed to 'successive judges' ability to absorb official illegality and turn it into part of the common law' (Ewing and Gearty 2000: 398).

Repressive powers were exercised by British governments in Northern Ireland throughout the twentieth century. The complicity of the courts is illustrated by the 1971 case of *McEldowney v Forde* ([1971] AC 632). The Civil Authorities (Special Powers) Act (Northern Ireland) 1922 allowed the Minister of Home Affairs for Northern Ireland to issue regulations 'for the preservation of the peace and maintenance of order'. The minister used this power to ban 'republican clubs' of all kinds and 'any like organisation howsoever described'. McEldowney was a member of a republic club, but there was no evidence that the club represented a threat to the 'peace' or 'order' or had engaged in any 'seditious … pursuits' ([1971] AC 632 at 647). Nevertheless, the House of Lords, by a 3–2 majority, ruled that the regulation was not so vague as to be beyond the minister's power.

The British working class remained a central target of emergency-style plans. Papers released by the UK's National Archives reveal that the Conservative government of Margaret Thatcher developed detailed plans to use the army to break the year-long 1984–85 miners' strike. Cabinet documents from 1984, partially published after 30 years, show that plans were drawn up to use troops to move coal stocks. Despite official policy ruling out the use of the armed forces, preparations were made to deploy 4,500 soldiers to drive vehicles, including 1,650 tipper lorries, capable of moving 100 kilotonnes a day of coal to power stations. Another plan, codenamed Operation Halberd, involved the use of troops in the event of a prolonged dockworkers' strike.

The 1984 papers confirm that the main concern of the government was to ensure that the miners remained isolated from other critical groups of workers. Following the outbreak of a national dockers' strike on 8 July as a result of efforts to break their embargo on moving scab coal, a special cabinet committee, held on 18 July, discussed 'possible strategies for the coal and docks dispute'. The committee discussed a plan to mobilise troops in 13 specialist teams that could be used to unload 1,000 tonnes a day at the docks. According to the documents, Armed Forces Minister John Stanley said that 'a considerably larger scale' operation could be organised. The meeting discussed that this would require a declaration of a state of emergency. The prime minister asked the Attorney General to advise on how far it was possible to use troops to unload the food imports under a state of emergency even though there was not an immediate threat to the 'essentials of life' (Travis 2014).

In other words, political considerations dictated the government's tactics, not legal niceties. Ultimately, Thatcher's cabinet did not have to resort to smashing the dockers' strike by force, as the Transport and General Workers' Union (TGWU) called off the strike within hours. A further dockers' strike in August was also speedily called off. Unofficial blocks on the movement of coal were imposed by railway workers and lorry drivers, but official secondary supportive strike action was opposed by the Trades Union Congress (TUC) and its affiliated unions.

These provisions are far from being of purely historical interest. Similar powers were created for peacetime in the first decade of the twenty-first century. As will be examined in Chapter 7, the Civil Contingencies Act 2004 empowers 'Her Majesty' by an Order in Council (in ordinary times, this means the senior cabinet ministers) to issue sweeping emergency regulations in any event that 'threatens serious damage to human welfare' or 'serious damage to the environment' or 'war or terrorism, which threatens serious damage to the security of the United Kingdom' (section 19). These regulations can, inter alia, 'enable the Defence Council to authorise the deployment of Her Majesty's armed forces' and 'make provision (which may include conferring powers in relation to property) for facilitating any deployment of Her Majesty's armed forces' (section 22(3)(l) and (m)).

From the American Revolution to the 'War on Terrorism'

The Dismantling of the Right to Revolution

The American Revolution of 1776 was necessary for the formation of the United States, which was to replace the United Kingdom as the ascendant capitalist power in the twentieth century. At the same time, it was based upon the rejection of British absolutism and monarchism. Reflecting its purposes, the American Declaration of Independence proclaimed the right of revolution to secure the 'inalienable' rights to life, liberty and the pursuit of happiness:

> [W]henever any Form of Government becomes destructive of these Ends, it is the Right of the People to alter or abolish it, and to institute new Government, laying its Foundation on such Principles, and organizing its Powers in such Form, as to them shall seem most likely to effect their Safety and Happiness.

That declaration stated that revolution can become the *duty* of the people, insisting that 'when a long train of abuses and usurpations, pursuing invariably the same Object evinces a design to reduce them under absolute Despotism, it is their right, it is their duty, to throw off such Government'.

Nonetheless, over time, the ruling elite in the US increasingly adopted measures designed to suppress any further or future such overturns. In particular, the emergence of the industrial working class and its struggles for political and social emancipation produced laws and powers designed to answer the perceived threat from below. These measures have been especially directed against socialists, above all, revolutionary Marxists who strive for a further social revolution.

As late as 1961, Justice Douglas, in his dissenting judgment in *Scales v United States* (367 US 203), quoted an 1848 address by Abraham Lincoln before the US House of Representatives, where Lincoln stated:

> Any people anywhere, being inclined and having the power, have the *right* to rise up, and shake off the existing government, and form a new one that suits them better. This is a most valuable – a most sacred right – a right, which we hope and believe, is to liberate the world.

Douglas, however, immediately commented: 'Of course, government can move against those who take up arms against it. Of course, the constituted authority has the right of self-preservation' (*Scales v United States* at 269–70).

In an appendix to his judgment, Douglas disassociated himself from the following language in the Supreme Court decision in *Dennis v United States* (341 US 494, 501), which suggested that the right to revolution only applied where no official mechanism existed for political change:

> Whatever theoretical merit there may be to the argument that there is a 'right' to rebellion against dictatorial governments is without force where the existing structure of the government provides for peaceful and orderly change.

Thus, Douglas upheld the right to rise up, even in defiance of official procedures for 'peaceful and orderly change'. Douglas maintained that the right of revolution is ultimately reserved to the people themselves, 'whatever formal, but useless, remedies the existing government may offer'. However, he emphasised that this does not mean the helplessness of the established government in the face of armed resistance, 'for that government has the duty of maintaining existing institutions'. He concluded that while legislatures and governments have the right to protect themselves, and may judge as to the appropriate means of meeting force directed against them, the propriety of the exercise of the ultimate right of revolution remained the prerogative of the population: 'As John Locke says, "The people shall be judge." Second Treatise on Civil Government, § 240' (*Scales v United States* at 276–8).

These propositions seek to distinguish between advocacy of the abstract right to revolution, which is arguably protected by the American Constitution, and actually engaging in, or even urging, revolution (Head 2011: chapter 2). In effect, the US Constitution, while it may recognise a 'right' to revolution, also recognises the 'right' and 'duty' of governments to put down actual rebellions. That repressive feature became ever more dominant in the second half of the twentieth century, and even more so in the opening years of the twenty-first.

Of course, during the Civil War of the 1860s, President Lincoln suspended the writ of habeas corpus, and military tribunals imprisoned or exiled political opponents who publicly condemned the president, the emancipation of slaves, conscription and the war.

This was the period in which the existence of the United States was most genuinely at risk, directly confronted by a military challenge from the slave-owning states. In many ways, the Civil War was the completion of the American Revolution, abolishing slavery, confiscating slave-derived wealth and clearing the way for the industrial development of American capitalism (McPherson 1990). Quite validly, some measures adopted in this 'war' period can be regarded as a necessary suspension of aspects of civil law in a battlefield context. A civil war necessarily produces conditions in which it may be difficult, if not impossible, to maintain civil law. As historian James McPherson observes: 'Martial law prevails over large parts of a country wracked by civil war; newspapers and other media of communication are often muzzled; enemy partisans and sympathisers are arbitrarily arrested and jailed, sometimes tortured and murdered (McPherson 1990: 57).

Rather than suspending the constitution, Lincoln suspended habeas corpus and permitted military commissions to try those accused of damaging the war effort. It is not known exactly how many civilians were arrested by military authorities during the Civil War. Estimates range from 13,000 to 38,000. Most of the arrests occurred, however, in states where the fighting was taking place, and most were for offences such as draft evasion, trading with the enemy, bridge burning and other forms of sabotage. On the whole, there was limited use of criminal prosecutions to stifle political expression during the war. The Lincoln administration enacted no sedition legislation, left most dissenters alone and quickly released those speakers arrested for seditious remarks (Stone 2004: 133).

Mounting Resort to Repressive 'Emergency' Powers

Fifty years later, however, the United States' controversial entry into the final stages of World War I in 1917 produced an almost immediate resort to politically repressive measures. Less than three weeks after voting for war, the US Congress began debate on what became the Espionage Act of 1917. Among those who were to be imprisoned were anti-capitalist defenders of the 1917 Russian Revolution like Mollie Steimer, the prominent pacifist Jane Addams, the Socialist Party presidential candidate Eugene V. Debs and the internationally famous anarchist Emma Goldman (Stone 2004: 138–44).

Before the war ended, Congress also passed the Alien Act of 1918, which authorised the government to deport any non-citizen, or even a naturalised citizen, who was a member of an anarchist organisation. The entire process was administrative, with no right of appeal, semi-secret proceedings and limited right to counsel. In 1918 alone, 11,625 people were deported under this Act (Stone 2004: 181).

After the war came the vicious Red Scare of 1919–20, aimed at crushing political dissent, particularly that inspired by the October 1917 Russian Revolution. The media was consumed with stories depicting Bolshevik rule as a descent into slaughter, confiscations and disorder. But membership of socialist and communist parties grew rapidly and, during 1919, the discontent of returning soldiers helped fuel a series of major strikes – a Seattle general strike, a Boston police strike, a national steelworkers' strike and a mineworkers' strike (Stone 2004: 220–22).

Mass arrests followed. Attorney General Palmer appointed J. Edgar Hoover to head a new General Intelligence Division within the Bureau of Investigations. It placed more than

200,000 people under surveillance and disseminated fabricated charges that communists and radicals had instigated violent strikes and race riots. By January 1920, more than 4,600 people had been arrested – virtually every known communist – and some 3,000 non-citizens were soon deported (Stone 2004: 231–2).

Resort to repressive executive powers reached new heights during World War II. One early indicator of what was to come was President Roosevelt's secret 1936 decision to authorise the J. Edgar Hoover-led FBI to investigate suspected fascists and communists in the US. Hoover regarded the assignment as an invitation to resume many of the activities he supervised during the Red Scare of 1919–20 (Stone 2004: 248). During 1940, before the US entered the war against Germany, the Congress re-enacted the Espionage Act of 1917, making its provisions applicable for the first time in peacetime. It then went further, passing the Alien Registration Act of 1940 (the Smith Act), which required all resident non-citizens to register with the government, streamlined deportation procedures and forbade any person 'knowingly or wilfully' to 'advocate, abet, advise, or teach the duty, necessity, desirability, or propriety of overthrowing or destroying any government in the United States by force or violence' (Stone 2004: 252).

During the war, almost 5 million non-citizens were registered under the Smith Act; about 900,000 Japanese, German and Italian nationals were classified as 'enemy aliens' and more than 9,000 were detained. By executive order, another 120,000 people of Japanese descent, two-thirds of whom were US citizens, were ordered to leave their West Coast homes to live in detention camps, even though there was not one documented act of espionage, sabotage or treason committed by anyone of Japanese descent residing on the West Coast (Stone 2004: 283–303). The Supreme Court sanctioned these internments in *Korematsu v United States* (323 U.S. 214 (1944)), commenting that 'hardships are part of war' (Stone 2004: 300).

The next period of 'war' – the Cold War – was part of a wider political confrontation. Internationally, it was a struggle for US global dominance, directed against the Soviet Union, and domestically it was aimed against communists and alleged 'fellow travellers'. The Cold War produced 'one of the most repressive periods in American history' (Stone 2004: 312). It was a period of red-baiting, blacklisting and McCarthyism, conducted under the long shadow of the House Un-American Activities Committee (Stone 2004: 312–426). Alongside the Communist Control Act of 1954, which 'outlawed' the Communist Party and stripped it of all rights, privileges and immunities, there were loyalty programmes, emergency detention plans, undercover surveillance, legislative investigations and criminal prosecutions (Stone 2004: 340).

Far from being an aberration, the abuses of the McCarthyite period were exceeded by those of the 1960s and 1970s, directed against the civil rights and anti-war struggles. Already, at the height of the urban riots by African American workers and youth in the 1960s, troops had been sent into Detroit and other cities (Hammond 1997). Another turning point came when four students were shot dead by National Guard troops during an anti-war protest at Kent State University in 1970 (Bills 1998; Caputo 2005). The Kent State killings were part of a wave of repression in the aftermath of the television announcement by President Nixon that US forces had crossed the border from Vietnam and invaded Cambodia. In response to an unprecedented nationwide student strike involving an estimated 4.3 million students, shutting down or disrupting more than 900 college campuses, National Guard troops were dispatched to 21 campuses, while police battled students at another 26. University officials closed down 51 campuses for the remainder of the term (Stone 2004: 465–6).

Throughout the Vietnam War, the FBI ran an expanded illegal counter-intelligence programme (COINTELPRO) that went beyond surveillance to active political harassment, infiltration, disruption, provocations, smear campaigns and frame-ups. Originally directed against the Communist Party in the 1950s, COINTELPRO was extended to the Trotskyist Socialist Workers Party, civil rights organisations and, prodded by the Johnson administration, the anti-war movement. The FBI's operation was accompanied by equally unlawful domestic operations by the CIA, in blatant violation of its legislative charter, which expressly forbid it from undertaking any 'internal security' role. Similarly illegal interventions were conducted by army intelligence, which mobilised 1,500 undercover agents to collect information on groups seeking significant change in the US, and by the National Security Agency (NSA). According to a subsequent Senate committee report, the FBI alone compiled more than half a million domestic intelligence files (Stone 2004: 488–500).

The Supreme Court effectively gave a green light to these activities. In *Laird v Tatum* (408 US 1 (1972)), the court, while invoking a principle against 'military intrusion into civilian affairs', ruled that the plaintiffs, who suspected they had been placed under army intelligence surveillance, lacked standing to challenge the infringement of their freedom of expression. The court found that they had not shown any direct injury, and that mere knowledge of military investigative activity fell short of a 'chilling' of their First Amendment free speech rights. In what amounted to a 'Catch-22' situation, the judges refused to order the military to stop collecting information about civilians unless plaintiffs could prove that they had been harmed by what the military was doing. On this basis, the court declined to rule on the constitutionality of army domestic intelligence activity (Stone 2004: 499, fn 311). This decision established a far-reaching precedent, as was seen 20 years later when a US district court, in *New Alliance Party v Federal Bureau of Investigations*, 858 F Supp (SD NY 1994), issued a similar ruling to strike down a challenge to FBI surveillance activities (Stone 2004: 499, fn 311).

The 'War on Terrorism'

This repressive record was outdone further following the terrorist attacks in the United States on September 11, 2001, which quickly became the trigger for previously prepared plans to invade Afghanistan and Iraq. Domestically, the Bush administration swiftly moved to assert far-reaching executive powers, combined with draconian legislation that, in the name of protecting ordinary people against terrorism, violated basic civil liberties. According to one summary, the measures included:

- indefinite detention, with no access to judicial review, of more than 1,000 non-citizens who were lawfully in the US and had not been charged with any crime;
- blanket secrecy concerning the identity of these detainees;

- refusal to permit many of these detainees to communicate with an attorney;
- an unprecedented assertion of authority to eavesdrop on constitutionally protected attorney–client communications;
- secret deportation proceedings;
- the incarceration of an American citizen, incommunicado, with no access to a lawyer, solely on the basis of an executive determination that he was an 'enemy combatant;
- new limitations on the Freedom of Information Act;
- expanded authority to conduct undercover infiltration and surveillance of political and religious groups;
- increased power to wiretap, engage in electronic eavesdropping and covertly review Internet and email communications;
- new powers to secretly review financial records; and
- expanded authority to conduct clandestine property searches (Stone 2004: 552).

Most egregious of all was the indefinite detention, without trial, of hundreds, if not thousands, of foreign citizens in military camps at Guantanamo Bay and elsewhere, including secret locations in allied countries, where detainees were 'rendered' for torture. These detainees were designated 'enemy combatants', an arbitrary classification that violates the Geneva Conventions, and subjected to brutalities that made a mockery of the international Convention Against Torture (Sands 2006: 143–223; Paust 2007).

Moreover, the USA PATRIOT Act (Uniting and Strengthening America by Providing Appropriate Tools Required to Intercept and Obstruct Terrorism) 'smuggled into law several investigative practices that have nothing to do with fighting terrorism, but that law enforcement officials had for years tried unsuccessfully to persuade Congress to authorise' (Stone 2004: 553). In addition, the limited guidelines promulgated in 1976 – after the exposure of the COINTELPRO and other programmes in violation of the First Amendment – restricting the FBI's authority to investigate political and religious activities were effectively dismantled. The FBI was authorised to monitor a wide range of constitutionally protected activities without having to show that any unlawful conduct might be afoot. Anti-war demonstrators were soon targeted, together with what the FBI termed 'anarchists' and 'extremist elements' (Stone 2004: 555–6).

While all these measures were ostensibly aimed at terrorists, or would-be terrorists, they set in place mechanisms for wider use in suppressing dissent, as well as defining terrorism in terms that can extend to many traditional forms of anti-government sentiment and activity (Stone 2004: 555).

The Supreme Court has again proven no fundamental obstacle. In 2008, just as it did in 1972 in *Laird v Tatum*, the court refused to hear an appeal brought by the American Civil Liberties Union (ACLU) and other groups challenging the Bush administration's warrantless domestic wiretapping programme conducted by the NSA, a military agency (ACLU 2008). The wiretapping programme began in 2001 but was first revealed to the public through a media leak in 2005. The programme, the full details of which are still not known, included domestic spying in breach of the Foreign Intelligence Surveillance Act (FISA).

In 2006, a US District Court judge had ruled that the programme violated the First and Fourth Amendments, the separation of powers and FISA. When that ruling in

ACLU v NSA was overturned on appeal, the challengers were caught in another Catch-22 situation. The government refused to identify the individuals targeted by the NSA programme, on the grounds that this information was secret. However, the appellate court upheld the government's argument that only those who could prove they had been specifically targeted by the programme could have standing to sue. The Supreme Court rejected a further appeal without comment.

In 2004, the Supreme Court, by a 6–3 majority, ruled that Guantanamo Bay detainees could seek writs of habeas corpus in US courts. The majority judgment, delivered by Stevens J, suggested that at stake were democratic conceptions dating back nearly 800 years to the Magna Carta of 1215 (*Rasul v Bush*; *Al Odah v United States*, 542 US 466 (2004)). Nevertheless, no detainees were released as a direct result of the decision. Four years later, in *Boumediene v Bush* (553 US 723 (2008)), the Supreme Court ruled 5–4 that Guantanamo detainees could immediately file habeas corpus petitions in US district courts challenging the legality of their confinement. Most had been held at the US naval base under brutal conditions – often enduring solitary confinement, water-boarding and other coercive techniques or torture – for more than six years, without having the merits of their cases reviewed by a court of law. However, the ruling did not question the executive branch's ability to declare someone an 'enemy combatant', a power the Supreme Court had upheld four years earlier in *Hamdi v Rumsfeld* (542 US 507 (2004)).

Later in 2008, a 5–4 decision by the US Court of Appeals for the 4th Circuit backed the Bush administration's contention that the president has such power. In *Al-Marri v Pucciarelli* (4th Cir. July 15, 2008), the court effectively overturned a decision reached by a three-judge panel of the same court in 2007, which compared the assumption of such sweeping powers to military rule and the oppression of the American colonies by King George III. The appellate ruling denied habeas corpus to Al-Marri, a legal resident of the US before the White House declared him an enemy combatant in 2003 and ordered the military to detain him in a navy brig in South Carolina. The government claimed that the Authorization to Use Military Force (AUMF) resolution passed by Congress in 2002 gave the president the power to carry out such detentions. Alternatively, it asserted that the commander-in-chief has unchallengeable authority to imprison anyone without charges for the duration of a global war on terror.

The post-9/11 practices were not simply the product of the Bush administration or the Republican Party. As discussed in the Introduction, the lawlessness, assertions of executive powers and blockages of judicial review went further under Obama, who claimed the right to assassinate people, including US citizens, via drone attacks.

Australia: From Martial Law to the Cold War

Martial Law and Military Mobilisations

In Australia, martial law was invoked several times during the nineteenth century against convicts, Aborigines and workers (Lendrum 1977; Windeyer 1979). Governor King declared martial law in 1804 in New South Wales to suppress an 'Irish insurrection'. Many participants in the revolt were tried by court martial, and a number were hanged (Lendrum 1977: 40). Another NSW governor, Darling, rejected the urging of his Attorney General to declare martial law in 1826 to use the military against Aborigines who were resisting seizures of their lands. Darling was of the view, however, based on advice from the British Secretary of State Lord Bathurst, that he could use troops against Aboriginal people without such a declaration, as if they were 'open enemies' against whom war could be declared (Lendrum 1977: 42).

Two of the most barbaric declarations of martial law came in 1828 and 1830, when Governor Arthur of Tasmania mobilised troops to drive Aborigines from settled areas. Arthur twice invoked martial law even though Aboriginal retaliation against their dispossession had taken the form of isolated attacks, not a general war (Lendrum 1977: 41; Calder 2008: 127–50). In 1840, Governor Gawler of South Australia cited martial law, although not formally declared, as well as the war of law, as the legal justifications for the summary execution of two Aboriginal people rounded up by troops in the Coorong area, near the mouth of the Murray (Lendrum 1977: 29, 34). As late as 1867, British authorities sent regulations to the Australian colonies providing for declarations of martial law, although it seems that these regulations were not put into practice (Clark 2007: 17, citing *Proposed Rules on the Subject of Martial Law*, SAPP No. 107 of 1867).

Without resorting to martial law, in 1854 soldiers were used alongside police to mount an attack on the Eureka Stockade, which miners had erected to resist the efforts of the authorities to collect licence fees. About 30 miners and four soldiers were killed in the ensuing battle, and many more were injured (McCulloch 2001: 36). The great strike struggles of the 1890s saw troops mobilised against specific demonstrations and gatherings, with orders to shoot to kill strikers and their supporters. In one infamous incident, Colonel Tom Price issued the following instruction to a volunteer unit during the extended Australian maritime strike of 1890:

> Men of the Mounted Rifles, one of your obligations imposes upon you the duty of resisting invasion by a foreign enemy, but you are also liable to be called upon to assist in preserving law and order in the colony … To do your work faintly would be a grave mistake. If it has to be done effectively you will each be supplied with 40 rounds of ammunition, leaden bullets, and if the order is given to fire, don't let me see any rifle pointed in the air; fire low and lay them out so that the duty will not have to be performed again. (McKinlay 1979: 377)

The turmoil of the 1890s led to section 119 being inserted in the constitution, to allow the military to be mobilised against 'domestic violence'. In the early years of the twentieth century, Australian state governments requested military intervention on at least six occasions to deal with such anticipated incidents as 'general strike riot and bloodshed', 'disturbances', wharf strike 'violence', 'labour troubles' and the 1923 Victorian police strike (Beddie and Moss 1982: 8–39). On each occasion, the Federal Government declined on the basis that the state police were capable of dealing with the threat (although troops were sent to guard federal buildings, including post offices, during the 1923 Victorian police strike) (Lee 1984: 201). Only one of those requests – by Queensland in 1912 – was formally made under s 119. Perhaps as a result of the legal and political difficulties experienced in invoking s 119, the section has never been applied.

Several of these episodes saw troops mobilised partially or assembled in substantial numbers without a formal call-out, however. Troops were also mobilised to break strikes on several occasions during the second half of the twentieth century, with Labor governments playing a leading role. When the Chifley government sent in soldiers against the coal miners' strike of 1949, the Labor government set a precedent that the Menzies government extended to establish a plan for systematic military involvement in breaking strikes under the cover of maintaining 'essential services' and defeating 'communism'.

The threat of military intervention was present during the constitutional crisis of 1975. Governor-General Sir John Kerr reportedly held his own meetings, as the titular commander-in-chief of the Australian Defence Force (ADF), with senior defence officials before dismissing the Whitlam government (Coxsedge, Coldicutt and Harant 1982: 35, 96).

The only major mobilisation of troops in an urban setting in Australia's history occurred in 1978. At 12.40 a.m. on 13 February 1978, a bomb exploded in a refuse bin outside the Hilton Hotel, the venue for the Commonwealth Heads of Government Regional Meeting (CHOGRM), a gathering of government leaders from former British colonies. Without any clear legal or constitutional authorisation (Head 2001a: 282–4), the federal Liberal government and the state Labor government deployed nearly 2,000 heavily armed troops, some with bayonets fixed, accompanied by armoured personnel carriers and helicopters. (For further detail on these or other military deployments in Australia, see Head 2009: 43–55.)

Wartime Internments and Political Repression

Emergency powers were adopted in Australia during both world wars, and were used to detain and incarcerate thousands of people of foreign descent, political activists and others, and more generally to suppress socialist and anti-war opinion. One study of the World War II national security legislation pointed out that it closely resembled its World War I equivalent, as well as the similar legislation in Canada, New Zealand and the United Kingdom (Douglas 2003).

The punitive use of these regulations against opponents of the war and conscription provoked several political confrontations during World War I. In 1915, a prominent International Workers of the World (IWW) leader, Tom Barker, was convicted of publishing posters likely to prejudice recruiting. He was charged under New South Wales state War Precautions Regulations. A magistrate ruled that a poster with the words 'Workers, follow your masters, stay at home' was prejudicial to recruitment, and, in effect, sentenced Barker to 12 months' jail. Amid protests, his conviction was quashed on appeal, with the court ruling that the state regulations were invalid in a field covered by federal law. The following year Barker was convicted again, this time under federal regulations, and his appeal was dismissed. His jailing triggered threats of IWW retaliation, including acts of sabotage which were then cited as evidence in the 1916 seditious conspiracy trial of the Sydney Twelve. In a bid to defuse discontent, the Governor-General cut Barker's sentence by nine months, and he was released after four months (Turner 1969: 16–17, 37–8).

There was a further controversy when the Australian High Court lent direct support to the use of the regulations to suppress dissent in a 1918 case. Ernie Judd, a member of the NSW Labor Council, the state's peak trade union body, was convicted under the War Precautions Act 1914–1915 (Cth) for successfully moving an amendment to a Labor Council resolution on the war effort. In the wake of the 1917 Russian Revolution, Judd's amendment set out the basis of socialist-minded opposition to the war, as well as the union movement's grievances against the conduct of the war. His amendment concluded:

> [We] refuse to take part in any recruiting campaign, and call upon workers of this and all other belligerent countries to urge their respective governments to immediately secure an armistice on all fronts, and initiate negotiations for peace. (Turner 1969: 217–18)

On appeal, the High Court unanimously rejected Judd's objection that the War Precautions Act required prosecutions to be personally authorised by the Attorney-General. Despite clear words in the Act forbidding indictments other than in the name of the Attorney-General, the judges delivered brief judgments simply declaring that the Act left the matter in the hands of the executive government. Only Justice Isaac Isaacs offered any explanation, saying the legislation:

> allowed the Executive to take steps for the safety of the Commonwealth and of the Empire which might be of a very drastic character, and the enforcement of regulations made under that Act might involve a great deal of discretion on the part of the public authority. (*R v Judd* [1919] HCA 9, (1919) 26 CLR 168)

Judd was later convicted on two further counts under the Act – for making anti-war statements during public meetings in the Sydney Domain. On one occasion, he said the fight of the Australian working class was not in France but 'right on the job'. On another, he invoked Christ's command: 'Thou shalt not kill' (Turner 1969: 218).

During World War II, wide-ranging powers were again conferred upon the executive by the National Security Act 1939–1940. Section 5 authorised the Governor-General to make regulations for securing the public safety and the defence of the Commonwealth and for prescribing all matters necessary or convenient for the more effectual prosecution of the war. The Australian High Court upheld the validity of section 5 in *Wishart v Fraser* ([1941] HCA 8; (1941) 64 CLR 470), where Justice Dixon emphasised the open-ended breadth of the judiciary's interpretation of wartime powers. He and fellow judges unanimously dismissed an argument that section 5 was unconstitutional because the subject matter handed over to the executive was so wide or uncertain that the legislation was not a law with respect to the defence power or any other head of legislative power in the constitution. Justice Dixon stated:

> The defence of a country is peculiarly the concern of the Executive, and in war the exigencies are so many, so varied and so urgent that width and generality are a characteristic of the powers which it must exercise.

Under the National Security Regulations, the federal government banned communist publications; outlawed the Communist Party of Australia and the Trotskyist Communist

League of Australia; and authorised police raids of offices and homes to enforce those proscriptions by seizing documents and arresting party members. Three members of the Trotskyist movement – Jack Wishart, Gil Roper and Allan Thistlewayte – were imprisoned for up to eight months for possessing or circulating dissenting material (Greenland 1998: 96–104).

The verdict in *Wishart v Fraser*, where Wishart challenged his conviction in the High Court, demonstrated the extent to which these powers were employed to silence and punish socialist opponents of the war. In essence, the judges unanimously upheld the imprisonment of Wishart for propagating the analysis of the Fourth International, the international Trotskyist movement, that the war was an imperialist one – that is, fought between the major world powers for economic and strategic supremacy – and for advocating the election of soldiers' committees to establish democratic control over the armed forces.

In another revealing case, *Francis v Rowan* ([1941] HCA 6 (1941) 64 CLR 196), the High Court unanimously overturned a magistrate's acquittal of Rowan on a charge, under the same National Security (General) Regulations, of endeavouring orally to influence public opinion in a manner likely to be prejudicial to the efficient prosecution of the war. Without a single dissent, the court reversed the verdict of the magistrate, who interpreted the word 'endeavour' in the regulations as requiring a conscious intention on the part of the accused to influence public opinion in the manner that the regulation prohibited. That is, the magistrate insisted on the normal criminal law requirement that the necessary intent, or *mens rea*, be proved.

Rowan's offence had been to address an anti-conscription public meeting and express a definite political opinion – that the war was being fought in the interests of the ruling capitalist elite. According to Acting Chief Justice Rich, the speech attacked 'the government, [Prime Minister Robert] Menzies and his followers'. The Acting Chief Justice quoted sections of Rowan's speech at some length, including the following excerpt:

> The men in control of this country form a minority government which is controlled by the big combines and industries and monopolies in this country, who by reason of their smoothness of tongue and suave manners have tricked the people of this country and have lulled them into a sense of false security. Also because I know that the people of this country have been tricked and robbed and forced into things by false statements and promises which have never been carried out. I consider it my duty to speak to you tonight to oppose conscription which Menzies and his followers wish to introduce into this country … men like Essington Lewis and other leaders of the big combines are preying upon the working class the same as the people in France and in every country in the world; the same little clique praying upon the masses.

The magistrate ruled that Rowan had not endeavoured to influence public opinion in a manner prejudicial to the efficient prosecution of the war, but the High Court judges insisted that such an intent was not necessary for guilt. In the words of Williams J: 'The offence would be committed if the statements he [Rowan] made were capable of influencing public opinion in the forbidden direction irrespective of any mens rea on his part.'

It was a highly political ruling. Not only did it effectively outlaw expressions of opposition to the Menzies government; it also prohibited reference to the economic class interests involved in the war. The judgments revealed concern that articulating anti-government and anti-capitalist sentiment could undermine public support for the war. Justice Williams found it objectionable that:

> [T]he defendant was making a number of statements calculated to create mistrust in the minds of his hearers as to the bona fides of the Government, suggesting that it was a minority government acting in the interests of one class of the community to the detriment of the general public, that it had fascist tendencies and that the army under its control would be more of a menace than an asset to the country.

At the same time, Justice Williams asserted that war made necessary a different approach to civil liberties. 'In time of war the necessity to protect the safety of the realm is paramount and must take priority over individual rights', he stated. This proposition suggests that courts should allow almost unlimited power to the executive to override traditional legal principles in periods of war or other alleged emergency.

In a study of the use of the World War II legislation, Douglas observed that some of the behaviour covered by the offences created by the national security regulations would also have constituted sedition (Douglas 2003). Seditious purposes under the then Crimes Act 1914 (Cth), sections 24A–E, included exciting disaffection against British, Dominion and Australian governments. However, for prosecutions, the emergency regulations had several advantages. First, defendants in sedition cases had a right to opt for trial by jury – a basic legal right enshrined in the Australian Constitution for indictable offences – and juries might be sympathetic to anti-war sentiment. By contrast, defendants charged under the wartime regulations were tried summarily. Second, there was no need to prove that statements were actually likely to arouse disaffection; only that they were calculated to do so. Third, there was no 'good faith criticism' defence under the regulations. A fourth advantage could be added. As illustrated by *Francis v Rowan*, there was no need to prove any intention to cause disaffection.

Douglas estimated that during World War II, governments approved the prosecution of at least 69 people, primarily communists, with some pacifists, fascists and a lone Jehovah's Witness (Douglas 2003). Of these, 61 were tried and 28 were jailed. However, a wider number of arrests were made, accompanied by 'massive' police raids and the seizure of literature. The Communist Party and the Trotskyist organisations were forced to dismantle and secrete their printing presses away.

Despite the severity of these measures, Douglas argued that wartime political repression was limited, with a degree of official tolerance toward anti-war opinion. However, he noted that enforcement was constrained by political considerations, most importantly government's need to secure the support of the Labor and trade union movement. Another major factor was the Communist Party's backflip to fervently support the war effort after the Nazi invasion of the Soviet Union in June 1941; from that point onward, prosecutions were rare. Douglas summarised the political calculations related to the trade unions as follows:

> Unions were willing to work with the government, but the price of cooperation was recognition of union sensitivities. Thus, union papers were treated more favourably than communist papers, notwithstanding that they sometimes published very similar articles. Communist union leaders could say certain things as union leaders, which they could not say as communists. Following the banning of the CPA, planning for raids proceeded on the basis that no prominent union officials were to be targeted. (Douglas 2003: 110–11, footnotes omitted)

The Labor government's highly partisan considerations are revealing. Rather than offering any guarantee of official tolerance, however, they point more generally to the politically calculating and discriminatory character of the application of such emergency powers.

'Cold War' Emergency Plans

There is no basis for concluding that the invocation of emergency powers, and their exploitation for definite political purposes, is confined to times of war, whether formally declared or not.

The Spy Catchers, volume one of the official history of the Australian Security Intelligence Organisation, or ASIO (Horner 2014), confirms that political calculations also loomed large with the onset of the so-called Cold War by the United States and its allies against the Soviet Union that began in the late 1940s. The Liberal-Country Party government of Prime Minister Robert Menzies that took office in late 1949 was committed to banning the Australian Communist Party, both for domestic and external reasons.

Internally, the Communist Party was influential in that the working class and trade unions that it led had been involved in post-World War II industrial action, notably the 1949 miners' strike in which workers fought for higher wages and better conditions. Externally, the formation of supposedly communist governments in Eastern Europe, followed by the 1949 Chinese revolution and the ensuing eruption of the Korean War in 1950, led to the deployment of Australian troops as part of US-led military mobilisations to combat what were perceived as developments that threatened the Western powers.

Under these conditions, according to *The Spy Catchers*, the Menzies government 'began organising for a possible global war', and needed ASIO to update the *Commonwealth War Book*, which set out plans for internments of 'aliens' (non-Australians) and political opponents (Horner 2014: 184). Outlining the purpose of the *Commonwealth War Book*, ASIO's official history states:

> This book, first prepared before the Second World War, set out the actions to be taken by government departments, both in the 'precautionary stage' before the outbreak of war, and during a war itself. The War Book stipulated, for example, that in the precautionary stage the Director-General of Security was to provide the Attorney-General with a list of people for whom he recommended detention or restriction orders be made. Once war was declared, the Director-General was to arrange for these people to be detained. Similarly, the Director-General was to provide lists of aliens (non-Australians or non-British subjects), and on the outbreak of war arrange for their internment. (Horner 2014: 184)

Clearly, these preparations involved the potential rounding up and imprisonment of many thousands of people. ASIO would have undertaken extensive surveillance, conducted surreptitiously, of wide layers of the population, not just Communist Party members, in order to provide the government with the required lists. In addition, other government departments would have been secretly involved in identifying the targets. Horner reports that on 28 July 1950, ASIO's chief, Director-General Charles Spry:

> [I]ssued his first policy statement on emergency measures, noting that 'in view of the uncertain international situation' they were to 'be undertaken immediately'. To avoid any misconception, 'the utmost discretion' was to be used and other government departments were to be advised that 'as a normal peacetime planning precaution we are accumulating certain information in case an emergency should arise'. (Horner 2014: 184)

Spry directed that, in addition to lists of 'aliens' to be interned, a list of 'British subjects' be drawn up, which would include the leaders of the Communist Party 'and other communists in key positions' (Horner 2014: 184–5). These preparations dovetailed with the Menzies government's move to outlaw the Communist Party, which would require ASIO and the police forces to seize the party's records and property and conduct mass arrests. In October 1950, as soon as the Communist Party Dissolution Act was signed into law, ASIO and state police officers raided Communist Party offices in Sydney, Melbourne, Perth, Hobart and Darwin. According to one ASIO record, officers seized 'more than half a ton of pamphlets, articles and other documents' (Horner 2014: 185).

These operations proceeded despite an ultimately successful High Court challenge to the Communist Party Dissolution Act: 'ASIO remained busy gathering information to apply the provisions of the act if it was found to be valid' (Horner 2014: 185). Moreover, these activities continued even after the High Court ruled the Act unconstitutional. Spry ordered ASIO officers to undertake 'the utmost effort, diligence, and ingenuity in order that we may produce clear legal proof that the ACP as an organisation or its individual members are engaged in activity prejudicial to the safety of the Commonwealth' (Horner 2014: 187–8).

In December 1950, Director-General Spry instructed ASIO's regional offices to prepare new lists of aliens to be interned, 'in the following order of priority': '1 Russians (excluding White Russians, who were considered anti-communist); 2 Chinese and North Koreans; 3 Albanians; 4 Bulgarians; 5 Romanians; 6 Poles; 7 Czechoslovakians; 8 Hungarians; 9 Yugoslavians (Horner 2014: 186). In addition, regional offices were to supply a list of Communist Party officials and 'Communist disrupters of industry'. Nearly 1,000 'communists' were to be locked up. Spry estimated that 'the immediate detention of about 750 selected Communists would render the party organisation innocuous for a period of time' (Horner 2014: 186).

These plans were explicitly politically biased against alleged 'communist' sympathisers, and in favour of former Nazis and fascists, who were now regarded as allies in the fight against communism. Spry directed that non-enemy aliens 'with an adverse pro-Communist security record should be listed automatically either for internment or restriction, depending on the degree of their subversive activities'; but it was 'not intended at this stage to intern former Nazis and Fascists' (Horner 2014: 186). ASIO knew who they were and could provide details to the government if required.

ASIO also participated in another secret government scheme, labelled Operation Alien, which was directed against industrial action by the working class. Military personnel would be used to maintain essential services in the event of strikes. ASIO's task was to inform the coordinating committee of Communist Party and trade union plans for industrial action (Horner 2014: 187). Without any clear legal authority, between 1952 and 1954, hundreds of troops were deployed on several occasions to load strikebound ships at various ports around the country, although public opposition forced the government to withdraw the soldiers from the sugar port of Bowen in 1953 (Head 2009: 47–8). A political precedent for using soldiers as strike-breakers had been set by the previous Labor government of Prime Minister Ben Chifley in 1949, when it mobilised troops to defeat a coal miners' strike (Head 2009: 47–8).

ASIO's internment plans were made in the closest association with the Menzies government, underscoring the intimate involvement of the political establishment in the surveillance activities and mass arrest plans of the security agencies. From early 1951, Spry held a series of meetings with Solicitor-General Kenneth Bailey, and sometimes Attorney-General John Spicer, to 'refine' the internment policy. ASIO estimated that it would need to consider the internment of about 3,100 people, including 2,000 enemy aliens, 100 other aliens and 1,000 British subjects and displaced persons (Horner 2014: 193). About 270 people were also listed for internment in the Australian colony of Papua New Guinea. Most were described as 'Asiatics' (Horner 2014: 194).

Even though the prospect of war receded after the end of the Korean War in 1953, ASIO maintained the Australia-wide list throughout the 1950s. By 1955, there were still 'approximately 982' Communist Party members targeted, along with 4,665 aliens. In 1957, Spry reported that the number of proposed internments had been reduced in a 'more liberal policy' (Horner 2014: 194).

ASIO's blatantly political role, in active partnership with the Menzies government, has now been confirmed by ASIO's official history. It documents Spry's personal discussion with the prime minister, offering to assist the government with its campaign for its 1951 constitutional referendum to gain the powers to ban the Communist Party, thus thwarting the High Court's ruling that the dissolution legislation was invalid. Via bugging devices and its many agents who had infiltrated the Communist Party, ASIO was able to gain full coverage of the party's national congress that year. Spry visited Menzies and told him:

> I would like to submit, for your consideration, whether it would be possible for you to cover certain matters which arose in this Congress during your forthcoming Referendum speeches. I feel, from the ASIO angle, that it would cause great perturbation, to say the least, within the hierarchy of the Australian Communist Party, if it was made known to them that the Government is aware of the details of their secret discussions. (Horner 2014: 190)

Menzies did, in fact, use ASIO's information in his opening speech of the referendum campaign, although he made several factual errors in doing so (Horner 2014: 190). Despite the defeat of the referendum, ASIO continued 'unrelenting' surveillance, infiltration and undercover provocations directed against the Communist Party (Horner 2014: 195–225). In 1954, it had 89 active agents and many more contacts inside the party (Horner 2014: 210).

New Zealand and Canada

During wars, major industrial struggles and political crises, extraordinary measures have also been imposed in other so-called advanced democracies with British-derived legal systems, notably in Canada and New Zealand, with the willing assistance of the courts.

In New Zealand, during World War II, dozens of communists were prosecuted for making or publishing subversive statements, most of whom received prison sentences; and numerous pacifists were arrested under the Emergency Regulations for holding illegal meetings and for publishing subversive literature. Overall, in 1940, there were 59 charges of making or publishing subversive statements, of which nine were heard in the New Zealand Supreme Court, where only one was acquitted. As in Australia, courts in Canada and New Zealand usually approached the regulations on the basis that, in wartime, executive powers were to be given a broad construction (Douglas 2003).

The extent of judicial embrace of such powers was exemplified in one case, *Stevenson v Reid* ([1942] NZLR 1), which involved an offence committed innocently against the Censorship and Publicity Emergency Regulations 1939. In the Supreme Court, Callan J not only upheld the regulations but also declared that, the executive having followed the prescribed statutory process, 'it would be quite impossible to challenge the validity of the regulations'. The concentration of power in the hands of the executive was a necessary wartime evil and the courts 'must submit to it' ([1942] NZLR 1 at 3). Callan J explicitly endorsed the alleged need to curtail political freedom:

> One of the, liberties which we enjoy in peace time and exercise very readily … is the liberty of criticizing … those persons … in positions of power and authority … That is one of the liberties, which may have to be curtailed in war time if it is exercised in a manner which conflicts with a true view of the public good. ([1942] NZLR 1 at 2)

That readiness to afford the executive near-absolute power was maintained well after World War II ended, during a major waterfront dispute in 1951. Waterside workers were locked out after banning overtime to fight against low wages and long working hours, and thousands of other workers went on strike to support them. The government declared an emergency and brought in the navy and army to work the wharves.

In *Hewett v Fielder* ([1951] NZLR 755), the Supreme Court held that the government's power, exercised by the Governor-General in Council under the oppressive Public Safety Conservation Act 1932 (NZ) to declare states of emergency and make emergency regulations, was virtually unlimited. The Governor-General's power to take such actions 'as he thinks necessary' was unable to be judicially restricted, proved that the decisions related to one of the very broad purposes of the Act and were taken in good faith ([1951] NZLR 755, at 760).

The Public Safety Conservation Act, which permitted the Governor-General to declare a state of emergency in any circumstances deemed to pose a danger to public safety or public order, remained on the books until 1987. Moreover, the Civil Defence Emergency Management Act 2002 (NZ) is hardly less arbitrary. It permits a minister to declare an emergency as the result of 'any happening, whether natural or otherwise' that threatens the safety of the public or property (section 4). Such a declaration hands extensive powers to the minister and to constables and Civil Defence Controllers, including to issue directives to people, control movement, requisition property, and forcibly enter premises (sections 84, 98–102).

There is a similar history in Canada. The War Measures Act of 1914 conferred extreme powers on the federal government, allowing it to effectively rule by decree when it perceived the existence of 'war, invasion or insurrection, real or apprehended'. The 'carte blanche' powers granted to the Governor in Council to do whatever was deemed 'necessary or advisable for the security, defence, peace, order and welfare of Canada' specifically included powers of censorship, arrest, deportation and property seizure (Lindsay 2014: 161). During World War I, more than 120,000 people were designated as 'alien enemies' and 7,762 of them were consigned to internment camps, often providing labour for government projects (Lindsay 2014: 162).

During the years before and after World War I, soldiers were also mobilised whenever strikes threatened the established order. In the words of two prominent labour historians: 'When strikes took the form of mass unrest involving unskilled workers, troops were deployed.' And during 1906, the use of military force 'spiked dramatically' when the troops were called out four times to deal with mass strikes by unskilled workers (Fudge and Tucker 2004: 18, 49).

The most notable strike of this period was the Winnipeg general strike of 1919. The 21 June confrontation with the Royal Canadian Mounted Police (RCMP, Mounties) and soldiers, following earlier arrests and confiscation of documents, resulted in 30 casualties, including one death. However, the use of troops was not confined to Winnipeg: they were also mobilised during the subsequent Vancouver general strike; against Quebec textile workers in 1920; coal miners in St Johns and Halifax in 1922; Sydney steelworkers in 1923; and Nova Scotia miners in 1925 (Heron 1998: 35–6, 67–8, 113).

The War Measures Act was used again in World War II to issue detailed regulations, including to limit the freedom of Canadians of foreign descent. About 22,000 Japanese-Canadians were detained in labour camps, and the government seized and sold their property to pay for their internment (Lindsay 2014: 163). By early 1940, two communist papers were banned and 64 people arrested for offences under the subversion regulations, of whom 19 were imprisoned. The Communist Party of Canada and 14 associated bodies were declared illegal in 1940, and more than 100 communists were interned. Hundreds of Jehovah's Witnesses were also arrested, and large numbers of people were prosecuted for making statements prejudicial to the war effort (Douglas 2003).

Further emergency powers legislation was introduced for the Korean War, but the War Measures Act remained in force throughout the Cold War period. In 1960, it was amended to declare that any action authorised by it would be deemed not to infringe any right or freedom recognised by the Canadian Bill of Rights (Lindsay 2014: 163).

On five occasions, troops have been used against Aboriginal peoples, from the Red River Rebellion of 1870 to Oka in 1990 (Haslip 2002: 4). Despite Canada's recent pacifist reputation, large-scale military interventions have occurred four times in the past four decades: the Front de Libération du Québec (FLQ) crisis (1963–70), the 1976 Olympic Games, the Oka standoff (1990) and disaster relief in Manitoba (1997) (Maloney 1997). After reviewing these experiences, a Canadian military historian concluded that the mechanisms for military assistance to civilian authorities were 'extremely flexible' and ensured that 'the military is not overburdened with legalities' (Maloney 1997: 145).

In the most convulsive confrontation, the War Measures Act was invoked to authorise a military intervention in a domestic crisis in October and November 1970, when a state of 'apprehended insurrection' was declared to exist in Quebec and emergency regulations were proclaimed in response to two kidnappings by the separatist FLQ (Maloney 1997: 138–9).

Under the emergency regulations, the FLQ was declared an illegal organisation, normal liberties were suspended, and arrests and detentions were authorised without charge. Ultimately, more than 12,000 troops were deployed in full battle order for a show of force to the citizens of Montreal. Airborne forces were brought in to conduct special operations, while soldiers conducted cordon and search operations jointly with Quebec provincial police. Over 450 persons were detained in Quebec, most of whom were eventually released without the laying or hearing of charges.

In all, 10 shots were fired, all warnings, without casualties. It could easily have been worse. At one point, Prime Minister Trudeau directed the Vice Chief of Defence Staff to place 'tanks on all the bridges in Montreal and men all over the city to show these pipsqueaks who has the power'. When troops arrived in Ottawa without Rules of Engagement and sought advice from the RCMP on what to do when approached by unknown individuals, they were told 'shoot them, but let us know afterwards so we can clean up the situation' (Lerhe 2004: 10).

In 1988, the powers contained in the War Measures Act were replaced by the Emergencies Act. It conferred extraordinary powers on the federal cabinet, allowing it to govern by decree when it perceives the existence of 'threats to the security of Canada', including acts of serious political violence or activities aimed at overthrowing the system of government (see Chapter 4).

During the late 1990s and early years of the twenty-first century, with the development of substantial anti-globalisation and anti-capitalist demonstrations against summits of world leaders, the Canadian Forces (CF) was mobilised regularly to assist police in preventing or suppressing protests at such gatherings. For the 2001 Summit of the Americas in Quebec City, some 1,200 CF personnel joined 6,700 police and hundreds of customs officers in the security operation, with another 3,000 soldiers on standby at nearby CF bases. Heavily armed police used tear gas, water cannon and rubber bullets, with CF troops maintaining a support role (Legras 2001). The 2002 G-8 Summit in Alberta saw the largest homeland mobilisation of troops since the 1970 FLQ crisis. More than 6,000 CF personnel and 4,500 police were deployed to enforce a 6.5-kilometre no-go zone around the summit venue, while three anti-aircraft missile batteries were set up and CF-18 fighter jets policed a 150-kilometre no-fly zone (Adelaide 2002).

Chapter 3

Martial Law, Emergency Doctrines, Official Lawlessness and Judicial Complicity

In addition to whatever emergency legislation is in place, and regardless of any limits supposedly placed on governments by that legislation, the English-derived common law provides considerable scope for dictatorial measures.

Firstly, the common law has been prepared to support recourse to the imposition of martial law, which is, in essence, the suspension of law altogether. Martial law declarations can pave the way for extensive military powers, including the right to summarily try and execute individuals, in order to put down civil unrest.

Secondly, over the past few centuries, the courts have developed the doctrines of revolutionary legality and necessity to justify draconian government actions or 'successful' revolutions that become new legal orders. It is beyond the scope of this book to fully explore these doctrines, but a brief examination is needed.

Thirdly, courts have recognised indemnities, immunities from prosecution and defences, such as self-defence and 'reasonable use of force'.

Fourthly, courts have protected governments from punishment for official lawlessness – acts of surveillance, harassment, violence or intimidation undertaken in the name of defending the state.

Martial Law

After the final defeat of the absolute monarchy in 1688 and up until the nineteenth century, martial law was regarded as an emergency suspension of the rule of law, strictly confined to cases of necessity in times of war, not in times of peace when ordinary courts were open (Capua 1977). Yet, this view seemed to shift somewhat during the nineteenth century.

At the beginning of that century, Blackstone conceded that the rules regarding the power to declare martial law were unclear and capricious. Writing in 1809, he said martial law was 'built upon no settled principle, but is entirely arbitrary in its decisions'. Indeed, it was 'in truth no law but something rather than allowed as law, a temporary excrescence bred out of the distemper of the state' (Blackstone 2001: 413).

Writing toward the end of the nineteenth century, however, Dicey asserted that the right to invoke martial law is 'a right inherent in government' (Dicey 2005: 543–5). Dicey, who is best known as a proponent of the concept of 'rule of law', said the term martial law was most accurately 'employed as a name for the common law right of the Crown and its servants to repel force by force in the case of invasion, insurrection, riot, or generally of any violent resistance to the law' (Dicey 2005: 288). It was a 'right, or power' that was 'essential to the very existence of orderly government, and is most assuredly recognized in the most ample manner by the law of England' (Dicey 2005: 155, citing *R v Pinney* (1832) 5 Car & P 254).

To justify this view, Dicey drew a dubious distinction between two types of martial law. One, martial law, 'in the proper sense of that term', meant the suspension of law and the government of a country or regions by military tribunals. This kind of martial was 'unknown to the law of England', and that was 'an unmistakeable proof of the permanent supremacy of the law under our constitution (Dicey 2005: 182, 183). Yet there was another meaning of martial law: the power of the government or citizens to 'maintain public order, at whatever cost of blood or property may be necessary' (Dicey 2005: 187). Pollock likewise stated: 'So-called "martial law", as distinct from military law, is an unlucky name for the justification by the common law of acts done by necessity for the defence of the Commonwealth when there is war within the realm' (Pollock 1902: 156). Pollock's view of martial law was more expansive than Dicey's. Pollock insisted that necessity, as determined by government, would make nearly all actions taken under martial law legal and immune from any subsequent challenge in the courts.

Halsbury's Laws of England states that martial law applies 'when a state of actual war, or of insurrection, riot, or rebellion amounting to war, exists' (Hailsham 1973: vol. 8(2), para. 821). Other authorities contend that a modified form of martial law can be declared in cases of internal insurrection or disorder that is beyond the power of the civil authorities to quell, applying the same test of necessity as applies to 'military aid to the civil power' (Wade and Phillips 1970: 409; Dicey 2005: 543). It seems to have been accepted that martial law allows the creation of military tribunals to administer summary justice (Ewing and Gearty 2000: 362–3).

Doubt remains as to the legal basis of martial law. It is said to be either an example of a common law right to employ force to repel force or, alternatively, a royal prerogative (Hailsham 1973: vol. 8(2), para. 821). Those contending that the royal prerogative has never been abolished can point to several eighteenth- and nineteenth-century Acts passed by parliament to suppress opposition to British rule in Ireland. They stipulated that 'nothing in this act contained shall be construed to take away, abridge or diminish, the acknowledged prerogative of his Majesty, for the public safety, to resort to the exercise of martial law against open enemies or traitors' (Campbell 1994: 127–8).

Regardless of this fundamental uncertainty about the doctrinal basis for martial law, the Privy Council in the 1902 *Marais* case, on appeal from Britain's Cape Colony, extended the power to declare martial law to even where the ordinary civilian courts were still sitting (*D.F. Marais v The General Officer Commanding the Lines of Communication and the Attorney-General of the Colony* [1902] AC 109). Their Lordships ruled that the Boer War was still underway, and this meant that the military authorities had unreviewable and hence untrammelled powers. They stated: '[O]nce let the fact of actual war be established, and there is an universal consensus of opinion that the civil courts have no jurisdiction to call in question the propriety of the action of military authorities' ([1902] AC 109, 110–12).

The court specifically dismissed the 1628 Petition of Right forbidding the monarchy from invoking martial law, ruling that its 'framers … knew well what they meant when they made a condition of peace the ground of the illegality of unconstitutional procedure' ([1902] AC 109, 114). In other words, as long as the authorities insisted there was no peace, military lawlessness could prevail.

Even more revealing was the massacre of anti-British colonial protesters in Amritsar, India, in 1919. Martial law was proclaimed and Brigadier-General Rex Dyer ordered his troops to open fire on 20,000 people who had gathered in defiance of regulations that prohibited meetings of more than four men (Simpson 2004: 64–6). The crowd was trapped within the walls of a meeting ground. Around 380 were killed and more than 15,000 wounded. Numerous in-camera trials followed, at which 180 people were sentenced to death and 264 to transportation for life. A committee of inquiry rejected Dyer's justification that the massacre was necessary to intimidate potential unrest elsewhere and he was condemned by the House of Commons, though not by the House of Lords (Simpson 2004: 64–6). Predictably, Dyer was never prosecuted, only invalided out of the army (Ferguson 2004: 276–9). According to Simpson, the committee might have adopted a Diceyan theory, according to which Dyer and others were 'personally liable, and risked trial and indeed conviction for murder' but there was 'no real sense in which this was or could ever be done' (Simpson 2004: 66). Simpson cited other examples of martial law and military brutality in Palestine, Egypt and South Africa (Simpson 2004: 62–71).

Martial law fell into disuse in Britain (but not its Irish colony) and most other 'advanced' countries during the twentieth century, usually replaced by more statutory forms of emergency or repressive powers (Simpson 2004: 69–71). Nevertheless, it remains in reserve. Martial law is still loosely described as 'the right to use force against force within the realm in order to suppress civil disorder' (Heuston 1964: 152). This formulation could justify dictatorial measures.

According to de Smith (a leading late twentieth-century authority on English constitutional and administrative law), if martial law arises, it is generally thought that the officer commanding the armed forces will become all-powerful and his actions 'non-justiciable and, for the time being, absolute, subject only to consultation (if this is feasible) with the civil power' (de Smith 1981: 511). 'Non-justiciable' means that the courts have no power to scrutinise the lawfulness of the actions taken.

In Australia, martial law was invoked several times during the nineteenth century against convicts, Aborigines and workers. In his work, *Emergency Powers*, Lee 'hazards a guess' that the power to resort to martial law continues in Australia as a creature of the common law. Lee considered that, while legislation was generally preferable, the doctrine of martial law should not be buried, 'for in the face of an extraordinary crisis it may come in useful ... it may be better to rely on a "shadowy, uncertain, precarious something" than nothing at all' (Lee 1984: 224).

This argument would seem to justify dispensing with the rule of law. The words quoted by Lee were taken from a nineteenth-century English judgment, where Chief Justice Cockburn stated: 'Martial law when applied to the civilian is no law at all, but a shadowy, uncertain, precarious something, depending entirely on the conscience, or rather on the despotic and arbitrary will of those who administer it' (*R v Nelson and Brand* (1867) F Cockburn Sp Rep 86).

Martial Law in the Twentieth Century: Ireland

How these propositions might apply in practice can be assessed from the experiences of British rule in Ireland, which provide a case study of the continuing operation of martial law during the twentieth century (Campbell 1994).

The first instance was triggered by the Easter 1916 Rebellion. The nationalist uprising was short-lived, lasting five days in Dublin, while the insurrection never even got off the ground elsewhere. Officially, 124 Crown forces were killed and 388 injured in the five-day counter-insurgency operation, compared to 180 civilians killed and 614 wounded (Ewing and Gearty 2000: 338–9). The Lord Lieutenant, Lord Wimborne, a cousin of Winston Churchill, proclaimed an immediate state of martial law in Dublin city and county. Under this authority, the British army commander-in-chief in the region, General Friend, swiftly issued martial law regulations that imposed a curfew and declared that any civilian carrying arms was liable to be fired upon without warning.

A day later, martial law was extended across the whole of Ireland, with British Prime Minister Asquith informing parliament that General Sir John Maxwell was being 'given plenary powers under martial law over the whole country'. By War Office instructions, Maxwell was empowered to 'take all such measures as may in his opinion be necessary for the prompt suppression of insurrection in Ireland' (Ewing and Gearty 2000: 339, 339n). A further proclamation brought into operation an emergency regulation that contemplated two types of military justice – a general court martial and a field general court martial – to try anyone charged with offences against the Defence of the Realm Regulations then in force throughout the UK. These tribunals, which sat in secret, could impose the death penalty where the intention of the accused was to assist the enemy, and, in other cases, prison sentences of up to life imprisonment (Ewing and Gearty 2000: 341). In the first few weeks of May 1916, 3,419 suspected Sinn Fein sympathisers were arrested by the military under internment and other emergency regulations, 188 civilians were tried by courts martial, 90 death sentences were passed and 15 people were executed (Ewing and Gearty 2000: 342).

No effort seems to have been made to challenge the legality of the executions, but one bid to challenge the closed-door conduct of the hearings was dismissed unanimously by a seven-member King's Bench court. Lord Chief Justice Viscount Reading considered that, having regard to the army commander-in-chief's opinion that it was necessary for public safety and the defence of the realm to exclude the public and the media, it was 'abundantly clear' that the in-camera proceedings were lawful. The readiness of the judges to dispense with the legal principle of open courts was voiced most vehemently by Justice Darling. He declared that it would have been 'grotesque' to invite 'the public to come and hear witnesses give evidence against rebels with whom a great many of that same public sympathised (*R v Governor of Lewes Prison, ex parte Doyle* [1917] 2 KB 254, 272, 274). One month after its proclamation, martial law was extended indefinitely. It was never formally revoked by proclamation, but simply ceased to apply when not judged essential by the UK government (Ewing and Gearty 2000: 339n).

Military tribunals re-emerged in Ireland in 1920 under the Restoration of Order in Ireland Act of that year, accompanied by an official policy of covertly authorised retaliation or reprisals. Entire towns were wrecked in revenge for the killing of army officers by the

Irish Republican Army (IRA), and troops fired indiscriminately into a Dublin football crowd, killing 14 men, women and children in Ireland's first 'Bloody Sunday' (Ewing and Gearty 2000: 358–60). Three weeks later, martial law was proclaimed once more, covering the four south-western counties. Two days after Lord French's declaration, the military commander-in-chief, Sir Nevil Macready, issued his first martial law proclamation. This made into capital offences, triable by the military, the unauthorised 'possession of arms, ammunition, or explosives', the wearing of military apparel and the harbouring or assisting of any rebels who were 'levying war' against the king. Within martial law areas, which soon included four further counties, a policy of 'official reprisals' was vigorously followed (Ewing and Gearty 2000: 360–61). Some confusion ensued because the ordinary courts continued to function alongside courts-martial operating under three distinct systems – martial law, the Defence of the Realm Consolidation Act 1914 and the Restoration of Order in Ireland Act 1920.

The willingness of the courts to legitimise martial law was demonstrated in three Irish King's Bench Divisional Court cases: *R v Allen* [1921] 2 IR 241; *R (Garde) v Strickland* [1921] 2 IR 317; and *R (Ronayne and Mulcahy) v Strickland* [1921] 2 IR 333. The first involved John Allen, who was sentenced to death by a military tribunal for possessing a revolver, ammunition and an IRA publication entitled 'Night Fighting'. Giving the unanimous decision of the court to uphold the sentence, even though it would not have been possible under the ordinary law or even the emergency legislation, Chief Justice Molony declared:

> It is the sacred duty of this Court to protect the lives and liberties of all His Majesty's subjects, and to see that no one suffers loss of life or liberty save under the laws of the country; but when subjects of the King rise in armed insurrection and the conflict is still raging, it is no less our duty not to interfere with the officers of the Crown in taking such steps as they deem necessary to quell the insurrection, and to restore peace and order and the authority of the law. ([1921] 2 IR 241, 242)

In that case, there was no challenge to the government's proclamation of the existence of a state of war, or to its claim that such a state of disorder existed when Allen was arrested. The court ruled that it was 'clear on the authorities that when martial law is imposed, and the necessity for it exists, or, in other words, while the war is still raging, this Court has no jurisdiction to question any acts done by the military authorities' ([1921] 2 IR 241, 269). Relying upon the 1902 precedent set by the Privy Council in *Marais*, the court held that the continued functioning of civilian courts in the martial law areas did not affect the legality of the military tribunals. And the lack of availability of the death penalty for these offences under the ordinary law was an objection 'rather for the consideration of Parliament than for this Court, which cannot, durante bello [during war], control the military authorities, or question any sentence imposed in the exercise of martial law' ([1921] 2 IR 241, 272). Allen was duly executed four days later, together with five others (Ewing and Gearty 2000: 364).

In the first *Strickland* case, death sentences imposed on seven men for levying war against His Majesty were challenged through writs of habeas corpus and certiorari on the basis that the military tribunal that had tried them had been improperly constituted. Chief

Justice Molony asserted that the court had 'the power and the duty to decide whether a state of war exists which justifies the application of martial law' ([1921] 2 IR 317, 329). But the court agreed with the military's assessment and therefore would not 'interfere to determine what is or what is not necessary' ([1921] 2 IR 317, 332). On the same day, in the second *Strickland* case, the court rejected an objection that the power to declare martial law had been 'surrendered or released' by the Restoration of Order in Ireland Act. In a one-page judgment, Chief Justice Molony and his fellow judges simply dismissed the submission as having 'no foundation in law' ([1921] 2 IR 333, 334).

Another judicial ruling, handed down in mid-1921, did call the continued application of martial law into question. *Egan v Macready* ([1921] 1 IR 265) was a further challenge to a military court's death sentence, this time for possessing ammunition. Significantly, the case was heard following the partition of Ireland, after sweeping electoral victories in the south for Sinn Fein and amid the announcement of a truce between the British forces and the IRA (Ewing and Gearty 2000: 365–6). Possibly influenced by the truce, Ireland's Master of the Rolls, Charles O'Connor, ruled that the power to declare martial law had been removed by the adoption of the Restoration of Order in Ireland Act – the very proposition rejected by Chief Justice Molony's Irish King's Bench court two months earlier. Master of the Rolls O'Connor insisted that the 'claim of the military authority to override legislation, specially made for a state of war, would seem … to call for a new Bill of Rights' ([1921] 1 IR 265, 275). He cited the then very recent House of Lords judgment in *Attorney-General v De Keyser's Royal Hotel* [1920] AC 508, which ruled that legislation could preclude the operation of prerogative powers by evincing an intention to cover the relevant field.

Master of the Rolls O'Connor's judgment led to an extraordinary confrontation with the military. General Macready refused to obey the habeas corpus order, and another in a similar case decided by O'Connor on the same day. The judge issued writs of attachment against the general and his deputy, as well as the governor of the prison where the men were held, declaring that their obstruction amounted to a 'deliberate contempt of Court – a thing unprecedented in this Court and the whole history of British law' ([1921] 1 IR 265, 280). The Crown argued that it had the right to hold the prisoners pending an appeal. General Macready threatened to 'arrest anyone, including the Master of the Rolls himself, who attempted to carry out the service of the writs'. A constitutional crisis was only averted when the government decided to release the men, telling parliament that the decision was 'based solely upon the existing situation in Ireland' and 'not due to any decision given by a Civil Court in Ireland', since the courts had 'no power to over-rule the decisions of Military Courts in the martial law area' (Ewing and Gearty 2000: 367). It seems that the government was driven by concerns about not upsetting the truce negotiations, rather than respect for the rule of law.

To say the least, the O'Connor affair left unresolved the claim for the primacy of martial law, and indeed called into question the principle of civilian control of the military. Moreover, a prominent constitutional scholar cast doubt on O'Connor's ruling, saying it 'has not met with approval' and appears 'to depend upon the view that the right to use martial law is a prerogative right' rather than 'simply an extension of the ordinary common law power to meet force with force' (Heuston 1964: 159).

In summary, even if the ordinary courts have jurisdiction to decide whether the state of disorder warranted martial law, there is no precise and settled body of law for answering that question, which seems to depend on judging whether order could only be restored by handing over power to the military authorities. If the courts decide that martial law is warranted, then the military's actions will be unreviewable, at least until the courts decide that the disorder has been pacified. Legal action could be brought against the military for manifestly unreasonable conduct and possibly for unnecessary use of force against people or property, but the law is unclear (de Smith 1981: 512). In de Smith's opinion, the legal uncertainty is academic in any case, because indemnity legislation would almost certainly be passed to exonerate those who acted in good faith to suppress an uprising (de Smith 1981: 514). The British parliament passed such an Act of Indemnity to cover the 1920 declaration of martial law in areas of Ireland (Rowe and Whelan 1985: 200).

'Necessity' and 'Successful' Coups

Two doctrines that British and American courts have fashioned over several centuries also underscore the readiness of the judiciary to accept the most extreme emergency measures, even when they involve patent illegality or coups that overturn constitutions. These doctrines are capable of upholding the imposition of dictatorial measures ('necessity'), or the outright seizure of power by the military or other authorities ('successful revolution').

As will be reviewed in Chapter 5, under the heading 'The Political Realist View and Doctrines of Necessity', these theories have been utilised to justify anti-democratic, military-backed coups, at least so long as the new regime accommodated the interests of British, American and other Western capitalist powers. Courts upheld the legality of various coups, including those in Pakistan (1958), Uganda (1966), Lesotho (1986 and 1989), the Seychelles (1977) and Grenada (1979) (Head 2001b: 545).

In most of these cases, the courts made reference to the 'principle of effectiveness' enunciated by Austrian legal philosopher Hans Kelsen in his work *General Theory of Law and State* (Kelsen 1946: 118–19). During the early 1930s, Kelsen and Carl Schmitt conducted a public debate in which Kelsen defended the place of judicial review against Schmitt's authoritarian views (Vinx 2015). Kelsen's conceptual framework had its own authoritarian implications, however. In essence, it justified the seizure of power by force. Quoting his writings, judges ruled that coups did not need to command 'universal adherence', simply 'a minimum of support'.

Indemnities

Historically, governments and other authorities have been willing to exploit vague and elastic phrases such as 'emergency', 'essential' and 'security' to act without clear legal authorisation and, if necessary, obtain retrospective indemnity. Dicey was a particular advocate of employing Acts of Indemnity to 'legalise' what was illegal (see Chapter 5).

Seven Indemnity Acts were passed in Ireland between 1796 and 1800 to protect the authorities against legal liability for their unlawful acts (Lee 1984: 222). Whelan traced this trend and gave some examples, one of which was the British government's media announcement during the 1926 General Strike:

> All ranks of the Armed Forces of the Crown are hereby notified that any action which they may find is necessary to take in an honest endeavour to aid the Civil Power will receive, both now and afterwards, the full support of His Majesty's Government. (Whelan 1985: 289–90)

Another example was Attorney-General Sir Hartley Shawcross's advice during the 1949 dock strike about the doubtful legal enforceability of the emergency regulations:

> I do not think that matters ... I have advised that this risk should be taken and that the Regulations should cover matters on which action is required without due regard to the niceties of the law. In an emergency the Government may have, in matters admitting of legal doubt, to act first and argue about the doubts later, if necessary obtaining an indemnification Act. (Whelan 1985: 289–90)

Shawcross's phrase, 'without due regard to the niceties of the law', illustrates the propensity and capacity of governments to dispense with the finer points of the 'rule of law' when confronted by serious political, social or industrial challenges to the established order.

Although the 1974 Heathrow operation was officially justified as a precaution against terrorism, the legal authority of the government to use the army was not clear (Lee 1984: 211). The editor of the *Criminal Law Review* proposed that resort be had to the royal prerogative to address the legal vacuum:

> If on a future occasion the legal powers of police and soldier prove inadequate, reliance may, in the last resort, have to be placed on the Royal Prerogative governing emergencies. That power, with its requirements of compensation, may be an acceptable means of filling in gaps in statutory and common law powers. (Lee 1984: 211–12)

Official Lawlessness

In the name of defending the state, governments or official security agencies may engage in unlawful surveillance, wars of aggression, military interventions, coups, assassinations, renditions and torture. Such practices have mushroomed in the twenty-first century. Considerable evidence has been produced of such crimes being committed from 2001 onward, both domestically and abroad. It is not possible to investigate or review these operations here. But it is important to note that those allegedly affected by these crimes have faced considerable difficulties in bringing law suits seeking to prosecute or obtain redress for such conduct.

Courts have dismissed legal actions on various grounds, including 'state secret' doctrines invoked by the government accused of being responsible. Two American cases decided in 2010 illustrate this development. One concerned the use of 'renditions' to secretly transport prisoners to locations in other countries where they could be tortured. The other involved the targeted assassination of people identified as terrorists.

In the first decision, the US Ninth Circuit Court of Appeals in a 6–5 en banc ruling dismissed a lawsuit by five victims of the Central Intelligence Agency's 'extraordinary rendition' programme against Jeppesen Dataplan, a unit of Boeing. The ruling relied on the 'state secrets' doctrine advocated by the Obama administration. The American Civil Liberties Union (ACLU) brought the suit, charging that defence contractor Jeppesen Dataplan knowingly facilitated the renditions, also known as 'torture flights', by providing flight planning and logistical support to CIA personnel. The suit, *Mohamed v Jeppesen Dataplan, Inc.* (9th Cir. Sept. 8, 2010), sought to expose a web of connections between top executives of defence corporations, foreign intelligence agencies and the US government.

The Ninth Circuit's ruling argued that 'there is precious little Jeppesen could say about its relevant conduct and knowledge without revealing information about how the United States government does or does not conduct covert operations'. On this basis, the court dismissed the case. Earlier, a three-judge panel of the Ninth Circuit had ruled against the Obama administration. Writing for the panel, Judge Michael D. Hawkins wrote that the 'state secrets' doctrine advocated by the administration 'has no logical limit'. The judge noted: 'As the Founders of this Nation knew well, arbitrary imprisonment and torture under any circumstance is a gross and notorious act of despotism.'

The Obama administration sought review of Hawkins' decision, which was overturned by the entire Ninth Circuit, in a judgment authored by Judge Raymond C. Fisher. While couching his opinion in the language of 'balancing' national security against individual liberties, Judge Fisher concluded, 'Courts must act in the interest of the country's national security to prevent disclosure of state secrets, even to the point of dismissing a case entirely' (Savage 2010).

In another 2010 decision, Federal District Judge John D. Bates dismissed a lawsuit that challenged the Obama administration's policy of targeted killings of individuals around the world, including US citizens. The administration had placed the name of US citizen Anwar Al-Aulaqi on a 'kill list', permitting any of the US government's military or intelligence agencies to carry out his assassination. Al-Aulaqi was reported to be in Yemen. The CIA had launched a cruise missile at a meeting Al-Aulaqi was attending there, but the intended victim survived.

In *Al-Aulaqi v Obama* (DDC Dec. 7, 2010), the ACLU and the Center for Constitutional Rights (CCR) filed a lawsuit on behalf of Al-Aulaqi's father, Nasser Al-Aulaqi, challenging the targeted killing programme. The Obama administration argued that the president had the power to order the killing of an American citizen without a trial or judicial review, despite this being a clear violation of international law and the US Bill of Rights. The Fifth Amendment to the US Constitution states: 'No person shall be … deprived of life … without due process of law.' The administration further argued that the case should not be allowed to proceed because it threatened to reveal 'state secrets'.

Judge Bates, in his ruling, acknowledged that the case raised 'stark' and 'perplexing' questions. He asked (at 2): 'Can the Executive order the assassination of a U.S. citizen without first affording him any form of judicial process whatsoever, based on the mere assertion that he is a dangerous member of a terrorist organization?' However, Bates concluded that the case could not proceed because Anwar Al-Aulaqi's father, Nasser Al-Aulaqi, lacked legal standing to bring the case.

This ruling implies that in order for the targeted killing programme to be challenged, the persons marked for death must appear themselves in the courts of the country that is trying to assassinate them. Bates included in his opinion a passage suggesting that in light of Anwar Al-Aulaqi's political and religious views, he should not be entitled to the protections of the US Constitution. The judge wrote that Al-Aulaqi has 'decried the US legal system and suggested that Muslims are not bound by Western law'. Accordingly, Bates wrote, Al-Aulaqi would not 'likely want to sue to vindicate his US constitutional rights in US courts'.

Judge Bates dismissed Al-Aulaqi's claims under international law because the doctrine of 'sovereign immunity' prevents the government from being the target of certain lawsuits without its express consent. Bates held that a judicial evaluation of the Obama administration's assassination programme would involve a 'political question' not subject to judicial review. Bates indicated that in light of his other rulings dismissing the case, it was unnecessary to decide whether the 'state secrets' doctrine applied.

Blocking Judicial Review: Three More Case Studies

Three cases decided during 2012 and 2013 – one in the United States, one in the United Kingdom and one by the European Court of Human Rights (ECHR) – provide a further revealing picture of the lengths to which the Obama administration, assisted by European governments, went to prevent any legal challenges to its assertion of far-reaching executive powers, such as to assassinate alleged enemies of the country, including US citizens, or to 'render' detainees to be tortured in other countries.

The three cases also demonstrate the readiness of the judicial authorities, and the judiciary itself, to facilitate these efforts. This is so even where judges themselves admit the Kafkaesque or 'Alice-in-Wonderland' character of their rulings in favour of official legal claims that effectively make it impossible for citizens to challenge violations of basic legal and constitutional rights. The results essentially permit government lawlessness, exposing the sham of traditional claims that Western legal systems are governed by a rule of law.

In just one of the three cases, that in the European court, did a victim of torture ultimately obtain some redress, albeit only against the government of the Republic of Macedonia, which had participated in the US torture programme, not against the government of the US itself. That limited victory also took 10 years, during which time the victim was frustrated and blocked by the governments and courts in Germany, Macedonia and the US.

Obama Administration Blocks Information Request on Assassination of US Citizens

In January 2013, as urged by lawyers for the Obama administration, US federal judge Colleen McMahon relied on expansive 'national security' provision in freedom of information legislation to deny requests by the American Civil Liberties Union and the *New York Times* for government records related to the assassination of US citizens.

The case originated as separate and independent requests under the 1966 Freedom of Information Act (FOIA) by the ACLU and *New York Times* journalists for information related to targeted killings, particularly of US citizens, in the wake of the September 2011 assassination of Muslim cleric and US citizen Anwar Al-Aulaqi in Yemen (discussed above and in Chapter 1).

The ACLU requested several broad categories of documents, including records pertaining to the presumed legal basis for assassination of US citizens and to the process by which US citizens could be targeted, including who was authorised to make such decisions and what evidence was needed to support them. The ACLU also requested documents related to the killing of Anwar Al-Aulaqi's 16-year-old son, Abdulrahman Al-Aulaqi.

By the beginning of 2013, the US government's 'targeted killing' programme, initiated under the Bush administration and expanded under the Obama administration, had already resulted in the deaths of thousands of people far from any battlefield, including at least three US citizens. The victims, as well as many bystanders, had been murdered without being charged with any crime and without trial or judicial review of any kind.

As discussed above, the Obama administration's ongoing programme was in violation of a core historic concept of the American legal system, which is contained in the Fifth Amendment of 1791: 'No person shall ... be deprived of life ... without due process of law.' The issue before the court, however, was not the legality of this programme, but the ability of the American people simply to have access to the legal and political arguments from the Obama administration seeking to justify it.

'I can find no way around the thicket of laws and precedents that effectively allow the Executive Branch of our Government to proclaim as perfectly lawful certain actions that seem on their face incompatible with our Constitution and laws, while keeping the reasons for its conclusion a secret', Judge McMahon, US District Judge for the Southern District of New York, wrote. The judge acknowledged the 'Catch-22' and 'Alice-in-Wonderland' nature of her ruling, but she attributed the 'paradoxical' outcome to 'contradictory constraints and rules' outside her control.

At issue was whether the administration would be ordered under the Freedom of Information Act to disclose to the public legal memos written by government lawyers defending the targeted killing of US citizens overseas who were suspected of involvement in terror operations.

'This Court is constrained by law, and under the law, I can only conclude that the Government has not violated FOIA by refusing to turn over the documents sought in the FOIA requests', McMahon said. Yet, despite this appeal to the rule of law, she concluded that the government could not be 'compelled by this court of law to explain in detail the reasons why its actions do not violate the Constitution and laws of the United States'.

By insisting on a constitutional separation of powers, the founders of the United States sought to avoid a government where one branch could wield the authority to act as judge, jury and executioner. 'Presidential authorization does not and cannot legitimize covert action that violates the Constitution and laws of this nation', McMahon wrote. 'So there are indeed legitimate reasons, historical and legal, to question the legality of killings unilaterally authorized by the Executive that take place otherwise than on a "hot" field of battle.'

Nevertheless, the judge ultimately ruled that virtually all the documents sought by the ACLU and the *New York Times* could be withheld from public disclosure under exemptions to freedom of information law.

McMahon's judgment cited extensively from documents and material from the period of the American Revolution, all of which confirmed that the framers of the US Constitution intended to forbid extrajudicial assassinations. Having reviewed these authorities, Judge McMahon quoted numerous public statements by Obama and senior administration officials that clearly indicated that the US government, with the direct involvement of Obama himself, was planning and carrying out such extrajudicial assassinations.

Citing 'national security' exceptions to the FOIA, government secrecy statutes and expansive executive privileges, the Obama administration not only failed to disclose the requested documents, but also refused to specify the documents that were being withheld, on the grounds that to acknowledge that any of the requested documents exist would compromise national security.

In her judgment, the judge referred to the sweeping powers that had been conferred on the presidency after the September 2001 terrorist attacks on the World Trade Center and the Pentagon. Congress passed a resolution entitled 'Authorization for the Use of Military Force' (AUMF) that empowered the president to:

> use all necessary and appropriate force against those nations, organizations, or persons he determines planned, authorized, committed, or aided the terrorist attacks that occurred on September 11, 2001, or harbored such organizations or persons, in order to prevent any future acts of international terrorism against the United States by such nations, organizations or persons. (Pub. L. No. 107-40, 115 Stat. 224 (2001))

That provision effectively gave the president carte blanche to take any action, without exception, he deemed necessary to pursue the indefinite 'war on terror' that has ensued ever since. Both the Bush and Obama administrations interpreted that power as extending far beyond the supposed primary field of battle, in Afghanistan and neighbouring Pakistan. Judge McMahon noted that the 'war on terror' exercise had been pursued 'far from any "hot" battlefield', including to Yemen, 'about 1500 miles from Afghanistan' and a country with which the US was not at war.

The Obama administration openly argued that it was perfectly legal and constitutional for the president to order the assassination of anyone, including a US citizen. The judge referred to the administration's 'vociferous insistence' that a US citizen could be 'targeted by the Executive Branch and still be accorded due process'. She said the government had gone so far as to mount an 'extensive public relations campaign' to convince the public that its conclusions were correct. Judge McMahon observed that the government had good reason to feel somewhat defensive about this assertion: 'Some Americans question the power of the Executive to make a unilateral and unreviewable decision to kill an American citizen who is not actively engaged in armed combat against this country.'

The judge noted that the administration held its view, notwithstanding the explicit language of the Fifth Amendment, as well as the Treason Clause of the Constitution, in which the framers, 'as leery of accusations of treason as they were of concentrating power in the hands of a single person or institution', prohibited any conviction for treason unless on the testimony of two witnesses to an overt act or a confession in open court. Despite thus drawing some attention to the overturning or erosion of historic principles, the judge deferred to the administration's demand for the protection, under freedom of information exemptions, of classified secrets, intelligence gathering methods and internal deliberative processes.

While the decision, on its narrowest basis, could be seen as resting only on the particular provisions of the FOIA, those sections of the Act, and how courts interpret them, are indicative of the wide-ranging and deferential approach of legislators and judges to executive secrecy claims based on 'national security'. Judge McMahon upheld, for example, the government's right to classify as secret, 'in the interest of national defense or foreign policy', the legal analysis that it asserts supports conduct such as targeted assassinations. As her judgment illustrates, such use of the classified documents provisions enables governments to shield their operations, no matter how unlawful, from public scrutiny and challenge.

In a footnote in her decision, Judge McMahon indicated that she had sent a draft of her decision to the Federal Bureau of Investigation (FBI) before issuing it, 'in order to give the Government an opportunity to object to the disclosure of any classified information that may have inadvertently found its way into this document'. The judge also issued a secret 'appendix' to her ruling that was not publicly available. She indicated in her decision that the secret appendix 'is being filed under seal and is not available to Plaintiffs' counsel'.

These practices indicate the readiness of judges to even seek government approval of their judgments before delivering them, and to withhold basic information from plaintiffs, depriving them of information they may require to challenge such rulings by governments and courts. The ACLU and the *New York Times* intended to appeal the decision.[1]

English High Court Rejects Inquiry into British Role in Pakistan Drone Strikes

In 2012, the High Court in London rejected a request for a judicial review of a decision by the Secretary of State for Foreign and Commonwealth Affairs to pass intelligence information from the United Kingdom's Government Communications Headquarters (GCHQ) to aid drone strikes by the United States in Pakistan's northwest region. The case was brought by Noor Khan, a Pakistani man whose father was killed, along with 49 other people, by a US drone attack on 17 March 2011. Khan's father, Malik Daud Khan, was chairing a peaceful *jirga* (tribal assembly) meeting to discuss chromite mining rights in North Waziristan when he was killed by several missile strikes.

In his legal submission, Khan asked the court to look into whether UK intelligence officials provided assistance in the killing of his father and if they were liable for prosecution under British law. Those providing such information could be committing

---

1 The consolidated cases are *New York Times v US Department of Justice* (11cv9336) and *ACLU v US Department of Justice* (12cv794), http://www.nysd.uscourts.gov/cases/show.php?db=special&id=251.

serious criminal offences, including conspiracy to commit murder (contrary to s 1, or 1A, of the Criminal Law Act 1977).

The ruling handed down by Lord Justice Moses, and supported by Justice Simon, decided strongly in favour of the Foreign and Commonwealth Office. It provided a legal justification for ensuring that the UK's role in assisting the US to carry out its drone assassinations would remain hidden from public exposure. Citing evidence from the Foreign Office, the ruling stated:

> [I]f the Secretary of State were required to make a substantive response to the claim, the likely consequence would be serious harm to national security and international relations. The United Kingdom Government would be compelled to express a definitive view on legal issues, complicating and damaging relations with our most important bilateral ally and, in consequence, damaging the United Kingdom's security. (*Khan v SSFCA [2012] EWHC 3728 (Admin)* at [17])

The ruling dismissed Khan's claim, stating that:

> [T]he real aim and target of these proceedings is not to inform GCHQ employees that if they were prosecuted, no defence of combatant immunity would be available. The real aim is to persuade this court to make a public pronouncement designed to condemn the activities of the United States in North Waziristan, as a step in persuading them to halt such activity. (*Khan v SSFCA [2012] EWHC 3728 (Admin)* at [57])

The ruling took note of legal proceedings that Khan had undertaken in Pakistan, in order to reiterate that under no conditions would the High Court make a ruling condemning the drone attacks or GCHQ's alleged role in them. Referring to Khan's plea to the court in Peshawar, Lord Justice Moses wrote:

> [H]e contends that the Government of Pakistan, and various Ministries, are under a constitutional obligation to take all necessary action to stop 'illegal drone strikes' and 'safeguard its citizens from target killing by an external force'. He pleads that 'the act of killing of innocent people on March 17 2011 was extra-judicial killing, more generally referred to as murder'. The prayer refers to criminal offences by those inside and outside Pakistan in drone operations.

He asserted: 'It is plain, from the nature of the claims, that the purpose of the proceedings in England and in Pakistan is to persuade a court to do what it can to stop further strikes by drones operated by the United States' (*Khan v SSFCA [2012] EWHC 3728 (Admin)* at [12–13]).

Lord Justice Moses dismissed the submission from Khan's legal team that clarification was required regarding the legal basis for the drone attacks carried out by the US in North Waziristan, in order to establish whether British officials could be secondary parties to murder or guilty of war crimes if they were providing critical information to the US. In its submission, Khan's team cited a *Sunday Times* article dated 25 July 2010. Written months before the attack that killed Khan's father and dozens of other innocent civilians, the information it contained, including quotes from a GCHQ official, confirmed that GCHQ passed vital locational and other intelligence to the United States on the whereabouts of what were described as 'leading militants in Afghanistan and Pakistan'.

The ruling noted that the *Sunday Times* article was one of a 'number of reports' that alleged that the drone strikes 'are linked to agents of the US Government and to United Kingdom employees of GCHQ'. Lord Justice Moses, however, refused to permit Khan to pursue his suit in order to determine whether these reports had a 'firm factual foundation'. He observed that, 'through no fault of the claimant, his case rests on a respectable but unconfirmed report' (*Khan v SSFCA [2012] EWHC 3728 (Admin)* at [11]).

The Secretary of State objected, first, that the court would be required to adjudicate on the acts of foreign sovereign states; second, that the claimant was seeking a declaration as to whether future conduct was proscribed by domestic criminal law; third, that the court should not be lured into giving an advisory opinion; and, fourth, that the case could not be tried at all in the absence of a statutory closed material procedure. In effect, after reviewing the claimant's arguments, the court accepted the first three objections, and said it was not necessary to rule on the fourth.

Lord Justice Moses cited *Kuwait Airways Corporation v Iraqi Airways Co (Nos 4 and 5)* [2002] 2 WLR 1353, 1362) as authority for 'the principle that the courts will not sit in judgment on the sovereign acts of a foreign state includes a prohibition against adjudication upon the "legality, validity or acceptability of such acts, either under domestic law or international law"' (*Khan v SSFCA [2012] EWHC 3728 (Admin)* at [15]). Once again, this doctrine, regularly relied upon by governments and courts to block any legal examination of military or intelligence operations in support of the United States, was utilised to prevent any exposure of, or accountability for, conduct potentially involving the most serious crimes.[2]

European Court Orders Damages for CIA Torture Victim

Late in 2012, the European Court of Human Rights in Strasbourg awarded damages of €60,000 to Khaled El-Masri, a German citizen of Lebanese origin. The judges accepted that Macedonian security services had illegally seized El-Masri at the end of 2003, subjected him to abuse and finally handed him over to agents from the CIA. The CIA then transported El-Masri to a secret prison in Afghanistan, where he was tortured and mistreated for months. The court said this was a serious violation of the European Convention on Human Rights, to which the Republic of Macedonia had acceded.

Although only representatives of the Macedonian government were accused, the verdict had broader significance. It was the first time that the unlawful renditions conducted by the US government and its European accomplices had been condemned by an international court for breaching international laws.

Previously, El-Masri's attempts to seek redress in Macedonia, Germany and the US had been systematically thwarted. Investigations, if they were conducted at all, were carried out

---

2 The court's judgment can be read at http://www.judiciary.gov.uk/Resources/JCO/Documents/Judgments/khan-v-SSFCA-approved211212.pdf.

reluctantly and half-heartedly; information was withheld by the investigating authorities citing state secrecy. The ECHR regarded all aspects of El-Masri's evidence as credible and supported by international investigations. His complaint that the measures taken against him, his handing over to CIA agents and the hindering of his attempts to seek legal remedies breached the central articles of the European Convention on Human Rights was sustained in every point by the court.

El-Masri had been arrested by security forces on his entry to Macedonia on 21 December 2003, and then taken to a hotel in Skopje, where he was held for 23 days without access to the outside world and under constant surveillance by secret service agents. Although he was not physically mistreated by the Macedonian secret service agents, they threatened to shoot him if he attempted to leave the hotel. On 23 January 2004, El-Masri was handcuffed and blindfolded, and taken to Skopje airport where he was handed over to masked CIA agents and abused physically and sexually. He was then forcibly taken onto a plane, thrown to the floor, chained and sedated.

Since this happened in the presence of Macedonian security officials, the Strasbourg court judged that the Macedonian authorities were jointly responsible for the torture that El-Masri suffered and guilty of breaching Article 3 of the European Convention, which prohibits torture as inhuman and degrading treatment. Also, according to the judges, the Macedonian security forces were aware that the CIA plane would transport El-Masri to Afghanistan, since they had access to the flight plans. It must therefore have been clear to them that El-Masri would face further torture, the judges said.

In Afghanistan, El-Masri was taken to the infamous 'Saltpit' prison, where he was further mistreated and questioned for extended periods. In May 2004, after four months, he was transported to Albania and then to Germany. The CIA had finally come to the conclusion that El-Masri was completely innocent and had been falsely detained.

The court in Strasbourg made the Macedonian government jointly responsible for the torture he suffered in Afghanistan. El-Masri was arrested on Macedonian territory, although there was neither an arrest warrant nor a valid extradition request from the US government. That El-Masri was detained in a hotel and his arrest was not logged was regarded by the court as additional proof of the illegality of the actions of the Macedonian authorities.

His illegal detention was regarded by the judges as a breach of the right to freedom and security of the person (Article 5) and – on the grounds of the illegitimacy of the measures taken against El-Masri – also as an illegal intervention into private and family life (Article 8).

The fact that the charges against persons unknown within the Macedonian security services filed by El-Masri were not pursued and eventually rejected was evaluated by the judges in Strasbourg as the hindering of a valid legal complaint, that is, a breach of Article 13.

The Macedonian government initially claimed that El-Masri's papers had merely been checked in Macedonia on the suspicion they may be counterfeit. Later, he was said to have travelled to Kosovo. The Strasbourg court possessed a written statement by the then Macedonian Interior Minister, Hari Kostov, who confirmed that El-Masri was arrested by the Macedonian security authorities, held in Skopje without contact with the outside world under the supervision of intelligence officials and was later handed over to a CIA team.

As well as El-Masri's evidence, the judges also based their verdict on the statement by the former Macedonian Interior Minister and primarily on inquiries conducted by Dick Marty, the special investigator of the European Council. Marty had produced detailed reports in 2006 and 2007 showing the involvement of various European states in the crimes organised by the CIA under the guise of the 'war on terror'. El-Masri's case was characterised as a 'documented transfer' because his transportation was well researched. Nevertheless, El-Masri had been previously frustrated by all the courts in which he sought justice.

In the US, a suit filed by the American Civil Liberties Union against CIA Director George Tenet and other CIA agents was rejected by the courts in 2005. This was then upheld by the Supreme Court in 2007, which ruled that the 'state interest in protecting state secrets' outweighed 'the individual claim for justice by El-Masri'. In 2008, the state prosecutor's office in Skopje rejected El-Masri's legal complaint against unknown Macedonian judicial officials.

In Germany, despite the involvement of the Munich state attorney's office in the case and a parliamentary committee of inquiry, as well as a mountain of evidence, no charges were filed. German Interior Minister Otto Schily, who was informed about the case by the American ambassador, Dan Coats, remained silent. In 2005, Justice Minister Brigitte Zypries said that 'everything constitutionally possible was done to resolve the case'. Before that, Federal Prosecutor Kay Nehm had rejected that the case fell within the jurisdiction of the Attorney General on the legally dubious grounds the El-Masri case was not one of 'political abduction'.

But even that was not enough, and the Munich public prosecutor had since effectively branded El-Masri as a criminal, ordering his surveillance. The phones of his lawyer, Manfred Gnjidic, were tapped for months, breaching the constitutionally enshrined lawyer–client privilege.

The Munich state attorney's office, which had received an official legal complaint from El-Masri in 2004, finally issued an arrest warrant against 13 CIA agents at the beginning of 2007. But this was never served, since the federal government refused to lodge an extradition request with the American authorities. Berlin wanted to avoid straining relations with Washington under all circumstances, and therefore thwarted all El-Masri's attempts to seek justice.

The diplomatic cables from the US embassy in Berlin in January/February 2007, published by WikiLeaks, show the compliance of the German authorities in covering up the crimes against El-Masri. For example, the then deputy US ambassador, John Koenig, warned the German government that it should carefully weigh up the consequences to bilateral relations when issuing international arrest warrants.

In December 2010, a Cologne court finally dismissed El-Masri's lawsuit against the federal government that had sought to enforce the extradition warrants against the CIA agents. As far as the German judiciary was concerned, the case was now at an end.

El-Masri also met a wall of silence at the parliamentary committee of inquiry, which until 2009 had been investigating the involvement of the German Secret Service in the Iraq war and German participation in the crimes of the US secret service.

Although the committee's final report came to the conclusion that El-Masri's presentation of the case was credible, it did not accept there had been any German involvement. In fact, the committee had been denied access to many files, on the grounds it might damage 'state secrets'. Thus evidence of the involvement of German security forces in the mistreatment and transportation of El-Masri could not be pursued.[3]

3 The judgment in *Case of El-Masri v The Former Yugoslav Republic of Macedonia (Application no. 39630/09)* can be read at http://www.lawfareblog.com/wp-content/uploads/2012/12/CASE-OF-ELMASRI-v.-THE-FORMER-YUGOSLAV-REPUBLIC-OF-MACEDONIA1.pdf.

Chapter 4
Legality and Semi-Legality: 'Models of Accommodation' and 'Business as Usual'

Most traditional or liberal approaches to emergency powers maintain that extraordinary or exceptional provisions are compatible with legality, or at least can be made so. Blatant or unfettered recourse to authoritarian measures are depicted as being kept within the bounds of law, even if the legal framework is stretched in totalitarian directions or partially suspended to deal with perceived or purported crises that challenge the existing socio-economic order. These models are also generally presented as preserving the constitutional order, regardless of whether they, in fact, enable violent repression of popular discontent and/or help pave the way for more authoritarian forms of rule.

According to the typology of Gross and Ní Aoláin, two broad positions exist among these approaches. *Models of accommodation* were said to 'countenance a certain degree of accommodation for the pressures exerted on the state in times of emergency, while, at the same time, maintaining normal legal principles and rules as far as possible'. On this view, 'when a nation is faced with emergencies, its legal, and even constitutional, structure must be somewhat relaxed (and perhaps even suspended in parts)' (Gross and Ní Aoláin 2006: 9). The focus is on upholding and legitimising the prevailing order by sanctioning supposedly temporary resort to dictatorial measures.

Business as usual models insist that 'ordinary legal rules and norms continue to be followed strictly with no substantive change even in times of emergency and crisis' (Gross and Ní Aoláin 2006: 10). As Gross and Ní Aoláin noted, such models are often criticised for disregarding 'the reality of governmental exercise of extraordinary measures and powers in response to emergencies'. Both models rely on 'an assumption of constitutionality that tells us that whatever responses are made to the challenges of a particular exigency, such responses are to be found and limited within the confines of the constitution' (Gross and Ní Aoláin 2006: 10). Such assumptions are predicated on restoring the stability and political legitimacy of the capitalist economic and legal system.

'The Principle of Legality'

While various tactical debates occur within this framework, the underlying concern is to maintain the edifice of legality. Characteristic in this respect was a volume of essays entitled *Emergencies and the Limits of Legality* (Ramraj 2008). Despite the manifold differences that the 16 authors had with each other, they shared a common commitment, 'in some fashion', to 'the principle of legality' (Ramraj 2008: 3). The editor explained that central to their conceptions of legality was 'the notion that any power exercised by the state must be authorised by law. This is the essence of modern, constitutional government' (Ramraj 2008: 4).

Ironically, the editor chose as his authority for that proposition Professor A.V. Dicey, the British constitutional writer of the late nineteenth and early twentieth century. Dicey's apologetics for the British doctrines of necessity, martial law and Acts of Indemnity, adopted to protect brutal exercises of state repression, both at home and abroad, are considered later in this chapter.

Another extraordinary claim was that, 'wartime courts' aside, 'the importance of upholding legality in times of crisis has been eloquently defended by judges around the world', even if 'sometimes in lone dissent' (Ramraj 2008: 5). Actually, the overwhelming record of the judiciary, whether in declared periods of war or not, has been to agree with, or accede to, the draconian actions of governments. Oftentimes they have formally recited the need to respect the 'rule of law' while handing down judgments that either sanctioned the abuses in question or stopped carefully short of impeding the executive in practice. In other cases, as documented in Chapter 3, they have blocked attempts to challenge abuses.

Many other examples could be cited of judicial complicity. While a US Supreme Court majority eventually upheld the right of Guantanamo Bay detainees to mount habeas corpus challenges to their incarceration, no prisoners had to be released as a result (*Boumediene v Bush* 553 US 723 (2008)) (see Chapter 8). Likewise, in a pivotal case on unlawful detention, the English House of Lords declared, by an 8–1 majority, that the courts had to defer heavily to the views of the executive government in 'assessing the strength of a general threat to the life of the nation' (*A v Secretary of State for the Home Department* [2004] UKHL 56) (see Chapter 10). And the Australian High Court upheld the use of control orders, a form of detention without trial, on the basis that the court was obliged to accept as 'notorious facts' that the Commonwealth faced unparalleled dangers from terrorism after 9/11 (*Thomas v Mowbray* [2007] HCA 33) (see Chapter 9). The 'Jamaican affair', discussed in this chapter, is yet another damning illustration of the historic role of the judiciary.

Whatever their divergences, the essayists were concerned to counter Carl Schmitt's open assertion that a state confronted with a violent emergency cannot remain faithful to law. Schmitt was described as a 'Nazi philosopher' (Ramraj 2008: 4). This is to erect a straw man. In reality, Schmitt was not simply a Nazi. He was a defender of the Weimar Republic of 1919 to 1933. Amid the revolutionary convulsions that followed the horrors of World War I, he developed his totalitarian arguments in an attempt to maintain that so-called 'democratic' capitalist order, particularly against socialist-minded workers. After the 1929 Wall Street crash ushered in the worldwide Great Depression of the 1930s, Schmitt also sought to forestall the Nazis, but ultimately preferred their dictatorship, which he worked energetically to legitimise, to the threat of a working-class uprising (see Chapter 5).

The inspiration for the range of theoretical and practical responses contained in the volume was said to be the Gross–Dyzenhaus debate, which advanced 'competing models for preserving legality in times of emergency' (Ramraj 2008: 6–8). Gross articulated the extra-legal measures model that provided that officials must occasionally step outside the constitutional order to deal with grave threats, so as to strengthen the legal order.

Dyzenhaus objected that this model permitted egregious departures from 'the principle of legality'. He urged faith in the capacity of judges and the 'moral resources' of the law to sustain a 'rule-of-law project' even when the legal and political order was under great stress. That was so, even if this project required 'imaginative experiments in institutional design' to transcend a rigid separation of powers in order to enable cooperation between the judiciary, executive and legislature (Dyzenhaus 2008: 64–7).

Some contributors to the volume, such as Tushnet and Lazar, contended that factors apart from law – including politics, informal power and discretion – regulate and constrain state power in emergencies, partly because of the poor record of the courts. Lazar conceded that formal adherence to legality can camouflage arbitrary abuses of power (Lazar 2008: 166–70). Other authors gave greater weight to political and sociological calculations; but all argued for legality, although often as an issue of expediency and political legitimacy. Pointing to Irish experiences, Colm Campbell cautioned that indiscriminate use of emergency powers 'can have radicalising effects by reinforcing a sense of membership of a victimised community, particularly in quasi-ethnic conflicts'. A visible commitment by the state to legality can have an 'indirect damping effect' on conflicts (Campbell, C. 2008: 186, 188).

The 'Ordinary Law' Approach

In the same volume, Tom Campbell stated his preference for a 'business as usual' model, provided that it permitted some 'extreme measures' in the name of combating the supposedly extraordinary threat of contemporary terrorism (Campbell, T. 2008: 202). In keeping with his 'prescriptive legal positivism' approach, he weighed in against expanding the 'rule of law' concept beyond the enforcement of 'authoritative rules' that can be applied without drawing on moral judgments. Campbell contended that judicial review on the basis of fundamental constitutional rights, by 'out of touch constitutional courts', may be 'insufficiently responsive to changed and catastrophic circumstances' (Campbell, T. 2008: 221). He rejected the positions of both Dyzenhaus and Gross:

> Dyzenhaus fears that Gross would leave us in a legal grey hole, that is, a sphere of executive power that is largely without legal constraint. Yet, the alternative he presents is arguably worse in that it creates a political grey hole in which unaccountable judicial power is exercised in a way that undermines political responsibility. Within democratic theory the Gross-Dyzenhaus debate does not represent us with an acceptable choice. (Campbell, T. 2008: 228)

By 'democratic theory', as he made clear earlier in his essay, Tom Campbell meant the prevailing parliamentary order. He argued that emergency legislation could be drafted to appropriately anticipate a broad range of emergencies, and supported Tushnet in calling for parliaments, as well as courts, being required by any emergency legislation to endorse an executive declaration that a state of emergency existed (Campbell, T. 2008: 219). Another alternative, Campbell suggested, was that offered by Kent Roach.

In his essay, Roach maintained that the 'ordinary law of emergencies', as illustrated by the US National Emergencies Act, the UK Civil Contingencies Act and the Canadian

Emergencies Act, had proven that it could effectively supervise the state and hold it accountable for its use of emergency powers. However, he also proposed that where such 'ordinary' laws are deemed by the legislature to be insufficient, there should be formal provision for executive derogations from rights, subject to subsequent legislative and judicial review. That would allow for situations where 'governments conclude that it is necessary to go beyond reasonable limits on rights and dispense with rights altogether' (Roach 2008: 230). While conceding that 'routine derogations could lead to tyranny', the optimal approach was to provide for 'explicit and democratic derogations from rights' (Roach 2008: 257). This, he contended was preferable to Gross's extra-legal measures model because it was 'designed to maximize both political and legal deliberation about the justifications for derogation' (Roach 2008: 257).

Despite his advocacy of an 'ordinary law' approach, Roach criticised the US National Emergencies Act, noting: 'In its single-minded focus on the power of the President to declare an emergency or an exception as opposed to the principles that might govern the declaration and conduct of the emergency, the Act is Schmittian' (Roach 2008: 235). However, Roach presented the UK Civil Contingencies Act as 'an admirable attempt to outline some broad legal principles to govern emergency governance rather than simply consigning these questions to the discretion of the sovereign' (Roach 2008: 240). This claim flew in the face of the potentially dictatorial powers enabled by the Act, as well as the preservation of royal prerogative powers (see Chapter 7). Roach considered the Canadian Emergencies Act to be 'carefully drafted' and 'not a Schmittian exercise of unrestrained power'. Indeed, it 'demonstrates how there can be a creative blurring of all three branches of government that may be particularly helpful to supervise the state during emergencies' (Roach 2008: 240, 241–2, 244). Those assertions are belied by the sweeping powers granted by the Act, and also the preservation of the royal prerogative power (see the Canadian case study below).

Who is the Audience?

In summing up the volume of essays, Ramraj posed the question of who the intended primary audience was for the authors involved. Dyzenhaus was addressing the judges, urging them to 'take seriously their role in constraining state power'. The arguments of Gross, who assumed, as a matter of empirical fact, that the judges tend to defer to the executive in times of crisis, appeared to be directed at public officials in the executive branch of government, encouraging them to make 'considered and deliberate' decisions. In part, according to Ramraj, Gross's arguments were aimed at 'the people' who must stand in judgment of such decisions (Ramraj 2008: 27). Essentially, the debates were regarded as directed to those holding power within the state. 'The people' – a term that lumps all members of society together, regardless of their wealth, class and socio-economic status – were relegated to a largely passive role, supposedly judging the emergency measures once they were completed by those in power.

Ramraj also partly acknowledged the limited scope of the essays:

> One limitation is the focus in many chapters on liberal-democratic states with a stable and developed legal-political infrastructure and an entrenched – though perhaps severely strained – culture of accountability. How much relevance does this discourse have for the developing world, where emergencies connote insurgency and prolonged armed conflict or military government? Or where a prolonged and complex process of post-conflict reconstruction involves, as if often does, the introduction of unfamiliar forms of wielding and constraining state power, the reduction or elimination of traditional forms of power and a direct challenge to the existing political elites? (Ramraj 2008: 28–9)

These were questions that 'must be conformed squarely', but that was a task 'for another day' (Ramraj 2008: 29). In truth, the assumed paradigm of a stable politico-legal system in a 'liberal-democratic state' is not just a narrow one, but a false one. Capitalism globally is increasingly beset by economic breakdown, growing social inequality and escalating geo-strategic conflicts between the major powers that threaten to lead to another world war. Under these conditions, even the most seemingly stable corporate, military and legal elites will confront the mounting likelihood of popular unrest, uprisings and war. Any serious examination of emergency powers must be undertaken in that context.

Models of Accommodation

Gross and Ní Aoláin outline several models of accommodation – classical, constitutional, legislative and interpretive. As reviewed in Chapters 2 and 3, the *classical* models are the Roman dictatorship, the French state of siege, Article 48 of the German Weimar Constitution and the British doctrine of martial law. *Constitutional* models are countries or states – such as the Netherlands and Portugal, and some states of the United States – that have explicit provisions in their constitutions for extraordinary executive measures in the event of an 'emergency'. *Legislative* models consist of legislation enacted to hand exceptional powers to the executive, such as the US, UK and Canadian emergencies legislation, as well as the far-reaching World War I and II regulation-making powers adopted in Britain. *Interpretive* models are those that permit the judiciary to interpret legal powers in ways that authorise emergency measures or actions by the executive.

Six Basic Flaws

Before examining these models, it must be said that they all share fundamental flaws. *First*, as established in Chapters 2 and 3, the classical models proved to be far from exemplars of constrained and delineated recourse to emergency powers. Rather, they gave way to totalitarian and brutal methods of rule to deal with upheavals produced by the rise of an exploited class – the slave revolts that shook Rome and the working-class rebellions that challenged the capitalist orders in France, Germany and Britain. Most acutely, the record of the Weimar Republic demonstrated the hollowness of formal constitutional constraints on emergency powers under capitalism, and how such constitutions serve as antechambers of authoritarianism when the ruling elite feels fundamentally threatened by discontent from below.

Second, there are obvious problems of definition. How are emergencies defined? Who has the power to decide whether a fact scenario, or alleged fact scenario, fits the definition? What powers can be exercised? As discussed in the Introduction, emergency is an inherently 'elastic' concept, open-ended and politically manipulable. From the 1933 Reichstag Fire, seized upon by Hitler to justify decree-making power, to the false claims of 'weapons of mass destruction' utilised by the US and its allies to invade Iraq in 2003, governments have inflated or fabricated pretexts for supposedly pre-emptive emergency measures.

Former President Richard Nixon's claim of unfettered presidential authority to determine the legality of any emergency action, regardless of constitutional and statutory provisions, underscored this reality. Interviewed by David Frost in 1977, Nixon was asked whether 'there are certain situations … where the President can decide that it's in the best interests of the nation or something, and do something illegal'. Nixon replied:

> Well, when the President does it, that means that it is not illegal … If the President, for example approves something because of the national security, or in this case because of a threat to internal peace and order of significant magnitude, then the President's decision in that instance is one that enables those who carry it out, to carry it out without violating the law. (Gross and Ní Aoláin 2006: 52–3)

The difficulties of definition and lawlessness are highlighted by constitutions that distinguish between different kinds or levels of emergencies. Portugal's, for instance, makes an unclear distinction between a 'state of siege' and a 'state of emergency'. The former may be declared 'in cases of actual or imminent aggression by foreign forces, serious threat to or disturbance of the democratic constitutional order or public calamity' (Article 19(2)). A state of emergency can be declared 'where the circumstances mentioned in the preceding paragraph are less serious' (Article 19(3)). Guatemala's constitution lists no less than five types of emergency: state of prevention, state of alarm, state of public catastrophe, state of siege and state of war (Article 139).

Written with overtones of Karl Loewenstein (see below), the German Basic Law provides for an 'internal emergency', a 'state of tension' and a 'state of defence'. An internal emergency can be declared 'to avert an imminent danger to the existence or free democratic basic order of the Federation or of a Land'. No definition is provided for a 'state of tension' (Articles 91, 87a(4), 12a(5)–(6), 80a, 115a–l).

Canada's constitutional remit is even more sweeping, extending to the making of laws 'for the Peace, Order and Good Government' of the country (section 91 of the Constitution Act of 1867). The Supreme Court of Canada has interpreted this power as permitting the national parliament to legislate for national emergencies (Forcese 2008: 63). In keeping with that seemingly open-ended power, the Emergencies Act 1988 authorises the federal government to declare four different types of emergency: 'public welfare', 'public order', 'international' and 'war'. A public order emergency, one that arises from 'threats to the security of Canada', can be directed against various forms of political dissent (see the case study on Canada at the end of this chapter).

Third, there is the phenomenon of 'militant' or 'intolerant' democracies that claim to stand for the defence of core values of a democratic order. On that basis, these states provide for the forfeiture of fundamental democratic rights from citizens who allegedly seek to undermine or destroy the 'democratic' constitution. In other words, in the name of democracy, democratic rights are eviscerated.

This has the effect of adopting a sweeping exceptional power to suppress opposition by preventing targeted people or political parties from exercising civil or political rights.

Article 18 of the German Basic Law, adopted after World War II, allows for people to be stripped of political rights for supposedly abusing these rights in order to combat the 'free democratic basic order'. Article 21(2) of the Basic Law provides for the declaration as unconstitutional of any political party that allegedly has similar goals. The German Federal Constitutional Court has used this power to ban two parties, the Socialist Reich Party and the Communist Party, and Israeli courts have invoked similar reasoning to proscribe parties that deny the existence of the state of Israel (Gross and Ní Aoláin 2006: 39–40).

Such an anti-democratic principle is incorporated into the European Convention for the Protection of Human Rights and Fundamental Freedoms. Article 17 states:

> Nothing in this Convention may be interpreted as implying for any State, group or person any right to engage in any activity or perform any act aimed at the destruction of any of the rights and freedoms set forth herein or at their limitation to a greater extent than is provided for in the Convention.

The notion of an 'intolerant' democracy contains definite shades of Carl Schmitt. Indeed, his theorising about the supposed need to block parties that opposed the existing 'democratic' order via exceptional, anti-democratic measures found echoes that spread across the Atlantic during the 1930s. Karl Loewenstein, a German constitutional scholar who emigrated to the US after the Nazis assumed power in Germany in 1933 – and later became a US government adviser during and after World War II, particularly in Latin America and Germany – proposed draconian measures for so-called liberal democracies to combat perceived enemies of democracy.

Loewenstein's basic proposition was that foes of democracy could hide behind a Trojan Horse of protection of individual rights to serve their cause and ultimately subvert the politico-legal order (Loewenstein 1937, 1938). He argued that the liberal democratic order was designed for normal times, and that the 'exaggerated formalism of the rule of law' had to be cast aside during periods of political crisis (Loewenstein 1937: 432). 'Democratic states' had to assume dictatorial methods to survive. By this doctrine, while expounded in the name of upholding democracy, democracy itself was expendable, or subservient to the retention of political power in the hands of the existing order. 'The statute-book is only a subsidiary expedient of the militant will for self-preservation' (Loewenstein 1937: 657). Employing conceptions that could have been invoked by Schmitt, Loewenstein wrote:

> Where fundamental rights are institutionalized, their temporary suspension is justified. When the ordinary channels of legislation are blocked by obstruction and sabotage, the democratic

> state uses the emergency powers of enabling legislation which implicitly, if not explicitly, are involved in the very notion of government. Government is intended for governing … If democracy believes in the superiority of its absolute values over the opportunistic platitudes of fascism … every possible effort must be made to rescue it, even at the risk and cost of violating fundamental principles. (Loewenstein 1937: 432)

Like Schmitt, while Loewenstein's concept of a 'militant democracy' was directed against fascist parties, it was above all aimed against communist parties that represented, even in a distorted form, the threat of working-class revolutions inspired by Marxist ideas of genuine socialist democracy: 'The central focus of Loewenstein's ire was first and foremost communism' (Greenberg 2015: 201). During World War II and the subsequent Cold War against the Soviet Union, Loewenstein became a much-utilised ideologist of US officials in Latin America, where his theories justified severe political repression, including arbitrary deportations of political dissidents, and in Germany, where his views were instrumental in the drafting of the German Basic Law and the court rulings to outlaw the Communist Party (Greenberg 2015: 169–210). In Germany, Loewenstein became a lauded political figure in US-backed ruling circles:

> The occupation's educational and cultural affairs departments therefore sponsored Loewenstein's tours throughout German cities to recruit the local support for an anti-communist campaign. Across the ruined country, Loewenstein called on Germans to combine the creation of democratic institutions with a vigilant suppression of Communist activities. (Greenberg 2015: 201)

Notably, Loewenstein's authoritarian concepts, like Schmitt's, have enjoyed a revival since the declaration of the 'war on terrorism'. They have been invoked by both legal scholars and European courts to justify measures such as preventative arrests and suspension of rights of targeted activists, initially Islamic fundamentalists (Greenberg 2015: 208).

Fourth, more broadly, there is the reality that the claims of governments to represent or to be defending democracy may be fraudulent. As reviewed in the Introduction, capitalist governments today function more as plutocracies than democracies, and also sponsor and benefit from anti-democratic regimes elsewhere.

In any case, these models of accommodation are premised upon the existence of democracy. They can just as well serve the interests of a military, absolute monarchy or other dictatorship, as currently exists in Egypt, Saudi Arabia and the Gulf States.

Fifth, models of accommodation may be quite accommodating toward models of semi-legality or extra-legality.

Significantly, Gross and Ní Aoláin, who generally favoured models of accommodation, concluded that in 'particularly exceptional circumstances' the 'Extra-Legal Measures model may be utilized to respond to the particular exigencies posed by terrorist threats' (Gross and Ní Aoláin 2006: 421). According to one of the authors, 'certain catastrophic cases' may indeed 'call for' the invocation of the Extra-Legal Measures model Gross and Ní Aoláin 2006: 377).

The authors also maintained that 'the intersection of legal systems in times of crisis is a fluid one, where state legal responses can move between the various legal models' (Gross and Ní Aoláin 2006: 421). Their book ended on the following revealing note:

> That fluidity is essential both to retain the applicability of law to crisis and to acknowledge that the law applied in times of crisis may vary in substance and content, a quality dependent on the nature and intensity of the crisis itself at any particular point. (Gross and Ní Aoláin 2006: 421)

In other words, in order to preserve the alleged relevance of law in times of crisis, the law must be malleable. This is an entirely circular conclusion: the law must be preserved for the sake of the law. It renders worthless the notion of the rule of law, because the law must permit whatever is asserted to be required by 'the nature and intensity of the crisis itself'. This remarkable outcome would leave no protection against authoritarianism.

In fact, Gross went so far as to embrace the use of torture, in blatant violation of international and domestic law, as well as the most fundamental human rights. Employing a logic reminiscent of Schmitt and Loewenstein (and the White House), he insisted, without specifying the 'truly catastrophic' circumstances to which he was referring:

> In such extreme situations, denying the use of preventative interrogational torture may be hypocritical, cold hearted, detrimental to long-term notions of the rule of law, and may, in fact, lead to more, rather than less, radical interference with individual rights and liberties. (Gross and Ní Aoláin 2006: 382)

If torture, which is absolutely and unconditionally prohibited under all major human rights and humanitarian law conventions, is permitted, what is left of the 'rule of law'?

Sixth, legislatures and courts exhibit a pronounced tendency to embrace or rubberstamp executive assertions that crises exist and necessitate exceptional measures.

According to Gross and Ní Aoláin, 'experience demonstrates that legislatures tend to abdicate responsibility in times of emergency' (Gross and Ní Aoláin 2006: 64). Arguably, the problem is not one of abdication, but basic agreement, based in common interests.

Examples include the rapid passage, within seven weeks of the 9/11 attacks, of the far-reaching and Orwellian-titled USA PATRIOT Act (Uniting and Strengthening America by Providing Appropriate Tools Required to Intercept and Obstruct Terrorism Act). Another instance was the passage by the British House of Commons of the first Prevention of Terrorism (Temporary Provisions) Act of 1974, less than 24 hours after pub bombings in Birmingham.

This complicity has been attributed to a supposed 'rally round the flag' effect, the alleged popularity of decisive and patriotic actions, 'party loyalties' and the asserted superiority of the executive to judge national security risks (Gross and Ní Aoláin 2006: 64–6). In reality, the 'loyalties' involved are rooted more fundamentally in underlying class and material interests, with legislatures invariably dominated by members of the ruling elites as much as the executives. For instance, more than half the members of the US Congress are millionaires, an analysis of personal financial disclosure data by the Center for Responsive

Politics revealed in 2014. These figures do not include the value of legislators' personal residences, automobiles and artwork (Center for Responsive Politics 2014).

The same goes for the judiciary, whose ranks are drawn, almost without exception, from similar privileged layers of society, with deep-vested interests in maintaining the existing socio-economic order. The majority of US Supreme Court judges are also millionaires (Consider the Source 2013). International experience demonstrates that when faced with perceived national crises, the judges tend to 'go to war' (Gross and Ní Aoláin 2006: 77).

One prominent example was the mass internment of Japanese, German and Italian nationals and people of Japanese descent in the US during World War II. The Supreme Court sanctioned these internments in *Korematsu v United States* (323 US 214 (1944)), commenting that 'hardships are part of war' (Stone 2004: 300). President Franklin Roosevelt's Attorney-General, Francis Biddle, referring to Roosevelt's Executive Order 9066, which authorised the evacuation of people of Japanese ancestry from the West Coast, commented: '[T]he Constitution has not greatly bothered any wartime President' (Gross and Ní Aoláin 2006: 95).

One Supreme Court judge stated: 'There is … a good deal to be embarrassed about, when one reflects on the shabby treatment civil liberties have received in the United States during times of perceived threats to its national security' (Gross and Ní Aoláin 2006: 78). But the suppression of fundamental legal and democratic rights in every period of political and social unrest in the US has been the norm since the early twentieth century, not a matter of aberration (Head 2011: 37–63). Gross and Ní Aoláin summed up the performance of the judiciary as follows:

> [P]ractice shows that domestic courts tend to support the government's position either by invoking such judicial mechanisms as the political questions doctrine and standing to prevent themselves from having to decide a case on its merits, or, when deciding a case on its merits, accepting the government's position. That tendency of the courts becomes even more pronounced when they deal with cases *durante bello* [during the war] as opposed to deciding them when the crisis is over. This constitutional experience, which is shared by nations worldwide, may suggest that judicial review of emergency powers ought to be welcomed by governments as it confers a certain degree of legitimacy on the government's actions without exposing the executive to substantial risk that its actions may be curbed by the judiciary. (Gross and Ní Aoláin 2006: 63)

This cynical conclusion indicates that judicial review – a key tenet of the rule of law – is regarded as a vehicle to whitewash and sanctify dictatorial measures.

'Legality Model': Dyzenhaus, Dicey and the 'Jamaica Affair'

One of the champions of the claim that emergency powers can, and must, be constrained by law is David Dyzenhaus. In his *The Constitution of Law: Legality in a Time of Emergency* (Dyzenhaus 2006), he contended that there is an unwritten constitution of law, exemplified in the common law constitution of British Commonwealth countries. Based on examination of cases decided in the United Kingdom, Australia and Canada, he argued that even in the absence of a constitutionally entrenched bill of rights, the law provided a moral resource that could inform a 'rule-of-law project' able to respond to severe legal and political crises. Moreover, Dyzenhaus insisted that judges play an important role in this rule-of-law vision, but it also required the participation of the legislature and the executive.

Significantly, in opposing Carl Schmitt's doctrine of exception, Dyzenhaus relied heavily on the conceptions advanced by a figure no less reactionary than Schmitt – Albert Dicey, long regarded as the protagonist par excellence of the 'rule of law'. Against Gross and Ní Aoláin's 'models of accommodation', Dyzenhaus suggested that 'Dicey's legality model' offered a superior solution (Dyzenhaus 2008: 46).

As interpreted by Dyzenhaus, Dicey preferred that legislatures adopt statutes that give officials the authority they need to respond to emergencies in a 'spirit of legality'. However, in the absence of such statutory provisions, officials should have two options. One was to raise a defence of necessity to justify going outside the law by being able to prove to a judge that what they did was 'strictly necessary to deal with an emergency'. The second was to count on an Act of Indemnity to legalise their illegality, 'as long as what they did was both reasonable and not recklessly cruel, again factors that a judge will be entitled to review' (Dyzenhaus 2008: 46–7).

The most obvious point to make about this schema is that it leaves enormous scope for authoritarian, draconian and brutal measures. What is meant by 'strictly necessary'? Or 'an emergency'? What is 'reasonable'? 'Recklessly cruel'? These terms are full of unstated political and value assumptions. Moreover, why should judges be entrusted with the task of arbitrating on the outcome, especially given the well-documented track record of courts rubberstamping repressive emergency actions?

Before probing the Diceyan model of retrospective indemnification, it is essential to place it within the context of Dicey's political and class standpoint as a member of the British establishment. Writing in the late nineteenth and early twentieth century, Dicey was a vehement and voluble opponent of Irish independence, female suffrage and votes for Negroes (Ford 1985). In 1913, he agreed with the Conservatives that the monarch could refuse the royal assent to the Home Rule Bill for Ireland, a power not exercised since 1707 (Bogdanor 1995: 132). Thus, Dicey's 'rule of law' clearly embraced the deployment of autocratic powers to defend the interests of the British Empire and its ruling elites.

Above all, Dicey's legalism abhorred any collective struggle by working people, and he supported violent force to suppress strikes. Dicey denounced the British Trade Disputes Act 1906, which gave some limited protection to the right to strike, as 'opposed to every principle of justice' (Cosgrove 1980: 209). During a 1912 miners' strike, Dicey wrote to a friend that this use of 'force' by the miners should be met with force, even if the result was bloodshed (Cosgrove 1980: 209–10). Again, his 'rule of law' envisaged bloody repression of working people.

Dicey equated collectivism with socialism, and was preoccupied with the threat of 'socialist revolution' (Dicey 1962: 17, 259). He claimed that collectivism threatened 'the gravest danger to the country (Dicey 1962: 398). Dicey's insistence that the judiciary was the bulwark of liberty was bound up with his knowledge that its members were drawn from the wealthy layers of society, well-versed in the sanctity of private property and 'freedom of contract'.

Dyzenhaus conceded that Dicey was aware that his claims for an exceptionless rule of law did not reflect the reality of the British Empire. Dicey certainly knew that his theories of no recourse to martial law, and for Acts of Indemnity to be confined to 'reasonable' abuses of power, were by no means adhered to by British authorities. That is because Dicey referred to the 'Jamaica affair' in his writings on martial law.

This 'affair' concerned the savage suppression unleashed by Governor Edward John Eyre's proclamation of martial law in reaction to the Jamaica uprising of 1865 (Kostal 2005). Britain's former slaves and their descendants, while formally freed from bondage 32 years earlier, lived in dire poverty, exacerbated by a government plan to clear squatters from land that planters wanted to use for sugar production.

In October 1865, a protest outside the courthouse in Morant Bay, a town in Jamaica, turned violent (Kostal 2005: 95–8). Eyre declared martial law in the Morant Bay area and sent troops to suppress the insurrection. While the rebellion was effectively over in a few days, Eyre maintained martial law for a month, during which time his forces killed 439 black people (either shot on the spot or after a perfunctory court martial); flogged 600 black men and women; and destroyed about 1,000 cottages and huts. Despite having no hand in the uprising, George Gordon – an educated, half-caste landowner, former magistrate and a member of the Jamaica House of Assembly – was found guilty of treason and executed within two days, without being allowed to make a proper defence.

When Eyre returned to Britain in August 1866, his supporters held a banquet in his honour. Eyre defiantly asserted that his actions were not only constitutionally appropriate but also politically necessary. The governor had a prerogative authority, he declared, located in the unwritten constitution, to proclaim martial law and put down unrest. In Jamaica that constitutional authority was confirmed by a local colonial statute. Nevertheless, Eyre ensured that an Act of Indemnity was passed to cover everything that he and his officials had done.

A Royal Commission of Inquiry was sent to Jamaica, which issued a report critical of the duration of martial law and the measures adopted to enforce it. As expected, however, prosecutions within Jamaica of officials and military officers failed in the hands of British settler judges. The British government also refused to bring criminal proceedings. Concerned about the sustainability of such methods of colonial rule, a Jamaica Committee, including leading liberals, such as John Stuart Mill (a vehement supporter of colonialism), initiated private prosecutions of Eyre and two military officers; but these failed too, essentially because of the judges' instructions to the juries.

The political atmosphere in ruling circles can be gauged from remarks by the prominent historian Thomas Carlyle. He denounced the judges who heard the prosecutions as part of the 'knot of rabid Nigger-Philanthropists, barking furiously in the gutter', who would, if successful, place a 'rope around [the] … neck' of any governor attempting to put down the frightfullest Mob-insurrection' (Carlyle 1867: 324).

In his charge to a jury, Lord Chief Justice Cockburn, who has been depicted as taking Dicey's approach, admitted that claims about the end of prerogative-based martial law could not be made about Ireland. Moreover, he pointed out that the illegality of the actions taken in Ireland had been rectified through Acts of Indemnity and, in any case, 'nobody can deny for a moment the power of Parliament to enact that martial law shall be put into force' (Cockburn 1867: 3). The judge also suggested that he understood why, in the circumstances of the uprising and in the light of Gordon's political record, officials could honestly think that Gordon was both a cause of the uprising and that his punishment would bring an end to the insurrection (Cockburn 1867: 152). A study of the affair concluded that Cockburn 'surely scuttled' any chance that a jury of 23 'affluent and (presumably) conservative men' were going to convict the defendants (Kostal 2005: 339).

The Lord Chief Justice added a postscript to the published edition of his charge that he not only 'accepted the fact of empire and the need to use force to preserve it' but also would not 'categorically condemn martial law' and 'made just one recommendation – for the "necessity of legislation if martial law is ever again to be put into force"' (Kostal 2005: 367, 483–4).

The other judge, Justice Blackburn, interpreted the Jamaican colonial statute as proving for the common law to be entirely suspended, allowing for martial law to be exercised 'in the fullest sense' (Finlason 1868: 79).

Several Jamaicans sued Eyre in tort, and found the same judicial determination to shield the former governor. Justice Willes held that Eyre could not be sued for his conduct in Jamaica, for two reasons. First, the alleged conduct must 'be of such a character that it would have been actionable if it had been committed' in the local jurisdiction. Second, 'the act must not have been justifiable by the law of the place where it was done'. Due to the Indemnity Act that Eyre passed just before leaving Jamaica, the act was found to be justifiable by the law of Jamaica. The Indemnity Act retrospectively legalised illegality, but the judge brushed aside the common law presumption against retrospective force. 'The court will not ascribe retrospective force to new laws affecting rights unless by express words or necessary implication that such was the intention of the legislature'; but in this case Eyre's intention was clear (*Phillips v Eyre* (1870) LR 6 QB 1, Exchequer Chamber).

Despite these unequivocal outcomes, Dyzenhaus drew the lesson that the Jamaica affair proved that, 'for all the participants … the compulsion of legality was a given' (Dyzenhaus 2008: 49). This conclusion was said to be based on three observations. The first was that 'Eyre scrupulously took legal advice from his chief law officer before he declared martial law.' Even though the governor saw no need for further advice once the military operation began, he believed 'he could do as he pleased once he had the initial warrant'. Hence, the politics of the suppression were 'understood and transacted in terms of law and legality' (Dyzenhaus 2008: 49, citing the final quote from Kostal 2005: 30).

This was remarkable logic. It gave credence to Eyre's justification for the slaughter, barbarity and violation of fundamental legal rights that was inflicted on the long-suffering Jamaicans. If Eyre initially took legal advice, that would have been only to protect himself, not his victims. Moreover, to cloak brutality in the veil of legality was not a sign of respect for the 'rule of law' but of the perceived need to use pseudo-legal camouflage for brazen abuses. 'Legality' here became an ideological pretext for outright repression, a common practice to this day.

Dyzenhaus's second argument was even more revealing. It was that the Jamaica Committee 'was not primarily motivated by concerns about black Jamaicans'. From this, Dyzenhaus concluded that those involved were preoccupied with the implications of the case for legal accountability within Britain and their supposed struggle for full male suffrage at home. They were embarked on a 'democratic, political project' in England (Dyzenhaus 2008: 49). If all this were so, surely it would be a damning indictment of the committee's lack of concern for the basic legal and democratic rights of the butchered Jamaicans and an exposure of the kind of 'democracy', built on imperialist plunder, that Mill and other liberals favoured.

Dyzenhaus's third contention was that the outcome of the 'affair' was 'indeterminate' (Dyzenhaus 2008: 50). In reality, there was nothing inconclusive about it. Mass murderers got away scot-free, with the help of the judicial elite in which Dyzenhaus has placed such store. After discussing the Jamaican affair, Dyzenhaus restated his belief in the role of judges in fighting, ostensibly on behalf of the public, the 'storm' of illegality, or at least acting as 'weathermen' doing their duty to 'alert the public as to the storm clouds on the horizon' (Dyzenhaus 2008: 51). On the contrary, the judges who absolved Eyre and his officers of all criminal and civil liability were acting on behalf of the state, as part of the state apparatus itself.

Rather than Dicey, in his remarks about martial law and the English Constitution, assuming 'a victory that had not yet been secured' (Dyzenhaus 2008: 50), the lauded professor was putting a gloss on the British ruling elite's long record of brutality, from Jamaica to South Africa, Ireland and the United Kingdom itself. In a footnote, Dyzenhaus claimed to agree with Simpson's verdict that Dicey's claim about martial law was 'grossly and perversely misleading' (Dyzenhaus 2008: 50, citing Simpson 2004: 60). But Dyzenhaus still maintained that Dicey's claim was an aspirational normative one, not meant to be a scientific description of the historical record. Yet, Dicey never condemned the atrocity in Jamaica, nor any of the other crimes committed by British colonialism.

Dyzenhaus, Dicey and Acts of Indemnity

As part of his case for Dicey as a pillar of legality, Dyzenhaus pointed to the professor's support for Acts of Indemnity, arguing that this represented a means of bringing officials 'within the law', albeit retrospectively. Dyzenhaus maintained this position even as he conceded that Dicey insisted that 'in a time of emergency, officials should also be given some margin for error' (Dyzenhaus 2008: 47). That is, their evaluation of the necessity for their actions need not be correct, just 'reasonable'. Such an interpretation, essentially that made by the judges in his cases, certainly suited Governor Eyre.

In backing Dicey's support for such retrospective grants of immunity, and claiming that this practice upheld legality rather than trampling over it, Dyzenhaus argued:

> [A]n Act of Indemnity should not purport to provide a blanket immunity for all illegal activity, nor should it provide expressly that it covers bad faith acts or acts of reckless cruelty. The Act is meant to secure the rule of law, not to undermine it. While the rule of law includes a principle of non-retrospectivity, that principle can be outweighed by other principles of the rule of law, in this situation, the need to preserve legal order. (Dyzenhaus 2008: 47–8)

This is a recipe for sanctioning violent and lawless repression, so long as judges subsequently agree that it was not carried out in 'bad faith' or with 'reckless cruelty'. Again, the historical record demonstrates that such legislation provides, in effect, a 'blanket immunity for all illegal activity', and one thoroughly embraced by Anglo-American jurisprudence. Dicey's own formulations were unequivocally in favour of upholding the authority of the state. He was a strong advocate of Acts of Indemnity to 'make lawful acts which when they were committed were unlawful' (Dicey 2005: 142):

> There are times of tumult or invasion when for the sake of legality itself the rules of law must be broken. The course which the government must then take is clear. The Ministry must break the law and trust for protection to an Act of Indemnity. (Dicey 2005: 272)

Dicey observed, pointing to historical experience, that the expectation of executives that such Acts would be passed 'has not been disappointed' (Dicey 2005: 144). As seen in Chapter 3, no less than seven Indemnity Acts were passed in Ireland between 1796 and 1800 to protect the British authorities against legal liability for their unlawful acts (Lee 1984: 222), and this trend was on display during major twentieth-century strikes in Britain.

Finally, it must be noted that the South African apartheid regime drew on this doctrine, complete with 'good faith' provisos, to shield itself from culpability for its two most notorious massacres – Sharpeville in 1961 and Soweto in 1976. The Indemnity Act of 1961 protected the government from any legal repercussions of the Sharpeville massacre and other violent repression that followed. It prevented the courts from hearing any criminal charges or civil claims against the government, its leaders or its employees for actions taken between 21 March 1960 and 5 July 1961. The Indemnity Act of 1977 did the same for the suppression of the Soweto uprising against the forced use of Afrikaans in schools:

> With retrospective effect between 16 June 1976 and 16 March 1977, this Act indemnifies the government, its officers and all other persons acting under their authority in respect of acts done, orders given or information provided in good faith for the prevention or suppression of internal disorder, the maintenance or restoration of good order, public safety or essential services, or the preservation of life or property in any part of the Republic. (du Bois-Pedain 2007: 28)

Dyzenhaus, Dicey and Martial Law

One of Dyzenhaus's central contentions is that Dicey opposed martial law as 'utterly unknown to the constitution' (Dyzenhaus 2008: 42) and this proved his fidelity to legality. In his often-cited work on the English constitution, Dicey stated:

> 'Martial law' in the proper sense of that term, in which it means the suspension of ordinary law and the temporary government of a country or parts of it by military tribunals is unknown to the law of England ... This is unmistakable proof of the permanent supremacy of the law under our constitution. (Dicey 2005: 283–4)

According to Dicey, as interpreted by Dyzenhaus, the English Constitution recognised martial law only in two other, 'very different' senses. There was the law that governed the military both in war and in peace; and there was the common law defence of necessity, which could be invoked by any citizen who responded appropriately to an immediate threat to peace and order. However, Dicey also asserted the legitimacy of Acts of Indemnity, which amounted to the 'legalisation of illegality' (Dicey 2005: 233) and claimed this as proof of his claim that the English Constitution did not know martial law (see Chapter 3).

Simpson described Dicey's claim about martial law as 'grossly and perversely misleading' because under martial law 'precisely what happens is the suspension of ordinary law, followed by the government of the relevant area by the military' (Simpson 2004: 60). In particular, Dicey's 'absurd legal theory' could not account for punishment and reprisal as central techniques of British colonialism's martial law (Simpson 2004: 54–90).

Despite the supposed nicety of the distinctions drawn by Dicey and Dyzenhaus, the history of the use of martial law in Britain and throughout the British Empire is barbaric. One example – from the period in which Dicey was writing – is the repeated imposition of martial law in Egypt, which was occupied by Britain from 1882.

Significantly, the first declaration of martial law, in 1914, was bound up with Britain's formal assertion of sovereignty over Egypt. The British government proclaimed Egypt a 'protectorate' that year in the context of World War I and the British offensive against the Ottoman Empire, of which Egypt had been a province for four centuries (Reza 2006: 535). Thus British rule commenced with martial law, which was instrumental to the assertion of sovereignty itself.

During the war, the British poured masses of foreign troops into Egypt; conscripted over 1.5 million Egyptians into the Labour Corps; and requisitioned buildings, crops and animals for the use of the army (Vatikiotis 1992: 246). A British governor was placed in command of the Egyptian military, and its actions were removed from the jurisdiction of the courts (Reza 2006: 535).

That imposition cannot be dismissed simply as a wartime measure, even if that were to be regarded somehow as an exceptional circumstance. Martial law continued after World War I, directed against the 1919 uprising of Egyptian nationalism, and ended only temporarily after Britain declared the country nominally independent in 1922 (Reza 2006: 535). By mid-1919, about 800 Egyptians had been killed by Allied (mainly Australian) troops and twice that number had been wounded (Jankowski 2000: 112). Australia's official war memorial website whitewashes and glorifies the suppression as follows:

> In early March 1919, demonstrations in Cairo, mainly by students, initiated an outburst of anti-British rioting, which within a few days spread through all the lower provinces and extended to upper Egypt. The situation was exacerbated by the local civil service's declaration of a general strike and the rapid suspension of railway and telegraph services. In the absence of a large British force in Egypt, elements of the Australian and ANZAC Mounted Divisions, then awaiting embarkation to Australia, were instructed to restore order. Within a month of the uprising order had been restored and principal political agitators imprisoned. The flexibility and mobility of the ANZAC forces involved were principal factors in the suppression of the rioting. (Australian War Memorial)

No one was held to account for the killings. Instead, the British government sent a commission of inquiry, known as the Milner Mission, to Egypt in December 1919 to determine the causes of the uprising, and to make a recommendation about the political future of the country. Lord Milner's report, published in February 1921, recommended that the protectorate status of Egypt be abandoned (Daly 1988: 249–50).

In effect, although the independence movement was crushed, ongoing popular resistance forced the British to grant a modicum of independence to Egypt in 1922. The British kept control over the strategic and lucrative Suez Canal, however, and continued to dictate Egyptian policy through a proxy ruler (Vatikiotis 1992: 264).

A 1936 Anglo-Egyptian treaty, which guaranteed the British a military presence in Egypt, permitted the British government to request declarations of martial law under the 1923 Egyptian constitution, which was modelled on the Belgian constitution. A 1939 declaration of martial law remained in place throughout World War II. Another declaration, from 1948 to 1950, accompanied the outbreak of the first Arab–Israeli war. It was reimposed in 1952 after protests against the British control of the Suez Canal led to the killing of dozens of people by British troops, and riots broke out in Cairo. This declaration lasted until 1956, until the consolidation of the victory of the 1952 Free Officers Revolution led by army colonel Gamal Abdel Nasser (Reza 2006: 535–6).

Another example, also from the period before Dicey died in 1922, was the 1919 massacre carried out by British troops at Amritsar in India (see Chapter 2).

Dyzenhaus, Torture and the 'Unlegalisable'

In his version of the 'rule of law', Dyzenhaus regarded some government actions taken on the pretext of emergency as 'unlegalisable'. Such actions were 'by definition' in 'extra-legal space'. By this circular reasoning, these 'emergency situations' could 'never amount to a state of emergency' (Dyzenhaus 2008: 52).

Even so, this category of behaviour was very narrow, possibly consisting only of blatant torture and 'lengthy or indefinite security detention', and perhaps not even that. Everything else was legalisable. Dyzenhaus stated:

> At most, and I do not mean to concede that the following comment applies to torture, there can be a brute act of politics that uses law to legalise past illegality because it is considered that, in this exceptional situation, there was reason for society to immunise the individual from legal sanctions. (Dyzenhaus 2008: 54)

To legalise 'brute acts', whether retrospectively or in advance, obviously leaves wide scope for violent repression under the banner of legality. The experiences in Jamaica, Egypt, India and Ireland, all rubberstamped by the courts, testify to that. Dyzenhaus's only caveat was that this immunity could not be the basis for a 'principled model'.

But Dyzenhaus also suggested that even torture was being brought within the claimed boundaries of legality. He referred to official and judicial decisions that were 'chipping away at the consensus' that torture was absolutely prohibited. These instances were recent US official practices (see Chapter 10); Canada's Supreme Court pronouncement that exceptional 'national security' grounds could justify a decision to deport a person to be tortured (*Suresh v Canada (Minister of Citizenship and Immigration)* [2002] 1 SCR 3); and the UK Court of Appeal's dictum that evidence obtained by torture might be admissible under certain circumstances (*A v Secretary of State for the Home Department (No. 2)* (2005) 1 WLR 414).

As for indefinite detention, it was not yet clear whether it was 'unlegalisable' because of ongoing litigation over the practice in the US, the UK and Canada. Still, Dyzenhaus insisted that these were 'inapt examples' because they were 'legally and morally doomed to take place in extra-legal space' (Dyzenhaus 2008: 53). Again, this is circular, self-defining, reasoning.

'Business as Usual'

According to the 'business as usual' model, a state of emergency does not justify a deviation from 'normal' legal powers. No 'special' emergency powers are to be introduced, either on a permanent or ad hoc, or retrospective, basis. Or, at least, governments cannot lawfully take any measures to combat crises unless such measures are explicitly provided for by the constitution. However, a 'soft' version of this model argues that constitutional powers can be interpreted as justifying more far-reaching measures during emergencies (Gross and Ní Aoláin 2006: 10, 86–109).

As outlined above, Tom Campbell and Kent Roach advocated 'business as usual' or 'ordinary laws' models. Tellingly, both called for allowance for 'extreme measures' (Campbell) or 'explicit and democratic derogations from rights' (Roach) within their conceptions of normalcy.

As discussed in examining American emergency law in Chapter 8, one of the judicial rulings most cited as an exemplar of this approach is Justice Davis's majority opinion in the US Supreme Court case *Ex parte Milligan* (71 US 2 (1866)), handed down a year after the end of the Civil War. In a judgment once hailed as a 'landmark decision in the protection of individual rights' (Gross and Ní Aoláin 2006: 94, citing Fridlington), Davis led the court in issuing a writ of habeas corpus to order the release of Lambdin Milligan, who had been sentenced by a military commission to be hanged for inciting an insurrection.

As a matter of statutory interpretation, the judges ruled that the Habeas Corpus Act of 1863, which authorised the president to suspend the writ of habeas corpus when he deemed it necessary, did not authorise military trials. Davis's majority opinion went further. He declared:

> The Constitution of the United States is a law for rulers and people, equally in war and in peace, and covers with the shield of its protection all classes of man, at all times, and under all circumstances. No doctrine, involving more pernicious consequences, was ever invented by the wit of man than that any of its provisions can be suspended during any of the great exigencies of government. (*Ex parte Milligan*, 71 US (4 Wall.) 2 (1866) per Davis J at 120–21)

Yet, the opinion left the door open to sweeping and authoritarian measures by insisting that all the powers to preserve the nation's existence lay within the constitution itself. The judgment also affirmed the power to invoke martial law if 'in foreign invasion or civil war, the courts are actually closed' (*Ex parte Milligan*, 71 US (4 Wall.) 2 (1866) per Davis J at 126).

Furthermore, the facts of *Milligan* differed little from cases decided during the Civil War itself, such as *Vallandigham* (68 US (1 Wall.) 243 (1863)), where the Supreme Court permitted military arrests and trials. For a speech denouncing the war, Vallandigham was charged with making 'treasonable utterances', tried and convicted by a military commission, and sentenced to imprisonment for the remainder of the war (Stone 2004: 82). It is not known exactly how many civilians were arrested by military authorities during the Civil War. Estimates range from 13,000 to 38,000 (Stone 2004: 124).

The *Milligan* majority sought to justify the disparity by stating that during the war, 'the temper of the times did not allow that calmness in deliberation and discussion so necessary to a correct conclusion of a purely judicial question', but a different outcome was possible 'now that public safety is assured' (71 US (4 Wall) at 109). This produced accusations of judicial hypocrisy. Because the judges had refused to resist executive power during the actual conflict itself, *Milligan* was characterised as 'mere rhetorical jousting at accomplished wartime deeds' (Rossiter and Longaker 1976: xi).

At the first next test, during World War I, moreover, in *Wilson v New* (243 US 332 (1917)), the Supreme Court effectively reversed Justice Davis's view in favour of a 'soft' version. While maintaining that a state of emergency could not create powers that did not already exist, the majority of judges insisted that a crisis could widen the scope of existing powers. As reviewed in Chapter 8, this pliable interpretation of constitutionality provided a legal justification for the expansion of presidential power throughout the ensuing century, including mass wartime internments during World War II, sanctioned by the Supreme Court in *Korematsu v United States* (323 US 214 (1944)) (see also Head 2011: 41–63).

One revealing line of argument by defenders of the 'business as usual' model is that it retains a symbolic, educational and even mythical value, despite being proven false in practice during times of crisis. 'One may acknowledge the unrealistic attributes of the model and still contend that upholding the myth of regularity and control by normal constitutional principles, even under circumstances of emergency, is socially beneficial' (Gross and Ní Aoláin 2006: 101). This cynical view amounts to maintaining the illusion, in the minds of the public, that the ruling elite stands committed to the 'rule of law', when in fact the opposite applies whenever there is a perceived threat to the prevailing socio-economic order. Gross and Ní Aoláin themselves concluded:

> Thus, the Business as Usual model assumes important symbolic and educational functions. Maintaining an unbending commitment to existing legal norms, the constitution, and the ideal of the rule of law – maintaining a 'mood of veneration' toward them – helps us answer the question of what are and what are not 'necessary' measures in a particular state of emergency. (Gross and Ní Aoláin 2006: 102)

Such reasoning suggested that the critical task of theorising about emergency powers was to find models that befuddled ordinary working people with myths that encouraged them to 'venerate' the legal system, while the truth was that those in the corridors of power had no such respect for legality. Gross and Ní Aoláin echoed Dicey and Dyzenhaus, and other scholars, in insisting that the model was valuable as a 'theoretical construct', even though its assumptions held true 'in no historical society' and did not 'comport with any specific number of empirically observable phenomena' (Gross and Ní Aoláin 2006: 102–3).

Case Study: Canada

Canada provides an example of the extent to which a model of constitutional and legislative accommodation can be used, in reality, to overturn basic civil liberties and democratic rights. This includes the outlawing of socialist and anti-war political parties; the internment of communists and foreigners; and the domestic deployment of military forces to suppress unrest.

The War Measures Act of 1914, adopted as Canada's government joined World War I as part of the British Empire, conferred extreme powers on the federal government, allowing it to effectively rule by decree when it perceived the existence of 'war, invasion or insurrection, real or apprehended'. During both world wars, the Act was used to outlaw dissent and issue detailed regulations limiting the freedom of Canadians of foreign descent (see Chapter 2).

In 1988, the powers contained in the War Measures Act were replaced by the Emergencies Act. It conferred extraordinary powers on the federal cabinet, allowing it to govern by decree when it perceives the existence of 'threats to the security of Canada', including acts of serious political violence or activities aimed at overthrowing the system of government.

The Act permits the Canadian government to rule by executive orders and regulations in any 'national emergency', which is defined broadly as 'an urgent and critical situation of a temporary nature' that 'seriously endangers the lives, health or safety of Canadians' or 'seriously threatens the ability of the Government of Canada to preserve the sovereignty, security and territorial integrity of Canada'.

Four kinds of emergency are provided for: public welfare (natural disasters); public order (internal security); international (external threats to security or territorial integrity); and war (war or other armed conflict, real or imminent). Considerable scope exists for domestic military intervention under the other three headings, but 'public order emergencies' explicitly relate to suppressing certain types of political opposition.

A public order emergency, covered by Part II of the Act, is one that arises from 'threats to the security of Canada' as defined by the Canadian Security Intelligence Service Act. Section 2 of that statute refers to espionage, sabotage, foreign influenced activities; 'acts of serious political violence' for the purpose of achieving a 'political, religious or ideological objective' within Canada or a foreign state; and activities 'directed toward or intended ultimately to lead to the destruction or overthrow by violence' of the Canadian system of government. Although the definition exempts 'lawful advocacy, protest or dissent', unless linked to any of the proscribed activities, the section leaves open considerable scope for emergency rule directed against various forms of political dissent, particularly if they can be depicted as potentially violent.

Once a public order emergency has been declared, the Governor in Council (normally on behalf of the federal cabinet) can issue far-reaching orders, including banning public assemblies; stopping travel and seizing control of public services; and imposing summary convictions for up to six months' imprisonment. There are no unlimited search and seizure powers, previously available under the War Measures Act, for a public order emergency, but they remain for an international emergency.

Emergency powers can last initially for 30 days and be continuously renewed. Ministers and other personnel exercising emergency powers 'in good faith' are protected from personal legal liability, although government liability and compensation remain. Parliamentary scrutiny is weak and belated: either House of Parliament can revoke an emergency declaration, but only after a delay of at least seven sitting days (Emergencies Act, sections 3, 16–26, 47–8, 58–9).

The statute states that it does not confer on the government the power to detain, imprison or intern Canadian citizens or permanent residents 'on the basis of race, national or ethnic origin, colour, religion, sex, age or mental or physical disability' (Emergencies Act, section 4). This proviso, however, does not preclude detention on political or ideological grounds; nor does it apply to non-citizens without permanent residency status.

One limitation on use of the Act compared to its predecessor, the War Measures Act, is that under section 25(3), the Governor in Council cannot declare a public emergency unless requested by a province or the emergency extends to more than one province. For that reason, there have been calls from within military and police circles for the Act to be amended (Lerhe 2004: 17).

One scholar stated that it is doubtful whether the Act could be used, as the War Measures Act was in October 1970, to abridge fundamental civil liberties. He explained that the Act's preamble says that the 'special temporary measures' are subject to the Charter of Rights and Freedoms, the Canadian Bill of Rights and 'must have regard to the International Covenant on Civil and Political Rights, particularly with respect to those fundamental rights that are not to be limited or abridged even in a national emergency' (Forcese 2008: 124). However, such preambles are not legally binding and the Charter and the Bill of Rights provide no secure protection of basic rights in the context of an alleged national security emergency.

Neither of these two statements of basic rights expressly prohibits or curtails the domestic mobilisation of the Canadian Forces to suppress political or social unrest. They do not allow for abridgement of rights during emergencies, but they do permit parliament to circumscribe at least some of the rights. Section 33 of the Charter allows the federal and provincial legislatures to exclude most Charter provisions by stating that a statute operates 'notwithstanding' the Charter. No parliament has utilised this power in an emergency situation, but it remains possible for this to happen in a crisis (Forcese 2008: 35, 120–22).

Otherwise, section 1 of the Charter guarantees the rights and freedoms set out in it 'subject only to such reasonable limits prescribed by law as can be demonstrably justified in a free and democratic society'. This protection is far from absolute. In the event of a crisis involving military deployment, the issue of what are 'reasonable limits' may well arise. In *Operation Dismantle v Canada Inc* ([1985] 1 SCR 441), Wilson J of the Supreme Court said the concept of 'right' used in the Charter had to 'take account of the fact that the self-contained political community which comprises the State is faced with at least the possibility, if not the reality, of external threats to both its collective well-being and to the individual well-being of its citizens' (at 489–90). While these remarks related to external threats, a similar claim could be made about internal threats.

Section 2 of the Charter recognises 'fundamental freedoms' of conscience and religion; thought, belief, opinion and expression; peaceful assembly; and association. Other sections set out certain democratic, mobility, equality and legal rights, some of which may limit military powers. For example, a person cannot be deprived of the 'right to life, liberty and security of the person' except 'in accordance with the principles of fundamental justice'. Everyone has the right 'to be secure against unreasonable search or seizure' and 'not to be arbitrarily detained or imprisoned'.

These provisions can restrict violations of democratic rights, at least where the rules of procedural fairness have not been followed. In *Suresh v Canada (Minister of Citizenship and Immigration)* ([2002] 1 SCR 3, 2002 SCC 1), the Supreme Court ruled that deportation to face torture was generally, but not always, unconstitutional and therefore Suresh was entitled to a fair hearing with procedural safeguards before being deported. However, the Canadian courts have generally treated military and national security considerations as overriding procedural fairness (for example, *Chiarelli v Canada (Minister of Justice)* [1992] 1 SCR 711). Moreover, the phrases 'reasonable limits', 'unreasonable' and 'arbitrarily' in the Charter leave considerable scope for military intervention, provided it is authorised by legislation, common law or judicially recognised prerogative powers. In a number of cases, the Supreme Court has suggested that the right to life, liberty and security of the person can be tempered or violated in times of war, national emergency or other security exigencies (Forcese 2008: 37).

Similar issues arise with the Bill of Rights, which declares 'human rights and fundamental freedoms' that include life, liberty, security of the person and enjoyment of property, except where deprived by due process of law. Other rights listed in section 1 of the Bill are equality before the law and the protection of the law; and the freedoms of religion, speech, assembly and association, and the press. However, the protection of these rights and freedoms is far from guaranteed. Section 2 of the Bill merely specifies that federal statutes be construed and applied as not to abrogate, abridge or infringe any of the rights or freedoms, unless expressly provided otherwise by an Act of Parliament. Therefore, it remains possible for federal legislation to override these provisions, as happened with the War Measures Act prior to its repeal by the Emergencies Act in 1988 (Forcese 2008: 119).

One scholar of Canadian national security law concluded: 'In Canadian constitutional law, it seems clear that Charter protections may be tempered where national security threats are at issue' (Forcese 2008: 35). The same appears to apply to the Bill of Rights.

Canadian courts have also recognised the continued existence of the royal prerogative as a source of executive power, encompassing 'the powers and privileges accorded by the common law to the Crown'. Legislation can override or abrogate prerogative powers, but only if the statute makes this clear by explicit language or necessary implication. From some court rulings, doubt may still exist about whether a legislative scheme has replaced prerogative powers (Forcese 2008: 67–8).

The first decade of the twenty-first century also saw a reminder of the potentially anti-democratic reserve powers exercised in the name of the Canadian Governor-General. Within the space of 13 months, parliament was twice prorogued by the Governor-General to overcome a perceived political impasse (Heard 2009).

In addition, the events of 9/11 were exploited to introduce the Public Safety Act 2004, which gave ministers powers to issue interim orders. The Emergency Management Act 2007 also sets out the federal government's emergency management roles and responsibilities (Lindsay 2014: 164). Provincial governments have extensive emergency powers that can overturn basic civil rights as well (Lindsay 2014: 167–71).

Chapter 5
Models of Extra-Legality and Illegality: Carl Schmitt's Lengthening Shadow

This chapter focuses on Carl Schmitt and others who can be considered as exponents of either 'extra-legal' or 'realist' models of emergency powers. The realist school, examined in the final section of this chapter, insists that 'legal rules and norms are too inflexible and rigid to accommodate the security needs of states' (Gross and Ní Aoláin 2006: 11). The Extra-Legal Measures model 'suggests that under extreme circumstances, public officials may act extra-legally when they believe that such action is necessary for protecting the nation and the public in the face of calamity, provided that they openly and publicly acknowledge the nature of their actions' (Gross and Ní Aoláin 2006: 11).

Gross and Ní Aoláin argued that this extra-legal model, in which they found attractive features, was qualitatively different from Schmitt's doctrine of exception because it served to ultimately preserve the rule of law. This distinction, in reality, is artificial and cosmetic. To appreciate that, it is first essential to further examine the role played by Schmitt's theories in the transition from the German Weimar Republic, which he initially sought to uphold, and Hitler's fascist regime, which Schmitt served, relatively seamlessly.

The Rehabilitation of Carl Schmitt

Carl Schmitt's jurisprudence has been described as a 'dark shadow' (Gross and Ní Aoláin 2006: 162). It must be said that the shadow is getting longer. It is not just that Schmittian conceptions are echoing through the assertions of exceptional executive power in Washington and other capitals. Nor is it just that legal theorists are having difficulty finding models of emergency powers that differ fundamentally from those of Schmitt. Attempts are being made to positively rehabilitate Schmitt and make his authoritarian views respectable. Even if his views are still not embraced positively, some scholars (for example, Salter 2012; Croce and Salvatore 2013) insist that his theories deserve respect, and even admiration.

Croce and Salvatore argue that Schmitt's legal theory needs to be reassessed and more greatly appreciated 'in its own right' rather than in the light of his 'political thinking'. They complain that 'too often the literature about him and his works fails to notice the central role played by law in his theory' (Croce and Salvatore 2013: 1–2). This is to suggest that Schmitt's jurisprudence can be understood outside the context in which he sought to first justify the frequent anti-democratic resort to rule by presidential decree under the Weimar Republic, and then the fascist dictatorship of the Nazis.

Moreover, Croce and Salvatore contend that in his 1934 work, *On the Three Types of Juristic Thought*, Schmitt acknowledged the flaws in his previous 'decisionist' approach and partly abandoned it in favour of an 'institutional' perspective. They reached this conclusion despite conceding that Schmitt retained the conviction that 'the decision of the sovereign is a basic pillar of every political community' (Croce and Salvatore 2013: 1). This also buries the real politico-legal content of Schmitt's contortions. As will be discussed in this chapter, Schmitt's 1934 work, produced amid his period as the Nazis' most favoured jurist, was part of his efforts to lay down a theoretical framework to ensure a homogenous and disciplined legal profession and judiciary, and therefore a more stable foundation for Hitler's dictatorship.

Salter goes further. He portrays Schmitt as a valiant anti-Nazi who, by supporting an expansive interpretation of the emergency powers of the German president under Article 48 of the Weimar Constitution, sought to 'enhance constitutional bulwarks directed precisely against extreme unconstitutional movements such as Nazism and Communism' (Salter 2012: 10). Salter favourably emphasises Schmitt's 'ambitions of becoming a leading constitutional adviser' to General von Schleicher, with whom Schmitt 'contrived' to 'outmanoeuvre Hitler' (without mentioning Schleicher's own plans for a military dictatorship). Further, Salter asserts of Schmitt:

> Attempts to read his subsequent embrace of the Nazi-Conservative coalition as if this represented the logical culmination of the allegedly Nazi implications of his earlier studies, involves a gross falsification of the historical record … Nothing in his work actually reveals a necessary transition from Schmitt's conservative-statist anti-liberalism to totalitarianism and Nazism. (Salter 2012: 10, 12)

The kernel of Salter's claim is that Schmitt's backing for authoritarian forms of rule by the German corporate and military elite between the defeat of the 1919 revolution and the handing over of power to Hitler in 1933 was somehow incompatible with his enthusiastic backing for Hitler's despotic rule as 'Führer'. For Salter, Schmitt was perfectly justified in asserting that the 'modern state was duty-bound to fight off and, if need be, defeat by authoritarian means' all challenges with a particular political agenda, such as 'both Communist and Nazi movements aspiring to destroy democracy from within' (Salter 2012: 11). Salter attributes Schmitt's subsequent direct service to the Nazis as merely 'shameless political opportunism' (as if they were irrelevant to Schmitt's theorising), although he concedes that Schmitt 'never public apologised, or accepted any personal responsibility for, his complicities' (Salter 2012: 14–15).

Such views are not new, but they are resurgent. Since the 1980s, in particular, efforts have been made to make Schmitt respectable. Bendersky and Schwab are among those in that period who depicted Schmitt as respectful of some features of the rule of law, and basically hostile to core Nazi doctrine (see Bendersky 2014; Schwab 1992). Even Schmitt's anti-Semitism has been described as mere 'lip-service' to fascism (Scheuerman 1997: 1744). Commentaries of an 'apologetic' character emerged in stark contrast to the post-World War II denunciations of Schmitt's role. Most notable was a special issue of *Telos*, a journal of 'critical theory', in 1987 devoted to Schmitt's work. According to the

Telos editors, 'the left can only benefit by learning from Carl Schmitt' (Piccone and Ulmen 1987: 14). Further *Telos* editions devoted to appraisals of Schmitt appeared in 1996, 2002, 2005, 2009 and 2010 (Salter 2012: 17).

To say the least, apologias for Schmitt are attempts to rewrite history. In reality, as will be demonstrated in this chapter, Schmitt's Weimar-period writings not only helped pave the way, both politically and legally, for the German elite's transfer of power to the Nazis, but a clear thread runs through Schmitt's writings before and after Hitler's anointment as German chancellor in January 1933. Above all, Schmitt sought to bolster the power of the German capitalist state, both against the threat of socialist revolution at home and against Germany's great power rivals, notably the United States.

How to Categorise Schmitt

The difficulties that legal academics have in differentiating their emergency powers frameworks from those of the German Weimar Republic and Nazi-era jurists are hinted at in Gross and Ní Aoláin's summation:

> Some have argued that the Extra-Legal Measures model resembles, and follows in the footsteps of, another seemingly extra-legal model of emergency powers, namely Carl Schmitt's theory of the exception … We suggest that, if anything, Schmitt's theory of the exception is akin to models of constitutional necessity. (Gross and Ní Aoláin 2006: 162)

The very fact that Schmitt's doctrines can be considered as analogous to the theories of necessity found in Anglo-American law underscores one of the central theses of this book – that every capitalist constitution, no matter how formally liberal and democratic, contains within it the capacity to authorise dictatorial rule in the name of saving the existing order from domestic threats, as well as external ones.

Indeed, there is much to be said for this categorisation of Schmitt as an advocate of accommodating necessity within a constitutional model. Schmitt himself saw his theories as essential to maintaining the German state against the danger of either a communist-led working-class revolution or a Nazi-led seizure of power. Ultimately, the inherent logic of his views saw him accommodate himself to the fascist regime, as a means of ensuring the strength of the state against its domestic left-wing opponents and foreign rivals, particularly Britain, the United States and the Soviet Union. The Nazis, in turn, found his theories useful as a means of seeking to justify and sanctify their violence and tyranny. Despite the Weimar Republic's formal adherence to democracy and civil rights, there was an underlying political continuity between it and the Nazi regime, which were both directed against the working class and the prospect of socialist revolution.

Nevertheless, Schmitt's conceptions will be examined here as an equally logical outcome of models of extra-legality which presuppose an unlikely return to democratic normalcy, or at least some form of popular mandate, after emergency rule. Regardless of whatever claims are made by proponents of extra-legal measures models about a totalitarian regime eventually having to be accountable to the population for its repressive conduct, such theories are conducive to terrifying, intimidating or coercing people into accepting anti-democratic outcomes. Schmitt's role and the evolution of Hitler's reign serve as illustrations of that reality.

Significantly, when Hitler was sworn in by President Paul von Hindenburg as German chancellor in January 1933, the Nazi leader made a short speech pledging to uphold the Weimar Constitution, respect the rights of the president and return to normal parliamentary rule after the next elections (Kershaw 1998: 423). Within one month, those vows were ditched, following the Reichstag Fire, when Hindenburg authorised an emergency decree to suspend the constitution's civil liberties; and within 18 months, Hitler had usurped the powers of the presidency after Hindenburg's death.

Schmitt's notorious embrace of, and legitimisation of, the Nazi regime after Hitler was appointed German chancellor was reviewed in the Introduction. What must be emphasised is that Schmitt's theories were developed during the Weimar Republic of 1919–33, which was imposed on Germany in the wake of the German Revolution of 1918–19. That revolution first saw the overthrow of the Kaiser and the monarchy; the taking of power of a Social Democratic government; and then the bloody suppression by that government of the further socialist-led workers' uprisings of 1919 (see Chapter 2).

Schmitt was a trenchant critic of the concessions made to liberalism in the Weimar Constitution of 1919, which enunciated a long list of fundamental civil liberties and rights. He indicted it for pretending that legality determined the holding of political power rather than sovereignty, which included the power to suspend the entire existing constitutional order. While he lambasted the naivety and deceitfulness of liberal democracy, and its weakness in the face of revolutionary uprisings, his theories dovetailed with, and helped to consecrate, the frequent resort to emergency decrees during the Weimar period. As reviewed in Chapter 2, Article 48 of the Weimar Republic, which provided for presidential declarations of emergency, was invoked more than 250 times in this period, starting from the outset with the inaugural Weimar president, the Social Democrat Friedrich Ebert.

Moreover, both politically and legally, this anti-democratic and draconian mechanism helped clear the road for the Nazis. It placed power in the hands of small number of individuals acting on behalf of the business, landowning and military elites. The National Socialists not only politically exploited the disillusionment of broad layers of people with the fraud of liberal democracy (Kershaw 1998: 379–427). Hitler also took full advantage of Article 48 and other presidential powers incorporated in the Weimar Constitution to initially cloak his dictatorship in legality and then lever himself into supreme power. Schmitt was not initially a Nazi, but he joined up in 1933 and became an apologist for the horrors of fascism, including the persecution of the Jews, as well as the communists, socialists and trade unionists.

Thus, there is a clear political and legal logic to Schmitt's trajectory from an authoritarian critic of Weimar constitutionalism to a jurisprudential handmaiden of Nazism. His theories were aimed originally at bolstering the capacity of the German capitalist state to thwart the threats of the perceived 'extremes' of the left and right – communism and fascism. But his doctrines, by legitimising the anti-democratic and repressive measures of the beleaguered Weimar ruling class, assisted in laying the political and legal groundwork for Hitler. Schmitt's subsequent enthusiastic support for Hitler's 'Führer' principle, as documented in the Introduction, cannot credibly be separated from the entire trajectory of his jurisprudence.

Schmitt: A Handmaiden to Fascism

More than that, a brief review of the historical record demonstrates that Schmitt was not simply a legal theorist, but a direct participant in the political plots and counter-plots that led to Hitler's appointment as chancellor in January 1933.

Schmitt accepted a professorship at the University of Berlin in 1928, having left his previous position at the University of Bonn. At this point, he was still primarily a law professor and legal scholar; and while highly regarded in his fields of endeavour, he was not actively involved in the highest echelons of the ruling elites. In 1929, however, as the economic crisis intensified in Germany and internationally following the Wall Street Crash, Schmitt became personally acquainted with General Kurt von Schleicher, an adviser to President von Hindenburg.

Schleicher was no ordinary general. In 1919, amid the turmoil of the post-World War I German revolution, he helped form the *Freikorps* units that were used to crush the Spartacus League-led communist uprising and murder its two foremost leaders, Rosa Luxemburg and Karl Liebknecht (Wheeler-Bennett 1967: 35).

Schleicher, who by 1929 wielded considerable power, with the military hierarchy's backing, found much of value in Schmitt's theories: in particular, the assertion that implied authoritarian powers co-existed with the 1919 Weimar Constitution and that, anyhow, the Weimar Constitution provided only for rules, not the requirements of governing. Schleicher took this to mean that a regime could dispense with democracy as long as it acted within the letter of the law, or at least gave the appearance of acting within the law (Feuchtwanger 1993: 218).

There was nothing innocent about this outlook. Like the 1919 repression, it was above all aimed at preserving the power of the ruling class against the threat from below. In the words of one historian, the succession of autocratic presidential governments that began in March 1930 constituted a creeping coup d'état by which the government, acting in the interests of the traditional elites, become more authoritarian and less democratic, a process that culminated with the Nazi regime in 1933:

> In light of the sources it can now be firmly stated that the fateful transition from parliamentary government to the presidential regime was well and carefully planned in advance. The protagonists, and Schleicher in particular, were not compelled by circumstances or by the hopelessness of the political situation; they acted with cool deliberation and with the intention of drastically altering the constitutional system and the balance of social forces in favour of old élites of the army, bureaucracy and big business. (Kolb 2005: 117–18)

Like the rest of the *Reichswehr* (military) leadership, Schleicher saw democracy as an impediment to military power, and was convinced that only a dictatorship could make Germany a great military power again (Nicholls 2000: 163–4). At the same time, Schleicher shared Schmitt's concerns that the lack of a stable government would lead to civil war or seizure of power by the Nazis or communists. These fears accelerated after the economic catastrophe erupted in 1929. Schleicher devised a plan for a presidential government comprised of a chancellor and cabinet ministers that combined with the power of the army, and the provisions of Article 48 of the Weimar Constitution would be able to essentially bypass the badly divided parliament and more effectively address Germany's severe economic distress and prevent civil disorder or revolution.

Schmitt's writings in this period corresponded with that approach. He spoke out against changes in the constitution of Weimar during its final years, believing that tampering with the constitution during a time of crisis would undermine the legitimacy of the entire system and invite opportunistic exploitation of the constitutional processes by the communists or fascists. His continued defence of the anti-democratic presidential powers granted by Article 48 was always intended as an effort to preserve the existing constitutional order.

Well before Hitler was handed the chancellorship in 1933, Schmitt was arguing for an authoritarian ruler who could claim plebiscitary support, a method later utilised by the Nazis. He depicted parliamentary democracy, based on secret ballots, as a fraud while invoking plebiscitary rule, sanctioning decisions already proposed by dictatorial methods, as a more authentic form of democracy. He wrote in 1926:

> The stronger the power of democratic sentiment becomes, the more certain seems the knowledge that democracy is something other than a system of registering secret ballots. For a democracy in the vital, not technical, sense, a parliament tied to liberal thinking, appears as a mere contrivance, while dictatorial methods can be not only sustained by popular acclamation but be seen as a direct expression of democratic substance. (Schmitt 1985b: 16–17)

This was a script ready-made for the would-be fascist dictator Hitler, even if Schmitt would have preferred a more traditional military-based dictatorship headed by his mentor, Schleicher. The Nazis, too, presented themselves as champions of democracy, in the sense of being the authentic embodiment of the popular will. Schmitt's version of democracy went hand in hand with his conception of a racially homogenous polity (see below). He dismissed 'liberal democracy' as 'just another form of liberalism intended not for self-identified communities but for the entire human race'.

After 1931, when the Nazis and the communists in the Reichstag could block other parties' efforts to form a government, Hindenburg ruled by emergency decree. His impressive re-election in 1932, against Hitler, signified for Schmitt a mandate for the powerful executive rule. Schmitt urged Hindenburg to govern as a 'constitutional dictator', preserving the state under extended use of Article 48, until the threat to the German state had passed. The fallout effects of the German Depression, the spread of street violence and the meteoric rise of Nazi and communist electoral strength in 1931 and 1932 all argued for the need for steady national leadership, able to rise to the challenge of exceptional events.

Schmitt published *Legality and Legitimacy* in 1932, warning of the means by which the constitutional order itself could be overthrown through the abuse of ordinary legal and constitutional processes. Most specifically, Schmitt opposed methods of constitutional interpretation that would permit allegedly anti-constitutional parties such as the National Socialists (NSDAP) or the Communist Party of Germany (KPD) to have the 'equal chance' to assume power legally. If such a party were to be allowed to gain control of the apparatus of the state itself, it could then use its position to destroy the constitutional order.

Schmitt counselled against interpreting the constitution in ways that allowed laws to be passed through formalistic means whose essence contradicted the wider 'values' represented by the constitution. He argued that a political constitution should be interpreted according to its internal essence, rather than strict adherence to its technical provisions, and applied according to the conditions imposed by the 'concrete situation' at hand.

On the advice of General Schleicher, President Hindenburg replaced Heinrich Brüning as chancellor with Franz von Papen on 30 May 1932. Papen, who was later to serve as Hitler's vice-chancellor for 18 months, soon took an action in Prussia, Germany's most populous state, that led to Schmitt's personal participation in a revealing constitutional law trial in Germany's Supreme Court.

In the 'Rape of Prussia' on 20 July 1932, Schleicher had martial law proclaimed and called out the *Reichswehr* to oust the elected Prussian government of Social Democratic Party (SPD) Premier Otto Braun. Using Article 48 of the Weimar Constitution, Hindenburg named Papen the *Reich* Commissioner of Prussia. The SPD called for a general strike, but the trade union leaders – believing in Schleicher's promises to include them within a reconstituted government – ordered their members to stay at their jobs (Wheeler-Bennett 1967: 253–5; Kershaw 1998: 369).

The justification for the martial law declaration was the Prussian regional government's alleged inability to maintain order in the face of civil unrest. Prussia was the largest of the German states, containing two-thirds of Germany's land mass and three-fifths of its population. Though the state government was controlled by the Social Democrats, the Nazis made significant gains in the April 1932 election. The Social Democrats made considerable efforts to block the rise of the Nazis with legal restrictions on their activities and various parliamentary manoeuvres, but fascist violence continued.

Papen, himself an anti-Nazi rightist at this point, regarded the imposition of martial law as having the multiple purposes of breaking the power of the Social Democrats in Prussia; controlling the Communist Party; placating the Nazis by removing their Social Democratic rivals; and simultaneously preventing the Nazis from becoming embedded in regional institutions, particularly Prussia's huge police force.

The Prussian state government appealed Papen's decision to the Supreme Court and a trial was held in October 1932. Schmitt was among three jurists who defended the Papen government's policy before the court. Schmitt argued that the Prussian state government had failed in its foremost constitutional duty to preserve public order. He further argued that because Papen had acted under the authority of President Hindenburg, Papen's actions had been legitimate under Article 48.

In keeping with his theory of exception, Schmitt insisted that the office of the president was sovereign over the political parties and was responsible for preserving the constitution, public order and the security of the state itself. Schmitt argued that with the Prussian state's failure to maintain basic order, the situation in Prussia had essentially become a civil war between the political parties. Therefore, imposition of martial law by the chancellor, as an agent of the president, was necessary for the restoration of order.

Flowing from his conception of a normless exception, Schmitt further argued that it was the president, rather than the court, that possessed the ultimate authority and responsibility for upholding the constitution, as the court possessed no means of politically enforcing its decisions.

Ultimately, the court decided that it, not the president, was responsible for the legal defence of the constitution; but the situation in Prussia was severe enough to justify the appointment of a commissarial government by Papen, though Papen had not been justified in outright suspension of the Prussian state government. Essentially, the Papen government won, as martial law remained in Prussia, and the state government continued to exist in name only (Wheeler-Bennett 1967: 253–5; Kershaw 1998: 369).

General Schleicher's Prussian coup, explicitly championed by Schmitt, laid the basis for Hitler's installation as German chancellor six months later. In fact, Schleicher had been prepared to anoint Hitler in the immediate aftermath of the Prussian coup. On 5 August 1932, Hitler and Schleicher held a secret meeting, in which Hitler demanded that he become chancellor and the Ministries of the Interior and Justice go to Nazis; Schleicher could remain as Defence Minister. Schleicher was willing to accept Hitler's arrangement, but Hindenburg refused, preventing Hitler from receiving the chancellorship at that point (Wheeler-Bennett 1967: 257–8).

Throughout the following crucial months, Schleicher ousted Papen to become chancellor himself. He hoped to attain a majority in the Reichstag by gaining the support of sections of Nazis for his government (Turner 1996: 24). According to the historian Kershaw:

> Schleicher's aim was an authoritarian regime, resting on the *Reichswehr* [the military], with support from the National Socialists. The idea was to 'tame' Hitler, and incorporate the 'valuable elements' from his Movement into what would have been essentially a military dictatorship with populist backing. (Kershaw 1998: 366)

In the end, Schleicher's manoeuvres with sections of the Nazis led by Gregor Strasser collapsed in the face of Hitler's intransigence, whereupon President Hindenburg installed Hitler as chancellor to replace him (Kershaw 1998: 366–423).

During this crisis, Schmitt was once more heavily involved in the machinations. He backed an alternative dictatorial plan by Schleicher:

> By late January, when it appeared that either Papen or Hitler might become chancellor, Schleicher concluded that exceptional measures were required as a last resort. He requested that the president declare a state of emergency, ban the Nazi and Communist parties, and dissolve the Reichstag until stability could be restored. During the interim Schleicher would govern by emergency decrees … . (Bendersky 2014: 184)

The Schleicher plan was based in part on Schmitt's view that 'a constitutional system could not remain neutral towards its own basic principles, nor provide the legal means for its own destruction'. Yet the liberal, Catholic and socialist press received word of the plan and attacked Schleicher's plan, and Schmitt's ideas, as creating the foundation for a presidential dictatorship (Bendersky 2014: 183–8).

One scholar summarised Schmitt's role in this process, and Schmitt's ready and calculating switch to the Nazi camp, as follows:

> [D]uring the Republic Schmitt had lent his intellectual support to the attempts of successive authoritarian chancellors, Brüning, Papen, and Schleicher, to usurp the authority of the parliament and govern through the 'charismatically' and 'plebiscitarily' elected office of *Reichpräsident* Hindenburg. Schleicher, the figure Schmitt was most aligned to personally, had hoped to carry out such a scheme while outmaneuvering the Nazis, who were gaining popular support – a strategy that Schmitt supported publicly. After failing in this endeavor, Schleicher resigned in January of 1933. When Hitler subsequently became chancellor, Schmitt was invited by Papen, who himself had always been less wary of the Nazis than Schleicher was, to help legalise the new fascist coalition regime … He revised his previous work to conform with party dogma and authored treatises that, sometimes clumsily but always enthusiastically, integrated his Weimar theories into a justification for the power-consolidating National Socialist regime. (McCormick 1997: 266)

How Schmitt's Weimar Writings Justified His Role

Far from being divorced from his 'political choices', Schmitt's Weimar-period writings underpinned his active engagement in the crisis of German capitalist rule throughout the Weimar Republic and prefigured his part in helping hand power to the Nazis.

Many of the strands of his theorising, including his later justifications of fascism, were present in *Die Diktatur*, which appeared in 1921. Schmitt insisted that politics must have primacy over legality. More precisely, the state must have the power, and exercise the power, to suppress working-class struggles. Written in the wake of the suppression of the 1919 Spartacist-led uprising, this work makes crystal clear that, while Schmitt was concerned with defending the German state against the supposed extremes of communism and fascism, his central preoccupation was to crush any challenge from the German workers.

Die Diktatur was subtitled 'From the Beginning of the Modern Concept of Sovereignty to Proletarian Class Struggle'. He counterposed 'sovereignty' to 'class struggle'. The state had to be prepared to use extra-constitutional means to preserve itself against internal disorder (the 'class struggle') as well as external threats (Wolin 1990: 396).

Some authors have contended that Schmitt's work in general is posited in a sociological vacuum, devoid of socio-economic content or analysis. According to Teschke:

> Since Schmitt's method – be it decisionism, the friend-foe distinction, or concrete order thinking – is bereft of any sociology of power, decisionism lacks the analytics to identify what constellation or balance of socio-political forces can activate, in what kind of situation, the politics of the exception and fear. (Teschke 2011: 80)

This is very false. While Schmitt might have offered no *analysis* of which socio-political forces activated exceptional powers, his work had a definite socio-economic and class *content*. As *Die Diktatur* explicitly demonstrated, his theorising sought to defend the German capitalist nation-state, following the 1918 revolution that overthrew the monarchy and the 1919 anti-Spartacist counter-revolution, from ongoing working-class revolts and potential revolutions.

This was the essential class content of Schmitt's insistence that every government capable of decisive action must include a dictatorial element within its constitution. He was arguing on behalf of the ruling capitalist class: the powerful German manufacturing and military interests that were seeking to reassert their domination and hegemonic aspirations after the defeat of World War I and the 1918–19 revolutionary convulsions.

Schmitt was fully conscious of the fragility of the Weimar Republic, which was part of a wider instability following the horrors of the 'Great War' and the eruption of the October 1917 Russian Revolution. For Schmitt, crises and states of emergency were not exceptional, but the predominant form of the life of modern nations (Scheuerman 2006a). Rather than the constitution, it was the 'logic of the concrete exception' that formed the basis of the state. The state alone retained the ultimate power of decision to suspend political normalcy by declaring a state of exception (Wolin 1990: 396).

Schmitt drew a distinction between temporary dictatorship and despotism – between 'commissarial' and 'sovereign' dictatorship. The former could suspend the constitution, but not promulgate a new one. In order to avoid the shocks and instability that overtook Germany in 1918–19, Schmitt initially sought to uphold the Weimar Constitution, notably by legitimising the use of Article 48, supposedly to save the constitution. But the logic of his stance was to justify indefinite dictatorship.

Schmitt's *Political Theology*, published in 1922, directly reflected his forthright warnings to the crisis-ridden German establishment that emerged from the 1918 revolution not to be deluded into thinking that Weimar constitutionalism could withstand potentially revolutionary convulsions. That is the tenor of his infamous opening statement: 'Sovereign is he who decides on the exception' (Schmitt 1985a: 5). He insisted: 'It is precisely the exception that makes relevant the subject of sovereignty, that is, the whole question of sovereignty (Schmitt 1985a: 6). To acknowledge the very existence of exceptional situations is to refute the formal face of liberalism, which maintains that pre-established general norms cover all possible contingencies. The power to decide on what is exceptional and what exceptional measures are to be implemented underscores the central role of *political* power. Responses to the exception cannot be constrained by a priori rules (McCormick 1997: 133–41).

In effect, Schmitt's theory of exception embraced a sovereign dictatorship in which an exception permits the suspension of the entire existing legal order (McCormick 1997: 133–41). 'What characterises an exception is principally unlimited authority, which means the suspension of the entire existing order' (Schmitt 1985a: 12).

More than that, the sovereign dictator could overturn and transform the legal order, in whole or part. The norm became subservient to the exception, reversing the relationship between the two. The exception 'cannot be circumscribed factually and made to conform to a preformed law' (Schmitt 1985a: 6). Indeed, Schmitt eliminated the notion of the normal and replaced it with the exception. 'The rule proves nothing; the exception proves everything: It confirms not only the rule but also its existence, which derives only from the exception' (Schmitt 1985a: 15).

It is impossible to read Schmitt without sensing his reference to the convulsive, 'exceptional' and 'abnormal' situation that beset the Weimar Republic. Despite its murder of Rosa Luxemburg and Karl Liebknecht – the revolutionary socialist leaders, in 1919 – Ebert's government faced the constant danger of a resurgence of a working-class uprising, which was to erupt again in 1921 and 1923, as well as threatened coups by the military and the Nazis. In 1923–24, after an abortive coup by Hitler and a failed Communist Party-led revolution, Ebert's regime relied on the military generals to survive and rested on a virtual military dictatorship for months, legitimised by the Weimar Constitution (Broué 2006).

Schmitt argued that every legal norm presupposed a normal and ordinary state of affairs, and could only be applied as long as that normalcy continued. He insisted that 'This effective normal situation is not a mere "superficial presupposition" that a jurist can ignore; that situation belongs precisely to [the norm's] immanent validity'; and 'For a legal order to make sense, a normal situation must exist.' Crises undermine this factual basis and undermine the foundations needed for ordinary norms: 'There exists no norm that is applicable to chaos' (Schmitt 1985a: 12–13).

In practice, the sovereign dictator had unfettered discretion about both whether an exception existed and what counter-measures ought to be taken in response. These unlimited and indivisible powers were exercisable only in exceptional cases, but the logical outcome of Schmitt's model was that the dictator's powers were never turned off. He regarded contemporary politics as a permanent state of crisis. At any time, without warning, there could be a 'danger to the existence of the state' (Schmitt 1985a: 6).

Schmitt's anti-Semitism was central to his theory. As early as 1923, in *The Crisis of Parliamentary Democracy*, he declared that 'democracy requires, first homogeneity and second – if the need arises – elimination or eradication of heterogeneity' (Schmitt 1985b: 9). Racial and cultural homogeneity and the elimination of heterogeneity were the pillars of Schmitt's version of democracy. Interestingly, one of the examples he gave was the white Australia policy of barring entry to 'unwanted entrants'.

According to Schmitt, 'democratic' homogeneity, with a plebiscitary character, presupposed a common historical memory, common roots and a common vision of the future, which required a polity in which the people speak with one voice. 'As long as a people has the will to political existence, he wrote, 'it must remain above all formulations and normative beliefs … The most natural way of the direct expression of the people's will is by approvals or disapprovals of the gathered crowd, i.e., the acclamation' (Schmitt 1985b: 12).

It is revealing that Schmitt's *Crisis of Parliamentary Democracy* culminated in a glowing tribute to Italian fascism, already imposed by Mussolini in 1922:

> Until now the democracy of mankind and parliamentarianism has only once been contemptuously pushed aside through the conscious appeal to myth, and that was an example of the irrational power of the national myth. In his famous speech of October 1922 in Naples before the march on Rome, Mussolini said, 'We have created a myth, this

myth is a belief, a noble enthusiasm; it does not need to be reality, it is a striving and a hope, belief and courage. Our myth is the nation, the great nation which we want to make into a concrete reality for ourselves.' (Schmitt 1985b: 75–6)

Schmitt concluded that 'the theory of myth is the most powerful symptom of the decline of the relative rationalism of parliamentary thought', not least because it offered the possibility of establishing 'an authority based on the new feeling for order, discipline and hierarchy (Schmitt 1985b: 76).

In his 1927 work, *The Concept of the Political*, Schmitt went further in his conception of exception. He insisted that what ought to be considered was the not just the actual occurrence of an exception but the possibility of one (Schmitt 1976: 35). Moreover, he presented the exception as the purest expression of political considerations. And he bound those calculations up with drawing distinctions between friends and foes, which was in line with the identification of Marxists and Jews as the existential threat to the German state. He wrote: 'The specific political distinctions to which political actions and motives can be reduced is that between friend and enemy (Schmitt 1976: 26).

Schmitt's view of the necessarily normless and existential exception was bound up with his embrace of war as the ultimate and inherent presupposition of all politics. 'War, the readiness for death of fighting men, the physical annihilation of other men who stand on the side of the enemy, all that has no normative, only an existential meaning (Wolin 1990: 406). This, too, was a theme later taken to its logical end in Hitler's 'total war' against Britain and the Soviet Union for German domination over Europe.

In two essays in the early 1930s, Schmitt developed his theory of the 'total state'. He insisted that 'politics intervenes in all spheres of life, there is no neutral sphere'. This conception also flowed from the necessity for 'not only the military, but also the industrial and economic preparation for war' (Wolin 1990: 408). Schmitt's view led organically to his acceptance of a summons from the new Nazi-led government in April 1933 to draft the infamous *Gleichschaltung* legislation that dissolved provincial diets and excluded the Communist Party from the Reichstag, cementing the foundations of Nazi one-party rule (Wolin 1990: 408).

Schmitt's foremost contemporary rival, Hans Kelsen, accused Schmitt's exceptionalism of rendering constitutional provisions redundant and irrelevant, except for those relating to emergency powers. Kelsen said Schmitt's theory reduced the Weimar Constitution to nothing more than Article 48 (McCormick 1997: 144). That observation was somewhat limited, even though the frequent invocation of Article 48 helped lay a path for the Nazis. Schmitt's thesis went beyond any specific constitutional set-up. His view of the sovereign dictator's unstoppable powers was so sweeping that it defied any constitutional constraint. That conception proved valuable to the Nazis, at least initially, when Hitler took office.

Schmitt's Personal and Theoretical Service to the Nazis

After Hitler became German chancellor in January 1933, and effectively seized power a month later via an emergency decree following the Reichstag Fire, Schmitt wasted little time in embracing the Nazi regime. Having initially been invited by Papen to help legitimise the initial fascist-led coalition government, Schmitt joined the Nazi Party on 1 May 1933. He not only lent his credentials, as a prominent conservative jurist, to the fascists; he also became an enthusiastic and prolific booster of the Nazis. For joining the party, he was 'rewarded with a prestigious professorship in Berlin, the editorship of Germany's major legal publication, Die Deutsche Juristen-Zeitung, a leading post in the Nazi professors' guild and the position of State Councillor (Staatstrat) to Prussia' (Scheuerman 1997: 1743).

During Nazi rule, Schmitt became an even more active advocate for the fascists than he had been for the authoritarian measures of the Weimar period. This was his 'most prolific' period. Between 1933 and 1936 alone, Schmitt authored four books and more than 50 essays for both academic and political journals. He hailed Hitler's struggle to 'liberate' Germany from liberalism and Marxism; praised the emerging National Socialist legal order; lauded the 'national revolution' (which cost the lives of thousands of workers and left-wing figures) that made it possible; and issued 'crude anti-Semitic diatribes'. He extolled the Nuremburg racial laws as the foundations of a new German 'constitution of freedom' and helped stage a notorious conference on 'German Jurisprudence in Struggle Against the Jewish Spirit' (Scheuerman 1997: 1743).

In his first major work under the Nazis – *State, Movement, Folk* – Schmitt hailed the Enabling Act of 24 March 1933 as the overthrow of the Weimar Constitution. Far from a temporary, commissarial dictatorship, Schmitt perceived a sovereign or permanent one. Since the Weimar Constitution was incapable of distinguishing friend from enemy, it deserved to perish. He depicted the Reichstag elections of 5 March 1933 – in which the Nazis had still received only 43.9 per cent of the vote, despite their terrorising activities – as a 'plebiscite through which the German people recognized Adolf Hitler … as the political Fuhrer of the German Volk' (Wolin 1990: 409). This lauding of Hitler's dictatorship was the logical end-product of Schmitt's views, not any break from them. He declared: 'In the one-party state of National Socialist Germany, the danger of a pluralistic dismemberment of Germany … has been vanquished' (Wolin 1990: 409).

Schmitt's jump into the Nazi order was not merely, as some scholars have contended, a simple matter of ego and prestige, or personal cowardice. Other academics have argued that Schmitt's anti-Semitism was merely a matter of paying lip service to the regime (as if that were acceptable) and he remained a defender of aspects of the rule of law, and basically hostile to Nazi doctrines (Scheuerman 1997: 1744). In reality, his admiration for Hitler and the fascists flowed organically from his Weimar-period theories, and he sought to adapt those theories to serve the interests of the Nazi state. Under Weimar both forms of capitalist rule – the Weimar Republic and the National Socialist dictatorship – Schmitt's preoccupation was with fashioning a legal order that could withstand the danger of revolutionary overthrow. He ultimately saw in fascism the chance to develop just such a system.

One scholar, Scheuerman, documented the continuity between Schmitt's Weimar-period theorising and his Nazi-period rationalising. However, Scheuerman attributed this continuity to Schmitt's belief that a central problem of modern legal theory was 'the enigma of legal indeterminacy, according to which legal norms inevitably fail to provide meaningful guidance to legal decision makers' (Scheuerman 1997: 1744). In Scheuerman's view, Schmitt's 'most shocking' endorsement of the Nazis' 'radical anti-Semitism' also flowed from Schmitt's conclusion that this racism was an essential element of constructing an alternative legal system able to guarantee the determinacy allegedly missing from liberal law. This, on Scheuerman's analysis, was central to Schmitt's embrace of dystopian National Socialist visions of a racially and ethnically homogenous 'folk community' that provided the bedrock for an underlying common set of jurisprudential values for Nazi legislators, lawyers and judges.

This approach obscures the primary political purpose of Hitler's anti-Semitism, which was directed at making an amalgam between Jewishness and Marxism, and specifically, after the October 1917 Russian Revolution, Bolshevism. While Hitler, according to biographical accounts, may have imbibed anti-Semitism before the Russian Revolution, it was that Bolshevik-led revolution that spurred his incitement of anti-Semitism as a means of demonising Bolshevism and the prospect of a communist revolution in Germany. As Kershaw concluded in his biography of Hitler, it was Hitler's conception of the Russian Revolution that became the decisive factor cementing this linkage: 'These images appeared to have provided the catalyst to the merger of anti-Semitism and anti-Marxism in his "world view" – an identity which, once forged, never disappeared' (Kershaw 1998: 153).

In *Mein Kampf*, Hitler explained how his conversion to anti-Semitism flowed from his encounters with the labour movement. It was among the workers that Hitler first came into contact with Jews. He then discovered, to his amazement, that many Jews played prominent roles in the labour movement. Heiden, an early biographer of Hitler, noted: 'The great light dawned upon him. Suddenly the "Jewish question" became clear … The labour movement did not repel him because it was led by Jews; the Jews repelled him because they led the labour movement.' Heiden concluded: 'It was not Rothschild, the capitalist, but Karl Marx, the socialist, who kindled Adolf Hitler's anti-Semitism' (Heiden 1969: 66).

As is widely known, the first brutal wave of repression following the inauguration of the fascist regime was directed against the organisations of the workers' movement – above all, the social democrats, the communists and the trade unions. The smashing of the organised labour movement, in which there was a tradition of opposing anti-Semitism, was both a preparation and a precondition for the genocide of the Jews. Despite the terror unleashed by the Nazis, there was persistent and considerable opposition from socialist- and communist-minded workers:

> A sizeable minority of Social Democrats and Communists were not willing to knuckle under and to accept passively whatever the new regime might order them to do. The widespread terror accompanying the 'seizure of power' and the mass arrests of the early months told them enough. Large numbers responded by forming underground groups, producing and distributing underground leaflets and papers and disturbing Nazi propaganda as best they could. In 1933 and 1934 hundreds of clandestine groups sprang up all over Germany – and quite often they were equally quickly liquidated by the Gestapo … It has been reliably estimated that the KPD between 1933 and 1935 lost 75,000 members through imprisonment and that several thousands of them were killed. That means that about a quarter of the members registered in 1932 were lost. (Carsten 1995: 180)

Marxism was always Hitler's primary political preoccupation, and the basis of his appeal to Germany's powerful industrialists. For all their demagogy against the allegedly Jewish financial elite, the Nazis' programme consisted essentially of prosecuting the interests of German capitalism, both against the domestic threat of socialism and Germany's European and American rivals for geo-strategic power. In February 1933, shortly after being anointed chancellor, Hitler gave a speech before Germany's most powerful industrialists, which Kershaw described as follows:

> He assuaged his business audience, as he had done on earlier occasions, by upholding private property and individual enterprise, and by denying rumours of planned radical experimentation in the economy. The rest was largely a restatement of his views on the subordination of the economy to politics, the need to eradicate Marxism, restore inner strength and unity, and thus be in a position to face external enemies. (Kershaw 1998: 447)

In a radio address to the nation given that same month, Hitler shouted: 'Never, never will I depart from the task of eradicating from Germany Marxism and its accompaniments. One must be the victor here: either Marxism or the German people' (Kershaw 1998: 453).

Schmitt shared that commitment, even if his language was somewhat more muted. As Scheuerman noted, his Nazi-period writings 'emphatically emphasis[ed] his hostility to Marxist conceptions of a planned economy' and 'the essentially capitalist core of this model' (Scheuerman 1997: 1749). Likewise, Schmitt wrote in praise of the 1934 Nazi labour laws, which reclassified employees as 'disciples' and stripped them of basic workplace protections. According to Schmitt, this was the clearest possible real-life expression of 'concrete-order legal thinking', which was his proposed jurisprudential alternative both to liberal normativism and unregulated 'decisionism' (Scheuerman 1997: 1752–3).

Schmitt's concept of concrete-order thinking was also directly linked to his anti-Semitism. 'Concrete-order thinking' demanded that ethnic Germans free themselves from 'alien' legal and intellectual influences, notably 'Jewish' conceptions of the rule of law that emphasised formalistic protections and procedures. Liberal concepts of state sovereignty had to be jettisoned in favour of the notion of a concrete ethnically pure 'folk community' whose inherent values and dynamics belied the normative aspirations of liberal jurisprudence (Scheuerman 1997: 1753–4).

Schmitt's supposed theoretising provided a jurisprudential cloak for lawless Nazi repression, directed first against the workers' movement, then against the Jews. He claimed that the fascist preference for situation-specific legal rulings was superior and more attuned to modern conditions than purported adherence to general laws. In fact, National Socialism was a 'state for the twentieth century' (Scheuerman 1997: 1754).

Above all, Schmitt's writings during this period hailed the 'Leader State' in which the Führer possessed unlimited legislative and administrative authority. He declared that Nazism had heroically 'crossed the Rubicon' by systematically abandoning the remnants of the liberal democratic illusion that general norms were the best means to legally regulate complex activities (Scheuerman 1987: 1755).

Schmitt: A Defender of Legality?

Some scholars have argued that Schmitt nevertheless argued for the retention of a semblance of a rule of law. Dyzenhaus suggested: 'Schmitt could not bring his vision of law completely into line with Nazi ideology. Simply put, he still maintained a shred of hope for law as an autonomous element in politics' (Dyzenhaus 1997: 186). This flies in the face of the record.

While Schmitt, in keeping with his long-time concern to prevent political instability, cautioned that outright decisionism 'runs the risk of missing the stable content' in law, he insisted that National Socialist law, if built on the foundations of a homogenous 'folk community', need not be arbitrary. One of his services to the Nazis was to advocate the creation of a reliably indoctrinated state bureaucracy and judiciary that would unerringly and intuitively grasp and give effect to the core fascist values. The mere fact of ethnic purity would create a 'spiritually' homogenous jurisprudence (Scheuerman 1997: 1756–8). Adopting the slogan 'Reform of the Jurists Instead of Reform of the Law', he wrote:

> If there is still to be an independent judiciary despite the fact that a mechanical and automatic binding of the judge to a pre-existing set of codified norms is no longer possible, then everything depends on the nature and make-up of our judges and administrators. (cited by Scheuerman 1997: 1756–7)

In his capacity as a leader of the Nazi professors' guild, Schmitt lauded the purging of racially 'alien' faculty members, and the ethnic cleansing of university libraries and reading lists. This would help ensure that the values of National Socialism would be drummed into the minds of aspiring lawyers and judges. Because such judges would be 'bound' together with 'folk spirit' of the Führer, the supreme lawmaker, they could legitimately veer away from the express letter of the law to make sure that the Führer's will was respected, whatever the circumstances of the individual case. This, Schmitt proclaimed, would provide more legal regularity than any competing legal system in the world (Scheuerman 1997: 1757–64).

In *State, Movement, Folk*, Schmitt explicitly spelt out the connection between this conception and that of a racially purified 'legal community':

> [I]t is an epistemological verity that only those are capable of seeing the facts [of the case] the right way, listening to statements rightly, understanding words correctly and evaluating impressions of persons and events rightly, if they are participants in a racially determined type of legal community to which they existentially belong. (cited by Scheuerman 1997: 1750)

In sum, 'by systematically developing this line of argumentation, Schmitt offers a brand of jurisprudence particularly well-suited to the political needs of the National Socialist leadership' (Scheuerman 1997: 1759). After 1936, when Schmitt and his patrons in the Nazi leadership suffered defeats at the hands of factional rivals, he felt compelled to give up a number of posts and lost much of his influence. Nonetheless, his conceptions and his personal participation in the fashioning of a totalitarian legal profession and judiciary had a continuing impact. Judicial decisions in Nazi Germany proved to be overwhelmingly consistent with the 'spirit' of fascist ideology (Scheuerman 1997: 1766).

Although Schmitt relinquished some posts, he retained key positions and continued to serve the Nazis. He kept his position in the Nazi Party, his chairmanship of the Berlin law faculty and his seat on the Prussian State Council until the end of World War II. His post-1936 writings focused on the concept of 'Grossraum', modelled on the US Monroe doctrine of supremacy over the Americas. This was a pseudo-legal variant of the Nazi doctrine of 'Lebensraum' that underpinned the drive to conquer Eastern Europe and the Soviet Union (Wolin 1990: 410).

As for Schmitt's reputed retreat from his earlier decisionism and his bid to preserve a modicum of the rule of law, that seems a predictable recasting of his views to justify the supposed state of normalcy embodied in the fascist order. Moreover, Schmitt's revisioning of his model was explicitly based on the Nazi quest for a racially purified order, and his own racist conception of humanity. Once purged of 'organic, biological and volkish differentiations' the legal order could be stabilised. He stated in *State, Movement, Folk* that 'all questions and answers intersect with the demand for homogeneity, without which a total Fuhrer-state could not subsist for a day' (Wolin 1990: 411).

One can only agree with Wolin's condemnation of all those promoting 'the ahistorical illusion that Schmitt's theoretical positions can be innocently lifted out of the socio-historical context in which they originated and [be] applied unproblematically to contemporary world affairs' (Wolin 1990: 412).

The most important conclusion is that Schmitt's views, and his political trajectory, illustrate the reality that so-called models of extra-legality, which correctly apply to him, help pave the way for permanent dictatorships, regardless of any caveats about only seeking temporary ones, supposedly to uphold an underlying constitutional order.

Agamben and Post-Modernist Reflections on Schmitt

Several post-modernist academics have acknowledged the fully totalitarian logic of Schmitt's idea of the state of exception, and commented on its echoes in contemporary politics, especially since 9/11. Agamben argued that post-9/11 history witnessed the extension and normalisation of Schmitt's concept:

> [T]he state of exception has today reached its maximum worldwide deployment. The normative aspects of laws can thus be obliterated and contradicted with impunity by a government violence that – while ignoring international law externally and producing a permanent state of exception internally – nevertheless still claims to be applying the law. (Agamben 2005: 87)

Douzinas also suggested that the 'war on terrorism' employed and expanded Schmittian notions:

> According to Carl Schmitt, the Sovereign decides exceptionally and performatively about the exception, suspends the law in order to save it. In our recent wars, in a modification of Schmitt's law, the United States placed itself in the position of global Sovereign by suspending international law. There is more. The exception does not just create the rule; it also constitutes an imaginary global space over which the Sovereign will rule, it creates the terrain of its application, its laws and its space. (Douzinas 2009)

It is misleading, however, to say that in Schmitt's view 'the sovereign suspends the law in order to save it'. Schmitt's preoccupation was with saving the German state, not the law. This miscasting of Schmitt's position, which also ignores or downplays his political role in directly paving the way for fascism, points to a more underlying flaw.

Post-modernist interpretations present the wholesale adoption of emergency and dictatorial powers abstractly and ahistorically as a universal phenomenon, stripping it of any socio-economic and class content. According to Agamben, the state of exception has become a 'paradigm of government' (Agamben 2005: 1). He insisted that the state of exception was neither legal nor extra-legal but belonged to an undefined 'zone of indifference' (Agamben 2005: 23). After a brief historical survey he concluded: 'In every case, the state of exception marks a threshold at which logic and praxis blur with each other and a pure violence without *logos* claims to realize an enunciation without any real reference (Agamben 2005: 40).

Beneath these grandiose and sweeping assertions, however, there is no examination of the concrete economic interests and class dynamics involved, so that, ultimately, these claims serve to whitewash both the full dimensions of state repression and its legal and political implications. Indeed, potentially reactionary conclusions are drawn. The turn to totalitarian methods is portrayed as a continuous characteristic of modern society, particularly since the French Revolution of 1789–99, suggesting that the fault lies with humanity in general, or with those, such as Marxists, who fight for human progress, rather than with current socio-economic order based on corporate profit and rival capitalist nation-states.

Agamben's *State of Exception* certainly illustrated how the suspension of laws within a state of emergency or crisis can become a prolonged state of exception. Referring to the military order issued by President George W. Bush on 13 November 2001, whereby hundreds of detainees were labelled 'enemy combatants' and taken to be held indefinitely at Guantanamo Bay without trial, Agamben wrote:

> What is new about President Bush's order is that it radically erases any legal status of the individual, thus producing a legally unnameable and unclassifiable being. Not only do the Taliban captured in Afghanistan not enjoy the status of POWs as defined by the Geneva Convention, they do not even have the status of people charged with a crime according to American laws. (Agamben 2005: 3)

Agamben also referenced the Nazi state of Germany under Hitler's rule. He recalled that Hitler never *abrogated* the Weimar Constitution; he *suspended* it for the entire duration of the Third Reich via the February 1933 Reichstag Fire Decree:

> The entire Third Reich can be considered a state of exception that lasted twelve years. In this sense, modern totalitarianism can be defined as the establishment, by means of the state of exception, of a legal civil war that allows for the physical elimination not only of political adversaries but of entire categories of citizens who for some reason cannot be integrated into the political system. (Agamben 2005: 2)

Agamben's central argument, however, was that this totalitarian tendency began with the 'democratic-revolutionary' tradition of the French Revolution, thus seeking to blame the overthrow of the feudal monarchical and aristocratic *ancien régime* in France for the crimes later committed by the capitalist governments of the nineteenth, twentieth and twenty-first centuries. According Agamben, the initial legislative provision for states of siege by the French Constituent Assembly in July 1791 effectively amounted to an act of original sin that doomed humanity from that time on. He insisted that 'it is important not to forget that the modern state of exception is the creation of the democratic-revolutionary tradition and not the absolutist one' (Agamben 2005: 5).

Such was Agamben's conclusion, despite the exigencies that faced the revolution in 1791 – the ongoing threat of a violent royal counter-revolution, backed by Louis XIV's fellow European monarchs – and the fact that the state of siege power specifically sought to restrict the deployment of the royal army in a list of named municipalities (Brown 2007: 201). It was only after Napoleon Bonaparte's coup d'état of 1799, itself made possible by Napoleon's earlier military suppression of the Parisian masses, that a dictatorship was established (Lefebvre 1969: 71–92).

Agamben's potted history of France in the nineteenth century whitewashed the violent repression carried out by the ruling capitalist-military establishment against the 1848 revolution and the 1871 Paris Commune. He lumped together every 'constitutional crisis' in France during the nineteenth and twentieth centuries (Agamben 2005: 12), without actually examining their social and political roots. Thus, he stated uncritically that the Constituent Assembly put Paris in a state of siege in 1848 and assigned General Cavaignac 'the task of restoring order in the city' (Agamben 2005: 12). This glossed over the bloody repression of the Parisian masses conducted on behalf of the ruling elite, as related in Chapter 2. Compounding that misrepresentation, Agamben gave credence to the claim that the counter-revolution established some democratic control over declarations of states of siege by entrusting this power to the parliament, at least until Napoleon III transferred the power to himself (Agamben 2005: 12). Likewise, Agamben made no mention of the violent suppression of the Paris Commune in 1871, and echoed the political establishment's claim that exclusive parliamentary power to resort to a state of siege was restored in 1878 (Agamben 2005: 12).

For all the radical phraseology of post-modernism, Agamben presented Schmitt as a genuine and prescient scholar, brushing over his theoretical and personal service to both the reactionary Weimar state and the ensuing Nazi regime. He claimed that Schmitt justified President Hindenburg's frequent recourse to emergency powers by the idea that the president acted as the 'guardian of the constitution' (Agamben 2005: 15). This falsely depicted Schmitt as a constitutionalist when in fact he was working hand in glove with

General Schleicher and others to prepare a military dictatorship. Agamben concluded that the Weimar Republic demonstrated that a 'protected democracy' of the kind supposedly envisaged by Schmitt was not a democracy at all, but functioned as a transitional phase that led 'inevitably to the establishment of a totalitarian regime' (Agamben 2005: 15). But the real mechanisms whereby Schmitt assisted in that process, and then joined the Nazi regime, were swept under the carpet.

Wider Academic Deference to Schmitt

One of the issues tackled in this book is the tendency of legal academics, even those who claim to oppose open-ended executive or emergency powers, to embrace Schmitt's conceptions, or have difficulty in differentiating themselves from them. An example is Philip Bobbitt, a law professor at New York's Columbia University, and director of its Center for National Security Law. Bobbitt has served several US administrations, including as Associate Counsel to the President; Counselor on International Law at the State Department; Legal Counsel to the Senate Iran-Contra Committee; and Director for Intelligence, Senior Director for Critical Infrastructure and Senior Director for Strategic Planning at the National Security Council.

In his 2008 work, *Terror and Consent: The Wars for the Twenty-First Century*, Bobbitt discussed Bruce Ackerman's proposal for an 'emergency constitution' that would impose limits on US executive authority:

> (1) the president could not declare an emergency on his own, except for a period of a week or two while Congress debates the matter; (2) following this period, any emergency powers would lapse unless a majority of both houses of Congress voted to continue them, and this endorsement would be valid for two months; (3) for a reauthorisation, a supermajority of 60 per cent of both houses would be required; (4) after another two months, a supermajority of 70 per cent would be need to continue the emergency powers; (5) after another two months, and for every ensuing two-month extension, an 80 per cent supermajority would be necessary. (Bobbitt 2008: 413–14)

The first virtue of Ackerman's schema, Bobbitt wrote, lay in the political sphere. It maximised the need for collaboration between the two major parties, Republicans and Democrats. This would put a restraint on 'the political temptation to exploit emergencies for partisan benefit' (Bobbitt 2008: 414). It would also avoid the sincerity of the claims to be waging war against terror being doubted because of the president's evidence of partisanship and lack of a 'bipartisan war cabinet' (Bobbitt 2008: 414). This remarkable suggestion hardly seems any guarantor against the imposition of dictatorial conditions against the population. Rather, it seems to be a recipe for closing ranks within the political establishment in order to quell popular opposition and attach political legitimacy to the emergency declaration. All the legislation adopted for the 'war on terror', such as the USA PATRIOT Act of 2001, received bipartisan support within the twin parties of rule in the US Congress, even though it authorised a vast array of measures to boost the surveillance and other powers of the intelligence agencies (Head 2011: 199–201). In 2010, the USA PATRIOT Act, originally introduced by the George W. Bush Republican administration, was extended unamended by Congress and the Obama Democrat administration (Head 2011: 63).

After postulating the political merits of Ackerman's blueprint, Bobbitt wrote:

> Ackerman's proposal also has the profound consequence of strengthening the rule of law by relying on the rule of law. A number of constitutional commentators have argued that liberal democracies – and perhaps states of consent generally – are not up to the task of anticipating emergencies because such states depend on laws, and emergencies are too unpredictable to be adequately governed by law. This was the position taken by the fascist political philosopher Carl Schmitt, for example before World War II, and it finds echoes in a number of critical legal theorists at present. (Bobbitt 2008: 414)

Before going any further, two points need to be made. First, as we have seen, Schmitt was not simply a fascist theorist. His concept of exception, initially propounded in 1922, developed in pre-Nazi Germany, under ostensibly democratic political and legal orders, but proved amenable to fascist totalitarianism, which Schmitt then served. Second, Schmitt's critique of liberal democracies did not rest on their supposed inability to anticipate unpredictable emergencies. He insisted that sovereignty itself was based on decision, not legality, and the 'state of exception' was not a temporary or peripheral feature of a political order, but an essential characteristic of a viable society, particularly in suppressing, and if need be exterminating, anyone identified as a 'foe'.

Bobbitt sought to narrow the scope of Schmitt's thesis by arguing that Schmitt was reacting to a description of law as depicted by Hans Kelsen's legal positivism – 'rigid and formulaic as well as formalistic' in Bobbitt's words (Bobbitt 2008: 414). Presumably, a less formalistic concept of law could be compatible with Schmitt's outlook, and still qualify as a 'rule of law'. Bobbitt drew the following conclusion, referring to Lon Fuller's *The Morality of Law* (Fuller 1964):

> Ackerman (and before him, Lon Fuller) appears to believe that a legal system can retain its legitimacy even while compromising some of its precepts if it maintains its 'identity as a normatively defensible model of legality'. Whether he is right about this, Ackerman's approach – retaining the processes and procedures of lawmaking – is certainly the surest method of taming the threat posed by the fact that no legal code can effectively foresee all the measures that might be necessary in an emergency. In fact, if Schmitt is right that law unavoidably must sometimes be suspended in emergencies then this is merely a feature of law as it is, and the legitimacy of laws is not thereby necessarily jeopardized. It is when we fail to take precautions such as Ackerman's that emergencies can destabilize the legitimacy of the state of consent by exacting lawless remedies in crisis, including of course dispensing with the ways by which law itself is enacted in a liberal democracy. (Bobbitt 2008: 414–15)

Bobbitt thus made considerable concessions to Schmitt's view. Implicitly, at least, he adopted the view that the Nazis found so helpful in Schmitt's theory. The key sentence is: 'In fact, if Schmitt is right that law unavoidably must sometimes be suspended in emergencies then this is merely a feature of law as it is, and the legitimacy of laws is not thereby necessarily jeopardized.' It seems that Bobbitt's real concern was with the perceived 'legitimacy' of the state in the eyes of its subjects, not the protection of core legal and democratic rights.

Bobbitt then went further, condemning Ackerman's 'supermajority' escalator as reflecting a bygone era of legalism: 'the passing nation state, with its heavy reliance on legal regulation and its marked reliance on legal process'. Ackerman's mechanism was likely to thwart an effective response to a serious crisis, such as 'a truly horrific terrorist attack'. Thus, the future would make a mockery of such a 'very precise law' (Bobbitt 2008: 415).

Among Bobbitt's 12 modest proposals for radically overhauling the US constitutional framework were the introduction of compulsory biometric ID cards, so that police could readily identify any person, and the abolition of the Posse Comitatus Act, which restricts the domestic deployment of federal troops because 'many in uniform believe that the act precludes the use of U.S. military assets in domestic security operations in any but the most extraordinary situations' (Bobbitt 2008: 418). Bobbitt's veritable police-state blueprint also featured blanket authorisations of telecommunications data mining by the US National Security Agency and preventative detention orders that could be extended, without trial, for up to two years. Such proposals, he claimed, were necessary to avoid being 'propelled into an indefinite period of martial law' by mass atrocities or catastrophes (Bobbitt 2008: 425).

This is a distinct echo of Schmitt's arguments for exceptional powers, ostensibly to ward off the threat of fascist dictatorship, but in reality to suppress acute working-class discontent. That course cleared the path for the Nazis, whom Schmitt then joined and served.

Schlesinger's Model

An earlier extra-legality model was proposed by former Kennedy administration adviser Arthur Schlesinger in his 1973 book *The Imperial Presidency*. The book traced the history of the US presidency from its conception by the founding fathers into an institution that Schlesinger concluded was out of control and had exceeded the constitutional limits (Schlesinger 1973: x). But Schlesinger's attempt to suggest means to curtail that power remained as cosmetic and abuse-permitting as Bobbitt's.

Schlesinger noted that national emergency powers allowed a president unilaterally to control any business activity or person within the country. He proposed that once a national emergency was proclaimed, it should get Congressional approval within 30 days in order to remain in effect. A joint resolution of Congress should be able to cancel a national emergency (Schlesinger 1973: 320–21). By Schlesinger's scheme, the national emergency power could only be used when the nation was at risk of being lost. He considered that only the Civil War, World War II and possibly Kennedy's 1962 Cuban missile crisis qualified as true national emergencies.

Schlesinger argued that extra-legal powers should only be invoked if a crisis was 'genuinely imperious' in the eyes of Congress and the general public, as well those of the president: 'The president's view that the life of the nation is truly at stake must be broadly shared by Congress and the American people' (Schlesinger 1973: 459). However, Schlesinger provided no clear criteria or means for determining the existence of such a consensus. Moreover, his conception ignored the role of the political establishment and the corporate media in drumming up scare campaigns, fomenting nationalism and xenophobia and manufacturing the appearance of consensus. He set out eight 'stringent and persuasive conditions' that must exist for a legitimate use of the emergency prerogative. The hopelessly vague and ineffective character of the eight prerequisites can be gauged by examining the final three conditions:

> (6) Secrecy must be strictly confined to the tactical requirements of the emergency. Every question of basic policy must be opened to national public debate
> (7) The president must report what he has done to Congress. Congress, along with the courts, and ultimately the people, will serve as the judge of the president's actions.
> (8) None of the presidential actions can be directed against the domestic process and rights. (Schlesinger 1973: 459)

How are these conditions to be interpreted and enforced? How exactly are the people to be the judge? None of these questions were answered. The experience since 1973, reviewed in Chapter 8, has been that presidents have increasingly resorted to secrecy, in the name of national security; blocked congressional, judicial and popular oversight; and trampled over basic legal and democratic rights.

Gross and Ní Aoláin's Extra-Legality Model

Despite this historical track record, Gross and Ní Aoláin argued:

> Open acknowledgment of extra-legal measures taken by government agents will contribute to reasoned discourse and dialogue between the government and its domestic constituency, between the government and other governments, and between the government and non-governmental or international organisations. (Gross and Ní Aoláin 2006: 154)

The authors sought to distinguish this doctrine from that of Schmitt, on the basis that it opened the door for subsequent legal accountability, either via the parliament or judicial interpretation of an indemnity law. This accountability, by contrast, was 'entirely absent from Schmitt's theory' (Gross and Ní Aoláin 2006: 170). In reality, such accountability has been meaningless, or served only to legitimise lawless actions. Finally, Gross and Ní Aoláin contended that, unlike Schmitt, under the extra-legal measures model 'the final decision in such matters is given to the people' (Gross and Ní Aoláin 2006: 170). Exactly how 'the people' were to hand down their judgment was not specified.

Gross rejected Dyzenhaus's characterisation of the extra-legal measures model as a 'lawless void' – a legal black hole in which the state acted unfettered by law. Gross insisted that the model 'seeks to preserve the long-term relevance of, and obedience to, legal principles, rules, and norms' by showing that 'going outside the law in appropriate cases may preserve, rather than undermine, the rule of law in ways that constantly bending the law to accommodate emergencies and crises will not' (Gross 2008: 62).

To counter the charge of a legal void, Gross insisted that the law would remain intact, albeit only as one benchmark against which to judge the supposed emergency response, while conceding that the social and political assessment might be different from the legal one. He asserted an ethic of political responsibility on the part of governments and officials, anchored in answerability to the public and the uncertain prospect of after-the-event ratification. These were, Gross argued, powerful deterrents for public officials who were considering resort to extra-legal measures (Gross 2008: 62–4).

There is no evidence, however, of the seeds of any such ethic of political responsibility in the responses of governments, either in the historical past or since the turn of the century. On the contrary, the record has been one of whipping up fears of terrorism and other alleged threats; concocting lies and fabrications to provide pretexts for emergency measures; and inventing pseudo-legal justifications for activities such as 'enhanced interrogation' and drone assassinations.

A manifest flaw with this model is that it relies upon openness and acknowledgement of illegality by the executive: 'To be properly implemented, the model calls for candor on the part of government agents, who must disclose the nature of their counter-emergency activities' (Gross 2003: 1024). That requirement flies in the face of the record of secrecy, cover-up and half-truths that has characterised the response of one government after the other.

In the cases of the Bush and Obama administrations, the damning revelations of abuse at Abu Ghraib, torture at Guantanamo Bay, secret CIA renditions for detainees to be tortured in other countries, and mass electronic surveillance of millions of Americans and people around the world primarily became known because of the courageous exposures of whistleblowers such as Julian Assange, Bradley (Chelsea) Manning and Edward Snowden. Instead of being rewarded for their efforts in promoting transparency, they were vilified, persecuted, indicted and, in Manning's case, jailed for many years.

Commenting on the official furtiveness, Chesterman noted that the general tenor was set by Vice President Dick Cheney when he spoke of working 'on the dark side' and 'in the shadows of the intelligence world' and 'quietly, without any discussion' (Chesterman 2008: 320). After reviewing just some of the most egregious abuses that had become known publicly, Chesterman concluded:

> In each of these cases – torture, extra-judicial detention and warrantless surveillance – public deliberation was never intended by the relevant officials … It appears unrealistic, therefore, to put much hope in the prospect that such decisions will ever be made either openly or candidly. (Chesterman 2008: 326–7)

Chesterman also cited the findings of the Church Committee's investigations in the 1970s into the illegal activities of successive US governments and the security agencies. He noted that the official claims that secrecy was needed to protect the operations of the intelligence and armed forces led to a 'culture of tolerating secrecy' and 'soon expanded to mask decisions of the President and his senior staff' (Chesterman 2008: 327).

It must be said, however, that Chesterman's suggested solution was just as likely to permit lawless claims to extraordinary powers by governments and officials. He proposed the imposition of minimal penalties for any abuses found to have violated the law. As a paradigm he suggested a judicial form of Queen Victoria's commutation to six months' imprisonment of the death sentences imposed on the two shipwrecked men convicted of killing and eating their cabin boy in *R v Dudley and Stephens* ((1884) 14 QBD 273) (Chesterman 2008: 329–32).

Chesterman admitted himself that this prospect of a token punishment would not encourage any greater official candour. His only claim was that the possibility of prosecution and punishment would do more to 'improve behaviour' than the extra-legal model's alleged 'formalised endorsement of wrongdoing asserted to be in the national interest' (Chesterman 2008: 332). But it is unlikely that a judicial slap on the wrist would convince authoritarian administrations to 'behave', any more than it would encourage them to expose themselves to public scrutiny.

The Political Realist View and Doctrines of Necessity

Both with regard to domestic and international law, other doctrines exist to justify the outright overturning of legality, or the resort to coups to take or maintain control over a country. Two such schools of thought are briefly examined here. Arguably, they come closer than any other theoretical model to the reality of the use and abuse of political, economic and repressive power to retain or extend a ruling elite's grip over a society.

One is the *political realist school* – which mostly, but not exclusively, features in theories of international relations. According to this approach, legal and ethical considerations are largely irrelevant when the very existence of a state is under threat. By this view, legality is an unaffordable luxury when dealing with violent crises that endanger the survival or fundamental interests of the nation-state (Friedrich 1957). Concerns of legality, morality or democracy, even if taken into account for political or tactical reasons, are secondary or subordinate to the quest for continued existence. This approach is more pervasive than generally acknowledged. Maxims such as 'necessity knows no law' give vent to this outlook.

A blunt expression of this school of thought was Dean Acheson's justification for aggressive US actions against Cuba. Acheson, a former US Secretary of State, was an adviser to President Kennedy during the 1962 Cuban missile crisis. Speaking of the imposition of a military blockade on Cuba, he stated:

> [T]he propriety of the Cuban quarantine is not a legal issue. The power, position and prestige of the United States had been challenged by another state; and law simply does not deal with such questions of ultimate power – power that comes close to the sources of sovereignty. I cannot believe that there are principles of law that say we must accept destruction of our way of life … No law can destroy the state creating the law. The survival of states is not a matter of law. (Acheson 1963: 14)

Gross and Ní Aoláin sought to quickly dismiss this school. They asserted that such views cannot be acceptable to those who believe that law matters, especially in times of crisis, as a check against arbitrary actions and unlimited discretion. But that response, of course, assumes that law does, or could, provide protection against despotism. They also argued that this theory does not transfer to the domestic sphere. They maintained that domestic states 'do offer hierarchical political rule and monopoly over the use of forces that is, allegedly, lacking on the international sphere' (Gross and Ní Aoláin 2006: 111). Yet, this simply begs the real question. On what is that rule and monopoly of force based? Issues of power and sovereignty are just as fundamental domestically as they are globally.

It is impossible to so simply separate the domestic and international spheres. Acheson's questions of sovereignty and 'ultimate power' are definitely raised by revolutions, coups and other 'regime-change' operations. These can and frequently do determine who is in power domestically. Moreover, those events often involved foreign intervention, either overt or covert.

That issue is underscored by the second line of approach. Over the past few centuries, the British and American courts have developed the doctrines of *revolutionary legality and necessity* to supposedly distinguish between 'successful' revolutions or coups that become new legal orders, on the one hand, and those that fail, or are regarded as illegitimate, on the other hand. This can be a precarious dichotomy, with the outcome having little to do with legal niceties.

In the English and American revolutions of the seventeenth and eighteenth centuries, both of which involved the violent overthrow of the existing order, the courts recognised the legitimacy of the victorious side and generally sanctioned acts done in the name of their revolutions, dating back to the dates on which their rebellions commenced (see *Mokotso* [1989] LRC (Const) 24, 96). These revolutions – the so-called English Civil War of 1642–51 and the American War of Independence of 1775–83 – were fundamentally progressive eruptions, breaking up the old feudal-monarchical forms of rule and signalling the rise to ascendancy of the emerging capitalist classes (McPherson 1990; Hill 1940).

During the second half of the twentieth century, however, the doctrine of revolution was utilised to justify anti-democratic, military-backed coups, at least so long as the new regime accommodated the interests of British, American or global capitalism. Much of this modern history draws upon a 1951 parliamentary speech by the British Secretary of State for Foreign Affairs, Herbert Morrison, setting out the practice of the British government in deciding whether to recognise the outcome of a coup d'état (United Kingdom, 1951). The speech, cited in the leading English House of Lords decision (*Carl-Zeiss Stiftung v Rayner & Keeler Ltd (No 2)* [1966] 2 All ER 536, 548), stipulates that a new regime must have 'effective control' over most of the state's territory, where that control 'seems likely to continue' and is 'firmly established'.

This approach has been used to uphold the legality of various military or military-backed coups, including those in Pakistan (1958), Uganda (1966), Lesotho (1986 and 1989), the Seychelles (1977) and Grenada (1979) (Head 2001b: 545). In Pakistan, the Supreme Court has validated successive alternations between civilian rule and military coups, including the October 1999 coup by General Pervez Musharraf (Head 2001b: 545). For example, in a 1958 case, Chief Justice Munir stated:

> If the revolution is victorious in the sense that the persons assuming power under the change can successfully require the inhabitants of the country to conform to the new regime, then the revolution itself becomes a law-creating fact because thereafter its own legality is judged not by reference to the annulled Constitution but by reference to its own success. (*State v Dosso ([1958] 2 PLD SC (Pak) 533)*

Little regard was paid to democratic rights in these cases. In the 1989 Lesotho case of *Mokotso*, after exhaustively reviewing the authorities, Chief Justice Cullinan concluded that a military coup was legal because:

> [I]f the judge is satisfied that the new regime is firmly established and there is no opposition thereto, and that the people are acting by and large in conformity with the new legal order, signifying their acceptance thereof, for whatever reason, I do not see that the judge can hold that regime to be other than legitimate … If the people ultimately acquiesce, then the new regime is entitled to recognition by the courts. (*Mokotso* [1989] LRC (Const) 24, 131–3)

By contrast, where the usurpation of power cut across Britain's strategic interests, as happened when Rhodesia's Ian Smith's unilaterally declared independence from Britain in 1965, the Privy Council judges ruled that the regime failed the test of 'successful revolution'. They insisted that Britain remained the lawful power, ready and willing to resume control over Rhodesia, a stance backed by British economic and diplomatic sanctions designed to bring Smith to the bargaining table (*Madzimbamuto v Lardner-Burke* [1969] 1 AC 645, 725, 722–3, 725).

In most post-World War II cases on coups d'état, the courts referred to the 'principle of effectiveness' enunciated by Hans Kelsen in his work *General Theory of Law and State* (Kelsen 1946: 118–19). In essence, Kelsen's theory justified the seizure of power by force. Quoting his writings, judges ruled that coups did not need to command 'universal adherence', simply 'a minimum of support'. Kelsen applied a purely legal positivist approach to revolutions, arguing that a successful revolution creates its own legitimacy (Kelsen 1946: 117–19, 220).

Significantly, Kelsen was a rival of Schmitt during the Weimar Republic, and the pair conducted a public debate in the early 1930s. Kelsen defended the place of judicial review against Schmitt's authoritarian view of executive and political power. In his 1931 essay 'Who Should Be the Guardian of the Constitution?', Kelsen defended the importance of judicial review over and against Schmitt's concept of the state of exception (Vinx 2015). Nevertheless, Kelsen's conceptual framework had its own authoritarian implications.

Kelsen postulated the existence of a 'basic norm', or *Grundnorm*, which formed the foundation of the legal order of a nation. Kelsen's concept of the basic norm was vague – it could be a written constitution or an unwritten principle of government. However, if such a *Grundnorm* is overthrown by a successful revolution, then a new *Grundnorm* is established that forms the foundation of all subsequent law. Thus, 'a national legal order begins to be valid as soon as it has become – on the whole – efficacious; and it ceases to be valid as soon as it loses this efficacy' (Kelsen 1946: 220).

By this effectiveness doctrine, if a revolutionary government or a military junta succeeds in destroying the existing *Grundnorm* and putting its own legal order into effect, then it becomes the *de jure* government. This applies no matter what the motivation of the regime was in seizing power, or whether its rule can be considered just or unjust according to conventional standards of morality. Ironically, Kelsen developed this amoral theory in an attempt to devise a 'pure theory of law', devoid of all the moral, ethical, political and sociological factors that Kelsen considered 'impure'.

Courts that have adopted Kelsen's principle of effectiveness have generally required proof of two elements. First, the revolution must be successful. It must be in unchallenged control of the country with no pre-existing legitimate government contending for power. Second, it must be effective, in that it commands the obedience of the bulk of the population (Edelstein 2002: 61). Even where judges expressed concern about the authoritarian conclusions of Kelsen's principle, they ultimately drew similar conclusions. In the 1989 Lesotho case, Chief Justice Cullinan denied any requirement for a usurping regime to prove popular acceptance, stating:

> Throughout the course of history there have been regimes, indeed dynasties, holding sway for many years, indeed centuries, whose rule could not be said by any manner of means to be popular and could even be described as oppressive; but who is going to say that a new legal order was not created with their coming and going? (*Mokotso* [1989] LRC (Const) 24, 130)

The Privy Council made a similar observation in the Rhodesian case:

> It is an historical fact that in many countries – and indeed in many countries which are or have been under British Sovereignty – there are now régimes which are universally recognised as lawful but which derive their origins from revolutions or coups d'état. The law must take account of that fact. (*Madzimbamuto* [1969] 1 AC 645, 724)

Likewise, the doctrine of necessity has become a means of justifying the abrogation or suspension of legal rights. Most of the early cases on necessity arose from the American Civil War, in which the northern industrialists defeated the secessionist southern governments based on a slave-owning form of capitalism. The US Supreme Court upheld the legality of measures taken by the southern states to maintain order and economic life, even though these governments were engaged in rebellion against the US Government. In 1868, the Court declared:

> [A]cts necessary to peace and good order among citizens ... which would be valid if emanating from a lawful government, must be regarded in general as valid when proceeding from an actual, though unlawful government. (*Texas v White* (1868) 7 Wallace 700, 733)

These acts therefore had to be obeyed, even if they infringed the US Constitution.

In 1969, in the Rhodesian case, the Privy Council applied this doctrine to rule on the legality of the Smith regime's indefinite detention of political opponents under emergency powers. With Lord Pearce dissenting, a majority of the court held the detention invalid – but only on the ground that Britain remained the only legal authority. In principle, the law lords were prepared to sanction the use of emergency powers to override democratic rights, observing that '[u]nder pressure of necessity the lawful Sovereign and his forces may be justified in taking action which infringes the ordinary rights of his subjects' (*Madzimbamuto* [1969] 1 AC 645, 721–2, 726, 731).

Some scholars have argued that since the 1970s, courts have expressed discomfort at Kelsen's separation of law and justice. One commentator drew attention to a 1986 Grenada Court of Appeal ruling, where the court stated:

> [T]he Court called upon to decide the question [of the legality of a coup] should take into consideration both the reason why the old constitutional government was overthrown and the nature and character of the new legal order. Was the motivation mere power grabbing or was it a rebellion for example against oppression or corruption or ineptitude? And is the new legal order a just one? (*Mitchell v Director of Public Prosecutions* [1986] LRC (Const) 35, 67)

The author mentioned that the decision followed the US invasion of Grenada (Edelstein 2002: 62). However, he failed to explain that the court was upholding the legality of the regime that was installed by that invasion, which overthrew the nationalist New Jewel Movement. This context suggests that overthrow of an existing order is more likely to be legalised by a court if the outcome accords with the strategic objectives of the US or another major power.

The same must be said about the 2001 ruling of the Fiji Court of Appeal in the *Prasad* case (*Republic of Fiji v Prasad* [2001] FJCA 1), which Edelstein contended represents 'a fusion of the indestructible *Grundnorm* with Western democratic thought'. According to this view, the court rejected Kelsen's theories in unequivocal terms, noting that they 'might too readily reward a usurper' (Edelstein 2002: 64). Likewise, another scholar argued that *Prasad* was a 'legal landmark' that would 'make it extremely difficult for a tyrannical regime which violates basic human rights recognised at international law to gain judicial recognition' (Williams 2001: 149–50).

It is certainly true that the court declared that a military-appointed interim government failed to establish that it was the legal government. It ruled that the 1997 Fijian constitution remained the supreme law of the country and had not been lawfully abrogated by the military commander, Commodore Frank Bainimarama, when he effectively took power in 2000. In reality, however, the judgment in *Prasad* does not substantiate the claims made above. Rather, the court left the way open for the military's administration to remain in office, at least until it reorganised itself by conducting stage-managed elections. Moreover, the judges rejected the argument that a usurping regime must be judged by its acceptance of international human rights obligations and declined to require observance of democratic norms.

Arguably, the most significant new criterion suggested by the court was acceptance of a new regime by the 'international community', which, in the context, referred to the stance taken by major Western nations, notably Australia, New Zealand, Britain and the United States. The judgment may have set an international precedent for assessing repressive military regimes and their actions – but a precedent that will primarily assist the major powers to impose their requirements with the assistance of local elites, not one that will defend the democratic rights of ordinary people (Head 2001b).

Chapter 6
Capitalism and Dictatorial Powers: A Marxist Critique

The growing resort to emergency powers and other authoritarian measures, at the cost of core legal and democratic rights and principles, points to the fact that the capitalist state is an instrument of class rule. Its powers and massive resources are employed to defend the material interests of a relatively small wealthy elite, amid mounting militarism and social polarisation. As the mass surveillance disclosed by intelligence agency dissidents such as Edward Snowden demonstrates, the preoccupation of this apparatus is not handfuls of terrorists but the danger of social unrest and an uprising from below.

Karl Marx and Frederick Engels famously characterised the capitalist state as a 'committee for managing the common affairs of the whole bourgeoisie' (Marx and Engels 1973, 110–11). Engels described the emergence, at the heart of the state, of bodies of 'armed men' alongside 'material adjuncts, prisons and institutions of coercion' (Engels 1942, 167). He warned that this apparatus of force grew stronger as class antagonisms within the state became more acute and as tensions grew between rival international powers.

Writing after the October 1917 Russian Revolution, Vladimir Lenin made a telling observation about the facade of democracy erected by the capitalist class. He insisted that the new workers' state was far more democratic than the capitalist states that were organising military forces to overrun Soviet Russia. Drawing on the work of Engels in *The Origin of the Family, Private Property and the State*, he observed that behind the democratic face of modern capitalist states, with their formal undertakings to uphold freedom of assembly, freedom of the press and 'equality of all citizens before the law', there invariably existed provisions allowing for all these guarantees to be swept aside to suppress threats from below during periods of crisis:

> There is not a single state, however democratic, which has no loopholes or reservations in its constitution guaranteeing the bourgeois the possibility of dispatching troops against the workers, of proclaiming martial law, and so forth, in case of a 'violation of public order', and actually in case the exploited class 'violates' its position of slavery and tries to behave in a non-slavish manner. (Lenin 1970a: 30–31)

Even as a matter of law, the capitalist elite reserves the right to sweep aside basic constitutional protections and procedures when it perceives 'a clear and present danger' (in the words of the US Supreme Court) to its fundamental class interests. One of many examples of constitutional norms and democratic principles being overturned occurred in Australia in 1975, when the elected Whitlam Labor government was ousted by the queen's representative, the Governor-General.

As Engels, drawing on historical research, explained in *The Origin of the Family*, the state is not – as is traditionally presented – a neutral arbiter of social conflict. The very existence of a vast apparatus of control and repression testifies to the fact that society is split into irreconcilably antagonistic classes. The bourgeois state is an instrument that upholds the political and economic dictatorship of the capitalist class. In recent decades, the repressive mechanisms at the state's disposal have been immensely extended and strengthened.

Thus the contemporary American state apparatus, to take the most significant instance, has the largest prison system in the world, with more than 2 million people behind bars. There are heavily armed police forces and National Guards, and a judicial system that processes over 14 million arrests annually and has the power to inflict capital punishment. Then there is a nuclear-armed and lavishly funded military force, and a giant 'national security' apparatus that has extraordinary powers to spy on the entire population. Since 2001, torture and drone assassinations, along with frequent declarations of states of emergency, have become state policy, as documented in this book.

For Marxists, therefore, analysis of emergency powers cannot be separated from an examination of the socio-economic and class character of the state and government exercising the powers. An aristocratic or capitalist regime seeking to maintain itself against a mass popular movement from below must be judged differently from a government, especially a working-class socialist government, that takes power as a result of such a movement and needs to defend itself against counter-revolutionary violence by the ousted ruling class.

As Leon Trotsky observed in *Their Morals and Ours*, writing of Abraham Lincoln's use of the 'severe means' that were necessary to win the American Civil War and abolish chattel slavery:

> History has different yardsticks for the cruelty of the Northerners and the cruelty of the Southerners in the Civil War. A slave-owner who through cunning and violence shackles a slave in chains, and a slave who through cunning or violence breaks the chains – let not the contemptible eunuchs tell us that they are equals before a court of morality! (Trotsky 1968: 32)

Democracy and Resort to Dictatorship

Marx and his close collaborator, Engels, made some pungent remarks about the kind of democracy and 'rule of law' established by the capitalist class. While capitalist social relations, based on the exploitation of the labour power of workers, were best served by the stability and appearance of fairness provided by a parliamentary order, that democratic facade was cast aside in times of political and economic crises.

In his early work *The Conditions of the Working Class in England*, Engels noted that legality was always reinforced, whenever required, by brute force, starting with police batons:

> A word or two as to the respect for the law in England. True, the law is sacred to the bourgeois, for it his own composition, enacted with his consent, and for his benefit and protection. He knows that, even if an individual law should injure him, the whole fabric

> protects his interests; and more than all, the sanctity of the law, the sacredness of order as established by the active will of one part of society, and the passive acceptance of the other, is the strongest support of his social position. Because the English bourgeois finds himself reproduced in his law, as he does in his God, the policeman's truncheon which, in a certain measure, is his own club, has for him a wonderfully soothing power. But for the working-man quite otherwise! (Engels 1976: 514–15)

Marx and Engels also drew lessons from the 1848–49 revolutions in Europe and the 1871 Paris Commune. In these convulsive events, when the rising bourgeoisie felt threatened by the emerging working-class masses, it undertook or collaborated in ferocious repression that resulted in the deaths of thousands of people, as discussed in Chapter 2. They concluded that, to end this oppression, the working class had no choice but to carry through revolutions, and that those revolutions could only succeed if they were prepared to defend themselves against the inevitably violent counter-attack by the old order. Drawing on the Roman republican conception of a temporary dictatorship to deal with existential threats to the republic, Marx and Engels explained the need for a transitional 'dictatorship of the proletariat' (see below).

Lenin, who was to lead the October 1917 socialist revolution in Russia, further forewarned, in the lead-up to World War I, that the post-Paris Commune decades of history in which the capitalist classes of Europe's leading powers, such as Britain and Germany, were able to rule reasonably peacefully by making economic and political concessions to the working class at home was coming to an end.

Several years before the outbreak of the 'Great War' between the major powers, Lenin warned, in an article analysing the evolution of German social democracy, that a 'half-century phase' in history, in which conditions of political legality predominated, was giving way to another phase. Lenin explained that the ruling classes of Germany, ironically, had created the 'most stable constitutional legality' but were now unmistakeably coming to the point where 'this legality, *their* legality, *will have to be* shattered – so that the domination of the bourgeoisie may be preserved' (emphasis in original). He foresaw that objective conditions were leading to 'the destruction of *all* bourgeois legality', the first signs of which were 'panicky efforts on the part of the bourgeoisie to get rid of the legality which, though it is their own handiwork, has become unbearable to them' (Lenin 1977: 310–11).

In June 1914, just weeks before the world war erupted, Lenin examined the relationship between the two methods of rule employed by the capitalist class against workers – repressive violence and parliamentary democracy. He referred to the experiences of 1848–49 and 1871, as well as to the repression conducted against the Chartist movement that demanded popular voting rights in Britain during the 1840s:

> In all capitalist countries throughout the world, the bourgeoisie resorts to two methods in its struggle against the working-class movement and the workers' parties. One method is that of violence, persecution, bans, and suppression. In its fundamentals, this is a feudal, medieval method. Everywhere there are sections and groups of the bourgeoisie – smaller in the advanced countries and larger in the backward ones – which prefer these methods, and in certain, highly critical moments in the workers' struggle against wage-slavery, the *entire*

> bourgeoisie is agreed on the employment of such methods. Historical examples of such moments are provided by Chartism in England, and 1849 and 1871 in France.
>
> The other method the bourgeoisie employs against the movement is that of dividing the workers, disrupting their ranks, bribing individual representatives or certain groups of the proletariat with the object of winning them over to its side. These are not feudal but *purely* bourgeois and modern methods, in keeping with the developed and civilised customs of capitalism, with the democratic system.
>
> For the democratic system is a feature of bourgeois society, the most pure and perfect bourgeois feature, in which the utmost freedom, scope and clarity of the class struggle are combined with the utmost cunning, with ruses and subterfuges aimed at spreading the 'ideological' influence of the bourgeoisie among the wage-slaves with the object of diverting them from their struggle against wage-slavery. (Lenin 1972: 455–86)

Leon Trotsky, who led the Russian Revolution alongside Lenin and then led the Left Opposition against the degeneration of the Soviet Union at the hands of the Stalinist bureaucracy, later noted that in times of economic advancement, the capitalist class preferred, and could afford, to govern democratically, displaying tolerance toward political and industrial opposition in order to better stabilise and legitimise its rule. But in periods of economic stagnation or decline, such as the 1930s, the political 'safety valves' of democracy gave way.

In 1929, examining the breakdown of democratic institutions that was starting to unfold in Europe, giving way to fascism or dictatorship in major countries such as Italy, Germany and Spain, Trotsky explained that the move toward totalitarianism flowed from the fact that parliamentary democratic institutions could not stand the pressure of the class tensions internally, and the international political conflicts:

> By analogy with electrical engineering, democracy might be defined as a system of safety switches and circuit breakers for protection against currents overloaded by the national or social struggle. No period of human history has been – even remotely – so overcharged with antagonisms such as ours. The overloading of lines occurs more and more frequently at different points in the European power grid. Under the impact of class and international contradictions that are too highly charged, the safety switches of democracy either burn out or explode. That is what the short circuit of dictatorship represents. (Trotsky 1997: 53–4)

In 1936, Trotsky again drew attention to the use of 'detachments of armed men in defence of property':

> The bourgeoisie was able to tolerate the freedom of strikes, of assembly and of the press only so long as the productive forces were mounting upwards, so long as the sales markets were being extended, the welfare of the popular masses, even if only partially, was rising and the capitalist nations were able to live and let live. It is otherwise now. (Trotsky 1975: 15, 17)

Drawing on the work of Marx, Evgeny Pashukanis, perhaps the best-known early Soviet jurist, elaborated this conceptual framework. He contended that the capitalist state was bound up with the principle of commodity exchange, and hence the protection of dominant private interests (Head 2007). These interests required, as far as possible, limits on the power of the state, and an avoidance of dictatorial methods that could threaten personal and property rights. Thus, the character of the state as a seemingly independent apparatus standing above society was not a purely ideological construct for duping ordinary people; the appearance was rooted in the reality of maintaining an *impersonal* guarantor of *personal* rights. To best achieve that end, the state could not be the plaything of this or that tycoon or even dictator.

Pashukanis quoted Marx and Engels' famous characterisation of the capitalist state as a 'committee for managing the common affairs of the whole bourgeoisie' (Pashukanis 1978: 149). However in times of crisis, particularly when capitalist interests as a whole were threatened from below, the ideal of the constitutional state would be dispensed with:

> For the bourgeoisie has never, in favour of purity of theory, lost sight of the fact that class society is not only a market where autonomous owners of commodities meet, but is at the same time the battlefield of a bitter class war, where the machinery of state represents a very powerful weapon ... The more the hegemony of the bourgeoisie was shattered, the more compromising these corrections became, the more quickly the 'constitutional state' was transformed into a disembodied shadow, until finally the extraordinary sharpening of the class struggle forced the bourgeoisie to discard the mask of the constitutional state altogether, revealing the nature of state power as the organised power of one class over the other. (Pashukanis 1978: 149–50)

Pashukanis noted that in the face of exceptional revolutionary upheaval, the impersonal nature of public power could give way to the private or semi-private wielding of power, via the mobilisation of fascist and other violent militias:

> In our times of heightened revolutionary struggle, we can observe how the official machinery of the bourgeois state retires into the background as compared with the volunteer corps of the fascists and others. This further substantiates the fact that, when the balance of society is upset, it seeks salvation not in the creation of a power standing above society, but in the maximal harnessing of all forces of the classes in conflict. (Pashukanis 1978: 139, fn 10)

Sovereignty and Capitalism

Marx and Engels also pointed out that the rising capitalist classes employed military and dictatorial force at critical stages to establish their socio-economic power in the first place. Notably, this occurred in (1) the primitive accumulation of capital; (2) struggles for state power such as the English, American and French revolutions of the seventeenth and eighteenth centuries; (3) the abolition of chattel slavery via the American Civil War; and (4) the worldwide expansion of their realms to colonise and encompass the globe.

In other words, sovereignty was established via violent operations with definite economic and class content.

In order for capitalist social relations, based on the extraction of surplus value by employers via wage labour, to gain ascendancy over the previous feudal relations of aristocrats, serfs and peasants, the rural populations had to be dispossessed of land and driven into the cities. Marx called this 'the historical process which by divorcing workers from their means of production, converts them into wage workers' (Marx and Engels 1975: 293).

This was by no means simply a violent dispossession. Primarily, it was achieved by economic means, based on the superior productivity and wealth generated by breakthroughs in industrial technology. Capital accumulation relied primarily on 'the silent compulsion of economic relations [which] sets the seal on the domination of the capitalist over the worker' (Marx 1993: 493).

In capitalist society – by contrast to earlier forms of class society, such as slavery and feudalism – the extraction of surplus labour does not take place through fixed status or political means, but economically. That is, while there were myriad laws in feudal society, which spelt out the obligations of the peasant, there are no such laws under capitalism. There is no statute that compels the worker to sell his or her labour power to the owner of capital. In the final analysis, he or she is forced to do so by the pressure of economic necessity. And that compulsion arises from the fact that, unlike the peasant or small producer in feudal society, who retains a relationship to the land, the worker in capitalist society has been separated from the ownership of the means of production.

Capitalism could only emerge once society's technology and productive capacity – for example, steam power – had developed to the point where large-scale manufacturing could arise. Nevertheless, capitalism's hegemony was accompanied, where necessary, by force. In Marx's words:

> [A]s soon as ... adverse circumstances prevent the creation of an industrial reserve army, and with it the absolute dependence of the working class upon the capitalist class, capital ... rebels against the 'sacred' law of supply and demand, and tries to make up for its inadequacies by forcible means. (Marx 1976: 794)

These processes were later extended around the world, as the capitalist profit system restlessly and relentlessly sought new sources of resources, cheap labour and markets, either through direct colonisation or integration into its orbit through puppet or comprador regimes. In *Capital*, Marx graphically described this violent expansion of primitive accumulation, summing it up as follows:

> The discovery of gold and silver in America, the extirpation, enslavement and entombment in mines of the aboriginal population, the beginning of the conquest and looting of the East Indies, the turning of Africa into a warren for the commercial hunting of black-skins, signalised the rosy dawn of the era of capitalist production. These idyllic proceedings are the chief momenta of primitive accumulation. On their heels treads the commercial war of the European nations, with the globe for a theatre ... The different momenta of primitive accumulation distribute themselves now, more or less in chronological order, particularly over Spain, Portugal, Holland, France, and England. In England at the end of the 17th century, they arrive at a systematical combination, embracing the colonies, the national debt,

> the modern mode of taxation, and the protectionist system. These methods depend in part on brute force, *e.g.*, the colonial system. But, they all employ the power of the State, the concentrated and organised force of society, to hasten, hot-house fashion, the process of transformation of the feudal mode of production into the capitalist mode, and to shorten the transition … The colonies secured a market for the budding manufactures, and, through the monopoly of the market, an increased accumulation. The treasures captured outside Europe by undisguised looting, enslavement, and murder, floated back to the mother-country and were there turned into capital. (Marx 1976: 918)

Marx and Engels supported Lincoln's use of emergency powers to help win the American Civil War of 1861–65 against the slave-holding southern Confederacy. This victory resulted in the abolition of slavery in America, one of the largest expropriations of private property in world history. Both men saw the war as an extension of the American Revolution of 1776. Marx and Engels argued that Lincoln's Emancipation Proclamation and the North's arming of black soldiers transformed the Civil War from a purely constitutional war to preserve the country with slavery intact into a revolutionary war. They believed that it advanced the cause of all workers, both white and black, by destroying chattel slavery. The revolution armed former slaves; destroyed the institution of slavery without compensation to the slave-owners; and opened the way for a struggle between the working class and the capitalist class.

The British ruling class, in its support of the South and in its bitter opposition to the Emancipation Proclamation – which it feared could trigger insurrectionary movements at home – was at least in part restrained from intervening on the side of the South by domestic working-class opposition to any such plan. Marx wrote in a 1864 letter that a 'monster meeting in St. James' Hall' had 'prevented [Prime Minister Lord] Palmerston from declaring war on the United States, as he was on the point of doing'.

The working-class solidarity with the North and the slaves also nourished a spirit of internationalism developing among European workers and helped set the stage for the founding of the First International (or the International Workingmen's Association – IWA) the following year in London. In late 1864, Marx was tasked by the IWA with drafting a letter congratulating Lincoln on his re-election. Marx wrote:

> The workingmen of Europe feel sure that, as the American War of Independence initiated a new era of ascendancy for the middle class, so the American Antislavery War will do for the working classes. They consider it an earnest of the epoch to come that it fell to the lot of Abraham Lincoln, the single-minded son of the working class, to lead his country through the matchless struggle for the rescue of an enchained race and the reconstruction of a social world.

Socio-Economic Power and Law

While holding socio-economic and state power, the capitalist class needed to elaborate legal principles that have the appearance of internal coherence and universality, and to continually adjust those doctrines to meet changing economic circumstances. In a letter to J. Bloch (21 September 1890), Engels emphasised that the economic situation is the 'ultimately determining factor in history' but:

> [T]he various elements of the superstructure – political forms of the class struggle and its results, such as constitutions established by the victorious class after a successful battle, etc., juridical forms, and especially the reflections of all these real struggles in the brains of the participants, political, legal, philosophical theories, religious views and their further development into systems of dogmas – also exercise their influence upon the course of the historical struggles and in many cases determine their *form* in particular. (Engels 1975: 394–5. italics in original)

Further contradictions arose constantly from the ideological role of law – from the need of any modern ruling class in the epoch of mass politics to present its political order as just and impartial. In a letter to Schmidt, Engels stated:

> In a modern state, law must not only correspond to the general economic condition and be its expression, but must also be an *internally coherent* expression which does not, owing to internal conflicts, contradict itself. And in order to achieve this, the faithful reflection of economic conditions suffers increasingly. All the more, so the more rarely it happens that a code of law is the blunt, unmitigated, unadulterated expression of the domination of a class – this in itself would offend the 'conception of right. (Engels 1975: 399–402)

Even so, Marx and Engels emphasised the decisive role played by control over the state apparatus, including the legal system, at critical junctures in history, most notably during revolutionary struggles. Engels concluded his letter to Schmidt by posing the question: 'Why do we fight for the political dictatorship of the proletariat if political power is economically impotent? Force (that is, state power) is also an economic power!' (Engels 1975: 402).

Fundamental Marxist Conceptions

Marx and Engels wrote on the role of law in contemporary society, but usually tangentially to their broader examinations of class structure and dynamics. With the exception of Marx's early *Critique of Hegel's Philosophy of Right* (Marx 1970a) and Engels' later *The Origin of the Family* (1942), they only addressed the issues of the state and law as subjects in themselves in several letters. Marx twice wrote of his intention to develop a theory of state and law, but this project was set aside to concentrate on his study of political economy, presented in the three volumes of *Capital*.

Nevertheless, many of their works examined the role of law in society, and from these two underlying conceptions can be identified: (1) that, in general, all forms of law and the state are in the end derived from the development of the productive and hence cultural level of human society; and (2) that law and the state will wither away in the process of arriving at a genuinely communist society. That is, the need for formal, bureaucratic and repressive instruments of rule will only disappear with the creation of a bountiful, egalitarian and democratic world.

For all the major Marxist theoreticians the roles of law and the state – as key social institutions – were derivative and secondary, not primary, in the economic, social and political structure. The starting point for understanding this historical materialist view is Marx's 1859 Preface to *A Contribution to the Critique of Political Economy*, where he tentatively described the following propositions, derived from years of research and experience, as 'a guiding thread for my studies':

> In the social production of their life, men enter into definite relations that are indispensable and independent of their will, relations of production which correspond to a definite stage of development of their material productive forces. The sum total of these relations of production constitutes the economic structure of society, the real foundation, on which rises a legal and political superstructure and to which correspond definite forms of social consciousness. The mode of production of material life conditions the social, political and intellectual life process in general. It is not the consciousness of men that determines their being, but, on the contrary, their social being that determines their social consciousness.
>
> At a certain stage of their development, the material productive forces of society come in conflict with the existing relations of production, or – what is but a legal expression for the same thing – with the property relations within which they have been at work hitherto. From forms of development of the productive forces these relations turn into their fetters. Then begins an epoch of social revolution. With the change of the economic foundation, the entire immense superstructure is more or less rapidly transformed.
>
> In considering such transformations, a distinction should always be made between the material transformation of the economic conditions of production, which can be determined with the precision of natural science, and the legal, political, religious, aesthetic or philosophical – in short, ideological forms in which men become conscious of this conflict and fight it out. (Marx 1969b: 503–4)

This seminal passage contains three propositions that relate to law. The first is that law, like other aspects of the political superstructure, arises from definite relations of production and the forms of social consciousness forged by those relations. The second is that those relations are not static but are inevitably shattered by the further development of technology and production itself, ultimately leading to social revolution. The third is that law is one of the ideological forms in which people become conscious of the underlying conflicts and 'fight them out'.

As a young man, Marx studied law but soon rejected the 'metaphysics of law', which he saw as divorced from social reality. He turned initially to a study of the philosophy of law and then to the class and economic driving forces of social development. In his 1843 *Critique of Hegel's Philosophy of Law*, he criticised the 'speculative philosophy of law' for its 'disregard of real man'. This notion was elaborated in the Preface to his 1859 *A Contribution to the Critique of Political Economy*:

> Neither legal relations nor political forms can be comprehended whether by themselves or on the basis of a so-called general development of the human mind, but that on the contrary they originate in the material conditions of life, the totality of which Hegel, following the example of English and French thinkers of the eighteenth century, embraces within the term 'civil society'; that the anatomy of this civil society, however, has to be sought in political economy. (Marx 1977: 20)

This conception formed the kernel of his analysis of the role of law throughout his life, although his view was enriched by an exhaustive study of political economy. In *Capital*, his final work, he remarked upon Thomas Hodgskin's 1832 complaint that: 'The power of the capitalist over all the wealth of the country is a complete change in the right of property, and by what law, or series of laws, was it effected?' Marx commented: 'The author should have remembered that revolutions are not made by laws' (Marx 1970b: 702–3). In other words, it was not abstract legality that determined property rights, but the taking of economic and political power by a definite social class, in this instance the capitalist class.

'The Dictatorship of the Proletariat' and the Withering Away of the State

The concept of the dictatorship of the proletariat, in the writings of Marx and Engels, has a distinctly democratic content. It means the temporary and emergency political rule of the working class as the first stage in the transition to a classless, stateless society. This political rule must include the control by the associated producers – the working class, which constitutes the overwhelming majority of society – of the productive forces they themselves have created. In other words, the dictatorship of the proletariat means from the outset the establishment of genuine democracy, with the majority of the population exercising economic power.

The term 'dictatorship of the proletariat' as used by Marx and Engels does not mean tyranny or absolutism or rule by a single individual, a minority or even a single party – but political rule exercised by the majority of the population. This is clear from their analysis of the Paris Commune of 1871, which ruled Paris for a period of 72 days before being militarily crushed. In his 1891 introduction to the re-issue of Marx's analysis of the Commune in *The Civil War in France*, Engels explained that the Commune, which was the first attempt at establishing the dictatorship of the proletariat, began with the 'shattering of the former state power and its replacement by a new and truly democratic one' (Marx 1948: 17).

In *The Civil War in France*, Marx underscored its democratic character. The Commune abolished the 'whole sham of state mysteries and state pretensions' and made public functions the activities of working people instead of 'the hidden attributes of a trained caste'. Its tendency of development, Marx emphasised, was 'a government of the people by the people'. Marx declared the Commune to be a harbinger for a future communist society:

> When the Paris Commune took the management of the revolution in its own hands; when plain ordinary working men for the first time dared to infringe upon the governmental

> privilege of their 'natural superiors', and, under circumstances of unexampled difficulty, performed their work modestly, conscientiously, and efficiently – performed it at salaries the highest of which barely amounted to one-fifth of what, according to high scientific authority, is the minimum required for a secretary to a certain metropolitan school board – the old world writhed in convulsions. (Marx 1948: 58)

In the *Critique of the Gotha Program*, Marx distinguished between the two stages of socialism. In the first, it would be impossible – given the economic, intellectual and moral birthmarks of the old capitalist order from whose womb socialist society emerged – to go beyond the 'narrow horizon of bourgeois right', by which he meant the formal legal equality that invariably masks social inequality. 'Law can never stand higher than the economic order and the cultural development of society conditioned by it', Marx wrote (Marx 1970c: 10). That is, the law would inherently reflect the fact that society could not provide a plentiful and satisfying life for all. Only after individuals were no longer enslaved by others, labour had become a meaningful and enjoyable pursuit rather than a burden, and the productive forces had increased abundantly would the communist ideal be realised.

Central to this view, as first expounded by Marx and Engels in the *Communist Manifesto* and later by Lenin in *The State and Revolution*, was that the state and law must begin to fade away as soon as the dictatorship of the proletariat was established. That is, inherent in the seizure of political power and the establishment of a workers' state was the creation of a unique kind of government that would immediately begin to transfer society's administration to the hands of the population at large.

In the *Communist Manifesto*, Marx and Engels put it this way:

> When, in the course of evolution, the class differences have disappeared and all production has been concentrated in the hands of the associated individuals, the public power will lose its political character. Political power, properly so called, is merely the organised power of one class for oppressing another. If the proletariat during its contest with the bourgeoisie is compelled, by the force of circumstances, to organise itself as a class, if, by means of a revolution, it makes itself the ruling class, and, as such, sweeps away by force the old conditions of production, then it will, along with these conditions, have swept away the conditions for the existence of class antagonisms generally, and will thereby have abolished its own supremacy as a class. In the place of the old bourgeois society, with its classes and class antagonisms, we shall have an association, in which the free development of each is the condition for the free development of all. (Marx 1952: 78)

Thus, after the socialist revolution, the state becomes an anachronism, retained only for the purpose of suppressing the former propertied classes, and immediately begins to fade away, to be replaced by a free association.

In *Anti-Dühring*, Engels described an evolving withering away process: 'The interference of the state power in social relations becomes superfluous in one sphere after another and then becomes dormant of itself' (Engels 1959: 301). He elaborated on this point in a letter to August Bebel in 1875, insisting that the dictatorship of the proletariat would be a state, but at the same time not a state; or, at least, it would be a self-dissolving state.

Engels criticised the German Social Democratic Party for advocating the formation of a 'free people's state':

> As long as the proletariat still *needs* the state, it needs it, not in the interests of freedom, but for the purpose of crushing its antagonists; and as soon as it becomes possible to speak of freedom, then the state, as such, ceases to exist. We would, therefore, suggest that everywhere the word 'state' be replaced by 'community' (*Gemeinwesen*), a fine old German word, which corresponds to the French word 'commune'. (Marx and Engels 1975: 336, emphasis in original)

Engels returned to this theme in his 1891 Preface to Marx's *The Civil War in France*, which described the formation and suppression of the Paris Commune. Engels contrasted the Commune to all previous revolutions, which had replaced one oppressive state by another:

> From the very outset, the Commune was compelled to recognise that the working class, once come to power, could not go on managing with the old state machine; that in order not to lose again its only just conquered supremacy, this working class must, on the one hand, do away with all the old repressive machinery previously used against itself, and, on the other, safeguard itself against its own deputies and officials, by declaring them all, without exception, subject to recall at any time. (Marx 1948: 16)

Apart from the right of recall, Engels reviewed three other measures taken by the Paris Commune to prevent 'careerism': (1) election to all posts, administrative, judicial and educational; (2) restriction of the wages of all officials, high and low, to those paid to workers; and (3) binding mandates for delegates to representative bodies.

Engels scorned the reverence for the state as a font of eternal justice, cultivated under capitalism, and advocated reducing the role of the state as quickly as possible after a socialist revolution:

> In reality, however, the state is nothing but a machine for the oppression of one class by another, and indeed in the democratic republic no less than in the monarchy; and at best an evil inherited by the proletariat after its victorious struggle for class supremacy, whose worst sides the victorious proletariat, just like the Commune, cannot avoid having to lop off at once as much as possible until such time as a generation reared in new, free social conditions is able to throw the entire lumber of the state on the scrap heap. (Marx 1948: 18)

In other words, the state was an 'evil' remnant of class society which had to be dispensed with in order to pave the way for the achievement of communism itself.

Socialism and the State

These conceptions of the withering away of the state were bound up with the nature of socialism itself. For Marx and Engels, a genuine socialist revolution must be a massive social movement in which the working people themselves take control of society. It could not be a putsch, directed by an elite from above, which would then dictate the shape of social change. As Engels wrote in his 1895 Introduction to Marx's *Class Struggle in France*, the experience of previous failed or betrayed revolutions – including the European revolutions of 1848, as well as the ultimate defeat of the Paris Commune of 1871 – indicated that:

> The time of surprise attacks, of revolutions carried through by small conscious minorities at the head of masses lacking consciousness is past. Where it is a question of a complete transformation of the social organisation, the masses themselves must also be in on it, must themselves already have grasped what is at stake, what they are fighting for, body and soul. The history of the last fifty years has taught us that. (Marx and Engels 1990: 520)

This understanding is bound up with the underlying principle developed by Marx and Engels, that of the self-emancipation of the working class. Previously, in the writings of the utopian socialists such as Saint-Simon and Robert Owen, socialism was conceived as the work of an enlightened elite, uplifting the downtrodden. Marx and Engels explained that the working class, which was created by industrial capitalism, was the only revolutionary class and could only liberate humanity from the irrationality and oppression of capitalism by freeing itself. This principle was enshrined as the first premise of the Rules of the First International in 1864: 'Considering, That the emancipation of the working classes must be conquered by the working classes themselves' (Marx 1964: vol. 11, 288).

This classical Marxist approach has profound implications for the transition to socialism after a revolution. Contrary to the 'command economy' view later imposed by the Stalinist bureaucracy in the Soviet Union, Marx insisted that the development of a socialist society would not take place according to a series of prescriptions and rules laid down by an individual, a political party or a governmental authority. Rather, it would develop on the basis of the activity of the members of society who, for the first time in history, consciously regulate and control their own social organisation as part of their daily lives, free from the domination and prescriptions of either the 'free market' or a bureaucratic authority standing over them. Marx explained that the significance of the Paris Commune of 1871 was that it involved:

> [T]he reabsorption of state power by society as one of its own living forces instead of as forces controlling and subduing it, by the popular masses themselves, forming their own force instead of the organised force of their own suppression – the political form of their social emancipation, instead of the artificial force appropriated by their oppressors. (Marx and Engels 1971: 153)

In Marx's view, the precondition for such a society is the development of the social productivity of labour to such a point that the vast bulk of humanity does not have to spend the greater portion of the day merely trying to obtain the resources to live. The overturn of capitalist rule would not see the overnight abolition of the market. The price mechanism would still be needed for a period as a guide in the provision of information regarding the relative costs of alternative production methods. But increasingly it would be made subordinate to and eventually replaced by the conscious regulation of the economy according to a plan, decided on, checked and altered to meet changing circumstances through the involvement of workers and the population as a whole in the process of economic decision-making.

The emergence of the Stalinist bureaucracy in the early 1920s, and its complete usurpation, by 1927, of political power meant that genuine socialist – that is, democratic – planning could never be carried out in the Soviet Union. Such democratic input would have immediately threatened the privileged social position of the bureaucracy and its monopoly of political power. Against the Stalinist bureaucracy, Trotsky argued that the demand for Soviet democracy was an economic necessity not an abstract policy, much less the expression of a pure moral ideal. The establishment of a planned economy, he wrote, was:

> by its very nature insoluble without the daily experience of millions, without their critical review of their own collective experience, without their expression of their needs and demands and could not be carried out within the confines of the official sanctums. (Trotsky 1969: 96)

That is, bureaucratic planning would inevitably lead to terrible mismatches, dislocations, inefficiencies, crises and eventual economic collapse. Democratic participation was an essential prerequisite and ongoing requirement for the harmonious development of a genuinely socialist economy and the all-round growth of productive output, as well as social emancipation. This imperative has enormous implications for law, being a central component of the need to de-legalise social life as far as possible and facilitate the withering away of the state. One of the early acts of the Soviet government was to abolish the old courts, staffed by professional judges and serviced by lawyers, and introduce people's courts, with lay assessors and lay advocates (Head 2007: 91–9).

Lenin and the Transition to a Stateless Society

A theme running through Lenin's relevant writings is that law and the state machinery are not neutral and necessary instruments of social regulation, but historical products of class society. They are essentially mechanisms whereby the most powerful social class enforces its economic and political rule. From the moment of the revolutionary taking of power by the working class and other oppressed masses, leading to the eventual creation of a classless society, the need for law and an enforcing state apparatus begins to fade away.

In *The State and Revolution* – written during the months following the February 1917 revolution that ended the Tsarist dictatorship – Lenin saw the factory and soldiers' committees, the workers' militia and the soviets of workers, soldiers and peasants' deputies thrown up by the revolution as the seeds of a future socialist society. This new social order would be 'no longer a state in the proper sense of the term, for … these contingents of armed men are the masses themselves, the entire people'. In the future, it would be possible to 'cast "bossing" aside and to confine the whole matter to the organisation of the proletarians (as the ruling class), which will hire "workers, foreman and bookkeepers" in the name of the whole of society' (Lenin 1964: 86–95).

Quoting extensively from Marx and Engels, Lenin insisted that a socialist revolution could not adapt the old state machinery of capitalist society to its needs, but would have to abolish the existing legal and bureaucratic apparatus and create a unique new system. This regime would be required to overcome the resistance of the old ruling class; but it would be democratic for the majority of the population and it would be transitional, leading to the emergence of a classless society.

Beirne and Hunt postulated the existence in Lenin's texts of three distinct forms of the dictatorship of the proletariat. The first was the exceptional, quasi-military form required for the immediate seizure and defence of state power. The second was based on the need to completely abolish (smash) and replace the previous state machinery. The third was to actively promote and popularise the social relations and institutions needed for the transition to communism. With this categorisation, they suggest a tension or contradiction between the first two, 'negative' strands in Lenin's conception and the third, more long-term form (Beirne and Hunt 1990: 62).

Yet, Lenin emphasised that even under the temporary dictatorship of the proletariat, the state would immediately *begin* to die away and would *ultimately* 'wither away' altogether when communism was really achieved – that is, when the productive forces of man had developed and been rationally planned to the point where, for all practical purposes, scarcity and inequality were eliminated, and along with them the struggle for individual existence.

'According to Marx, what the proletariat needs is only a state in process of withering away, i.e., so constituted that it will *at once* begin to wither away and cannot help [but] wither away.' Further on he added: 'The proletarian state will begin to wither away *immediately* after its victory, since in a society without class contradictions, the state is unnecessary and impossible' (Lenin 1970b: 37, 43; my emphasis).

Lenin did not expect an isolated revolution in backward Russia, followed by a prolonged capitalist encirclement. Nevertheless, even in the most favourable circumstances, he did not expect the process of withering away to be automatic. Drawing from Marx's writings on the Paris Commune, he advocated the introduction of definite protections against the misuse of official power: political representatives would be paid no more than the average worker's wage; they would be subject to instant recall by their electors; and representatives would be obliged to participate in administrative work (Lenin 1970b: 62–3).

Only with the advent of true communism would the root causes of social antagonisms – private and conflicting ownership of the productive forces, the division of the globe into nation-states and the inherent social inequality produced by the capitalist market – be overcome. By then the great majority of working people would be accustomed to administering their own affairs and those of society without the need for legal and physical coercion. This would eventually dispense with the need for a state – that is, a separate body of politicians, bureaucrats, judges and armed personnel.

Lenin drew a further remarkable conclusion from Marx's analysis – that not only law but the workers' state itself would be 'bourgeois' in the period of transition to communism.

As regards the distribution of products of consumption, bourgeois law, of course, inevitably presupposes the *bourgeois* state as well, because law is nothing without a mechanism capable of *compelling* the observance of legal norms. It follows that under communism not only does bourgeois law remain for a certain time but so does the bourgeois state – without the bourgeoisie (Lenin 1970b: 138; Lenin's emphasis).

Lenin's analysis of the state remaining bourgeois, at least as regards the unequal distribution of production, provides a key to understanding the rise of privileged layers under Stalin, presiding over gross inequality. It points to the inherent danger that the state apparatus, as well as the law it enforces, will be used by a new elite against the interests of the broad masses of people.

Lenin insisted that this danger had to be consciously combated. In 1919, he wrote in his *Theses on Bourgeois Democracy and the Dictatorship of the Proletariat*, which was presented to the founding conference of the Communist International:

> Destruction of state power is the aim set by all socialists, including Marx above all. Genuine democracy, i.e., liberty and equality, is unrealisable unless this aim is achieved. But its practical achievement is possible only through soviet, or proletarian democracy, for by enlisting the mass organisations of the working people in constant and unfailing participation in the administration of the state, it immediately begins to prepare the complete withering away of any state. (Lenin 1987: 157–8)

Trotsky and the Stalinist Dictatorship

Trotsky was one of the foremost leaders of the October 1917 Revolution and of the fight against Stalin's bureaucratisation of Soviet society. His most complete exposition of the relationship between law and the state was written as part of his analysis of the degeneration of the Soviet Union, in *The Revolution Betrayed.* Chapter 3 of that work, entitled 'Socialism and the State', contrasts the evolution of the Soviet state into an ever more totalitarian regime under Stalin with the classical Marxist conception of the withering away of the state.

While basing himself on the writings of Marx, Engels and Lenin on law and the state, Trotsky developed their conceptions by examining them in the context of both the acute contradictions of the Russian Revolution and the increasingly integrated character of world economic life. Trotsky first set out to explain the unavoidable necessity for a socialist revolution to pass through a transitional regime in 'the lowest stage of communism' before the material and political conditions arose for genuine communism:

> The material premise of communism should be so high a development of the productive forces that productive labor, having ceased to be a burden, will not require any goad, and the distribution of life's goods, existing in continual abundance, will not demand – as it does not now in any well-off family or 'decent' boardinghouse – any control except that of education, habit and social opinion. (Trotsky 1991: 39–40)

This would be the case, Trotsky argued, even in an American socialist state, based on the most advanced capitalism. Even under those favourable circumstances, it would not be possible to immediately provide everyone with as much as he or she needed, and therefore everyone would initially have to be spurred or encouraged to produce as much as possible.

Moreover, Trotsky noted that Marx had expected the social revolution to commence in the most economically advanced capitalist countries, such as Germany and Britain. Instead, Russia, one of the least developed countries, had been thrust into the lead. By itself, Russia could not even reach socialism – that is, 'the lowest stage of communism' – because it was still trying to catch up with the capitalist powers. From this, Trotsky drew the conclusion that Soviet Russia could not be classified as a socialist regime, 'but a preparatory regime transitional from capitalism to socialism' (Trotsky 1991: 47).

Trotsky insisted that an essential task of the transitional proletarian dictatorship was to prepare for its own dissolution. Success in this 'fundamental mission' was bound up with overcoming both class distinctions and material contradictions (Trotsky 1991: 52). In *Anti-Dühring*, Engels had written that in order for the state to fade away, 'class domination and the struggle for individual existence' must disappear. But these two preconditions would not necessarily be achieved simultaneously. As the Russian experience demonstrated, the socialisation of the means of production did not automatically remove the struggle for individual existence:

> We have thus taken the first step toward understanding the fundamental contradiction between Bolshevik program and Soviet reality. If the state does not die away, but grows more and more despotic, if the plenipotentiaries of the working class become bureaucratised, and the bureaucracy rises above the new society, this is not for some secondary reason like the psychological relics of the past, etc. but is a result of the iron necessity to give birth to and support a privileged minority so long as it is impossible to guarantee genuine equality. (Trotsky 1991: 55)

Trotsky conceded that the first attempts to create a state cleansed of bureaucratism had suffered from the 'unfamiliarity of the masses with self-government' and 'the lack of qualified workers devoted to socialism'. At the same time, he pointed to more profound difficulties that soon emerged, arising out of the unfavourable global situation:

> That reduction of the state to functions of 'accounting and control', with a continual narrowing of the function of compulsion, demanded by the party program, assumed at least a relative condition of general contentment. Just this necessary condition was lacking. No help came from the West. The power of the democratic Soviets proved cramping, even unendurable, when the task of the day was to accommodate those privileged groups whose existence was necessary for defence, for industry, for technique and science. In this decidedly not 'socialistic' operation, taking from ten and giving to one, there crystallised out and developed a powerful caste of specialists in distribution. (Trotsky 1991: 59)

This clearly had immense implications for the legal system, whose function became, in large measure, the enforcement of social disparities. Trotsky related that the Left Opposition had warned in the early 1930s against accepting the predictions of the Soviet bureaucracy that, within five years, 'the last relics of capitalist elements in our economy will be liquidated':

> You must not limit yourself to the socio-juridical form of relations which are unripe, contradictory, in agriculture still very unstable, abstracting from the fundamental criterion: level of the productive forces. Juridical forms themselves have an essentially different social content in dependence upon the height of the technical level. 'Law can never be higher than the economic structure and the cultural level conditioned by it' (Marx). (Trotsky 1991: 60–61)

Trotsky and Democracy

In earlier writings, Trotsky defended the October 1917 Revolution and the initial actions of the Bolsheviks: including the seizure of power; the dissolution of the Constituent Assembly; the banning of parties that took up arms against the revolution; and other measures taken during the civil war of 1919–21. In *Terrorism and Communism: A Reply to Karl Kautsky*, Trotsky responded to Kautsky, previously a major figure in the Marxist movement, who accused the Bolsheviks of proceeding undemocratically. Members of the Austro-Marxism school – who, in some instances, claimed to be Marxist legal theorists – joined Kautsky's denunciation of the revolution. They included Karl Renner, Otto Bauer, Max Adler, Rudolf Hilferding and Friedrich Adler.

Trotsky insisted that the Soviet Revolution was far more democratic than the parliamentary apparatus defended by Kautsky. He pointed to the innate fraud of capitalist democracy, which leaves the economic power and control over the state apparatus in the grip of a ruling elite. Trotsky argued that this reality gave the working masses no other way but revolution to take charge of society:

> Violent revolution has become a necessity precisely because the imminent requirements of history are helpless to find a road through the apparatus of parliamentary democracy. The capitalist bourgeois calculates: 'while I have in my hands lands, factories, workshops, banks; while I possess newspaper, universities, schools; while – and this is most important of all – I retain control of the army: the apparatus of democracy, however you reconstruct it, will remain obedient to my will. (Trotsky 1975: 58)

Trotsky examined democracy from a theoretical and historical standpoint. He pointed to the degeneration of the democratic conception in the hands of the capitalist class and its jurisprudential theorists:

> As a battle cry against feudalism, the demand for democracy had a progressive character. As time went on, however, the metaphysics of natural law (the theory of formal democracy) began to show its reactionary side – the establishment of an ideal standard to control the real demands of the labouring masses and the revolutionary parties … In the real conditions of life, in the economic process, in social relations, in their way of life, people became more and more unequal; dazzling luxury was accumulated at one pole, poverty and hopelessness

> at the other. But in the sphere of the legal edifice of the state, these glaring contradictions disappeared, and there penetrated only unsubstantial legal shadows. (Trotsky 1975: 60–61)

Trotsky related the need for the dictatorship of the proletariat in the transition to communism to the political and economic tasks involved in overthrowing capitalism. He argued that genuine socialism and communism were impossible to achieve without the free and creative involvement of all people. The bureaucratic police state erected by Stalin was not only an affront to socialist democracy but also a suffocating barrier to the development of the productive and cultural capacities of society:

> The socialistic economy must be directed to ensuring the satisfaction of every possible human need. Such a problem it is impossible to solve by way of commands only. The greater the scale of the productive forces, the more involved the technique; the more complex the needs, then the more indispensable is a wide and free creative initiative of the organised producers and consumers. The socialist culture implies the utmost development of the human personality. Progress along this path is made possible not through a standardised cringing before irresponsible 'leaders', but only through a fully conscious and critical participation by all in a socialistic creative activity. The youthful generations stand in need of independence, which is wholly consistent with a firm leadership but rules out any police regimentation. Thus the bureaucratic system in crushing the Soviets and the party is coming ever more clearly into opposition with the basic needs of economic and cultural development. (Trotsky 1991: 9)

In line with Marx and Engels, Trotsky's emphasis was on the self-liberation of the entire population. This was the essence of communism, he insisted. Therefore, the task of the Soviet state was to encourage, not stifle, the maximum degree of conscious, well-informed and independent participation in political and administrative affairs.

These principles are maintained by the Fourth International, the world party founded by Trotsky to continue the struggle for Marxism against the betrayal of the Russian Revolution carried out by the Stalinist bureaucracy and its affiliated communist parties around the globe. The *Statement of Principles* of the Socialist Equality Party, the Australian section of the International Committee of the Fourth International, for example, states:

> The establishment of workers' power requires far more than the election of socialist candidates to the existing institutions of the bourgeois state. New forms and structures of genuine participatory democracy – arising in the course of revolutionary mass struggles and representative of the working-class majority of the population – must be developed as the foundations of a workers' government, that is, a government of, for, and by the workers. The policy of such a government, as it introduces those measures essential for the socialist transformation of economic life, will be to encourage and actively promote a vast expansion of democratic working-class participation in, and control over, decision-making processes. It will favour the abolition of existing institutions that either curtail democratic processes or serve as centres of conspiracy against the people (such as vice-regal representation, the standing army, the police, and the entire security-intelligence apparatus). These and other

necessary changes of a profoundly democratic character, to be determined by the masses themselves, are possible only in the context of the mass mobilisation of the working class, imbued with socialist consciousness. (Socialist Equality Party 2010: para. 18)

Chapter 7
Britain: 'Civil Contingencies' and Prerogative Powers

In Britain today, no less than in previous centuries, wide-ranging powers exist to declare emergencies. This can potentially take place under legislation, common law, prerogative powers or the doctrine of martial law. Although numbers of scholars have argued that the non-statutory powers have been curbed and subjected to greater democratic or judicial scrutiny and control in recent decades, the political and legal record speaks otherwise. Not only has the most sweeping emergency powers legislation in recent British history been introduced, but great care has been taken to preserve all the ancient and amorphous non-statutory powers derived from the British monarchy.

Britain provides a classic illustration of Lenin's observation that capitalist states, regardless of their democratic or 'rule of law' pretensions, invariably leave open recourse to dictatorial forms of rule to counter what are regarded as existential threats, notably political threats from within the mass of the population.

Potentially authoritarian powers remain, both via and beyond the legislation – the Civil Contingencies Act 2004 – that was introduced to ostensibly cover the field of emergency preparations, declarations and powers. In the first place, that Act provides what scholars have described as the 'most powerful and extensive' peacetime emergency powers ever enacted (Walker and Broderick 2006: 188).

Secondly, that Act, while itself containing vast powers (reviewed below), did not completely replace other far-reaching legislative provisions, notably the Emergency Powers Act 1964. Thirdly, the 2004 Act itself alludes to the continued application of royal prerogative powers. Section 22(3) stipulates that emergency regulations can make any provision that would be possible through an Act of Parliament or the royal prerogative.

Fourthly, in a 2009 review of the prerogative powers, the Ministry of Justice concluded, and the government of Prime Minister Gordon Brown readily agreed, that the possibility of using the prerogative powers should remain open. On the pretext that urgent emergency scenarios could make compliance with the Act's regulation-making procedures 'impractical', the review reached the conclusion that the Act, despite its sweeping provisions, would have to be cast aside. 'In practice, therefore', the report stated, 'the Royal prerogative might need to be relied on in place of the Civil Contingencies Act in particularly extreme and urgent circumstances' (Cabinet Office 2009: paras 70–72).

As reviewed below, this declaration of the need to bypass the Civil Contingencies Act was part of a wider retention of the prerogative powers to deal with both major domestic emergencies and decisions to declare war or conduct military interventions overseas.

Having already examined the immense scope of such executive powers and their exploitation historically in Chapters 2 and 3, we need to first consider the extent to which they have been either augmented or supplanted by the Civil Contingencies Act.

Civil Contingencies Act

Officially, the objectives of the Civil Contingencies Act 2004 were stated to be:

- To create a modern framework for coordinating contingency planning and response at the local level, codifying existing arrangements.
- To enhance cooperation and understanding in support of a regional level capability.
- To modernise the legislation under which the Government can respond to extreme emergency situations to turn it into a usable tool fit for the twenty-first century (Cabinet Office 2003).

The legislation was said to be responding to a need to clarify and reform the law:

> Whilst the use of the prerogative and common law to deal with matters of crisis and disturbance is well established, there is also wide agreement amongst observers as to the need for both clarification and reform. (Walker and Broderick 2006: 44)

In reality, far from 'clarification and reform', the legislation created a new Pandora's box of executive powers without overriding the existing murky prerogative and common law provisions.

The Act empowers 'Her Majesty' by an Order in Council (in ordinary times, this means senior cabinet ministers) to issue sweeping emergency regulations in any event that 'threatens serious damage to human welfare' or 'serious damage to the environment' or 'war or terrorism, which threatens serious damage to the security of the United Kingdom' (section 19).

Emergency powers can be triggered whenever the governing authorities, acting in the name of Her Majesty in Council, are 'satisfied' that an emergency has occurred, is occurring or is about to occur. The regulations can suspend, modify or override any other Act of Parliament, with the sole exception of the Human Rights Act 1998 (Walker and Broderick 2006: 44–5). Even statutes regarded as essential to civil liberties and basic constitutional rights – such as the Magna Carta 1297, the Bill of Rights 1688, the Parliament Acts 1911–49 and the Representation of the People Act 1983 – can be swept aside (Walker and Broderick 2006: 192).

Regulations can last for up to 30 days, and can be renewed. They must be laid before parliament 'as soon as is reasonably practicable' and shall lapse after seven days unless both houses of parliament approve them; but in the meantime their effect is immediate. Moreover, even these limited provisos would mean little if parliament could not or did not meet. Moreover, the Secretary of State has the power to rule whether an event or situation poses a threat to human welfare, and to amend the Act itself, subject to subsequent parliamentary approval.

Although the Blair government presented the Act as one concerned primarily with responding to disasters, the 2003 Queen's Speech specifically referred to terrorism, and the proposal was also driven by concerns about civil unrest, including the eruption of fuel price protests and pickets outside oil refineries in 2000 (Walker and Broderick 2006: xiii, 47).

The definitions of emergency are extensive, considerably wider than the previous provisions under the Emergency Powers Act, and allow for politically 'interventionist stances' toward potential crises (Walker and Broderick 2006: 63–76). Possible threats to 'human welfare' extend to 'damage to property' and disruption to supplies, communications or transport. No criteria are provided for the key tests of 'serious damage to human welfare' and 'war or terrorism, which threatens serious damage to the security of the United Kingdom'. 'Serious' is not defined; neither is 'security'. Ministers are given powers to specify that certain situations or events are emergencies.

Once an emergency has been declared, the authorities can assume 'almost boundless power' (Walker and Broderick 2006: 161). They can, among other things, prohibit assemblies, ban movement, create offences, deploy the armed forces and confer emergency powers on any individual. There are no specific powers of arrest or detention without trial, but the Act's sponsors refused to rule out such detention, which the courts have in the past been prepared to accept, even in peacetime 'civil emergencies' (see *Attorney-General of St Christopher, Nevis and Anguilla v Reynolds* [1980] AC 637).

In a briefing on the legislation, Liberty (the National Council for Civil Liberties) called it 'the most powerful piece of peacetime legislation ever proposed in the UK', and warned that 'it seeks to grant the Government unprecedented powers to make emergency regulations which are unavailable under existing laws'. Liberty expressed concern that 'it is in times of emergency that citizens' fundamental rights are at greatest risk' (Liberty 2004: para 4). Liberty also noted that the government had shown an increased willingness to declare an emergency, citing the declaration of a 'technical' emergency following the September 2001 attacks in the United States. This declaration enabled the government to derogate from article 5 of the European Convention on Human Rights, thereby permitting detention without trial under the Anti-Terrorism Crime and Security Act 2001 (Liberty 2004: para 5).

One detailed study of the Civil Contingencies Act described it as 'the most powerful and extensive peacetime legislation ever enacted', containing within it 'the tools for dismantling civil society', with 'the potential to inflict terrible damage on the constitution of the United Kingdom' (Walker and Broderick 2006: 188, 214). The authors also drew attention to the slim likelihood of any effective parliamentary or judicial review of actions taken under emergency powers. In effect, the legislation provides the framework for extra-constitutional and dictatorial forms of rule, backed by military force.

Nevertheless, official policy insists, and the reactions of successive governments have confirmed that even greater emergency powers continue to exist. In fact, these governmental responses indicate a disinclination to invoke the Civil Contingencies Act because of the perceived limitations and accountability mechanisms contained within it (Walker 2014b: 217–23). In other words, despite the breadth of the powers contained in the Act, and the ease with which they can be invoked, governments and state authorities prefer to leave open the option of utilising even more arbitrary and ill-defined powers.

Emergency Definitions and Powers under the Civil Contingencies Act

The Civil Contingencies Act has different definitions of emergencies in Part 1, which covers contingency planning and arrangements, and Part 2, which involves the powers and responsibilities invoked during emergencies. Section 1 of Part 1 itself confers three meanings to the word 'emergency':

1. Meaning of Emergency
   (1) In this Part 'emergency' means
      (a) an event or situation which threatens serious damage to human welfare in a place in the United Kingdom,
      (b) an event or situation which threatens serious damage to the environment of a place in the United Kingdom, or
      (c) war, or terrorism, which threatens serious damage to the security of the United Kingdom.
   (2) For the purposes of subsection (1) (a) an event or situation threatens damage to human welfare only if it involves, causes or may cause
      (a) loss of human life,
      (b) human illness or injury,
      (c) homelessness
      (d) damage to property,
      (e) disruption of a supply of money, food, water, energy or fuel,
      (f) disruption of a system of communication
      (g) disruption of facilities for transport, or
      (h) disruption of services relating to health.
   (3) For the purposes of subsection (1)(b) an event or situation threatens damage to the environment only if it involves, causes or may cause
      (a) Contamination of land, water or air with biological, chemical or radio-active matter, or
      (b) Disruption or destruction of plant life or animal life.

This definition is extremely broad. Apart from the vagueness of the term 'serious', the definition of 'human welfare' would permit an emergency to be construed in circumstances that go far beyond threats to life and safety. Disruption of health services, for example, could cover a nurses' strike, or disruption of transport facilities could cover industrial action by railway workers.

Moreover, section 1(4) permits a minister to declare, by order, that a specified event or situation falls within any of paragraphs (a) to (c) of subsection (1). A minister can also amend subsection (2) to provide that if an event or situation involves or causes disruption of a specified supply, system, facility or service, it is to be treated as threatening damage to human welfare.

Subsection (2) only marginally limits the words 'human welfare'. According to Walker and Broderick, this may have been due to a fear that the term 'might be taken to include such esoteric and immeasurable aspects of the human condition as spiritual welfare'

(Walker and Broderick 2006: 64). Likewise, subsection (3) places some slight limit on the term 'environment'. No such limitation at all applies to 'war', which could include various forms of armed conflict.

Under subsection (5) the event or situation can be inside or outside the United Kingdom. The qualifier in subsection 1(a) and (b) means it must affect a 'place' within the United Kingdom. 'Place' is obviously a rather broad term, rather than locality or region. No such qualifier is attached to subsection 1(c), covering war or terrorism.

By virtue of section 18, terrorism is given the same meaning as the Terrorism Act 2000, which is:

> the use or threat of action where it involves serious violence against a person, involves serious damage to property, endangers a person's life, other than that of the person committing the action, creates a serious risk to the health or safety of the public or a section of the public, or is designed seriously to interfere with or seriously to disrupt an electronic system. (Terrorism Act s 1)

The use or threat of action must be designed to influence the government or an international governmental organisation, or to intimidate the public or a section of the public; and the use or threat of action must be made for the purpose of advancing a political, religious racial or ideological cause.

The reference to 'threat', like the term 'threatened damage' in s 1, opens the way for emergencies to be designated even where no damage has yet occurred or has not been proven to be likely to occur. This terminology could possibly be explained as designating the purpose and objects of the Act to place obligations on emergency services and local authorities to assess risks and provide contingency plans. Part 1 also requires increased cooperation and information sharing between different emergency services ('Category 1 responders') and also non-emergency services ('Category 2 responders') that might have a role in an emergency, such as electricity companies.

In broad terms, Category 1 responders must assess the risks of an emergency occurring; maintain plans to respond to an emergency; publish the assessments and plans in so far as this is 'necessary or desirable'; and maintain arrangements to warn, inform and advise members of the public in the event of an emergency. They must also devise and maintain 'business continuity plans' to allow their operations to continue in the event of an emergency. These requirements are further elaborated in the Civil Contingencies Act 2004 (Contingency Planning) Regulations 2005. These plans are also subject to publication objectives and guidelines that include instruction to not alarm the public unnecessarily.

A Minister of the Crown may also issue guidance, and section 9 allows for monitoring by the government, giving ministers power to require a person to provide information about action taken or not taken under the Act. The duties of Category 2 responders are mainly to cooperate with, or to provide information to, Category 1 responders.

Part 2 of the Act is directed at when an emergency is no longer a threat but an actuality. Section 19(1) defines 'emergency' in the same sweeping manner as the purposes of Part 1. One difference is that for Part 1 the geographical context is 'place', while in Part 2 it is a 'part or region'. This is said to show the intent of Part 1 to focus on local arrangements, while Part 2 warrants a broader area of emergency.

Regions are specified in Schedule 1 to the Regional Development Agencies Act 1998. There are nine such regions: East Midlands, Eastern, London, North East, North West, South East, South West, West Midlands and Yorkshire and the Humber.

Again, the Secretary of State can amend the legislation by providing that, in so far as an event or situation involves or causes disruption of a specified supply, system, facility or service, it can be treated as threatening damage to human welfare.

Part 2 is said to involve a 'triple lock' system, relating to seriousness, necessity and geographical proportionality. Under section 21, conditions precedent to using the emergency powers are: that an emergency has occurred, is occurring or is about to occur (subsection (2)); it is necessary to make provision for the purpose of dealing with the emergency (subsection (3)); and the need for the provision is urgent (subsection (4)). Subsections (5) and (6) specify that it must be the case that existing legislation cannot be relied upon without the risk of serious delay, or it is not possible without the risk of serious delay to ascertain whether the existing legislation can be relied upon, or the existing legislation might be insufficiently effective.

Each of these 'locks' is, however, sufficiently vague to allow a government or state authorities to interpret them as they see fit.

Emergency regulations may be made under section 20 by the Order in Council if Her Majesty is satisfied that the conditions under s 21 are satisfied. If this is not possible – due, for example, to loss of communication with the Queen – a senior Minister of the Crown may make the regulations again under the conditions of s 21. Interestingly 'senior Minister of the Crown' includes the Commissioners of Her Majesty's Treasury, an anachronistic term which includes 'mere Government Whips in the House of Commons' (Walker and Broderick 2006: 155).

The emergency regulations themselves consist of any provision 'appropriate' for the purpose of preventing, controlling or mitigating an aspect or effect of an emergency. An extensive list of permitted purposes for regulations:

(a) protecting human life, health or safety;
(b) treating human illness or injury;
(c) protecting or restoring property;
(d) protecting or restoring a supply of money, food, water, energy or fuel;
(e) protecting or restoring a system of communication;
(f) protecting or restoring facilities for transport;
(g) protecting or restoring the provision of services relating to health;
(h) protecting or restoring the activities of banks or other financial institutions;
(i) preventing, containing or reducing the contamination of land, water or air;
(j) preventing, reducing or mitigating the effects of disruption or destruction of plant life or animal life;
(k) protecting or restoring activities of parliament, of the Scottish parliament, of the Northern Ireland Assembly or of the National Assembly for Wales; or
(l) protecting or restoring the performance of public functions.

Under subsection 22(3), any power that parliament could confer by Act or by exercise of prerogative power is bestowed upon the regulation maker. A non-exhaustive list follows. This includes requisition and confiscation and destruction of property; requiring or prohibiting movement to or from specified places; and the creation of offences of failure to comply with provisions or orders.

In their breadth of purposes and powers, these can only be described as police-state provisions. Regulations can be promulgated that override basic legal and democratic rights. The regulator need only 'be satisfied' regarding the appropriateness, proportionality and geographical scope of the regulations. Such a test is extremely difficult to enforce via judicial review.

There are few specific limits. Subsection 23(3) forbids forcible military service or prohibiting or enabling participation in relation to industrial action, and subsection (4) disallows imprisonment exceeding three months and heavy fines. Regulations lapse after 30 days but can be renewed. Under section 27, 'as soon as reasonably practicable', the regulations must be laid before parliament. The regulations then lapse after seven days unless adopted by a resolution from each House.

Section 25 covers the establishment of a tribunal, after consultation with the Council on Tribunals (subsection (1)), unless there is an urgent need. Tribunals may be set up to decide issues devolving from the regulations, for example appeals against quarantine measures or the issuing of licences or the assessment of compensation. This amounts to window dressing because a tribunal cannot overrule a minister.

While draft plans and emergency assessments under Part 1 are generally available to the public, there is no indication that draft regulations under Part 2 will be open to public scrutiny. According to the Joint Parliamentary Committee on the Civil Contingencies Bill, this is for three reasons: (1) the need for frequent change and amendment; (2) drafts are only a starting point; and (3) to conceal potential weaknesses and targets in the plans from terrorist agencies or 'disruptive' industrial action groups (Joint Committee 2003: Appendix 9). It is hard to reconcile the third point with the rule of law, and the first two points seem to hardly be a justification to avoid public debate.

In summary, the Act gives governments virtually unlimited powers to declare emergencies and adopt extraordinary regulations.

Other Legislative Powers

Despite the Civil Contingencies Act purporting to tie all emergency provisions together, other legislative frameworks provide for emergency powers. For example, in the case of a nuclear emergency, the Radioactive Substances Act 1993 and the Radiation (Emergency Preparedness and Public Information) Regulations 2001 set out the roles, powers and responsibilities of Nuclear Response Organisations. Further provisions specifying 'emergency' powers include the Energy Act 1976, section 3; the Railways Act 1993, section 118; the Animal Health Act 2002; the Food and Environment Protection Act 1985, Part 1; and a 'host of other examples' (Walker 2014b: 222).

Agencies that have separate legislative schemes include:

- Department of Health (DH)
- Health Protection Agency (HPA)
- Department for Environment, Food and Rural Affairs (Defra)
- Government Office for Science
- Environment Agency
- Food Standards Agency
- Government Decontamination Service (GDS)
- Cabinet Office
- Home Office
- Ministry of Defence (MOD)
- Department for Communities and Local Government (CLG)
- Representatives of the Devolved Administrations
- Met Office.

Numerous other agencies, including traffic regulators and education institutions, can also invoke pieces of legislation to trigger emergency protocols. There is also the Centre for the Protection of National Infrastructure (CPNI), which monitors 'critical infrastructure' and provides the government with annual confidential National Risk Assessments, covering three broad categories: natural events, major accidents and malicious attacks. A Cabinet Office Sector Resilience Plan for Critical National Infrastructure draws up plans, but these have been described as 'woefully brief' and lacking in indication of a role for Part 2 of the Civil Contingencies Act (Walker 2014b: 216).

The result of all this, according to one study, is 'club government' of emergency powers, which is informal, oligarchic and secretive (Moran 2003: 4).

Calling Out the Armed Forces

Over and beyond the Civil Contingencies Act, British government and military policy assumes that considerable powers exist to mobilise armed troops internally to deal with a variety of threats to 'public safety' or 'order'. The 2005 Ministry of Defence document *Operations in the UK: The Defence Contribution to Resilience* sets out policy guidelines for Military Aid to the Civil Power (MACP). It states:

> Based under common law, MACP is the provision of military assistance (armed if appropriate) to the Civil Power in its maintenance of law, order and public safety, using specialist capabilities or equipment, in situations beyond the capability of the Civil Power. (Ministry of Defence 2005: 4-1)

According to the guidelines, the legal basis for instructing armed forces personnel to provide MACP in the UK can be one, or a combination, of the following:

- Section 2 of the Emergency Powers Act 1964 (plus the Emergency Powers (Amendment) Act (Northern Ireland) 1964) enables the Defence Council to issue instructions to undertake 'work of urgent national importance'.

- Part 2 of the Civil Contingencies Act 2004 empowers the Queen or a senior minister, in particular circumstances, to issue emergency regulations which can in turn enable the Defence Council to deploy the armed forces.
- A common law tenet indicates that citizens should provide reasonable support to the police if requested to do so. All members of the armed forces have a duty to provide the support normally expected of the ordinary citizen. The same common law tenet enables a Defence Minister to direct the armed forces, on a case by case basis, to provide specialist support to the police.
- Queen's Regulations place an additional duty on military commanders to act on their own responsibility without a request by a civil agency where, 'in exceptional circumstances, a grave and sudden emergency has arisen, which in the opinion of the Commander demands his immediate intervention to protect life or property'.

Thus, the guidelines assume or assert that, alongside specific statutory provisions, there are potentially far-reaching common law and prerogative or executive powers to justify armed interventions. These can be invoked to deal with 'a varying range of criminal and malicious activities'. The request procedures envisage MACP operations for criminal investigations and major events (Ministry of Defence 2005: 4-2, 4B-2).

The Ministry of Defence suggests that the Emergency Powers Act and the Civil Contingencies Act 'provide a stronger basis for' MACP activity than the common law. It insists that the common law imposes a duty on every citizen, including service personnel, to assist in the enforcement of law and order when requested, where it is reasonable to do so, and that this requirement forms the 'main basis for the MACP mechanism'. However, the guidelines state that this duty is 'difficult to formulate and cannot be relied upon in all circumstances to provide a legal basis for a response, especially if commanders use it without Defence Council authorisation' (Ministry of Defence 2005: 4-2).

The Ministry of Defence's reference to the common law duty to provide military aid being 'difficult to formulate' points to the uncertain scope and character of this power and the associated legal rights and liabilities of called-out service personnel. As noted in Chapter 3, the last judicial guidance on this subject was provided in 1832 in *R v Pinney* ((1832) 170 ER 962). The mayor of Bristol and nine aldermen were unsuccessfully prosecuted by the Attorney-General for breaching their common law duty to assemble a sufficient force to put down three days of riots. A military major had advised the mayor that it would be 'imprudent to put arms in the hands of young troops'. But in the related case, *Charge to the Bristol Grand Jury*, Lord Tindal insisted that soldiers had a duty, as citizens, on their own authority, to do their utmost to 'put down riot and tumult'. Two officers who had refused to order the troops to fire without a magistrate's sanction were found guilty of neglect of duty, causing one to commit suicide (Babington 1990: 84).

In the 1890s, a parliamentary committee endorsed the common law duty. The 1893 *Report of the Select Committee on the Featherstone Riots* said resort to military assistance must be the 'last expedient' of the civil authorities, but when such a call was made, 'to refuse such assistance is in law a misdemeanour' (Babington 1990: 122–32).

Royal Prerogative Powers

Apart from referring to the Queen's Regulations, *Operations in the UK* makes no mention of the prerogative powers of the Crown. The relationship between these and the asserted common law tenet remains unclear. The royal prerogative powers are vast in scope – they are said to cover any situation not otherwise dealt with by statute – and effectively unreviewable by the courts (*Burmah Oil Co. Ltd. v Lord Advocate* [1965] AC 101; Whelan 1985: 287).

In *Chandler v Director of Public Prosecutions* ([1964] AC 763, 800), Lord Hodson stated: 'The Crown has, and this is not disputed, the right as head of State to decide in peace and war the disposition of its armed forces.' In *Burmah Oil Co Ltd v Lord Advocate* ([1965] AC 75, 100), Lord Reid said: 'There is no doubt that control of the armed forces has been left to the prerogative … subject to the power of Parliament to withhold supply and refuse to continue legislation essential for the maintenance of a standing army.'

Thus, some three centuries after the struggle for parliamentary and civilian supremacy over the British monarchy – and in a political system that professes to be democratic – the power of the government to call out the military still rests on vestiges of regal authority. In the words of one scholar, the prerogative power to control disorder 'is a dangerous mystery unwarranted in a democratic society' (Whelan 1985: 287). More to the point, such power is incompatible with genuine democracy.

Ordinarily, the Defence Council, which consists of military leaders as well as government ministers and officials, exercises the prerogative powers on behalf of the Crown. The council is based in the Ministry of Defence and is normally chaired by the Secretary of State for Defence.

These powers and arrangements operate above and beyond the Civil Contingencies Act. That is, they can be instigated without any formal declaration of a state of emergency under the Act (Walker and Broderick 2006: 251). Taken as a whole, considerable legal powers are said to exist to authorise calling out the troops to deal with a wide variety of alleged threats to society – including civil unrest, industrial action and acts of terrorism – and these measures have been augmented by the 'almost boundless power' that can be asserted under the 2004 Act.

Successive British governments have deliberately left open recourse to prerogative powers. Prime Minister Gordon Brown's government initially professed enthusiasm for constitutional reform to limit the royal prerogative powers (Walker 2014b: 216). It was under intense public pressure to do so, particularly with regard to the powers to declare war or commit troops overseas, after the exposure of the lies and fabrications of 'weapons of mass destruction' used by the US administration, the Blair government and other allied governments to justify the 2003 invasion of Iraq. However, ultimately, no abolition or even formal restriction of the prerogative powers took place (Blick 2014).

The final paper in the Brown government's review, *The Governance of Britain: Review of the Executive Royal Prerogative Powers – Final Report* (issued in 2009), declared that there were shortcomings in the Civil Contingencies Act because: 'The time needed to make emergency regulations under the 2004 Act could make compliance impractical in some emergency scenarios.' Therefore, it argued: 'These [prerogative] powers may provide a vital ability to act where there is insufficient time to put statutory provisions in place' (Cabinet Office 2009: paras 70, 75). The Brown administration accepted this recommendation, and the subsequent Cameron government showed no inclination to change that stance (Walker 2014b: 216).

Walker concluded that because of the availability of the prerogative powers, Part 2 of the Civil Contingencies Act, which has yet to be invoked, became the subject of official disdain and neglect. One reason was 'disinclination to comply with the mechanisms for limitation and accountability in Part 2' (Walker 2014b: 218–19). To substantiate his analysis, Walker compared the Act's provisions to some of those in terrorism legislation drafted in 2011, which envisaged, for example, 'enhanced' powers of detention and other deprivations of liberty during undefined 'exceptional circumstances'. Despite some parliamentary qualms about the arbitrary and open-ended character of that phrase, the government refused to insert a definition (Walker 2014b: 219–22).

A Brown government discussion paper, *The Governance of Britain*, noted that the executive had for hundreds of years 'been able to exercise authority in the name of the Monarch without the people and their elected representatives in their Parliament being consulted'. It concluded that such an arrangement was 'no longer appropriate in a modern democracy' (Secretary of State for Justice and Lord Chancellor 2007: para 14). The paper proposed a review to consider whether the royal prerogative as a whole should be 'codified or brought under statutory control' (Secretary of State for Justice and Lord Chancellor 2007: para 50). Yet, it specifically ruled out changes to the status of the 'legal prerogatives of the Crown or the Monarch's constitutional or personal prerogatives' (Secretary of State for Justice and Lord Chancellor 2007: para 24).

The only conclusion that can be drawn is that the ruling establishment in Britain is determined to retain unfettered emergency powers to deal with serious political, economic and social upheavals. For all the references to 'rule of law' and 'democracy', great care has been taken to preserve the royal prerogative powers, described by Dicey – one of the traditional authorities on the 'rule of law' and the British Constitution – as 'the residue of discretionary or arbitrary authority, which at any given time is legally left in the hands of the Crown' (Dicey 2005: 282).

There exists no definitive, let alone legally binding, list of prerogative powers. No comprehensive account is even provided in constitutional law texts, such as that produced by Bradley and Ewing (Bradley and Ewing 2010: Chapter 12). As part of the Brown government's review, the Ministry of Justice produced something approaching an official outline. It had four categories, with direct or potential relevance to emergencies. 'Ministerial prerogative powers' included the deployment of the armed forces and confiscation of private property (in times of 'grave national emergency'). 'Constitutional/personal prerogatives' featured dismissals of governments and an emergency right to 'require the personal services of subjects in case of imminent danger'. The third and fourth groups were 'powers exercised by the Attorney General' and 'archaic prerogative powers'. These covered such things as imposition of service in the Royal Navy and wartime internment of 'enemy aliens' (Cabinet Office 2009: 30–34).

Another review of prerogative powers related to the military found many that, while depicted as disused and 'obsolete', have not been abolished. They include the right to conscript subjects into the armed forces, billet members of the armed forces in people's homes and impose martial law (McBain 2011, 2012).

The refusal of governments to abolish these powers points to the fact that, far from being redundant, they may in fact be revived and utilised under conditions of acute domestic social tensions and/or war.

Martial Law, Immunity and Lawlessness

As reviewed in Chapter 3, British law also combines other legacies of the monarchy and absolutism, notably the doctrine of martial law, with traditional recourse to such extra-legal measures as the granting of indemnities to retrospectively validate unlawful repression and the invocation of rules to block legal challenges to lawless government actions.

Not only does martial law remain an option that has never been conclusively repudiated by legislation or judicial rulings, but also doubts exist about whether the ordinary courts have jurisdiction to decide whether a state of disorder warranted martial law. According to one authority, legal action could be brought against the military for manifestly unreasonable conduct and possibly for unnecessary use of force against people or property, but the law is unclear (de Smith 1981: 512). In any case, the legal uncertainty is academic because indemnity legislation would almost certainly be passed to exonerate those who acted in supposed good faith to suppress an uprising (de Smith 1981: 514). As noted in Chapter 3, the British parliament passed such an Act of Indemnity to cover the 1920 declaration of martial law in areas of Ireland (Rowe and Whelan 1985: 200).

It is likewise with unlawful acts of surveillance, harassment, violence or intimidation. As noted in the Introduction, those allegedly affected by such acts in Britain have found it almost impossible to prosecute or obtain redress for such conduct. Courts have dismissed legal actions on various grounds, including potential damage to 'national security' or 'international relations'. Thus, as outlined in one case study, in 2012, the High Court refused judicial review of a government decision to pass intelligence information from the Government Communications Headquarters (GCHQ) to aid drone assassinations, including of UK citizens, by the United States in Pakistan's northwest region. The court ruled that a legal challenge, accusing the government of conspiracy to murder, would compel the government to express a definitive view on the legal issues, 'complicating and damaging relations with our most important bilateral ally and, in consequence, damaging the United Kingdom's security' (*Khan v SSFCA [2012] EWHC 3728 (Admin)* at [17]).

Such rulings are a chilling indication of the readiness of the courts to embrace and rubberstamp draconian, murderous and repressive government activities, regardless of their apparent illegality, in the interests of 'national security' and military alliances.

Chapter 8

The United States: Presidential Powers and Declarations of Emergency

Despite its origins in the revolutionary overthrow of British tyranny, and the later adoption of a Bill of Rights that seeks to defend core legal and democratic rights against arbitrary government power, the United States has also increasingly seen an extraordinary expansion of executive powers. Both by pseudo-legal arguments and surreptitious actions, successive administrations have asserted emergency or emergency-type powers that are potentially dictatorial.

The Constitution has been wilfully interpreted in many different ways to insist that the president and the executive have emergency powers that do not need to be given by Congress, or even later approved by it. There have been actions and orders of past presidents that have been heavily criticised as being unconstitutional, yet their examples have been followed and extended by subsequent administrations, including that of Barack Obama.

According to a Congressional Research Service report, *National Emergency Powers*, issued on 18 September 2001, there are limits and restraints upon the president in his exercise of emergency powers. With the exception of the habeas corpus clause, the Constitution makes no allowance for the suspension of any of its provisions during a national emergency. Nonetheless, presidents have extensive emergency powers:

> Federal law provides a variety of powers for the President to use in response to crisis, exigency, or emergency circumstances threatening the nation. Moreover, they are not limited to military or war situations. Some of these authorities, deriving from the Constitution or statutory law, are continuously available to the President with little or no qualification. Others – statutory delegations from Congress – exist on a standby basis and remain dormant until the President formally declares a national emergency. These delegations or grants of power authorize the President to meet the problems of governing effectively in times of crisis. Under the powers delegated by such statutes, the President may seize property, organize and control the means of production, seize commodities, assign military forces abroad, institute martial law, seize and control all transportation and communication, regulate the operation of private enterprise, restrict travel, and, in a variety of ways, control the lives of United States citizens. (Congressional Research Service 2001: 1)

The Congressional Research Service report also pointed to political factors that had led to perceived limitations on presidential powers:

> Disputes over the constitutionality or legality of the exercise of emergency powers are judicially reviewable. Indeed, both the judiciary and Congress, as co-equal branches, can

> restrain the executive regarding emergency powers. So can public opinion. Furthermore, since 1976, the President has been subject to certain procedural formalities in utilizing some statutorily delegated emergency authority. The National Emergencies Act (50 U.S.C. 1601–1651) eliminated or modified some statutory grants of emergency authority, required the President to declare formally the existence of a national emergency and to specify what statutory authority, activated by the declaration, would be used, and provided Congress a means to countermand the President's declaration and the activated authority being sought. (Congressional Research Service 2001: i)

A closer examination reveals that these congressional oversights, along with scrutiny by the courts, have been incapable of providing any check on presidential power.

This chapter has four parts. The first examines how the federal executive power has been interpreted. While the events of September 11, 2001 marked a turning point in the way extensive emergency powers have been applied and used, previous presidents also ordered actions with little regard for either their constitutional validity or approval by Congress. Occasional formal reprimands by the Supreme Court have done little to restrain presidential actions.

The second part examines the National Emergencies Act, adopted in 1976. It required a president to declare formally the existence of a national emergency and provided Congress a means to countermand the declaration; but Congress has never chosen to exercise that power.

The third part reviews the creation and function of the Federal Emergency Management Agency (FEMA) and the National Incident Management System (NIMS). It explores the problems faced when federal authorities have given low priority to disasters and crises that are not terrorism-related, most particularly in the Katrina Hurricane disaster of 2005.

The fourth part outlines the sweeping scope of state emergency laws and their application, especially with reference to the emergencies declared in Ferguson, Missouri in 2014 and Baltimore, Maryland in 2015 to suppress protests against police killings.

Presidential or Executive Power

A president has substantial powers – both as chief executive, charged with seeing that laws are faithfully executed, and as commander-in-chief – to take emergency measures, including to mobilise the armed forces.

Presidents have also repeatedly invoked necessity to justify taking emergency measures, even if they violate constitutional dictates and statutory restrictions on their powers. Perhaps the most blatant public expression of this assertion came in former President Nixon's 1977 televised interview with David Frost. Asked if the president could decide whether something was in the nation's best interests and do something illegal, Nixon replied:

> Well, when the President does it, that means that it is not illegal … If the President, for example, approves something because of the national security, or in this case because of a threat to internal peace and order of significant magnitude, then the President's decision in

> that instance is one that enables those who carry it out, to carry it out without violating a law. (Gross and Ní Aoláin 2006: 52–3)

Despite the controversy over Nixon's claim, the extraordinary powers of the president have been, in effect, shielded and extended over the past four decades with the complicity of both the political establishment, as embodied in Congress, and the legal establishment, as embodied in the judiciary.

During the period from 1972 to 1976 – in response to the discrediting and resignation of Nixon over the Watergate bugging affair, the secret invasion of Cambodia and the failed intensification of the bombing of Vietnam – several congressional initiatives were taken to appear to curtail presidential emergency powers.

The 1972 Special Committee on National Emergencies and Delegated Emergency Powers established by the US Congress found '470 special statutes that could be invoked by the president at any time during a declared national emergency' (Church 1977: 198). The powers included:

> to seize property; to organize and control the means of production; to seize commodities; to assign military forces abroad; to institute martial law; to seize and control all transportation and communication; to regulate the operation of private enterprise; to restrict travel; and, in a plethora of other ways, to control the lives of all Americans. (Church 1977: 198)

Four decades on, these powers not only remain intact but have mushroomed. The National Emergencies Act 1976 (50 USC 1601–1651) was supposedly designed to limit and formalise the power of Congress to restrain the emergency powers of the president. It introduced procedural requirements for a president to declare a formal national emergency. The Act was meant to limit the number of national emergencies declared; but there are currently more than 30 persisting national emergencies, compared to the four that existed in 1976 (Thronson 2013).

According to a Senate committee, the existence of four presidentially declared states of emergency giving rise to vast emergency powers, dating back to 1933, made it 'distressingly clear' that 'our Constitutional government has been weakened by 41 consecutive years of emergency rule' (Thronson 2013: 739–40). Yet, the National Emergencies Act 1976, supposedly enacted to 'prevent numerous or indefinite declarations of national emergency has become part and parcel of their unmitigated propagation' (Thronson 2013: 740).

Not only does the national emergency declared by President Bush on 14 September 2001 remain in force – long after the killing of Osama bin Laden and the proclaimed destruction of Al Qaeda's infrastructure – so do at least 29 other emergencies. Congress, although formally required by the 1976 Act to vote every six months on whether a national emergency should continue, has done so only once (Thronson 2013: 738).

The number of emergencies in place almost certainly exceeds the 30 identified by research, because many presidential directives remain classified and others are likely to have been kept secret from the public (Thronson 2013: 742). A declaration of national emergency gives the president access to powers contained in at least 160 statutory provisions and dozens of executive orders, presidential directives and other regulations (Thronson 2013: 742–3).

As discussed in the second part of this chapter, the 1976 Act itself places no conditions on the president's ability to declare a national emergency. An original draft of the bill stated that the president could only be authorised to declare a national emergency if the president found it 'essential to the preservation, protection, and defense of the Constitution, and is essential to the common defense, safety or well-being of the territory and people of the United States'. That proviso was removed in order to leave in place the presidential powers bestowed by various statutory delegations (Thronson 2013: 749).

The Supreme Court has made it clear that the president does not require express congressional or statutory authorisation to exercise such powers domestically. If an emergency threatens the freedom of interstate commerce, transportation of the mail or some other federal government responsibility, he may call upon 'the army of the Nation, and all its militia … to brush away the obstructions' (*In re Debs*, 158 US 364 (1919) at 381).

As discussed in Chapter 2, such judicial rulings have left the way open for increasingly aggressive assertions of presidential, executive and prerogative powers to use military personnel and resources against civilians, flying in the face of the clear intent of the Constitution. In effect, the role of commander-in-chief has been transformed from a guarantor of civilian supremacy over the military to an instrument for utilising the armed forces against civil unrest and political dissent.

Constitutional presidential authority has been asserted to provide a broad basis for the mobilisation of military forces under the banner of homeland security. Particularly since 2001, the White House has asserted that the executive powers of the president and his position as commander-in-chief support wide-ranging exceptions to the Posse Comitatus Act, which generally prohibits the domestic use of the armed forces. Defense Department regulations assert another 'constitutional' exception to the Act, founded on the 'inherent right of the U.S. Government … to ensure the preservation of public order and to carry out governmental operations … by force, if necessary'.

The Civil Disturbance Statutes (10 USC, sections 331–5) allow the president to call up the armed forces and the National Guard (state militia) to suppress challenges to the political order, including insurrections, 'domestic violence', unlawful obstructions, combinations, or assemblages, and 'rebellion against the authority of the United States'.

The Department of Defense (DoD) Directive 3025.12, 'Military Assistance for Civil Disturbances (MACDIS)', provides for far-ranging use of the military against civil unrest:

> The President is authorized by the Constitution and laws of the United States to employ the Armed Forces of the United States to suppress insurrections, rebellions, and domestic violence under various conditions and circumstances. Planning and preparedness by the Federal Government and the Department of Defense for civil disturbances are important due to the potential severity of the consequences of such events for the Nation and the population … The President has additional powers and responsibilities under the Constitution of the United States to ensure that law and order are maintained. (MACDIS, 4 February 1994: 3)

DoD 3025.12 also states: 'Under reference (r), the terms "major disaster" and "emergency" are defined substantially by action of the President in declaring that extant circumstances and risks justify Presidential implementation of the legal powers in those statutes.'

Even greater authoritarian provisions have been introduced. The National Security Presidential and Homeland Directive (NSPD 51, HSPD 20) was promulgated in 2007. In the event of a 'catastrophic emergency', which the president can declare without congressional approval, NSPD 51 would institute virtual martial law under the authority of the White House and the Department of Homeland Security. It would suspend constitutional government under the provisions of Continuity of Government, leaving extraordinary powers in the hands of the president and vice-president. 'Catastrophic emergency' is loosely defined as 'any incident, regardless of location, that results in extraordinary levels of mass casualties, damage, or disruption severely affecting the U.S. population, infrastructure, environment, economy, or government functions'. 'Continuity of Government' is defined as 'a coordinated effort within the Federal Government's executive branch to ensure that National Essential Functions continue to be performed during a Catastrophic Emergency'.

How Have Such Powers Been Aggregated?

The framers of the Constitution saw the prerogative powers of the English monarchy as an insult to democracy. They felt that no one branch of the government should hold unchecked power, and were wary of the inherent powers given to the monarchy (Edelson 2013: Chapter 2). Nevertheless, many official and academic advocates of broad presidential power deny such intentions by the framers or look to emergency situations being outside the domain of any constitutional limitations (Gross and Ní Aoláin 2006: 72–3).

Broadly speaking, three approaches have been taken to seek to legitimise the president's emergency powers:

1. emergency presidential power authorised in advance by Congress;
2. limited unilateral emergency presidential power subject to retroactive congressional approval;
3. broad unilateral emergency presidential power defined by the president.

Article 1, section 8 of the Constitution expressly assigns to Congress the ability to declare war, raise armies and call forth the military to suppress insurrection and repel invasions. Of course, Congress may legislate to allow the president certain powers: 'When the President acts pursuant to an express or implied authorisation of Congress, his authority is at its maximum, for it includes all that he possesses in his own right plus all that Congress can delegate' (*Youngstown Sheet & Tube Co. v Sawyer*, 343 US 579, 635 (1952).

Despite these provisions, presidents have often independently exercised emergency power – sometimes with approval from Congress or the courts, sometimes with neither. The enumerated powers given to the president in the Constitution amount to little in terms of specific emergency provisions. However, a common argument is that the president must have unilateral emergency powers to repel sudden attacks or to defend the nation, even if that action must then be retroactively approved by Congress, thereby preserving the rule of law (Fisher 2010).

Then there are outright assertions of broad unilateral emergency power defined by the president. These views came to prominence after 9/11 in memoranda prepared by Bush administration lawyers. John Yoo, a law professor working in the Office of Legal Counsel, wrote the memorandum seeking to validate the president's actions after September 11 (Yoo 2001). Jay Bybee, the Assistant Attorney-General, co-authored the 'Yoo-Bybee' memorandum that concluded that 'enhanced interrogation techniques' (effectively torture) were permitted in interrogating terrorist suspects (Yoo and Bybee 2002). According to the memo, the brutal interrogation methods amounted to torture only if they caused the same level of pain as 'organ failure, impairment of bodily function or even death'. Even waterboarding, defined as torture by the US Code of Military Justice for more than a century, was permissible under this standard. Bybee was later appointed a federal judge.

The claim that the president has broad emergency power stems from the insistence on the existence of an inherent power beyond those granted in the Constitution. The president is also regarded as having exclusive power in the field of international relations (Edelson 2013: 9). This is further strengthened by the use of the state secrets doctrine and other legal machinations to stop the courts or Congress from reviewing such orders and actions.

Many legal academics have sought to portray the courts as placing limits on executive power. In *Beyond the Law*, Paust extensively catalogued the abuses of the US Constitution and international and domestic law by the George W. Bush administration 'authorized and abetted by previously secret memos, letters, directives, authorizations, and orders' (Paust 2007: x). Paust contended that 'during war and threats to national security, it is often the judiciary that has maintained the line between lawful and unlawful exercises of Executive power' (Paust 2007: xii).

In reality, US courts, like their counterparts globally, have tended to support the executive's position, either by invoking doctrines such as 'political question' or standing to reject jurisdiction over challenges to the executive's actions, or by siding with, or at least accepting, the government's assertions (Gross and Ní Aoláin 2006: 63). When faced with alleged national crisis, the judiciary tends to 'go to war' (Gross and Ní Aoláin 2006: 77). Examples from Lincoln to Obama highlight the Supreme Court's reluctance to completely deny the president emergency unilateral powers, while seeking to maintain the appearance of a rule of law.

From Lincoln to Roosevelt

During the Civil War, President Lincoln instructed his generals to suspend habeas corpus for the purposes of suppressing insurrections. Federal troops arrested John Merryman, a US citizen, in his home. Merryman managed to get hold of a lawyer, and a writ of habeas corpus was sought in the Supreme Court. In *Ex parte Merryman*, 17 F. Cas. 144 (1861), Chief Justice Roger Taney ruled that the president had acted unconstitutionally in suspending habeas corpus:

> He [the president] certainly does not faithfully execute the laws if he takes upon himself legislative power by suspending the writ of *habeas corpus* and the judicial power, also, by arresting and imprisoning a person without due process of law. Nor can any argument be drawn from … the necessities of government for self defence, in times of tumult and danger. The Government of the United States is one of delegated and limited powers.

Taney CJ noted that the framers of the Constitution withheld the plenary powers of the British Crown, which were deemed too broad and dangerous. Ultimately, Lincoln ignored the judgment, appealing instead to Congress for retroactive approval. In 1863 the Habeas Corpus Act exonerated the past suspension of the writ.

In the *Prize Cases*, the Supreme Court validated Lincoln's order of a blockade while Congress was out of session. Such an act is generally considered an act of war and thus must be approved by Congress. However the court ruled that Lincoln had implied constitutional power when the nation's security was at risk and immediate action was needed:

> If a war be made by invasion of a foreign nation, the President is not only authorised but bound to resist force by force. He does not initiate the war, but is bound to accept the challenge without waiting for any special legislative authority. And whether the hostile party be a foreign invader or States organized in rebellion, it is nonetheless a war although the declaration of it be 'unilateral'. (*The Prize Cases*, 67 US 635 (1863) per Grier J)

Edelson contends that the case is limited by its facts – 'rebellious states were engaged in military action against the federal government' (Edelson 2013: 46). Nevertheless, many officials, commentators and supporters of broad emergency powers cite the case as judicial authority for implied powers, not least in the 'war on terrorism'.

One of the most cited cases for the proposition that the courts will uphold legality is *Ex parte Milligan*, 71 US 2 (1866). Lambdin Milligan had been arrested, charged and convicted by a military commission of several offences, including kidnapping the governor of Indiana. He was sentenced to be hanged. Milligan believed he should have been tried before a civilian court, given that Indiana was 'not a theatre of war'. The Supreme Court held that as the actions took place in Indiana, and the courts were open, Milligan had the right to a jury trial in a civilian court. In words that have become famous, Justice Davis declared in that case:

> The Constitution of the United States is a law for rulers and people, equally in war and in peace, and covers with the shield of its protection all classes of man, at all times, and under all circumstances. No doctrine, involving more pernicious consequences, was ever invented by the wit of man than that any of its provisions can be suspended during any of the great exigencies of government. Such a doctrine leads directly to anarchy or despotism, but the theory of necessity in which it is based is false; for the government, within the Constitution, has all the powers granted to it, which are necessary to preserve its existence. (*Ex parte Milligan*, 71 US (4 Wall.) 2 (1866) per Davis J at 120–21)

This statement has been hailed as 'courageous' and 'one of the bulwarks of American civil liberty', while others have described it as an 'evident piece of arrant hypocrisy' (Gross and Ní Aoláin 2006: 90). The truth is that Justice Davis's words left ample room for presidential authoritarianism by insisting that all the powers to preserve the nation's existence lay within the Constitution itself. His judgment also affirmed resort to martial law under some circumstances:

> [T]here are occasions when martial rule can be properly applied. If, in foreign invasion or civil war, the courts are actually closed, and it is impossible to administer criminal justice according to the law, *then*, on the theatre of active military operations, where war really prevails, there is a necessity to furnish a substitute for the civil authority, thus overthrown, to preserve the safety of the army and society, and as no power is left but the military, it is allowed to govern by martial rule until the laws can have their free course. (*Ex parte Milligan*, 71 US (4 Wall.) 2 (1866) per Davis J at 126)

When the issue of presidential emergency power next came for testing during World War I, the Supreme Court effectively reversed Justice Davis's insistence that the source of such power had to be found strictly within the Constitution. While maintaining that a state of emergency could not create powers that did not already exist, the majority of judges insisted that a crisis could alter the scope of existing powers: '[A]lthough an emergency may not call into life a power which has never lived, nevertheless emergency may afford a reason for the exertion of a power already enjoyed (*Wilson v New* 243 US 332 (1917) per White CJ at 348). The majority's judgment approved the exercise of emergency powers under the aegis of the Constitution in a manner that under normal circumstances would be unconstitutional. This elastic interpretation of constitutionality provided a legal justification for the expansion of presidential power throughout the ensuing century. During World War I, President Wilson also asked Congress for authority to take repressive action, leading to two pieces of draconian legislation – the Espionage and Sedition Acts – whose roles were outlined in Chapter 2.

During the Great Depression of the 1930s, President Roosevelt utilised the *Wilson v New* emergency powers doctrine as a legal peg for much of the early New Deal legislation that was designed to rescue capitalism from a fundamental breakdown. Roosevelt's administration equated the acute economic crisis to wartime conditions. This was accepted by the Supreme Court, which declared that 'while emergency does not create power, emergency may furnish the occasion for the exercise of power'. It ruled that the US government's war power 'permits the harnessing of the entire energies of the people in a supreme cooperative effort to preserve the nation' (*Home Building & Loan Association v Blaisdell* 290 US 398 (1934) per Hughes CJ at 425–6).

In World War II, President Roosevelt both worked with congressional authority and instigated actions on his own, justifying them as emergency responses to threats abroad. In part, he relied upon the Supreme Court's dicta in *Curtis-Wright* (299 US 304 (1936)) that the president had plenary and exclusive powers in the field of international relations and could take unilateral action without congressional approval. In *Ex parte Quirin* (317 US 1 (1942)), two groups of German saboteurs had been arrested. Roosevelt ordered them to be tried by a military tribunal. The Supreme Court denied leave to file for habeas corpus. By the end of the war, Roosevelt's executive orders had enabled the incarceration of more than 110,000 Japanese-Americans in camps (Daniels 1993: 104). This regime was effectively upheld by the Supreme Court in *Korematsu v United States* (323 US 214 (1944)).

Referring to Roosevelt's Executive Order 9066, which authorised the evacuation of people of Japanese ancestry from the West Coast, Francis Biddle, Roosevelt's

Attorney-General, summed up the cynicism with which such issues are approached, and the confidence that administrations have in the acquiescence of the judiciary. Biddle commented:

> [T]he Constitution has not greatly bothered any wartime President. That was a question of law, which ultimately the Supreme Court must decide. And meanwhile – probably a long meanwhile – we must get on with the war. (Gross and Ní Aoláin 2006: 95)

From Truman to Obama

During the Korean War, President Truman tested the limits of emergency presidential power by committing American forces to support South Korea without congressional approval. When he made orders relating to the war that affected a domestic crisis, the Supreme Court placed limits on this emergency power; but the decision protected the property interests of big business, not democratic rights. A labour dispute over pay resulted in a national strike in the steel industry, an important producer of military material for the troops in Korea. Truman issued an executive order for the steel mills to be seized and operated. He also informed Congress that he did not need its approval, to which Congress was silent (Edelson 2013: 102). In *Youngstown Sheet & Tube Co v Sawyer*, 343 US 579 (1952) the court held in favour of the steel companies:

> Even though 'theater of war' be an expanding concept, we cannot with faithfulness to our constitutional system hold that the Commander in Chief of the Armed Forces has the ultimate power as such to take possession of private property in order to keep labor disputes from stopping production. This is a job for the Nation's lawmakers, not for its military authorities. (per Black J)

> His command power is not such an absolute as might be implied from that office in a militaristic system, but is subject to limitations consistent with a constitutional Republic whose law and policymaking branch is a representative Congress. The purpose of lodging dual titles in one man was to insure that the civilian would control the military, not to enable the military to subordinate the presidential office. (per Jackson J)

Despite such admonishments the 1950s and 60s continued to see an expansion in the use of presidential emergency power (Edelson 2013: 117). President Nixon stretched that power to use for espionage – wiretapping, opening mail, burglary, an 'enemies list' – and claimed the courts had no power over him. In *United States v Nixon* (418 US 683), Nixon refused to comply with a subpoena issued by the court, and the court rejected his claim to privilege (but only because there was no proof of the need to protect official secrets):

> Absent a claim of need to protect military, diplomatic, or sensitive national security secrets, we find it difficult to accept the argument that even the very important interest in confidentiality of Presidential communications is significantly diminished by production of such material for *in camera* inspection with all the protection that a district court will be obliged to provide.

After the Nixon administration, Congress passed the War Powers Act, the Foreign Intelligence Surveillance Act and the Independent Counsel Act in an attempt to head off public concern about untrammelled presidential power. Then the events of September 11 were exploited to institute an unprecedented enlargement of executive 'emergency' powers. Paust documented the resulting doctrine: 'a fundamentally antidemocratic and unconstitutional preference for a congressionally unchecked and judicially unreviewable Executive commander in chief power to override any inhibiting domestic law' (Paust 2007: 90).

After September 11, the Office of Legal Counsel drew up secret legal opinions, the administration believing that these would then indemnify its actions if they were later deemed criminal (Edelson 2013: 130). One, drafted by Yoo, stated:

> We conclude that the Constitution vests the President with the plenary authority, as Commander in Chief and the sole organ of the Nation in its foreign relations, to use military force abroad – especially in response to grave national emergencies created by sudden, unforeseen attacks on the people and territory of the United States … .
>
> Neither statute, however, can place any limits on the President's determinations as to any terrorist threat, the amount of military force to be used in response, or the method, timing, and nature of the response. These decisions, under our Constitution, are for the President alone to make. (Yoo 2001)

Another memorandum deemed terrorist suspects as neither prisoners of war nor enemy combatants, thus justifying the Bush administration's incarceration without trial of suspects. President Bush signed the Military Order of 13 November 2001, which denied access to civilian courts, allowed the military to hold suspects indefinitely anywhere in the world and instituted military commissions that could impose the death penalty. The government chose a naval base in Guantanamo Bay, believing it to be a legal quagmire because it was not US territory (Thompson 2010).

Two Supreme Court cases eventually ruled that prisoners could file petitions for habeas corpus, but neither decision resulted in the release of a prisoner. In *Hamdi et al. v Rumsfeld* (542 US 507 (2004)), it was stated:

> We reaffirm today the fundamental nature of a citizen's right to be free from involuntary confinement by his own government without due process of law, and we weigh the opposing governmental interests against the curtailment of liberty that such confinement entails … .
>
> We therefore hold that a citizen-detainee seeking to challenge his classification as an enemy combatant must receive notice of the factual basis for his classification, and a fair opportunity to rebut the Government's factual assertions before a neutral decision-maker … These essential constitutional promises may not be eroded.

The Department of Defense established Combatant Status Review Tribunals (CSRTs) in the wake of this decision, and expanded the definition of 'enemy combatant' to anyone who 'directly supported hostilities in aid of enemy forces' (Wolfowitz 2004). Congress then lent support by passing the Detainee Treatment Act of 2005, which allowed for only very limited review of CSRT decisions.

In 2006, the Supreme Court found that the military tribunals violated both US military law and the Geneva Conventions. In *Hamdan v Rumsfeld* (548 US 557 (2006)), the court said that the president did not possess unlimited power to decide how to try detainees, and that congressional support was necessary. Congress then passed the Military Commissions Act of 2006, which overcame the *Hamdan* ruling. The Act allowed the president to interpret the meaning and application of the Geneva Convention and allowed evidence to be hidden from detainees on national security grounds. The Act was challenged in court, but the Supreme Court only found section 7, denying prisoners the right of habeas corpus to federal courts, to be unconstitutional (*Boumediene v Bush* 553 US 723 (2008)).

While many had hoped the Obama administration would rein in such actions (candidate Obama had in fact called for the closure of Guantanamo Bay), the administration allowed such detention systems to continue, justified by similar memoranda (Edelson 2013; Thompson 2010).

In fact, President Obama continued the resort to emergency powers for political purposes that are remote from any genuine emergency. In 2015, for example, he issued an executive order declaring a 'national emergency' to deal with what he termed 'the unusual and extraordinary threat to the national security and foreign policy of the United States' posed by the Venezuelan government (see Chapter 1).

The National Emergencies Act

The 1976 National Emergencies Act (50 USC 1601–1651) eliminated or modified some statutory grants of emergency authority; required the president to declare formally the existence of a national emergency and to specify what statutory authority, activated by the declaration, would be used; and provided Congress a means to countermand the president's declaration and the activated authority being sought.

Among the basic problems with the Act are that it does not require a president to justify the declaration of an emergency. Nor does it outline the principles that should govern the president's decision to declare an emergency, or the executive response to the emergency. Thus, according to Roach:

> In its single-minded focus on the power of the President to declare an emergency or an exception as opposed to the principles that might govern the declaration and conduct of the emergency, the Act is Schmittian. (Roach 2008: 235)

Title II provided a procedure for future declarations of national emergency by the president and prescribed arrangements for their congressional regulation. The statute established an exclusive means for declaring a national emergency. Furthermore, emergency declarations were to terminate automatically after one year unless formally continued for another year by the president, but could be terminated earlier by either the president or Congress.

Originally, the prescribed method for congressional termination of a declared national emergency was a concurrent resolution adopted by both houses of Congress. This type of so-called 'legislative veto' was effectively invalidated by the Supreme Court in 1983 (*Immigration and Naturalization Service v Chadha*, 462 US 919 (1983)). The National Emergencies Act was amended in 1985 to substitute a joint resolution as the vehicle for rescinding a national emergency declaration.

In the event of an emergency declaration, Congress must consider such a joint resolution every six months (50 USC 1622). However, Congress has never ended an emergency, and rarely considers voting to do so (Roach 2008: 235).

When declaring a national emergency, the president must indicate, according to Title III, the powers and authorities being activated to respond to the exigency at hand. Certain presidential accountability and reporting requirements regarding national emergency declarations were specified in Title IV; and the repeal and continuation of various statutory provisions delegating emergency powers was accomplished in Title V.

The Act requires that executive orders, rules and regulations 'shall be transmitted to the Congress promptly under means to assure confidentiality where appropriate' (50 USC 1641). Yet it does not provide for methods of publishing, nullifying or amending such orders or regulations.

FEMA and Other Federal Agencies

Presidential power is not the only arena of rapidly expanding emergency decree-making. A wide range of federal agencies also exercise emergency powers or adopt emergency rules, bypassing normal legislative and judicial procedures for rule-making.

A study published in 2013 found there was a 'systemic shift' in the use of emergency powers by federal agencies after 2001. Federal agency emergency rule-making jumped threefold in a span of two years, and increased further in the ensuing decade (Boliek 2013: 3348–9). Judicial review of such rule-making was rarely sought and even more rarely granted, making it 'arguably inconsequential'. Of the nearly 5,000 such rules adopted between 1995 and 2011, only 74 were reviewed by courts, and just 18 were declared deficient – less than 0.4 per cent (Boliek 2013: 3350).

Primary federal responsibility for coordinating emergency responses is meant to lie with the Federal Emergency Management Agency (FEMA). Created by Executive Orders 12127 and 12448 on 1 April 1979 by President Carter, FEMA is the agency in charge of federal disasters and emergency relief and recovery. While the UK's Civil Contingencies Act focuses on local and regional agencies working together, FEMA is instead meant to 'take over' in times of emergency. A state simply needs to call a 'state of emergency' and formally request help from the president for FEMA to be mobilised to respond. It then has control over National Guards; funds for the building of emergency shelters and the logistics of food, medicine, controlling hygiene and preventing 'criminality' (looting, etc.); and the management of grants for the recovery period.

Following the September 11, 2001 attacks, the Homeland Security Act 2002 encompassed FEMA. It became part of the Department of Homeland Security, which was primarily charged with the targeting of terrorist suspects. FEMA's incorporation into the realm of the 'war on terror' via the Department of Homeland Security Act has been attributed to a 'policy window' (Brook and King 2007: 400) where the national mood had shifted after 9/11 from one of fear and acquiescence to overbearing government control (Jones 2003: 787).

FEMA was assigned broad and vague responsibilities. The legislation stated:

> Section 507:
>
> (a) In General. – The functions of the Federal Emergency Management Agency include the following:
>
> (1) All functions and authorities prescribed by the Robert T. Stafford Disaster Relief and Emergency Assistance Act (42 U.S.C. 5121 et seq.).
>
> (2) Carrying out its mission to reduce the loss of life and property and protect the Nation from all hazards by leading and supporting the Nation in a comprehensive, risk-based emergency management program –
>
> (A) of mitigation, by taking sustained actions to reduce or eliminate long-term risk to people and property from hazards and their effects;
>
> (B) of planning for building the emergency management profession to prepare effectively for, mitigate against, respond to, and recover from any hazard;
>
> (C) of response, by conducting emergency operations to save lives and property through positioning emergency equipment and supplies, through evacuating potential victims, through providing food, water, shelter, and medical care to those in need, and through restoring critical public services;
>
> (D) of recovery, by rebuilding communities, individuals, businesses, and governments can function on their own, return to normal life, and protect against future hazards; and
>
> (E) of increased efficiencies, by coordinating efforts relating to mitigation, planning, response, and recovery.
>
> (b) Federal Response Plan. –
>
> (1) Role of FEMA. – Notwithstanding any other provision of this Act, Federal Emergency Management Agency shall remain the lead agency for the Federal Response Plan established under Executive Order No. 12148 (44 Fed. Reg. 43239) and Executive Order No. 12656 (53 Fed. Reg. 47491).

The National Response Coordination Centre is also located within FEMA's headquarters. However, the National Disaster Medical System was transferred from the Department of Homeland Security to the Department of Health and Human Services under the Pandemic and All-Hazards Preparedness Act 2006.

Under the Robert T. Stafford Disaster Relief and Emergency Assistance Act (Public Law 93-288) which was consequently amended by the Disaster Mitigation Act of 2000, state, local and tribal governments are obligated to undertake risk mitigation measures (such as developing plans and protocols) as a precondition to receiving funds for non-emergency disaster assistance. The requirements are then set out in the Code of Federal Regulations as well as by FEMA issuing guidance through external memoranda of policy procedures.

However, as seen in crises such as Hurricane Katrina (considered below), this partnership is rocky at best, with many state authorities unsure and unclear of their role in conjunction with federal authorities. A clear example of such resistance to shared responsibility and planning occurred earlier with the 'Crisis Relocation Planning' that was meant to be a coordinated effort to plan ways to relocate people in large cities in the event of a nuclear attack. Many states refused to comply even though funding had already been provided for the effort (May 1985: 42).

FEMA has responded to many controversial disaster-type situations, including the dumping of toxic waste at Niagara Falls and the Three Mile Island accident. Its response to Hurricane Andrew in 1992 was criticised; but even more criticised was its response to Hurricane Katrina in 2005.

FEMA, Hurricane Katrina and the Gulf of Mexico Disaster

One of the five deadliest hurricanes in the history of the United States, Katrina devastated the Gulf Coast from central Florida to Texas. The most damage occurred in New Orleans, Louisiana, where a storm levee system failed, causing catastrophic flooding. Many people were stranded with no indication of any relief effort. Victims were also left with no shelter and few provisions (Pierre and Stephenson 2008).

Tens of thousands of survivors were forced into wretched conditions – hot, overcrowded makeshift emergency centres – deprived of the most fundamental provisions. Without food, water, medical care, nappies or toilets, more victims succumbed to the catastrophe. FEMA turned relief trucks away, cut emergency lines, and survivors were prevented from leaving the city. Victims were vilified and blamed for the social anarchy. Police and armed mercenaries were given the nod to gun down unarmed 'looters' or residents desperately seeking higher ground in the affluent neighbourhoods. As the situation grew more desperate, the Bush administration ordered in the military (World Socialist Web Site 2005).

Given that most of the victims were poor and African American, some analyses attributed the appalling response to racism (Reed 2007: 561–2). Others argued that an emphasis on terrorist-related incidents within the Department of Homeland Security contributed to FEMA's inability to handle all hazards:

> For years emergency management professionals have been warning that FEMA's preparedness has eroded. Many believe this erosion is a result of the separation of the preparedness function from FEMA, the drain of long-term professional staff along with their institutional knowledge and expertise, and the inadequate readiness of FEMA's national emergency response teams. The combination of these staffing, training, and organizational structures made FEMA's inadequate performance in the face of a disaster the size of Katrina all but inevitable. (FEMA 2006)

In 2006, a House of Representatives Select Bipartisan Committee to Investigate the Preparation for and Response to Hurricane Katrina report attributed the failure to a lack of 'initiative'. It said the response plans were inflexible and unable to adapt to a natural disaster outside forecast risks. Critical elements of the National Response Plan were executed late or not at all:

> [W]e found that while a national emergency management system that relies on state and local governments to identify needs and request resources is adequate for most disasters, a catastrophic disaster like Katrina can and did overwhelm most aspects of the system. (House of Representatives 2006: 5)

In response, Congress revised and reorganised the agency. Six statutes were passed, including the Post-Katrina Emergency Management Reform Act of 2006 ('Post-Katrina Act'), which had the most relevance to emergencies and disaster management. The Act sought to reinvigorate the agency and produce a 'new FEMA'. The Act provided for 10 regional offices as well as a National Integration Center. It also classified FEMA as a distinct entity within the Department of Homeland Security. While decoupling FEMA somewhat from the 'war on terror' focus, these changes were intended to bolster its capacity to intervene nationally in any declared emergency.

In the next major national emergency, however, the corporation responsible for the disaster was permitted to take charge of the response operation. FEMA was effectively sidelined by the Obama administration in the response to the 2010 explosion on the BP-run Deepwater Horizon oil rig in the Gulf of Mexico. The blast killed 11 workers, injured 17 more and led to the greatest single ecological catastrophe in US history. Some 206 million gallons of oil gushed out from the wellhead located deep beneath the ocean's surface, and about 80 kilometres from Louisiana's southeast coast. Millions more gallons of highly toxic chemical dispersant were dumped on the Gulf's surface or released underwater.

The spill directly impacted coastline stretching from Texas to Florida, including estuaries, marshlands and beaches. Hundreds of thousands of Gulf Coast residents faced financial hardship, including many thousands who lost their jobs as a result of damage to the fishing and tourism industries. In spite of the magnitude of the disaster and overwhelming evidence that basic safety concerns were flouted in order to speed the oil well into production, the Obama administration left BP itself in total control of the disaster site, clean-up and response, highlighting the subordination of government to powerful corporate interests. According to a Congressional Research Service report, FEMA 'has responsibilities with respect to the economic impacts of the spill; its role so far has been primarily that of an observer' (Hagerty and Ramseur 2010: 1).

State Emergency Powers

Governors and agencies in each of the 50 states hold vast and broad emergency-declaring and response powers. Inadequate reporting and data collection make it impossible to gauge whether the increasing exercise of such powers federally has been matched by the states (Boliek 2013: 3350–52). While the wording of emergency legislation and emergency rule-making measures varies from state to state (Boliek 2013: 3371–75), the powers are sweeping.

California, the most populous state, can be taken as an example. Its emergency power regime includes the California Emergency Services Act; the California Disaster Assistance Act; California Disaster and Civil Defense Master Mutual Aid Agreements; and other regulations. The California Emergency Services Act confers upon the governor and other officials a range of emergency powers, and sets up an Office of Emergency Services within the governor's office. The Act sets out three types of emergency:

1. State of war emergency. This does not need proclamation by the governor and occurs when the state or nation is attacked by an 'enemy of the United States' or upon receipt of a warning from the federal government that such an attack is 'probable or imminent'.
2. State of emergency. This means 'the duly proclaimed existence of conditions of disaster or of extreme peril to the safety of persons and property within the state caused by such conditions as air pollution, fire, flood, storm, epidemic, riot, drought, sudden and severe energy shortage, plant or animal infestation or disease, the Governor's warning of an earthquake or volcanic prediction, or an earthquake, or other conditions, other than conditions resulting from a labor controversy'.
3. Local emergency. This involves similar conditions to a state of emergency but within a narrower territorial limit (California Emergency Services Act s 8558).

During a state of war emergency or a state of emergency, the governor 'may suspend any regulatory statute, or statute prescribing the procedure for conduct of state business, or the orders, rules, or regulations of any state agency' (s 8571). The governor may also commandeer private property (s 8572) and 'may cooperate with the President and the heads of the armed forces and other agencies of the United States, and with officers and agencies of other states, on matters pertaining to emergencies; and he may take any steps he deems necessary to put into effect any rules, regulations, or suggestions made by such persons or agencies' (s 8573). Moreover:

> None of the provisions of this chapter shall limit, modify, or abridge the powers vested in the Governor under the Constitution or statutes of the state by proclamation, to declare any county, city and county, or city, or any portion thereof to be in a state of insurrection or to proclaim the existence of martial law and to exercise all the powers vested in him thereunder independent of, or in conjunction with, any of the provisions of this chapter. (s 8574)

Case Study: The States of Emergency Declared in Missouri in 2014

During 2014, in the space of three months, backed by the federal government, the governor of the US state of Missouri declared two states of emergency. One was in Ferguson, a working-class suburb of St. Louis. The other covered the entire state. Both gave sweeping powers to the police and the state's National Guard. The first emergency, in Ferguson in August, was to suppress protests that broke out over the police killing of Michael Brown, an unarmed 18-year-old. The second emergency, across the state in November, was imposed pre-emptively in order to put down anticipated unrest over an expected decision by a county grand jury not to lay charges against the police officer responsible for Brown's death.

On 9 August 2014, Brown was shot and killed by police officer Darren Wilson in Ferguson. His death, and the subsequent release of an autopsy, commissioned by his family, showing that he was shot six times – including twice in the head while apparently kneeling on the ground – triggered protests on local streets.

The emergency declarations, accompanied by mobilisations of the National Guard, provide a case study of the repressive and arbitrarily determined measures being adopted in the United States, from the White House down, to deal with protests and other expressions of social and political discontent. The mass media, and many of the politicians and other political players involved, generally depicted the Ferguson disturbances in purely racial terms, because Brown was African-American and the police officer who shot him was white. A probing of the circumstances, however, points to deeper tensions, of a class character bound up with the widening social gulf between the wealthy corporate elites in America and the falling living standards faced by working people, including in poor suburbs like Ferguson.

While racially polarised (its 21,000 residents are 67.4 per cent black, 29.3 per cent white and 3.3 per cent everything else), Ferguson is also a microcosm of the impoverishment and inequality prevailing in American cities. As a result of the post-2008 housing market collapse, on top of decades of de-industrialisation, Ferguson's median household income adjusted for inflation fell 25 per cent from 2000 to 2012, to less than $36,000 a year (Bloomberg 2014).

Fuelling the protests was also the understanding that Brown's death was not an isolated event. Despite a lack of comprehensive official data on homicides by police in the US, it is clear that hundreds of people die at the hands of police every year. According to a *Wall Street Journal* report in late 2014, national statistics provided by the Federal Bureau of Investigation do not report 25 per cent or more of police killings in the US. The newspaper analysed data from 105 of the largest police agencies in the country and compared the figures to the FBI statistics. More than 550 killings between 2007 and 2012 were not part of the FBI totals. Specifically, in these jurisdictions the *Journal* tallied at least 1,800 police killings, compared to only 1,242 reported to the FBI (Wall Street Journal 2014).

The newspaper said the full national scope of the underreporting could not be quantified. In the period analysed by the *Journal*, 753 police entities reported about 2,400 killings by police. The large majority of the nation's roughly 18,000 law enforcement agencies did not report any. One of the major causes of the discrepancy is the failure of many local police agencies to report homicides that are considered justifiable. As the Fairfax County, Virginia Police Department told the newspaper, such killings are not an 'actual offense', and they are not reported to the FBI (Wall Street Journal 2014).

The US Centers for Disease Control and Prevention (CDC) keeps data on deaths that occur across the country. One of its categories is homicide by 'legal intervention', a term that covers any situation where a person dies at the hands of anyone authorised to use deadly force in the line of duty. This category consists of all sworn police officers, but not private security guards. In just 16 states, there were 130 such deaths in 2009 (Centers for Disease Control and Prevention 2009).

In Ferguson, demonstrators and other residents soon found themselves confronted by heavily armed police who used military-style armoured vehicles, tear gas and stun grenades to break up protests. This repression further inflamed the unrest. According to an account by an American Civil Liberties Union (ACLU) staff attorney:

> Tear gas, rubber bullets, and assault weapons; free speech zones, gags, and press pens: This is the arsenal of the police state. Some of these tactics are physical. The other ones – all the more pernicious for their quiet coercion – impose a veil of silence over the actions of law enforcement. And each of these weapons has been unleashed on the people of Ferguson, Missouri, since the killing of Michael Brown.
>
> In the first few nights of protest, Ferguson and St. Louis County police responded with a truly inconceivable show of force. Officers suited up in DHS [Department of Homeland Security]-funded military hand-me-downs, outfitted with goggles, machine guns, sniper rifles, riot gear and gas masks. Distressing warzone-like images flickered into the public consciousness: photos of armed police cohorts pointing loaded automatic weapons at citizens with their hands in the air, women and children's faces streaming with tear gas and milk and white officers targeting black protesters like it's Selma circa 1964. (Rowland 2014)

The First Emergency Declaration

On 16 August, Missouri governor Jay Nixon issued an executive order declaring a state of emergency and authorising the Missouri State Highway Patrol to impose a curfew within the City of Ferguson 'in order to protect public safety and security' (Nixon 2014a). Titled Executive Order 14-08, the order was vague and sweeping, and invested the Missouri State Highway Patrol chief with open-ended powers. Governor Nixon's order stated, among other things:

> I do hereby direct the Missouri State Highway Patrol, through its Superintendent, to command all operations necessary to ensure public safety and protect civil rights in the City of Ferguson and, as necessary, surrounding areas during the period of this emergency. (Nixon 2014b)

The order also gave the Highway Patrol superintendent the power to call on the support of 'other local law enforcement agencies, as deemed necessary', and directed the imposition of a curfew 'under such terms and conditions deemed necessary and appropriate by the Superintendent'. No time limit was set for the emergency. Instead, 'This order shall be terminated upon execution of a subsequent Executive Order.'

The order provided no objective evidence that an emergency existed. The governor simply asserted, without reciting any detail, that the conditions necessary to declare the existence of an emergency pursuant to the relevant Missouri law, Chapter 44, RSMo, had been found to exist. This is reminiscent of Carl Schmitt's insistence that the sovereign is the person who decides on the exception.

Two days later, Governor Nixon signed Executive Order 14-09, mobilising the Missouri National Guard 'to help restore peace and order and to protect the citizens of Ferguson'. That order stated that 'additional resources of the State of Missouri are needed to help relieve the conditions of distress and hazard to the safety and welfare of the citizens of the City of Ferguson'. Again, the order was indefinite and the powers granted were sweeping:

> [B]y virtue of the authority vested in me by the Constitution and laws of the State of Missouri, including section 41.480, RSMo, [I] order and direct the Adjutant General of the State of Missouri, or his designee, to forthwith call and order into active service such portions of the organized militia as he deems necessary to aid the executive officials of Missouri, to protect life and property. (Nixon 2014c)

Further, the order authorised 'the Superintendent of the Missouri State Highway Patrol to take such measures, including but not limited to, restricting and/or closing streets and thoroughfares in the City of Ferguson, to maintain peace and order'. This order was also premised, without further elaboration, on the assertion that a state of emergency existed and had been duly declared.

The legislation that purports to provide and delineate this power is sweeping. Missouri State Law RSMo Chapter 44 contains the powers to declare a state of emergency. In particular, section 44.010 defines a state of emergency and section 44.100 sets out the governor's emergency powers during a state of emergency. Both are extraordinarily broad. 'Emergency' is defined as:

> any state of emergency declared by proclamation by the governor, or by resolution of the legislature pursuant to sections 44.010 to 44.130 upon the actual occurrence of a natural or man-made *disaster of major proportions* within this state when the *safety and welfare* of the inhabitants of this state are *jeopardized*. (emphasis added)

The italicised words provide great leeway for an emergency to be declared. No criteria are set for determining the meaning of 'major proportions'. The phrase 'safety and welfare' is likewise open to many interpretations, as is the word 'jeopardized'.

Section 44.100 lists 11 groups of powers exercisable by the governor, enumerated (a) to (k). These include powers to 'take action and give directions to state and local law enforcement officers and agencies as may be reasonable and necessary for the purpose of securing compliance with the provisions of this law'. Other powers refer to seizing or requisitioning transport, communications, fuel, housing and medical facilities; and rationing or otherwise directing the distribution of essential supplies and services. The most potentially far-reaching power in the Governor's hands is (j):

> Perform and exercise such other functions, powers and duties as may be necessary to promote and secure the safety and protection of the civilian population.

This power could be used to exercise semi-dictatorial control over the population, in the name of promoting or securing its 'safety and protection'.

The capacity of these measures to violate core legal, constitutional and democratic rights, and the unwillingness of the courts to prevent that from happening, was demonstrated when the American Civil Liberties Union initiated a number of emergency proceedings. One of these cases challenged, as unconstitutional, an arbitrary 'keep moving' rule imposed by the police on residents and journalists on public sidewalks in Ferguson.

The ACLU brief said the police adopted the tactic of patrolling the sidewalks in groups and shouting 'keep moving' at anyone standing in their way. Those who did not move quickly enough were tackled and arrested. Standing still for as little as five seconds was sufficient to be taken to the ground and handcuffed. Hundreds of arrests, including of journalists, were made for 'failure to disperse'.

This tactic clearly sought to intimidate people and obstruct the exercise of basic constitutional rights such as freedom of speech, freedom of the press and freedom of assembly. The legal challenge was issued on behalf of Mustafa Abdullah, who was repeatedly told to 'keep moving' by police. As part of the emergency proceedings, *Abdullah v County of St. Louis et al.*, the ACLU applied for a temporary restraining order that would have required the police to stop using the tactic while the lawsuit was pending. According to the ACLU brief:

> On five separate occasions within a period of approximately one hour at different locations, Plaintiff [Abdullah] was ordered by law enforcement officials to refrain from gathering or standing for more than five seconds on public sidewalks and threatened with arrest for non-compliance ... Plaintiff was at no time violating any law. Numerous other individuals in the area, including members of the media, were similarly ordered by law enforcement officials to refrain from gathering or standing for more than five seconds on public sidewalks and threatened with arrest for non-compliance. They, too, were violating no law.
>
> When inquiries were made to law enforcement officers regarding which law prohibits gathering or standing for more than five seconds on public sidewalks, the officers indicated that they did not know and that it did not matter ... The officers further indicated that they were following the orders of their supervisors, whom they refused to name. (Gillerman 2014)

The ACLU argued that the police tactic 'restricts First Amendment activity'. The First Amendment, part of the 1791 Bill of Rights, guarantees freedom of the press, freedom of speech, freedom of assembly and freedom to petition the government to redress grievances. Arbitrary police rules that lead to harassment, detention or arrest of demonstrators and journalists exercising their First Amendment rights arguably violate the US Constitution.

Missouri Attorney-General Chris Koster defended the 'keep moving' rule, however, and opposed the ACLU petition, arguing that the police tactics were 'designed to protect public safety'. He cited alleged 'gunfire and violence' in the areas where the protests were taking place. This invocation of 'public safety' to suspend democratic rights mirrors the invocation of 'national security' at the national level. It is an elastic justification for the implementation of extraordinary measures. In any case, it was the police who were perpetrating 'gunfire and violence', having shot an unarmed teenager and menaced demonstrators.

Federal District Judge Catherine D. Perry of the Eastern District of Missouri denied the application for a temporary restraining order. The judge was satisfied with assurances from the authorities that a 'free speech zone' had been established where the 'keep moving' rule would not be invoked. Her ruling effectively sanctioned the denial of First Amendments rights, banishing residents and journalists to a police-designated zone designed to shut down or sideline protests and prevent on-the-spot reporting of incidents taking place elsewhere in Ferguson.

Another legal action challenged the police practice of ordering journalists and others to turn off their cameras and stop recording. That lawsuit was apparently resolved with a vaguely worded agreement that the police could be filmed as long as the filming did not represent a threat to 'public safety' and did not interfere with the officers' performance of their official duties (Gillerman 2014).

These measures were clearly endorsed by the Obama administration. On 14 August, two days before the state of emergency was declared, President Barack Obama told a press conference that he had spoken to Governor Nixon to express his 'concern over the violent turn that events have taken on the ground'. Obama praised Nixon as 'a good man and a fine governor' and stated: 'I'm confident that, working together, he is going to be able to communicate his desire to make sure that justice is done and his desire to make sure that public safety is maintained in an appropriate way' (Obama 2014a).

At a press conference on 18 August, two days after the declaration of emergency, President Obama condemned 'those who are using the tragic death as an excuse to engage in criminal behavior' by 'looting or carrying guns and even attacking the police'. While acknowledging that the population had certain constitutional rights – including the 'right to speak freely, to assemble and to report in the press' – the president made no criticism of the police response. Asked if he agreed with Governor Nixon's decision to send in the National Guard, Obama aligned himself with the decision, while claiming that he had sought assurances from Nixon that the National Guard would be used in 'a limited and appropriate way' (Obama 2014b).

Attorney General Eric Holder visited Ferguson on August 20, two days later, met local FBI officials involved in the police crackdown and posed for a photo opportunity with Missouri Highway Patrol captain Ron Johnson, who was in command of the operation (Damon 2014).

The Second Emergency Declaration

On 17 November 2014, Governor Nixon declared a second state of emergency, this time on an even more far-reaching basis. He announced what amounted to a pre-emptive state of emergency throughout St. Louis and across the entire state. It was not predicated on either the existence of violence or any specific decision by the grand jury; rather it was based only on the 'possibility' of 'unrest'.

Nixon's declaration stated that 'regardless of the outcomes of the federal and state criminal investigations, there is the possibility of expanded unrest' (Nixon 2014d). This rationale for invoking emergency powers and deploying a branch of the armed forces was so broad that it could be used under a broad range of conditions in an American city. The opening clauses of the order stated:

> WHEREAS, the City of Ferguson and the St. Louis region have experienced periods of unrest over the past three months; and

> WHEREAS, the United States Department of Justice and St. Louis County authorities are conducting separate criminal investigations into the facts surrounding the death of Michael Brown; and
>
> WHEREAS, the United States Department of Justice and St. Louis County authorities could soon announce the findings of their independent criminal investigations; and
>
> WHEREAS, regardless of the outcomes of the federal and state criminal investigations, there is the possibility of expanded unrest; and
>
> WHEREAS, the State of Missouri will be prepared to appropriately respond to any reaction to these announcements; and
>
> WHEREAS, our citizens have the right to peacefully assemble and protest and the State of Missouri is committed to protecting those rights; and
>
> WHEREAS, our citizens and businesses must be protected from violence and damage; and
>
> WHEREAS, an invocation of the provisions of Sections 44.010 through 44.130, RSMo, is appropriate to ensure the safety and welfare of our citizens. (Nixon 2014e)

As with the initial emergency, sweeping powers were handed to the police and National Guard. The governor's order directed 'the Missouri State Highway Patrol together with the St. Louis County Police Department and the St. Louis Metropolitan Police Department to operate as a Unified Command to protect civil rights and ensure public safety in the City of Ferguson and the St. Louis region'. It further ordered that the Unified Command 'may exercise operational authority in such other jurisdictions it deems necessary to protect civil rights and ensure public safety'. It also authorised the deployment of the National Guard to 'take such action and employ such equipment as may be necessary to carry out requests processed through the Missouri State Highway Patrol and ordered by the Governor of the state to protect life and property and support civilian authorities'. The order was to expire in 30 days, but could be extended in whole or in part by a subsequent executive order (Nixon 2014e).

Governor Nixon later more than tripled the number of National Guard troops in the St. Louis region, from 700 to 2,200. On 28 November, the governor indicated a prolonged operation by calling a special legislative session to provide ongoing funding for 'ongoing Ferguson-related security measures'. In his letter to members of the General Assembly, Nixon pointed to the use of the National Guard in a wide range of everyday civilian locations. He stated that 'in addition to providing security at nearly 100 locations around the region, including at police stations, fire houses, utility substations, hospitals, shopping malls and stadiums, guardsmen are also performing roving and static patrols in the Ferguson area' (Nixon 2014f).

These measures were coordinated with the Obama administration, which also sent 100 FBI agents to Ferguson before the grand jury decision. Two weeks after the emergency declaration, 1,268 guardsmen remained stationed in the St. Louis region, still conducting extensive patrols (Nixon 2014g).

Amnesty Documents Human Rights Violations

The initial crackdown on peaceful protesters by police in Ferguson, Missouri violated numerous US and international laws, according to a report published in October 2014 by Amnesty International. The report documented systematic acts of police violence against peaceful protestors, and the arrest of media and international observers. It detailed the suppression of rights protected under the US Constitution, international law and international human rights agreements (Amnesty 2014).

Police confronted protesters while 'armed with semi-automatic weapons and leashed police dogs', the report noted: 'Officers moved among the protesters using armored vehicles which are more commonly seen in a conflict zone rather than the streets of a suburban town in the United States' (Amnesty 2014: 10).

In one incident, 'Amnesty International witnessed an officer with the St. Ann Police Department in Missouri point his AR-15 semi-automatic rifle at a group of journalists and threaten to kill them' (Amnesty 2014: 10). The report noted that the practice of pointing firearms at peaceful protestors violated US law and international conventions, including the UN's Basic Principles for the Use of Force and Firearms by Law Enforcement Officials.

The report concluded that the police sought to 'collectively punish' local residents and peaceful protestors. It noted that the imposition of a curfew 'limited not only the rights of those who were demonstrating peacefully, but also the freedom of movement of the general public in Ferguson, who were required to be off of the streets after midnight each night'. The report stated: 'In all, more than 170 individuals were arrested during the first 12 days of protests since Michael Brown's death.' More than three quarters of arrests were for the ad hoc charge of 'failure to disperse' (Amnesty 2014: 12).

Law enforcement officials repeatedly fired tear gas and rubber bullets at protesters (Amnesty 2014: 13). On one occasion, the Amnesty International delegation 'witnessed officers aboard [an] armored truck in full riot gear, including helmets, vests, masks, and boots. Some of the officers had their guns drawn with no names, badges, other identifying information visible' (Amnesty 2014: 13).

The report also documented attacks on free speech and the media. 'Legal and human rights observers as well as members of the media have repeatedly been obstructed' by police, it noted. Some were assaulted or arrested:

> From August 13 through October 2, at least 19 journalists and members of the media were arrested by law enforcement, with others subjected to tear gas and the use of rubber bullets … Reporters for CNN, Al Jazeera America and other outlets report being harassed or physically threatened. (Amnesty 2014: 16)

Another Case Study: The Baltimore Emergency of 2015

In April 2015, the death in police custody of 25-year-old Freddie Gray – only one of a wave of police killings around the country – triggered clashes with police in Baltimore, Maryland, demonstrations that spread to other cities and a virtual police-military occupation that lasted several weeks. Gray died after suffering fatal spinal injuries at the hands of the police. The unarmed man was arrested for making eye contact with a police officer and allegedly running away. After being tackled by six officers, thrown into a police van and denied medical assistance, Gray fell into a coma and succumbed a week later.

Confronted by protests and isolated incidents of looting, Maryland governor Larry Hogan, a Republican, at the request of Baltimore mayor Stephanie Rawlings-Blake, a Democrat, signed an executive order declaring a state of emergency in Baltimore City (Hogan 2015). The declaration allowed Governor Hogan to activate the National Guard, announcing plans to deploy 5,000 troops to support local and state police troops. In addition, Mayor Rawlings-Blake established a city-wide, week-long curfew from 10 p.m. to 5 a.m. City schools, state offices, colleges and universities and courts within the city issued shelter-in-place orders or closed altogether.

Baltimore, only 40 miles from the nation's capital, was effectively occupied, with heavily armed units placed in key public locations throughout the city, accompanied by armoured vehicles and military helicopters. In a show of force, heavily armoured vehicles – including Mine-Resistant Ambush Protected vehicles (MRAPs) returning from Afghanistan and other war zones – dispersed crowds. More than 300 protesters were arrested.

President Obama, who was in close contact with Maryland and Baltimore authorities, indicated his support for the crackdown. At a White House press conference, he said it was 'entirely appropriate' for the mayor and governor to work 'to stop that senseless violence and destruction'.

Conditions in Baltimore exemplify America's social inequality. As a whole, it is ranked the sixth poorest city in the country. In the Sandtown-Winchester area where Gray was arrested, more than half of the working-age population is unemployed, and a third of all residential properties are vacant or abandoned. A report published by the city in 2011 found that nearly a third of all families in the neighbourhood live in poverty.

The emergency declaration (Hogan 2015) cited part of its authorising power as coming from Title 14 and Section 13-702 of the Public Safety Article within Maryland State Code. Title 14 includes a broad grant of governor's powers generally, as well as some powers given under the Maryland Emergency Management Act and the state's Catastrophic Health Act to execute a number of actions if necessary to protect the 'public health, welfare, or safety' during a declared state of emergency.

Such authority may include, among other things, the right to suspend any statute, rule or regulation of the state; to compel evacuation of an affected area; to establish curfews; and to control entry and exit from an emergency area, as well as the movement of people in that area. Similarly, Section 13-702 specifically gives the governor authority to order the State Militia into active duty in times of, or in reasonable apprehension of, circumstances such as public crisis, disaster, rioting, tumult or breach of peace.

In the declaration, the governor authorised the Maryland Emergency Management Agency or other appropriate agency to 'engage, deploy, and coordinate available resources' during the emergency period (Hogan 2015).

Chapter 9

Australia: Vague Emergency Plans

In Australia too, vast scope has been retained for the invocation of emergency powers, both by legislation and non-statutory means. There is no federal emergency legislation; but the vagaries of the legal doctrines inherited and utilised from Britain, including the application of royal prerogative powers and martial law, can be combined with equally amorphous and expansive powers attributed by the 1901 Australian Constitution to the federal executive, including the Governor-General (such as the defence and 'aliens' powers).

As seen in Chapter 2, martial law was declared several times in the early years of the British colonisation of the continent and, as in Britain, resort to this authoritarian form of rule remains legally possible. Since the formation of the Australian Commonwealth in 1901, the use of emergency powers on a large scale has been confined to periods of war. Emergency powers were adopted nationally during both world wars, and were used to arbitrarily intern thousands of people and suppress socialist and anti-war dissent and activities.

However, such measures have also been prepared during peacetime. As discussed in Chapter 2, it is now known from the first volume of the official history of the Australian Security Intelligence Organisation (ASIO), published in 2014, that detailed plans for similar sweeping emergency measures were drawn up in the 1950s, during the 'Cold War' directed against the Soviet Union (Horner 2014). These preparations were said to be necessary for an 'emergency' in connection with a possible war; but it seems that they could have been activated without any formal declaration of war.

Moreover, new peacetime scope for the defence power was opened up by the High Court in 2007 in the context of the 'war on terrorism'. In the first decade of the twenty-first century, federal governments also invoked executive powers to deploy the military domestically, for example against refugee arrivals, and legislation was adopted to facilitate military call-outs by the executive to counter undefined 'domestic violence'. Further, in 2009, in the wake of the global financial crisis that erupted in 2008, the High Court opened the way for wider executive powers to be exercised in response to 'financial' emergencies and potentially other events judged to threaten the national state. The full scope of these and other executive powers remains unclear, as can be seen by numerous High Court judgments.

In addition, state and territory legislation provides for sweeping powers to be handed to governments and police forces in many other emergency or emergency-type measures. The early years of the twenty-first century saw more frequent exercise of those powers, particularly at the state level, in the context of dealing with incidents of social unrest or alleged terrorism. This chapter primarily focuses on the federal arena; but two emergency declarations in the northern state of Queensland during the first 15 years of the current century are examined as contemporary examples of the resort to emergency provisions by state governments.

No Federal Emergency Powers Legislation

Successive governments have declined to introduce federal emergency or disaster management legislation in Australia – that is, except for the Defence Act 1903 (Cth), which provides for the military to be called out to deal with undefined 'domestic violence' and gives the government and military commanders extraordinary powers when a call-out occurs (Head 2009). The role and implications of that legislation, which are potentially vast, are briefly considered below.

As a result of the lack of specific emergency powers legislation, the preparations for responding to national crises – including severe political crises, terrorism and natural disasters – rest on the assumed executive powers of the Australian Commonwealth, as well as cooperation with the state governments. This creates a situation of considerable murkiness about emergency powers, a legal lacuna that has been maintained despite calls – such as by the federal government-funded Australian Strategic Policy Institute (ASPI) (Templeman and Bergin 2008) – for legislation or some other legal instrument to clarify the arrangements.

As a consequence, the Australian situation resembles that of the United States, where federal emergency powers largely rest on the allegedly elastic executive powers of the president (as discussed in Chapter 8).

In part, Australia's legal vacuum can be explained by the constitutional division of powers, which leaves many responsibilities in emergency management in the hands of the states. Issues of disaster and emergency management are not mentioned in the 1901 Constitution, and therefore, as 'residual' powers, remain with the states. And there are doubts about the extent of the applicability of s 119 of the Constitution, which states: 'The Commonwealth shall protect every State against invasion and, on the application of the Executive Government of the State, against domestic violence' (see the discussion below on the military call-out powers.)

The federal government could seek a referral of powers from the states under s 51 (xxxvii) of the Constitution, as it has done in the field of terrorism. Or it could rely on various other powers that are assigned to the Commonwealth by s 51 of the Constitution – such as 'defence', 'external affairs', 'trade and commerce', 'telegraphic, telephonic and other like services', 'meteorological observations' and 'insurance' as well as the 'incidental' power. The Commonwealth also has full constitutional legislative power over the territories: the Australian Capital Territory (ACT – the seat of federal government), the Northern Territory and offshore Australian territories in the Indian and Pacific oceans and Antarctica.

Yet, none of these avenues appear to have been explored by successive governments. Recommendations for legislation have been made for many years, including by Lee in his treatise *Emergency Powers* (Lee 1984: 193). Nevertheless, not even the federal agency formally responsible for disaster prevention and management has been given any legislative foundation. An ASPI report noted:

> The states and territories have constitutional responsibilities for emergency management and control most of the functions essential for effective disaster prevention, response and

> recovery. There is still some uncertainty, however, on who will be in charge in the situation of a major national disaster in Australia and how the response would be coordinated across borders … The Commonwealth agency seen to be responsible for this, Emergency Management Australia (EMA), has no mandate, legislation or Cabinet endorsement with which to take command. (Templeman and Bergman 2008: 7)

Another summary of the legal position noted:

> In Australia, the Commonwealth Attorney-General is responsible for the Commonwealth's counter-disaster arrangements. Notwithstanding this, the Attorney-General has no statutory mandate to require other government departments, responders or the private sector to prepare emergencies nor is there a specific power to coordinate the Commonwealth response to an emergency. The Attorney-General has no specific mandate or authority to bring the states and their agencies together or to require Commonwealth agencies to release resources for the response to an emergency. (Eburn 2014: 147)

In its 2008 report, ASPI called for 'an instrument of delegation issued by the federal government, with the constitutional agreement of jurisdictions'. This authority, ASPI said, would be two-fold: first, to direct action within the Commonwealth's jurisdiction; and, second, when a state or states agreed that the severity of an emergency warranted overall federal command and control (Templeman and Bergin 2008: 8). The exact form such an 'instrument' would take was not specified.

Significantly, ASPI's report proposed a greater role for the military in disasters. It suggested that the government consider:

> [Whether] contemporary approaches to securing the nation now require disaster response by our military to be regarded as core business, along with its war-fighting role and if so what would that mean for the selection of military equipment and dispersal and interoperability of military assets around Australia. (Templeman and Bergin 2008: 12)

This call relates to the potential use of the military call-out powers, discussed below.

Vague Existing Emergency Plans

Judging by the existing national emergency plans, or at least those that are open to public scrutiny, two features stand out. One is the assumption that virtually open-ended emergency powers exist. The second is that successive governments and the emergency agencies have deliberately not sought to clarify precisely on which legal or constitutional powers they rely.

The ASPI report referred to the Commonwealth Government Disaster Response plan (COMDISPLAN), which provides a structure for inter-jurisdictional requests, approval authority and coordination mechanisms (Templeman and Bergin 2008: 21). However, according to ASPI, that plan does not detail the precise national authorities, roles and responsibilities in a major disaster. ASPI added that a 2008 meeting of the federal-state Ministerial Council for Police and Emergency Management endorsed Australian Emergency Management Arrangements, but these did not 'confer any additional authority' (Templeman and Bergin 2008: 21). The ASPI report also mentioned a 'National Emergency Protocol' that describes the communications arrangements, between the prime minister, state premiers and territory chief ministers 'designed to ensure leaders coordinate key messages to the public during a national emergency' (Templeman and Bergin 2008: 17).

COMDISPLAN is certainly a vague and brief (16-page) document. Its coverage is not confined to natural disasters, but could extend to any serious civil unrest or political crisis. It states that the plan can be activated for 'any disaster or emergency regardless of the cause' (Australian Government 2014: 6). The only proviso is that before a request is made for federal assistance, 'a jurisdiction must have exhausted all government, community and commercial options' (Australian Government 2014: 6). Requests are made by designated state or territory emergency controllers, and can be approved by the federal Attorney-General or minister responsible for emergency management (Australian Government 2014: 7–9).

Military assistance is part of the plan, but only under the rubric of 'assistance to the civil community' (and seemingly not military call-out for 'aid to the civil power' as discussed below). That can include the deployment of aircraft, engineers, search and support teams and communications (Australian Government 2014: 14).

Even more vague is the National Strategy for Disaster Resilience (COAG 2011), adopted by the Council of Australian Governments (COAG) in 2011. It provides a policy statement on developing 'community resilience' to natural disasters, calling for contributions from business, non-government organisations and individuals, without clarifying any of the issues of government power and legality.

Another more detailed and far-reaching plan exists to deal with 'catastrophic natural disasters' that overwhelm the existing resources of governments or the capacity of their executives to function. This National Catastrophic Natural Disaster Plan (NATCATDISPLAN) is couched in terms of extreme natural disasters, but refers to the existence of contingency plans, including for unelected officials to assume control of governments (Australian Government 2010). Such contingency, or 'succession', planning points to wider arrangements for crises that allegedly threaten to disable governments, and not only natural disasters.

The NATCATDISPLAN defines a 'catastrophic natural disaster' as 'an extreme hazard event that affects one or more communities, resulting in widespread, devastating, economic, health, social and environmental consequences, and that exceeds the capability of existing State or Commonwealth Government emergency and disaster management arrangements' (Australian Government 2010: 1). That definition, by adopting the generic term 'extreme hazard event', is capable of extending beyond purely 'natural' disasters. The NATCATDISPLAN's 'concept' is stated as follows:

> The great majority of emergencies, including catastrophic disasters, can be managed under existing plans and arrangements. The NATCATDISPLAN specifically provides for those events where the ability of a government to carry out its emergency management

> responsibilities is significantly affected either through insufficient resources due to the size of the disaster or the incapacity of the Executive. (Australian Government 2010: 2)

The NATCATDISPLAN's 'principles' specify that 'States have primary responsibility for the management of emergencies within their jurisdictions and are responsible for determining their own internal coordination mechanisms'; and 'States retain overall responsibility for executive decision making and State legislation remains in place at all times' (Australian Government 2010: 2). Nonetheless, the plan envisages action that would seem to call upon unstated legal powers to reconstitute 'executive governments' that have been 'incapacitated'.

Without elaborating, the plan states that: 'The Commonwealth and States have plans for continuity of government. To minimise the disruption to the Executive Government, all continuity of government arrangements should provide necessary succession planning (Australian Government 2010: 3). In order to implement these 'continuity arrangements', if necessary, the NATCATDISPLAN states:

> Recognising that the law of the affected government(s) remain in place, the NATCATDISPLAN provides for the collaboration of all other governments to support the affected jurisdiction(s) by:
>
> - Supporting the reconstitution or rebuilding the capacity of the Executive Government(s) where it has been incapacitated;
> - Coordinating national support in the response to, and recovery from the emergency including in relation to policy, strategy and public messaging, in support of an affected jurisdiction;
> - Coordination of public information in line with the *Model Arrangements for Leadership during Emergencies of National Consequence* and existing arrangements to support the National Crisis Committee (Australian Government 2010: 2–3).

Activation of the NATCATDISPLAN will occur 'upon agreement between the Prime Minister and the First Minister(s) of the affected jurisdiction(s), or their representative(s)' or 'at the direction of the Prime Minister, or most senior elected Commonwealth Government representative or public official, in instances where no legitimate representative of the Executive Government can be readily contacted due to the impact of a catastrophic natural disaster and where it appears to be clear that significant assistance to the jurisdiction is required' (Australian Government 2010: 3).

Upon activation of the plan, 'the National Crisis Committee (NCC), chaired by the National Security Adviser, will be convened and will support the Prime Minister and First Ministers in the coordination of strategic support to the affected jurisdiction(s) to assist in the response to and recovery from a catastrophic natural disaster' (Australian Government 2010: 4).

The NATCATDISPLAN further provides for the appointment of a coordinator to effectively take charge, with unspecified powers:

> Where the Executive Government of a State has been incapacitated or severely affected as a result of a catastrophic natural disaster, by agreement between the Prime Minister and First Minister(s) of the affected governments(s), or their legitimate representative(s), a coordinator may be appointed to support the jurisdiction's administration to ensure that response and recovery needs are met. (Australian Government 2010: 4)

Attached to the NATCATDISPLAN is the *Model Arrangements for Leadership in Events of National Consequence*. These arrangements replace the 'National Emergency Protocol of February 2006'. The three-page document is very sketchy. It states that in the event of an 'emergency of national consequence': 'the Prime Minister and the affected First Minister(s) will consult as necessary to coordinate the response to, and recovery, from the emergency including in relation to policy, strategy and public messaging, in support of an affected State or Territory'; and 'the Prime Minister and the affected First Minister(s) will consult on, and deliver the key leadership messages to be conveyed to the public' met (Australian Government 2010: 7).

These are extraordinary and potentially dictatorial powers that have no legislative basis whatsoever. Eburn summed up the situation as follows:

> In the absence of counter-disaster legislation there is no process for a formal declaration of disaster or emergency at the national level, and no clear authorisation to waive the application of the 'normal' law or to take extraordinary action that is warranted by the emergency. The Commonwealth may be forced to rely on the historical prerogative power of the Crown, now encompassed in the phrase 'the Executive power of the Commonwealth' and provided for in section 61 of the Australian Constitution. (Eburn 2014: 149)

The Cyclone Tracy Precedent

Eburn pointed to an historical precedent for the assertion of such powers. After the northern city of Darwin was devastated by Cyclone Tracy on Christmas Day 1974, the federal Whitlam government appointed a serving military commander, Major General Alan Stretton, to take supreme command of recovery operations. Stretton had a few months earlier been made Director-General of the newly established Commonwealth Natural Disasters Organisation (NDO) – now the EMA.

Officially, a supreme commander was appointed 'because the situation in Darwin was a national disaster of major dimensions' (Eburn 2014: 150). As Darwin was in the Northern Territory, the government could possibly have relied on its power, under s 122 of the Constitution, to make laws with respect to the territories. According to Stretton, however, that was not the basis of his appointment (Eburn 2014: 151). Instead, the government is assumed to have exercised executive or prerogative powers. Stretton was given total command, answerable only to Prime Minister Gough Whitlam (Robertson 1999: 56).

Because of the extreme popular sensitivities to the mobilisation of troops for domestic purposes, Stretton made it clear during Cyclone Tracy that he was acting in his civilian capacity as director of the NDO. He refused to declare martial law, earning him criticism from other military figures at the time (Head 2001a: 273). Another consideration was the legal unclarity surrounding the deployment of soldiers against civilians. Stretton stipulated that troops not carry arms; that they be accompanied by a police officer; and that the soldiers' authority would stem from a citizen's supposed duty under common law to assist in maintaining order (Head 2001a: 273).

There is no doubt, however, that Stretton asserted and exercised authoritarian powers. More than 35,000 people were evacuated from the city, not always voluntarily, leaving a skeleton population. Stretton regulated access to the city by means of a permit system. Permits were only issued to those who were involved in either the relief or reconstruction efforts, and were used to prevent the early return of those who were evacuated. Within six days, Darwin's population had been reduced to 10,500, and the emergency was declared over (Robertson 1999: 58). Stretton recommended that full civilian control should resume in Darwin, ending a short but far-reaching imposition of emergency powers.

The sweeping and uncertain nature and scope of the government's executive and prerogative powers is discussed below. But first, it is necessary to consider the related question of the extent of the military call-out powers, which have been augmented since 2000 by specific legislation but which also rely on 'the executive power of the Commonwealth'.

Military Call-Out Powers

The internal use of troops against citizens is normally associated with military dictatorships and other authoritarian regimes. Yet, the opening years of the twenty-first century have been marked by developments in Australia, and comparable countries such as the United States and Britain, that raise serious issues about the domestic use of the armed forces. Alongside a turn to military interventions, most notably in the Middle East and Central Asia, has come a greater use of the defence forces for internal purposes (Head 2009).

In Australia, legislation was introduced in 2000, and extended in 2006, giving federal governments and the chief of the Australian Defence Force (ADF) explicit peacetime powers to call out the troops if 'domestic violence is occurring or is likely to occur' that 'would be likely to affect Commonwealth interests' or require the protection of a State or Territory.

'Domestic violence' is a vague, anachronistic and seemingly incongruous term which in contemporary parlance normally refers to violence in the home. The expression is taken from section 119 of the Constitution, which states: 'The Commonwealth shall protect every States against invasion and, on the application of the Executive Government of the State, against domestic violence.'

But 'domestic violence' is not defined in the Constitution, or in the Defence Act 1903 (Cth) or regulations. No judicial definition exists either. Likewise, there is nothing in the law about how grave or widespread 'domestic violence' must be before the ADF is mobilised. Enormous discretion has thus been placed in the hands of the government and the ADF itself to intervene against civil unrest.

Under Part IIIAAA of the Defence Act, the government has wide powers to call out the ADF. In a 'sudden and extraordinary emergency' the prime minister alone, or two other 'authorising ministers' acting together, can give the order, which does not even need to be in writing – it can be made via a quick phone call. Moreover, the government can issue standing orders for the activation of the ADF whenever the chief of the armed forces deems it necessary.

The ministers can also call out the ADF in the name of 'preventing acts of violence' against 'critical infrastructure', even if the relevant state or territory government does not agree to the intervention (in seeming contradiction of s 119 of the Constitution). There is no definition of 'critical', except that damage or disruption would 'directly or indirectly endanger the life of, or cause serious injury to, other persons'. 'Infrastructure' is defined broadly enough to cover a vast range of ordinary domestic facilities such as roads, railways, buildings, sporting arenas, schools, universities, hospitals, telephone and power lines, dams and water pipelines, mass media outlets and computer networks.

These provisions give extraordinary powers to a handful of politicians and military officers to launch military mobilisations (Head 2009).

Once deployed, military officers can order troops to open fire on civilians, as long as they determine that it is reasonably necessary to prevent death or serious injury, or to protect or stop a threatened disruption of any 'critical infrastructure'. Soldiers will have greater powers than the police in some circumstances, including the right to shoot to kill someone escaping detention; search premises without warrants; detain people without formally arresting them; seal off areas; and issue general orders to civilians. They can also shoot down aircraft, sink ships, interrogate civilians and seize documents. (For a detailed outline and analysis of these powers, see Head 2009: 100–118.)

No call-out has yet occurred under the legislation. Nevertheless, military forces, including elite Special Air Services (SAS) units, have been deployed with increasing regularity for major political and sporting events. Growing use has been made of the ADF on many civilian fronts, including the Northern Territory Aboriginal intervention; the turning back of refugee boats; the patrolling of neighbourhoods in Afghanistan, Iraq, East Timor and the Solomon Islands; and counter-terrorism exercises.

It has been generally assumed that these operations have been validly conducted under executive power. It is therefore quite possible that future call-outs could be conducted under a claim of executive power, rather than the Defence Act. This raises two largely neglected issues. One is whether the call-out legislation covers the legal field. Can executive or prerogative powers – derived from common law or the Constitution – still be invoked to deploy the armed forces? If so, can such call-outs exceed or extend the powers defined by the Defence Act? The second major question is: What role can the Governor-General play as the commander-in-chief of the armed forces? No definitive answers exist to these questions.

On the first question, the Defence Act, the Defence Force Regulations and the National Counter-Terrorism Plan all assume that other call-out powers exist. Despite the extensive and intricate drafting of the 2000 and 2006 amendments to the Act, no attempt was made to define or circumscribe these non-statutory powers. Instead, s 51Y of the Act states: 'This Part does not affect any utilisation of the Defence Force that would be permitted or required, or any powers that the Defence Forces would have, if this Part were disregarded.'

What sources of power could be invoked to trigger these provisions? Three main possibilities seem to exist. One is the executive power of the Commonwealth, formally vested in the Governor-General by s 61 of the Constitution, and possibly augmented by s 68, which nominates the Governor-General as the commander-in-chief of the military forces. Another is the residual prerogative power of the Crown, essentially derived from the history of the British monarchy. The third is common law power, perhaps based upon that exercised by English magistrates and ministers during the eighteenth and nineteenth centuries (Head 2009).

Beyond that, there is another issue: does legal scope still exist to declare martial law, bypassing both the Defence Act and the Regulations?

Troops have been called out domestically on numbers of occasions since Federation in 1901, notably during strikes and in 1978 following the Hilton bombing. On none of those occasions was s 119 of the Constitution invoked; nor were the operations authorised by any legislation. Instead, it is widely assumed that these deployments were valid exercises of the executive power of the Commonwealth. Commenting on the 1978 call-out, Blackshield, citing earlier High Court judgments, concluded that the government invoked the 'nationhood' principle and its 'amorphous and unexplored bundle of attributes of sovereignty', "inherent in the fact of nationhood and of international personality"' (Blackshield 1978: 10).

However, if this 'amorphous' power were invoked today to justify a military call-out, another question would arise: has the power been extinguished or at least curtailed by the introduction of Part IIIAAA of the Defence Act?

The issue of whether legislation overrides executive power in the field of national security arose in the *Tampa* case (*Ruddock v Vadarlis* (2001) 110 FCR 491). The High Court effectively permitted the federal government to deploy military personnel, including SAS troops and sailors, to turn away 433 asylum seekers and forcibly transport them to Nauru, a remote Pacific island, even though the relevant legislation, the Migration Act, required suspected unlawful entrants to be detained in an Australian immigration facility. A panel of three justices refused to consider an appeal from a 2–1 decision of the Full Federal Court upholding the lawfulness of the detention and expulsion of the *Tampa* refugees. The Federal Court majority held that the government has executive or prerogative power under s 61 of the Constitution to detain and remove 'aliens' and take any other action it considers necessary to protect 'national sovereignty'. By analogy, similar reasoning could be applied to a troop deployment to protect 'national sovereignty'.

However, the authority of the *Tampa* case is not clear on this question because the High Court did not consider the issue, instead rejecting the appeal application on the ground that the asylum seekers were no longer in Australian jurisdiction.

A similar approach was taken by Barwick CJ and Jacobs and Mason JJ in *Barton v Commonwealth of Australia* ([1974] HCA 20; (1974) 131 CLR 477), where the issue was whether extradition legislation superseded any prerogative power to request a foreign government to surrender an alleged offender. Mason J said a statute would not abrogate a prerogative of the Crown unless it did so by 'express words or by implication'. Barwick CJ went further, saying that even though he strongly suspected that the draftsman of the extradition legislation intended it to be all-embracing, the words of the statute did not clearly and unambiguously express an intention to displace the prerogative.

Reliance on Executive and Prerogative Powers

Section 61 vests the executive power of the Commonwealth of Australia in the monarch, exercisable by the Governor-General; and s 68 specifically vests the command of the naval and military forces of the Commonwealth in the royal representative, the Governor-General. In his *Emergency Powers*, Lee asserted that '[a] reading of s 61 and s 68 would suggest some legal basis to justify the assertion that the power to invoke military aid unilaterally is also an attribute of the executive power' (Lee 1984: 206).

Lee also argued that s 61 encompasses a judicially recognised royal prerogative, referring to two British Privy Council cases. In *Chandler v Director of Public Prosecutions* ([1964] AC 763, at 8), Lord Hodson stated: 'The Crown has, and this is not disputed, the right as head of State to decide in peace and war the disposition of its armed forces.' In *Burmah Oil Co. Ltd v Lord Advocate* ([1965] AC 75), Lord Reid said: 'There is no doubt that control of the armed forces has been left to the prerogative … subject to the power of Parliament to withhold supply and refuse to continue legislation essential for the maintenance of a standing army.'

It is revealing that, some three centuries after the struggle for parliamentary and civilian supremacy over the British monarchy – and in a political system that professes to be democratic – the power of the government to take emergency action is said to rest on vestiges of regal authority. Furthermore, if this is so, the possibility arises that the vice-regal power can be invoked independently of, or even contrary to, the decisions of the elected government – a possibility illustrated by the Governor-General's dismissal of the Whitlam government in 1975 (see the discussion below on the Governor-General's role).

Moreover, there is the problem, as Lee acknowledged, that these Privy Council cases relate to unitary systems of government. Under the Australian Constitution, the prerogative power must be 'divided' along federal–state lines. Lee argues that because s 114 of the Constitution forbids the states from raising or maintaining any naval or military force without the consent of the Commonwealth Parliament, 'the Crown' in the military context can only mean the federal executive power. Yet, part of that power still clearly lies in the hands of the states, at least because a state request is required under s 119 before the armed forces can be deployed to protect a state against domestic violence.

Most recognised constitutional scholars now seem to accept that the executive power of the Commonwealth corresponds to, but can extend beyond, the express grant of legislative power set out in s 51 of the Constitution. Lane has suggested that 'there is also an inherent self-protecting power in the Federal Government, as there is in any sovereign state', and therefore 'the Government could use the armed forces to maintain law and order and the running of the government' (Lane 1974: 77). Dixon J's comments in the *Communist Party Case* are regarded as providing the relevant principle:

> It is within the necessary power of the federal government to protect its own existence and the unhindered play of its legitimate activities. And to this end, it may provide for the

> punishment of treason, the suppression of insurrection or rebellion and for the putting down of all individual or concerted attempts to obstruct or interfere with the discharge of the proper business of government. (*Australian Communist Party v Commonwealth* (1951) 83 CLR 1 at 188)

There is no shortage of judicial and academic opinion to the effect that the scope of the prerogative power, in particular, is uncertain (Renfree 1984: 389, 394) and cannot be confined to a list of powers or subject matters (Blackshield and Williams 2006: 523, 525). Equally, there is a general view that the prerogative power, derived from those of the monarchy, extends to where there is 'a national emergency, an urgent necessity for taking extreme steps for the protection of the Realm' (*Burmah Oil Co. Ltd v Lord Advocate* per Lord Hodson at 136).

This prevailing view could easily justify resort to dictatorial forms of rule, either on the assertion that the state itself is threatened or that parliamentary rule has become dysfunctional or inoperable. According to Lee's *Emergency Powers*:

> [A] special or emergency prerogative lies dormant in the fabric of executive powers. Such a prerogative awaits activation in the face of extreme necessity … Another assertion … is that a case can be made for an extraordinary prerogative which extends to the assumption of legislative power when the legislative arm of government is paralysed. (Lee 1984: 322)

Likewise, Renfree's *The Executive Power of the Commonwealth of Australia* concluded:

> The prerogative of the Crown … arises from a general principle that in time of emergency the law arms Crown and subject alike with the right of intervening, and sets public safety above private right … Apart from natural disasters and political crises, there are two main crises that may confront a nation – attack from abroad and domestic violence within. (Renfree 1984: 466)

In a more recent statement of the broad and undefined scope of the executive power, French CJ said in *CPCF v Minister for Immigration and Border Control*, [2015] HCA 1:

> Any consideration of the non-statutory executive power must bear in mind its character as an element of the grant of executive power contained in s 61 of the Commonwealth Constitution. The history of the prerogative powers in the United Kingdom informs consideration of the content of s 61, but should not be regarded as determinative. The content of the executive power may be said to extend to the prerogative powers, appropriate to the Commonwealth, accorded to the Crown by the common law. It does not follow that the prerogative content comprehensively defines the limits of the aspects of executive power to which it relates. (at [42])

Strictly speaking, French CJ's statement was *obiter* (not necessary for the decision), but it was typical of the expansive and elastic view of executive power taken by High Court judges, especially since 2001.

Expanding Executive Power Since 2001

As during both world wars and the Cold War, the twenty-first century has seen the use of another 'war' – the 'war on terrorism' – to justify extraordinary legal measures, accompanied by official assertions of the need to expand the non-statutory powers of the executive. In Australia, as in the United States and Britain, far-reaching 'anti-terrorism' legislation has been introduced. Vague and sweeping definitions of terrorism have been coupled with provisions that impose severe prison sentences for offences such as 'advocating terrorism' and that erode many basic legal and democratic principles, including that of no detention without trial (Head 2012: 179–205).

Even beyond that, the highly charged political atmosphere created since the September 11, 2001 terrorist attacks in New York and Washington has produced government demands for extensions of executive power. Courts in Australia have generally permitted such claims. One early sign came in November 2001, when the High Court refused to consider an appeal from a split decision of the Full Federal Court upholding the lawfulness of the detention and expulsion of refugees who had been rescued by the *Tampa*, a container cargo ship (*Vadarlis v MIMA and Ors* M93/2001).[1]

By ruling that the refugees had been taken outside the jurisdiction of the court by being forcibly removed to the remote Pacific island state of Nauru, the High Court effectively sanctioned the federal government's use of executive power and military force to remove asylum seekers from territorial waters and transport them to detention camps on remote Pacific islands. This was despite provisions in the Migration Act 1958 (Cth) that required suspected unlawful entrants to be brought ashore and detained in Australia (Head 2002a).

The Commonwealth Solicitor-General, David Bennett QC, told the High Court that a contrary decision could restrict the government's ability to avoid such disasters as the attack on the World Trade Center. Despite the significance of the case, the judges summarily dispensed with it after a hearing that lasted less than two hours, followed by a bare 15-minute recess. In a one-page judgment, they declared that the claim for a writ of habeas corpus had been 'overtaken by events' – namely the government's forced transfer of the *Tampa* refugees to another country, Nauru.

In the Federal Court, the majority had held that the government's actions were authorised by section 61 of the Australian Constitution, which invests the government with executive power, including the so-called prerogative powers formerly exercised by the British monarchy. French J interpreted the scope of executive power widely, giving governments room to override legislation in the name of defending 'national sovereignty'. Parliament could, by legislation, circumscribe executive power; but 'the greater the significance of a particular executive power to national sovereignty, the less likely it is that, absent clear words or inescapable implication, the parliament would have intended to extinguish the power' ([2001] FCA 1329 at [185]). This reasoning could allow a government to resort to a range of extra-parliamentary measures, particularly in pursuing the 'war on terror (Head 2002a: 30–32).

1 See http://www.austlii.edu.au/au/other/hca/transcripts/2001/M93/2.html.

The constitutional scope for Australian federal governments to use the defence power for domestic purposes was extended in 2007 when the High Court upheld the validity of an interim control order imposed on a Melbourne worker, Jack Thomas, sanctioning one of the central features inserted into the Criminal Code (Cth) by the Anti-Terrorism Act 2005 (Cth). In effect, in *Thomas v Mowbray* [2007] HCA 33, by a 5 to 2 majority, the court legitimated the anti-terrorism legislation that the Commonwealth and State governments have introduced since 2002. In doing so, by a margin of 6 to 1 (Kirby J dissenting alone on this aspect) the court also condoned the extension of the Commonwealth parliament's defence power under s 51(vi) of the Constitution beyond war and external threats.

When *Thomas v Mowbray* was argued in the High Court, Solicitor-General Bennett declared that anyone who opposed an almost unlimited interpretation of the defence power was displaying 'September 10 thinking'. He insisted that the High Court had to take 'judicial notice' of the September 11, 2001 attacks, and the growth of 'fanatical ideological movements which compass the destruction of Western civilisation' ([2007] HCATrans 76 and 78).

The High Court essentially endorsed these assertions. Kirby and Hayne JJ dissented, but only Kirby J rejected the radical widening of the defence power. Led by Gleeson CJ, the majority gave the federal government enormous scope to use the power for 'military and naval defence' for domestic purposes. In a joint judgment, Gummow and Crennan JJ spoke of 'the defence of the realm against threats posed internally as well as by invasion from abroad by force of arms'. These propositions are broad enough to sanction the use of the military to suppress political protests and civil unrest.

The majority judgments declared that the court was obliged to accept as 'notorious facts' that the Commonwealth faced unparalleled dangers from terrorism. The judges broadened the concepts of 'constitutional facts' and 'judicial notice' to accept all the assertions made by the federal and state governments and their security and spy agencies, such as ASIO. The decision tore asunder the half-century-old proposition, adopted by the High Court in *Australian Communist Party v The Commonwealth* [1951] HCA 51; 85 CLR 30, that the government cannot simply assert a danger to national security in order to invoke the defence power for domestic political purposes during peacetime.

Ordinarily, courts require evidence to substantiate the claims made by litigants, including governments. In criminal cases, it is up to the prosecution to prove its charges 'beyond a reasonable doubt'; and in cases involving deprivation of liberty it has been accepted, until now, that governments must prove their allegations. In *Thomas v Mowbray*, however, the judges effectively embraced the executive's view.

Callinan J, for example, declared it was 'blindingly obvious' that 'groups of zealots forming part of, or associated with Al Qa'ida' were 'making common cause of hatred against communities posing no threat to them' and 'planned to undertake violent, literally suicidal attacks upon even the institutions and persons of those communities'. Callinan J acknowledged that the evidence was 'hearsay' – not normally admissible in a court of law ([2007] HCA 33 at [543–4]).

In the *Communist Party Case* of 1951 the High Court rejected the attempt of the Menzies government to ban the Communist Party during the Korean War. After winning the 1949 election in the wake of the coal miners' strike, Prime Minister Robert Menzies claimed a 'political mandate' to place Australia on a 'semi-war footing' against communism.

Against a backdrop of global anti-communism, the Communist Party Dissolution Bill was the incoming government's first piece of legislation. The Bill's recitals claimed that its measures were required for the 'security and defence of Australia' in the face of a dire threat of violence, insurrection, treason, subversion, espionage and sabotage.

In the *Communist Party Case*, however, the High Court rejected the use of these recitals to validate the government's claim to be exercising the defence, incidental and executive power of the Commonwealth. The judges warned of the corrosive dangers of unfettered executive power. Dixon J stated:

> History and not only ancient history, shows that in countries where democratic institutions have been unconstitutionally superseded, it has been done not seldom by those holding the executive power. Forms of government may need protection from dangers likely to arise from within the institutions to be protected. ((1951) 85 CLR 30 at 187)

In effect, that stand was vindicated when Prime Minister Menzies called a referendum to override the decision and was defeated, despite his efforts to whip up a red-baiting campaign in the context of the Cold War. None of the judges in *Thomas v Mowbray* mentioned the referendum, which gave a clear public verdict against the unfettered use of the defence power. In dissent, Kirby J commented: 'I did not expect, during my service, I would see the *Communist Party Case* sidelined, minimised, doubted and even criticised and denigrated in this Court' ([2007] HCA 33 at [386]).

Kirby J said the majority view was 'further evidence of the unfortunate surrender of the present court to demands for more and more governmental powers, federal and state, that exceed or offend the constitutional text and its abiding values' ([2007] HCA 33 at [386]).

In his book *Emergency Powers*, Lee took a wide view of the defence power, although he did not consider the issue at length. He quoted Dixon J's dictum from the 1949 sedition case, *R v Sharkey* ((1949) 79 CLR 121), where Dixon J cited Quick and Garran's annotated *Constitution of the Australian Commonwealth* as follows:

> The maintenance of order in a State is primarily the concern of the State, for which the police powers of the State are ordinarily adequate. But even if the State is unable to cope with domestic violence, the Federal Government has no right to intervene, for the protection of the State or its citizens, unless called upon by the State Executive. If, however, domestic violence within a State is of such a character as to interfere with the operations of the Federal Government, or with the rights and privileges of federal citizenship, the Federal Government may clearly, without a summons from the State, interfere to restore order. Thus if a riot in a State interfered with the carriage of the federal mails, or with interstate commerce, or with the right of an elector to record his vote at federal elections, the Federal Government could use all the force at its disposal, not to protect the State, but to protect itself. Were it otherwise, the Federal Government would be dependent on the Government of the State for the effective exercise of its powers. ((1949) 79 CLR 121 at 151)

Financial 'Crises' and Other 'Disasters'

Arguably, the global financial crisis that erupted in 2008 has led to a further expansion of 'emergency' executive power, as outlined in *Pape v Commissioner of Taxation* (2009) 238 CLR 1. In their joint judgment, Gummow, Crennan and Bell JJ said the challenged tax bonuses, part of the government's stimulus packages, could not be authorised by the federal government's spending power under s 81 of the Constitution, but were within the power of the executive to defend the Australian body politic in the event of a 'crisis'.

The majority of judges in *Pape* noted that, like defence power, the nationhood power was elastic, and could expand in times of national emergency (Kerr 2011: 39). Thus, it could now be used to justify declarations of emergency and the installation of supreme commanders and the deployment of the military, as occurred in Darwin after Cyclone Tracy. The global financial crisis happened over several months and involved no physical danger to individuals or property. By comparison, other purported emergencies might arise quickly and be said to threaten lives or massive destruction of property. As uses of the nationhood power are asserted on a case-by-case basis, a range of emergencies could come within the scope of the *Pape* doctrine (Kerr 2011: 39).

The minority judges in *Pape* objected that 'emergency' was an extremely vague category of events, too broad to underpin a major constitutional doctrine – but that is arguably what now exists.

After noting that the parties had agreed that there was a global financial and economic crisis, Gummow, Crennan and Bell JJ stated:

> It can hardly be doubted that the current financial and economic crisis concerns Australia as a nation. Determining that there is the need for an immediate fiscal stimulus to the national economy in the circumstances set out above is somewhat analogous to determining a state of emergency in circumstances of a natural disaster. The Executive Government is the arm of government capable of and empowered to respond to a crisis be it war, natural disaster or a financial crisis on the scale here. This power has its roots in the executive power exercised in the United Kingdom up to the time of the adoption of the Constitution but in form today in Australia it is a power to act on behalf of the federal polity. (at [233])

Notably, the judgment gave no consideration to whether a legislative power existed to make laws regarding national emergencies. The other member of the majority, French CJ, said it was not necessary to decide whether s 61 of the Constitution confers power on the executive to respond to national emergencies. Nevertheless, he said the executive power extended to 'short-term fiscal measures to meet adverse economic conditions affecting the nation as a whole', where such measures were peculiarly within the capacity and resources of the federal government (at [133]).

Moreover, the Chief Justice opined that the executive power must be given a wide and flexible interpretation in order to deal with emergencies of 'all sorts' that might arise. He cited testimony to a 1929 Royal Commission on the Constitution by Sir Edward Mitchell KC, who stated:

> Of course, the executive government cannot be confined, like a manager of a business might, merely to those specific matters which come within the provisions enumerating what it is authorised to bring before Parliament to legislate about. It is clear that all sorts of emergencies may arise, and all sorts of things may happen as to which the executive government must have a free hand. (at [125])

French CJ also set out an expansive and potentially expanding role for the executive power, drawing on s 61 of the Constitution:

> The collection of statutory and prerogative powers and non-prerogative capacities form part of, but do not complete, the executive power. They lie within the scope of s 61, which is informed by history and the common law relevant to the relationship between the Crown and the Parliament. That history and common law emerged from what might be called an organic evolution. Section 61 is an important element of a written constitution for the government of an independent nation. While history and the common law inform its content, it is not a locked display cabinet in a constitutional museum. It is not limited to statutory powers and the prerogative. It has to be capable of serving the proper purposes of a national government. (at [127])

The only reservation that French CJ placed on this evolving function of the executive power was that the exigencies of 'national government' should not be invoked to set aside the distribution of powers between the Commonwealth and the states and between the executive, legislature and judiciary, nor to abrogate constitutional prohibitions (at [127]). Citing earlier High Court judgments, he further pointed out that the scope of the executive power of the Commonwealth had 'often been discussed but never defined (at [131]).

Members of the minority in *Pape* voiced significant concerns, which only served to underscore the breadth of the propositions embraced by the majority. Hayne and Kiefel JJ stated:

> Reference to notions as protean and imprecise as 'crisis' and 'emergency' (or 'adverse effects of circumstances affecting the national economy') to indicate the boundary of an aspect of executive power carries with it difficulties and dangers that raise fundamental questions about the relationship between the judicial and other branches of government. (at [352])

Hayne and Kiefel JJ noted that no party or intervener in *Pape* disputed that there was a financial crisis, and therefore it was not necessary to examine whether it was for the court to decide what constitutes a 'crisis' or an 'emergency', or whether it was sufficient that the executive had concluded that circumstances warranted such a description:

> If it is for the Court to decide these matters, questions arise about what evidence the Court could act upon other than the opinions of the Executive, and how those opinions could be tested or supported. Yet, if it is to be for the Executive to decide whether there is some form of 'national emergency' (subject only to some residual power in the Court to decide that the Executive's conclusion is irrational), then the Executive's powers in such matters would be self-defining. (at [353])

'Real and radical difficulties' were presented by such an understanding of executive power, the two judges said. They said talk of 'crisis' and 'emergency' necessarily invoked the *Communist Party Case*, where Dixon J spoke of the source of the legislative power to put down subversive activities and endeavours as 'the necessary power of the federal government to protect its own existence and the unhindered play of its legitimate activities'. But, as Dixon J cautioned, such a power cannot be self-defined by the executive, so that it becomes 'unexaminable, to apply as the Executive Government thinks proper' (at [354]).

By implication, that is the logic of the majority decision in *Pape*: to give the executive the power to define for itself 'crises' or 'emergencies' that justify the imposition of emergency measures, or bow to the difficulties in the High Court itself trying to decide whether an existential 'crisis' had erupted and what evidence to rely upon in making such a ruling. Hayne and Kiefel JJ did not make the further point that in cases involving another elastic term, 'national security', the High Court has invariably deferred to the executive's assessment.

Heydon J, the other dissenting judge, made a pregnant observation, warning of the danger of claims of crisis being abused for political purposes:

> Modern linguistic usage suggests that the present age is one of 'emergencies', 'crises', 'dangers' and 'intense difficulties', of 'scourges' and other problems. They relate to things as diverse as terrorism, water shortages, drug abuse, child abuse, poverty, pandemics, obesity, and global warming, as well as global financial affairs. In relation to them, the public is endlessly told, 'wars' must be waged, 'campaigns' conducted, 'strategies' devised and 'battles' fought. Often these problems are said to arise suddenly and unexpectedly. Sections of the public constantly demand urgent action to meet particular problems. The public is continually told that it is facing 'decisive' junctures, 'crucial' turning points and 'critical' decisions. Even if only a very narrow power to deal with an emergency on the scale of the global financial crisis were recognised, it would not take long before constitutional lawyers and politicians between them managed to convert that power into something capable of almost daily use. The great maxim of governments seeking to widen their constitutional powers would be: 'Never allow a crisis to go to waste.' (at [551])

In the teeth of these objections, the *Pape* decision has given an unprecedentedly broad peacetime interpretation to the executive power. In the words of one constitutional lawyer:

> [I]t has left an implied executive nationhood power floating untethered above the Constitution, to be used in the future as a justification for Commonwealth legislation on anything that the Commonwealth regards as an 'emergency' that it considers can best be addressed by the Commonwealth financial power. (Twomey 2010: 343)

Governor-General's Powers

With regard to the prerogative or executive power, another issue arises: does the Governor-General, the vice-regal representative, retain reserve powers to intervene? The language of s 68 differs from that of other sections of the Constitution referring to the Governor-General. Former High Court justice and major general Sir Victor Windeyer noted in his advice to Justice Hope after the 1978 military call-out:

> Some provisions of the Constitution refer to 'the Governor-General in Council' – which section 63 stipulates is to be construed as the Governor-General acting with the advice of the Federal Executive Council: but other provisions refer simply to 'the Governor-General'. The distinction is significant. Section 68 states that 'The Commander in Chief of the naval and military forces of the Commonwealth is vested in the Governor-General as the Queen's representative' – not in the Governor-General in Council. It follows that orders by the Governor-General to the Defence Force, including calling it out, are given by virtue of the authority of command in chief. That does not mean that His Excellency may act without ministerial advice. He must act on the advice of a responsible minister; but not necessarily by an Order-in-Council after a meeting of the Executive Council. (Windeyer 1979)

Why the 'significant' distinction was made between the two types of vice-regal power, Windeyer did not explore. He simply concluded that the armed forces can be called out on ministerial advice, without the need for a formal Executive Council and the issuing of an Order-in-Council. This assumed relationship is reflected in the Defence Act's call-out provisions. Thus, s 51A of the Act states that if the authorising ministers are satisfied that domestic violence is occurring, or is likely to occur, that would be likely to affect Commonwealth interests, the 'Governor-General may, by written order, call out the Defence Force and direct the Chief of the Defence Force to utilise the Defence Force to protect the Commonwealth interests against the domestic violence'.

There have been well-placed expressions from within the military-strategic establishment of the view that the Governor-General has some independent authority over the armed forces, in the nature of overall command. In a 1983 Canberra Paper on Strategy and Defence, a senior military officer, Air Vice Marshall Geoffrey Hartnell, suggested that the Governor-General had a responsibility of 'ensuring that the armed services do not become the political tool of government, i.e., to avoid the creation of a Parliamentary army'. Arguing that the Governor-General was vested with the powers of the British monarch, the writer continued:

> As an extreme example of this the Sovereign has power to influence or even to deny the use of the armed forces if it is clear that the government of the day intends that the armed services should be used for purely political ends of a domestic nature. Such a safeguard reduces the possibility of a Russian type army being developed under the Westminster system. (Hartnell 1983: 88)

While this view invokes the vice-regal powers as a protection against the armed forces being mobilised for political purposes, it necessarily contemplates a Governor-General issuing orders to the military that contradict or conflict with the decisions or instructions of an elected government. Such a proposition leaves the door open for a Governor-General to claim the right to order the armed services to defy a government in circumstances of political or constitutional crisis. Such a crisis indeed occurred in 1975, when Sir John Kerr dismissed the Whitlam government. Hartnell made an oblique reference to the 1975 dismissal. He pointed out that one of the arguments advanced by Edmund Barton against amending s 68, during the debate at the final Constitutional Convention, held in Melbourne in 1898, was that no one would dream of adding the words 'in Council' to s 5 of the Constitution, which empowers the vice-regal representative to summon and dissolve parliament. Hartnell observed that Australian history may have been altered had s 5 required the Governor-General to exercise that power on the advice of a responsible minister.

During the 1898 debate, Alfred Deakin, a future prime minister, moved that, to place the matter beyond doubt, the proposed s 68 should be amended to include the words 'acting under the advice of the Executive Council'. He said the issue was of such importance that it had to be clarified, noting instances in which governors of Australian colonies, particularly in Victoria and New South Wales, had exercised or attempted to exercise actual military command and control. In one case, a battery of artillery had been offered for service in South Africa without the knowledge of the NSW premier, Sir Henry Parkes. In Victoria, it had taken a 10-year fight to settle the question. One delegate expressed fears that s 68 could allow 'military despotism'.

Barton, another future prime minister (and High Court justice), opposed the amendment because he thought the words already had that effect. He argued that there would be a 'revolution' in England if the Queen sought to declare war or peace without the sanction or advice of a responsible minister. By this argument, the power of the vice-regal representative is determined by political, rather than legal, considerations. Another delegate supporting Barton's position insisted that ministerial control over the armed services would be 'subversive to discipline' and could lead to a 'mutinous sergeant or non-commissioned officer, calling for support from Trades Hall to insist that a minister disallow a court-martial sentence. Significantly, the debate occurred against a backdrop of convulsive strikes in the 1890s. Ultimately, after a somewhat heated debate, the amendment was defeated without a formal vote being recorded.

Johnston has argued that the subjugation of the military to civil authority is a 'great constitutional principle' recognised in s 68. He suggested that s 68, combined with the references of Brennan and Toohey JJ in *Re Tracey; Ex parte Ryan* ((1989) 166 CLR 518) to the historic struggle for civil control over the armed forces, could amount to an implied constitutional limitation against the deployment of the military for domestic law enforcement (Johnston 1990: 80–85).

Relying upon a vice-regal power as the foundation for an implied constitutional limitation is a contradiction in terms. It only highlights the Constitution's reservation of undemocratic powers to the Governor-General.

A tradition seems to have developed where Governors-General do enjoy special relations with military commanders. Sir Zelman Cowen voiced his agreement with his successor Sir Ninian Stephen's 'close relationship of sentiment'. By way of amplification, he recalled that he had been aboard a Leopard tank, sailed in almost every type of naval vessel and flown in RAAF aircraft. Moreover, he had had 'substantial discussions' with senior officers, including one about terrorism with General Meyer, a US Army chief (Cowen 2001: 21–2).

Cowen went on to discuss the 'reserve' powers of the Governor-General, including the one exercised by his predecessor, Sir John Kerr, to dismiss a government, saying that the events of November 1975 'focussed attention on the exercise of constitutional and political power by a Governor-General'. Significantly, Cowen denied that the office had a purely ceremonial character, asserting that on the basis of his five years of experience in the post, 'by the exercise of functions and influence within acceptable limits, a Governor-General can, in an appropriate case, exercise an effective influence on the processes of government'. Without specifying the 'acceptable limits', Cowen outlined a 'vigilant and inquiring' role for the Governor-General, including questioning ministers and requiring clear and ample explanations for their proposals. He concluded: 'Approval of a document or of a course of action which falls within his purview is not to be regarded as a mindless, unenquiring, mechanical endorsement' (Cowen 2001: 25).

Before making his decision to remove Whitlam in 1975, Kerr not only held meetings with senior defence officials. He also sought the opinion of the Law Officers of the Crown (the Attorney-General and the Solicitor-General). Their opinion, given to Kerr on 6 November, five days before the dismissal, denied that the Governor-General was under a duty to dismiss a government that could not secure budgetary supply in the Senate, as the Opposition had contended, but expressly declined to examine his reserve powers. The opinion was signed by Solicitor-General Maurice Byers, yet it remains unclear whether it represented the concluded view of Byers or Attorney-General Kep Enderby.

On 10 November, Kerr controversially consulted the Chief Justice of the High Court, former Liberal Party cabinet minister Sir Garfield Barwick, without Whitlam's approval. On the same day, Barwick CJ advised Kerr that he had constitutional authority to withdraw the prime minister's commission (Winterton 2003: 238).

At Kerr's request, Barwick CJ sought and obtained the concurrence of another High Court judge, former Solicitor-General Sir Anthony Mason. It seems that Kerr had also directly consulted Mason, a personal friend, on more than one occasion (Winterton 2003: 248).

These extraordinary, informal and secret exchanges made two senior members of the High Court complicit in the removal of an elected government, and pre-empted any legal challenge. In his letter of advice, Barwick justified his willingness to advise on the ground that he was advising only on issues which, though constitutional, were 'purely political' and 'unlikely to come before the court'. Later, he asserted that Kerr's actions 'could never come before the High Court in any shape or form' and that the issue was 'non-justiciable'.

However, as Winterton has pointed out, this view is no means clear; and, in any case, the question of whether a matter is justiciable is itself a justiciable issue. Barwick CJ's involvement was not unprecedented. Chief Justices, State and Commonwealth, gave advice on every major exercise of the reserve powers in Australia during the twentieth century (Winterton 2003: 249).

This record of collaboration between senior judges and vice-regal representatives underscores the undemocratic character of the reserve powers. Because of the controversy surrounding the High Court's participation in the 1975 dismissal, subsequent Chief Justices and Governors-General have declared that such advice will not be sought or given again (Winterton 2003: 250).

However, these statements provide no formal guarantee, and indeed, given the past record, little assurance that similar collaboration will not occur behind the scenes in a future political crisis, including one that may involve the deployment of the armed forces. Barwick argued in 1983 that Whitlam's dismissal could be justified under s 61 of the Constitution, which imposes on the Governor-General an implied duty to 'maintain' the Constitution by preventing 'chaos' (Barwick 1985: 41).

Drawing on the opinions of other constitutional scholars, Winterton rejected this argument on two legal grounds and because, 'were such a power to be accepted, Australian government could end up resembling the French quasi-presidential system' (Winterton 2003: 247).

What of parliamentary or political challenges? After dismissing Whitlam on 11 November, Kerr that afternoon refused to comply with a House of Representatives resolution expressing no confidence in the new government formed by Malcolm Fraser and requesting that Kerr call on Whitlam to form a government (Winterton 2003: 239). Kerr purported to exercise the reserve powers of the monarchy to dismiss Whitlam, yet declined to consult the Queen, in order to shield her from controversy. Parliament, or at least the House of Representatives, parliament's most directly elected house, proved impotent in seeking to overturn Kerr's assumption of power.

Massive demonstrations and strikes erupted across the country, and lasted for several days but were eventually wound down by the Labor Party and trade union leaders, notably Whitlam and Australian Council of Trade Unions (ACTU) president Bob Hawke, who urged working people to save their rage for the ballot box (Workers News 1975). An *Australian* editorial marking the 20th anniversary of the dismissal, noted by Winterton, concluded that 'Australian democracy survived these momentous events. There was no blood on the streets and no national strike' (Weekend Australian 1995: 22). In reality, mass demonstrations and strikes did occur. If the Labor Party and union leadership had not ultimately demobilised the tumultuous protest movement, the full implications of the anti-democratic reserve powers may have been laid bare.

Following the footsteps of the 1890 to 1898 conventions that drafted the Constitution, the 1998 Constitutional Convention decided to preserve the unclarified reserve powers. While its resolution on presidential powers recommended that the non-reserve powers be 'spelled out so far as practicable', the reserve powers and the conventions governing them were merely to be incorporated by reference. Proposals to adopt the Republic Advisory Committee's partial codification of these conventions were abandoned. Not even the basic proposition that the prime minister must enjoy the confidence of the House of Representatives was to be specified (Winterton 1998).

Martial Law and Common Law Powers to Suppress Riots

It is doubtful that the common law power of ministers and local magistrates to use soldiers to put down riots is still intact. An English study has suggested that the powers have been lost in Britain, at least since the adoption of the Emergency Powers Act 1920, which permitted the central government to use troops for such purposes as the maintenance of law and order, provided that the government first declared a state of emergency (Greer 1983: 574–8, 598).

However, as already discussed, the British authorities still assert that a common law tenet exists enabling the government to direct the armed forces to intervene. Moreover, until the 2000 amendments to the Defence Act, the various instruments governing military force in aid of civil power in Australia assumed the existence of 'riot' powers, and were in fact modelled on the archaic provisions of the Riot Act 1715 (UK), which itself was repealed in 1973 (Bronitt and Stephens 2007: 270). Measures derived from the UK Riot Act remain on the books in a number of Australian jurisdictions (for example, the Western Australian Criminal Code, Chapter IX).

Revealingly, the supposedly inherent power to resort to martial law may still also exist; or at least Lee, a prominent scholar, supports that view. In his work, *Emergency Powers*, Lee 'hazards a guess' that the power to resort to martial law continues in Australia as a creature of the common law (see Chapter 3).

State and Territory Powers

While no federal emergency powers legislation exists in Australia, each state and territory has statutes that give extraordinary powers to their executive governments, individual ministers and police chiefs to override basic legal and democratic rights after declaring states of emergency. Little attention has been paid to these provisions. Only an overview is possible here, but the measures are far-reaching and have the potential to be applied in draconian and repressive ways.

Under the Australian Constitution, the states retain authority over police and emergency services. The states and territories have extensive legislation covering emergency and disaster management, creating response agencies and providing for emergency powers (Eburn 2013). Each state has its own police force, state emergency service and firefighting services.

According to Eburn, 'each state also has an emergency plan' and 'there is a standing appointment of local, regional and state emergency controllers (usually police officers) who can take control of the response arrangements' (Eburn 2014: 151–2). In fact, police commissioners are almost invariably the state emergency controllers, investing them with considerable powers to declare emergencies and to take authoritarian measures in dealing with them.

Drawing a comparison with the British Civil Contingencies Act 2004 (see Chapter 7), Eburn sums up the sweeping nature of the emergency powers in the hands of state governments as follows:

> In Australia extensive powers are vested in the relevant ministers and/or the state coordinator and are largely spelt out as standing powers – that is, they are already set out in the relevant legislation. This allows agencies to plan for, and understand in advance, what powers they will have during a declared state of emergency, disaster or alert. There is in each case a general power to do whatever is necessary or make such orders as are required to ensure an effective response, but the general powers to require people to evacuate, to commandeer

> private assets, to require people to assist in the emergency response or to take and use water and the like are set out well in advance of any particular emergency. (Eburn 2014: 152)

Basic civil rights and liberties can be extinguished or suspended by government decrees or police orders under the legislation in each state and territory. In his text *Emergency Law*, it takes Eburn more than 50 pages to detail the command and control blueprints and powers across the nine jurisdictions (Eburn 2013: 156–214). Generally speaking, each government has similar powers at its disposal to declare emergencies and take whatever actions are deemed necessary in response – including to issue orders and directives, and arrest and charge anyone who fails to comply.

In Victoria, if the state premier declares a 'state of disaster', the emergency services minister can even suspend the operation of other legislation. The minister has the power to suspend any Act, regulation, rule or other instrument that sets out the 'functions, powers, duties and responsibilities' of a government agency if compliance with that law or rule 'would inhibit response to or recovery from the disaster (Emergency Management Act 1986 (Vic) s 24).

Queensland's Public Safety Preservation Act 1986 provides a typical example of the emergency powers at the disposal of state governments and police chiefs. An open-ended power exists to declare an emergency, and for an undetermined period. Section 5 states that:

> [I]f at any time a commissioned officer (the emergency commander) is satisfied on reasonable grounds that an emergency situation has arisen or is likely to arise the commissioned officer may declare that an emergency situation exists in respect of an area specified by the commissioned officer.

Such a declaration 'shall continue until revoked by the emergency commander or, if the emergency commander is unavailable, another commissioned officer of the same or more senior rank'.

The phrases 'satisfied on reasonable grounds' and 'is likely to arise' clearly vest considerable discretion in the hands of the emergency commander. Moreover, this discretion will be extremely difficult to challenge in the courts, particularly during an alleged ongoing emergency.

The Act's dictionary does provide a definition of 'emergency situation', but the width of the definition also leaves great scope for an emergency declaration. 'Emergency situation' means:

> (a) any explosion or fire; or (b) any oil or chemical spill; or (c) any escape of gas, radioactive material or flammable or combustible liquids; or (d) any accident involving an aircraft, or a train, vessel or vehicle; or (e) any incident involving a bomb or other explosive device or a firearm or other weapon; or (f) any impact of a naturally occurring event such as a flood or a landslide; or (g) any other accident; that causes or may cause a danger of death, injury or distress to any person, a loss of or damage to any property or pollution of the environment.

A long list of powers is available to the emergency commander during a declared emergency. Under s 8 of the Act, they include to seize or take control of resources; use force to evacuate or exclude people from any premises; block roads; forcibly enter premises; search premises and seize property; and issue directions. Anyone who fails to comply with a direction faces up to one year's imprisonment, 'unless the person has a reasonable excuse'. In addition, the government, ministers and officials are immune from liability for acts done under the Act 'in good faith and without negligence'.

The Act has further parts for declaring, extending and ending 'terrorist emergencies' and 'chemical, biological and radiological emergencies'. These also contain extensive powers for more specific emergency situations.

These provisions do not exhaust the powers of the state government and the police. Section 4A of the Act states: 'This Act does not prevent a person from declaring a state of disaster or another emergency under another Act.' In addition: 'The existence of another declaration under another Act does not prevent the making of a declaration, or the exercise of powers, under this Act.' The Disaster Management Act 2003 is given as an example of another Act by which an emergency can be declared.

State Emergency Declarations: Two Queensland Case Studies

Two events in Queensland since the turn of the century give a picture of how such powers can be used for repressive and deadly purposes, including in highly charged political situations.

In 2004, anger over the death of an Aboriginal man in highly suspicious circumstances boiled over on Palm Island, 65 kilometres north of Townsville. Residents stormed the island's police station, barracks and courthouse after the death in police custody of Cameron Doomadgee, 36. The events were triggered by the Queensland State Coroner's partial release of an autopsy report on the death of Doomadgee, whose body was found in a police cell just an hour after he had been locked up for the minor 'drunk and disorderly' offence of 'causing a public nuisance' (Hooper 2009).

Doomadgee's death was one of hundreds of deaths of indigenous people in police custody or prisons over the past four decades. Despite official promises of a speedy, full and frank disclosure of the circumstances of his death, the coronial findings were withheld for a week, fuelling suspicions of a police–government cover-up. When finally given to the family, the material revealed that Doomadgee had died of internal bleeding after suffering four broken ribs and a ruptured spleen and liver – wounds consistent with having been assaulted by police officers (Hooper 2009).

As soon as the unrest erupted, far from seeking to calm the situation, the police invoked emergency powers and flew in at least 80 officers, including heavily armed members of the paramilitary Special Emergency Response Team (SERT). Backed by the Labor Party government of Premier Peter Beattie, an emergency situation was declared under the Public Safety Preservation Act 1986 (Qld). Police took control of the island's airport, school and hospital, closed roads and launched terrifying raids on homes. Amid large-scale arrests, school classrooms became temporary holding cells, offices and police dormitories (Head 2004).

In 2014, SERT officers shot a 42-year-old man in a hail of automatic gunfire in the Brisbane working-class suburb of Inala. The police turned a confrontation with the man into a four-hour siege. They declared an 'emergency situation' under the Public Safety Preservation Act 1986 and locked down residential areas extending hundreds of metres. Traffic was blocked from the 'exclusion zone' and residents told to remain indoors, creating an atmosphere of alarm.

Despite police commanders indicating that the man had made no threats to anyone, the SERT team was mobilised. It used an armoured 'Bearcat' vehicle and squads of police marksmen to besiege the man in a car parked at the front of a block of apartments. The emergency declaration was revoked after five hours.

It was the second 'emergency situation' declared in Brisbane on that day. Earlier, police invoked emergency powers in Ipswich, another large working-class community, after an abandoned suitcase was reported at a bus stop. Surrounding streets near the Ipswich City Mall were cordoned off and several buildings evacuated. The supposed bomb scare proved to be false. Police said the suitcase contained only 'personal items' and the emergency was revoked about two hours later (Head 2014a, 2014b).

Both emergencies took on the appearance of shows of force conducted in an atmosphere of fear of terrorism generated by governments and the media. The Inala shooting was the first in a series of fatal police shootings in and around Brisbane in the lead-up to the G20 Leaders Summit in the city during November 2014, which also saw the mobilisation of thousands of police and military personnel (Head 2014).

Chapter 10
International Human Rights Law: No Protection

International law has proven no barrier to the imposition of totalitarian, draconian or human rights abuses, even torture, which is absolutely prohibited by global conventions.

In the first place, international law reserves to the national state the power to override most basic legal and democratic rights in alleged emergencies or dire challenges to the stability of the state. In the Universal Declaration of Human Rights, the International Covenant on Civil and Political Rights (ICCPR) and other related instruments – such as the European Convention on Human Rights and Fundamental Freedoms ('European Convention') and the UK Human Rights Act – the listed civil and legal rights are mostly subject to far-reaching exemptions or derogations, including for 'national security', 'public safety' and 'public emergency'. This leaves considerable leeway for draconian measures, including seemingly permanent ones such as detention without trial and other provisions imposed in the name of fighting the endless 'war on terrorism'. Thus, Article 4 of the ICCPR states:

> 1. In time of public emergency which threatens the life of the nation and the existence of which is officially proclaimed, the States Parties to the present Covenant may take measures derogating from their obligations under the present Covenant to the extent strictly required by the exigencies of the situation, provided that such measures are not inconsistent with their other obligations under international law and do not involve discrimination solely on the ground of race, colour, sex, language, religion or social origin.
> 2. No derogation from articles 6, 7, 8 (paragraphs 1 and 2), 11, 15, 16 and 18 may be made under this provision.

These exceptions to derogation relate to killing, torture, slavery, trial by law and freedom of religion.

Under the European Convention, however, even the right to life is carefully circumscribed to permit killing by state forces in order to make arrests, prevent escapes from detention and quell riots and insurrections (Article 2). As with the ICCPR, governments can derogate from most obligations under the European Convention 'in time of war or other public emergency threatening the life of the nation' (Article 15). Particularly since the declaration of the 'war on terrorism' in 2001, courts have tended to give executive governments much leeway to use these provisions.

The Genocide Convention and the Convention Against Torture permit no exceptions or derogations. However, the latter has certainly not stopped governments, notably that of the United States, resorting to torture or secretly 'rendering' detainees to be tortured in other countries. No US official has been prosecuted or held to account, legally or politically, in any manner for the hideous programme of torture and abuse documented by the US Senate Intelligence Committee's report on CIA torture. A heavily redacted summary of the report was finally released in late 2014, but the Obama administration and US courts blocked the release of the full report itself.

The subsequent political, media and judicial whitewash of the Senate CIA torture report – marked by the refusal of the Obama administration, the United Nations human rights agencies and the US courts to take or permit any action to place those responsible on trial – provides a damning case study of the reality of immunity from international law (see the case study below: 'US torture and political and judicial coverup').

Courts in other jurisdictions too have been complicit in the violation of international law. The UK Court of Appeal indicated that evidence obtained by torture might be admissible under certain circumstances (*A v Secretary of State for the Home Department (No. 2)* (2005) 1 WLR 414); and Canada's Supreme Court pronounced that exceptional 'national security' grounds could justify a decision to deport a person to be tortured (*Suresh v Canada (Minister of Citizenship and Immigration)* [2002] 1 SCR 3).

The reality is that international human rights law provides little or no protection against the abuse of emergency powers, regardless of any violation of basic legal and democratic rights. In any case, because the nation-state system still prevails globally, international law is not legally binding domestically unless it is incorporated into national legislation. Even where that happens, with some exceptions – such as the US Constitution's Bill of Rights and the Canadian Charter of Rights and Freedoms – domestic human rights measures are not constitutionally entrenched, and can therefore be abridged, amended or repealed by legislatures.

Some domestic human rights provisions simply require courts to interpret all legislation, where possible, consistently with enumerated human rights, generally drawn from the ICCPR. If the legislation under consideration cannot be interpreted consistently with a human right, the court may only declare that an incompatibility exists, and report the issue to the legislature. Such a declaration does not affect the validity of the legislation in question.

Furthermore, under provisions like the UK Human Rights Act, the courts are instructed to permit limits to human rights if the limits are 'demonstrably justified in a free and democratic society'. This proviso, which English judges have described as one of proportionality, leaves scope for governments to brush aside or whittle down democratic rights of minorities in the name of upholding the democratic rights of the majority.

An Exceptional Case?

One judicial ruling sometimes cited as demonstrating the capacity and readiness of courts to hold governments to account according to the standards of international law is that of the English House of Lords in 2004 in *A v Secretary of State for the Home Department* ([2004] UKHL 56). The case concerned 'counter-terrorism' legislation that overturned the principle of habeas corpus in order to allow a terrorist suspect to be held in police custody without charge for up to 28 days. This power was reminiscent of the measures used in Ireland, where internment without trial was reintroduced during the 1970s. A person arrested under section 41 of the Terrorism Act 2000 (on suspicion of terrorist-related activity) could be held by police for 48 hours, and courts could extend the detention for 28 days.

In order to justify these powers, the British government derogated from Article 5 of the European Convention, which provided the right to liberty, subject only to lawful arrest or detention. The government invoked Article 15 of the Convention, which permitted derogation 'in time of war or other public emergency threatening the life of the nation'. In its ruling, the House of Lords accepted that indefinite detention without trial of foreign national terrorist suspects, unable to be prosecuted or deported, could be permissible under Article 15, in the context of the 9/11 attacks in the United States.

However, the majority ultimately declared the particular circumstances to be discriminatory and disproportionate to the exigencies of the public emergency. In a dissent on the threshold issue of whether the threat of terrorism constituted a 'public emergency threatening the life of the nation', Lord Hoffmann stated that the gravest threat to Britain arose not from potential terrorist attacks, but from legislation such as that resorted to by the government:

> This is one of the most important cases which the House has had to decide in recent years. It calls into question the very existence of an ancient liberty of which this country has until now been very proud: freedom from arbitrary arrest and detention. The power which the Home Secretary seeks to uphold is a power to detain people indefinitely without charge or trial. Nothing could be more antithetical to the instincts and traditions of the people of the United Kingdom … Whether we should survive Hitler hung in the balance, but there is no doubt we shall survive Al Qaeda. The Spanish people have not said that what happened in Madrid, hideous crime as it was, threatened the life of the nation. Their legendary pride would not allow it. Terrorist crime, serious as it is, does not threaten our institutions of government or our existence as a civil community … The real threat to the life of the nation, in the sense of a people living in accordance with its traditional laws and political values, comes not from terrorism but from laws such as these. ([2004] UKHL 56, [86–97])

Nonetheless, the 8–1 majority view was that the courts had to defer heavily to the executive government's assessment of national security. In the words of Baroness Hale:

> Assessing the strength of a general threat to the life of the nation is, or should be, within the expertise of the Government and its advisers … If a Government were to declare a public emergency where patently there was no such thing, it would be the duty of the court to say so. But here we are considering the immediate aftermath of the unforgettable events of 11 September 2001. The attacks launched on the United States on that date were clearly intended to threaten the life of the nation. ([2004] UKHL 56, [226])

In part, this solidarity with the government reflected the political and ideological impact of the 9/11 attacks (see below). Lord Nicholls, however, pointed to underlying deference to the executive, above and beyond the immediate circumstances of 9/11. He stated:

> All courts are very much aware of the heavy burden, resting on the elected government and not the judiciary, to protect the security of this country and all who live here. All courts are acutely conscious that the government alone is able to evaluate and decide what counter-terrorism steps are needed and what steps will suffice. Courts are not equipped to make such decisions, nor are they charged with that responsibility. ([2004] UKHL 56, [79])

The ruling illustrated the consistent record of courts in giving executive governments great scope to take actions that are asserted to be essential to the 'security' or survival of the national state.

Broad Definitions of 'Public Emergency'

One of the means by which international law facilitates emergency powers is by generously interpreting the 'public emergency' derogation tests in favour of governments. Hence, in *Lawless v Ireland* (1 Eur. Ct HR (ser. B) at 56 (1960–61), a nine-member majority in the European Commission of Human Rights defined the term for the purposes of Article 15 of the European Convention as 'a situation of exceptional and imminent danger or crisis affecting the general public, as distinct from particular groups, and constituting a threat to the organised life of the community which composes the State in question (para. 90, at 82).

Some of the five dissenting members proposed narrower definitions. One indicated that the linkage between war and emergency in Article 5 – 'in time of war or other public emergency' – meant that the emergency must be interpreted as 'tantamount to war' (para. 93, at 95). Another member suggested that a public emergency only existed when the constitutional order of the state had broken down and the different branches of government could no longer function (para. 95, at 101). But the European Court of Human Rights affirmed the majority's decision.

Despite the amorphousness of words such as 'threat to the organised life of the community' and their capacity to be used to suppress dissent, Gross and Ní Aoláin concluded, after considering several such definitions, that: 'Notwithstanding differences in nuance and emphasis, they accentuate the capacity for definitional agreement and the possibility for meaningful and robust oversight and accountability over claims of "public emergency"' (Gross and Ní Aoláin 2006: 251–3).

Applied in practice in British-ruled Northern Ireland, the European Commission's approach legitimised abuses that amounted to torture. In 1971, the British government reintroduced internment, and at least five detainees were interrogated using 'five techniques' – hooding, standing against a wall, subjection to noise, deprivation of food and water, and deprivation of sleep (Gross and Ní Aoláin 2006: 276). In *Ireland v United Kingdom* (1976 YB Eur. Conv. On HR (Eur. Comm on HR)), the Commission decided that, although the five techniques amounted to torture, a 'public emergency' existed (at 584–6). Yet, the ruling referred to a 'lasting crisis' that had begun in 1966 – that is, a decade before the case came before the Commission. In effect, the Commission approved a semi-permanent derogation permitting torture – far from a temporary, exceptional deviation from human rights law.

In their analysis of numerous cases, Gross and Ní Aoláin concluded, among other things, to international courts and tribunals giving 'greater leeway in derogation cases to democratic states than to non-democratic or illiberal states'. As discussed in Chapter 5, the categorisation of major capitalist powers as 'democratic' is most dubious. In practice, however, the courts and tribunals are applying double standards in their favour.

The record of the UN Human Rights Committee, the agency charged with scrutinising compliance with the ICCPR, is no better. Gross and Ní Aoláin stated that the committee had 'traditionally failed to assess the existence of emergency in certain states and has frequently declined to endorse the principle of proportionality in its examination of state practice', although 'the committee has shown greater gumption in this area in the past few years'. In particular, 'problem emergencies, and specifically permanent emergencies, have managed to escape the net of thorough examination' (Gross and Ní Aoláin 2006: 302).

The UN and the 'War on Terrorism'

The UN Security Council took unprecedented action following the September 11, 2001 terrorist attacks. Within 24 hours, Security Council Resolution 1368 had been adopted, unanimously condemning the attacks and sanctioning military responses. Two weeks later, Resolution 1373 obligated all member states to take far-reaching legislative and executive action in order to combat terrorism.

Far from demonstrating the effectiveness of the UN, however, the response to 9/11 demonstrated that it functioned as a conduit for the strategic and economic interests of the major powers, notably the United States. Indeed, the twin resolutions effectively paved the way for military unilateralism, starting with the US invasion of Afghanistan, and for equally self-interested domestic responses, with governments seizing upon the declared 'war on terrorism' – and the lack of any definition of terrorism by the UN – to introduce repressive measures that served their own political purposes.

Under the thinly veiled threat of potential retribution from Washington if they failed to cooperate – US President George W. Bush had declared in an address to a joint session of Congress on 20 September 2001 that 'Either you are with us, or you are with the terrorists' (White House 2001) – governments of all stripes around the world complied with the UN resolutions, while often utilising them to deal with their own political foes. Thus, for example, China cracked down on dissent, including by the banned Falun Gong spiritual movement and the Uighur people (Head 2005: 84–91); and Indonesia introduced authoritarian measures reminiscent of the Suharto dictatorship on the pretext of targeting Islamic fundamentalists (Head 2005: 77–84).

The response reflected the reality that the UN remains dominated by the five veto-wielding powers that emerged victorious from the last world war, and that it is constituted by nation-states, each of which has its own political, commercial and strategic interests to protect. Resolution 1368, passed the day after 9/11, recognised 'the inherent right of individual or collective self-defence' as a legitimate response to terrorism for the first time. By doing so, the Security Council effectively removed itself from further decision-making about the legitimacy of the use of military force by the US and its partners in Afghanistan under the banner of combating terrorism. Given Washington's adoption of a pre-emptive intervention doctrine that asserted a sweeping right to act unilaterally, the US seemed to be handed a 'carte blanche' (Boulden and Weiss 2004: 11–12).

Resolution 1373, adopted two weeks later, appeared to offer a contrast. It detailed requirements that necessitated significant actions by member states, including legislative changes, making the Security Council arguably intrusive in domestic affairs. The resolution left open the definition of terrorism, however, allowing wide latitude for interpretation – in effect another carte blanche. Various states have used the international legitimacy conferred by Resolution 1373 and other UN provisions to de-legitimise political opponents and demonise them as terrorists. Thus, the terrorist label has been attached to Uighur separatists (China), Chechen rebels (Russia), Kashmir militants (India), Papuan separatists (Indonesia) and Palestinians (Israel). A Maldives opposition politician was sentenced to 10 years' imprisonment on terrorism charges for peacefully protesting against rights violations by the government; and in Uzbekistan, 15 men were convicted of terrorism offences for organising public demonstrations (Saul 2006: 50–51).

On the one hand, member states were ordered to criminalise all terrorist-related acts, and were instructed to provide compliance reports within three months. Some 117 reports were submitted on time – 'by all historical standards, a remarkable response' – and by December 2002 this number had increased to 175 (Oudraat 2004: 162). Paragraph 8 of Resolution 1373 expressed the Council's 'determination to take all necessary steps in order to ensure the full implementation of this resolution'. The absence of any compliance procedure, however, opened the door to unilateral responses both internally and externally. The US was not alone in asserting its right to attack a supposedly non-compliant state. Russia threatened to intervene against Georgia for its 'glaring violation' of Resolution 1373 in failing to halt rebel raids into Chechnya (Oudraat 2004: 163–5).

The United States was widely credited with initiating Resolution 1373, which was adopted unanimously on September 28, 2001 after a Council meeting that officially lasted just three minutes (SC Res. 1373, 28 September 2001, S/RES/1373 (2001)). The resolution was adopted under Chapter VII of the United Nations Charter, and is therefore binding on all UN member states. It marked a shift in international law, which was previously presumed to be valid only if a state had voluntarily signed the relevant international treaty, whereas the Security Council imposed Resolution 1373 on all member states.

Resolution 1373 obliged governments to ensure that terrorist acts are established as serious criminal offences in domestic laws and regulations, and that the seriousness of such acts is duly reflected in sentences served. It further requires all states to prevent and suppress the financing of terrorism, as well as criminalise the wilful provision or collection of funds for such acts. The funds, financial assets and economic resources of those who commit or attempt to commit terrorist acts or participate in or facilitate the commission of terrorist acts, and of persons and entities acting on behalf of terrorists, must also be frozen without delay. Further, states must prohibit their nationals or persons or entities in their territories from making funds, financial assets, economic resources, financial or other related services available to persons who commit or attempt to commit, facilitate or participate in the commission of terrorist acts.

States must also refrain from providing any form of support to entities or persons involved in terrorist acts; take the necessary steps to prevent the commission of terrorist acts; and deny safe haven to those who finance, plan, support, commit terrorist acts and provide safe havens as well. Moreover, states must prevent those who finance, plan, facilitate or commit terrorist acts from using their respective territories for those purposes against other countries and their citizens. Perhaps, most significantly of all, states must ensure that anyone who has participated in the financing, planning, preparation or perpetration of terrorist acts or in supporting terrorist acts is 'brought to justice'.

States were required to afford one another the greatest measure of assistance for criminal investigations or criminal proceedings relating to the financing or support of terrorist acts, and to prevent the movement of terrorists or their groups by effective border controls. States were obliged to intensify and accelerate the exchange of information regarding terrorist actions or movements; forged or falsified documents; traffic in arms and sensitive material; use of communications and technologies by terrorist groups; and the threat posed by the possession of weapons of mass destruction. States were also called on to exchange information and cooperate to prevent and suppress terrorist acts and to take action against the perpetrators of such acts. States were instructed to become parties to, and fully implement as soon as possible, the relevant international conventions and protocols to combat terrorism.

The Security Council's Counter-Terrorism Committee (CTC) monitored implementation, including through mandatory state reporting. This process became increasingly demanding, with governments under pressure to take ever-greater actions to prove compliance. In 2002, the CTC chairman, UK Ambassador Jeremy Greenstock, stated: 'Do not expect us to declare any member state compliant, because 1373 is open-ended, and the threats posed by various forms of terrorism will evolve' (Saul 2006: 237).

As a result of these processes, during the first decade of the twenty-first century, in jurisdictions around the world, counter-terrorism laws and prosecutions became some of the most prominent measures directed against perceived threats to the social order and the interests of the state itself. Long-standing legal principles – including habeas corpus, the presumption of innocence and freedom of thought and association – were overridden or eroded. Novel concepts such as 'preventative' punishment, offences of 'praising' or 'glorifying' terrorism (itself defined in broad terms) and detention without trial were introduced.

Anti-terrorism legislation has been officially justified as being aimed at protecting members of society against violent acts. However, it is almost invariably targeted at conduct that is motivated by a political, ideological or religious purpose in a manner that challenges, disturbs or seeks to change the established order. Nearly all legal definitions of terrorism refer to such motives, even if the inherently political character of such classifications has prevented any commonly agreed international definition.

The classification of 'terrorist', like that of 'saboteur' or 'traitor', is notoriously susceptible to abuse for political purposes. African National Congress leader Nelson Mandela, for example, was sentenced to life imprisonment and was imprisoned for 27 years for conduct that would today fall under anti-terrorism law. He was convicted on four charges of sabotage for planning armed actions against the apartheid regime, before being released in 1990 to enter negotiations with the regime, leading to a power-sharing political and economic system. Mandela was later awarded a Nobel Peace Prize. Other groups, when involved in an armed struggle, have been labelled 'terrorists' by the Western governments or media, only to be later called 'national leaders', 'statesmen', 'heroes' or even 'peace-makers'. Another example, and Nobel Peace Prize laureate, was Menachem Begin, a Zionist anti-British terrorist who later became an Israeli prime minister (Coady and O'Keefe 2002).

Today's primary 'terrorist' targets – Al Qaeda-linked groups – were yesterday's 'freedom fighters' in the eyes of the Western powers and mass media during the guerrilla war against the Soviet-backed regime in Afghanistan. Billions of dollars were siphoned into Osama bin Laden's Islamic fundamentalist movement by the Carter, Reagan and George Bush senior administrations until the early 1990s (Blum 2002: 155). Likewise, ousted Iraqi president Saddam Hussein was also once a close ally of Washington, particularly during the fratricidal Iran–Iraq war of the 1980s (Blum 2002: 133–4, 145–6).

All legal definitions of terrorism exclude what has been termed state terrorism – acts of violence or intimidation organised, supported or sanctioned by governments or government agencies. These may include wars of aggression, military interventions, coups, assassinations, renditions and torture. Past practices of this variety were conducted by the Nazi regime in Germany, and by the US-backed dictatorships of Suharto in Indonesia and Pinochet in Chile. Intensive, but unsuccessful, efforts were to bring some of those allegedly responsible, including General Augusto Pinochet and former US Secretary of State Henry Kissinger, to justice (Tigar 2007: 27–74).

The Ideological Impact of 9/11

The political and ideological impact of the 'war on terrorism' on theorists of emergency law can be gauged through the response of Gross and Ní Aoláin. They presented the threat of terrorism as calling into question previous assessments of how governments react to crises: first because of the allegedly particularly catastrophic nature of the dangers involved; and second because the 'global counter-responses' – presumably a reference to the UN Security Council resolutions – may require the activation of special powers (Gross and Ní Aoláin 2006: 377). Describing this issue as 'complex', the two authors were split on their approach:

> [W]hile one of us views the existing legal regimes as providing sufficient cover to respond adequately to the nature of the threat posed by transnational groupings such as al Qaeda, the other co-author argues that certain catastrophic cases may justify, and indeed call for, the invocation of the Extra-Legal Measures model. (Gross and Ní Aoláin 2006: 377)

Regardless of their divergence, both authors suggested that a broader reconsideration of international law was required. They proposed that 'the episodic but catastrophic nature of current terrorist violence (New York, Madrid and London) means that emergency powers facilitated domestically by international derogation privileges are not sufficient to contain the global threat of terrorism (Gross and Ní Aoláin 2006: 379).

Gross specifically advocated relaxing the absolute prohibition on torture under international law. His contention mirrored, quite directly, the claims made by the US administration for permitting so-called enhanced interrogation techniques (see the case study below: US torture and political and judicial coverup):

> [O]ne of us has argued that there may be circumstances – truly catastrophic cases – when the appropriate method of tackling extremely grave national dangers and threats may call for public officials going outside the legal order, at times even violating the otherwise entrenched absolute prohibition on torture, anchoring this position in the framework of the Extra-Legal Measures model of emergency powers. In such extreme situations, denying the use of preventative interrogational torture may be hypocritical, cold hearted, detrimental to long-term notions of the rule of law, and may, in fact, lead to more, rather than less, radical interference with individual rights and liberties. (Gross and Ní Aoláin 2006: 382)

The charge of hypocrisy, directed against anyone upholding the decades-old prohibition on torture, was a truly remarkable one. The opposite is true. Overturning the prohibition serves only to sanctify the 'radical interference with individual rights and liberties' already committed by US governments at Guantanamo Bay, Abu Ghraib and secret torture camps where detainees were rendered. The US Senate Select Committee report on CIA torture, released in a heavily redacted and truncated form in 2014, laid bare just some of the degrading horrors perpetrated by the United States (again, see the case study below: US torture and political and judicial coverup). Those who hypocritically defend torture in the name of upholding 'individual rights and liberties' bear responsibility for this horror and its likely continuation in the period ahead.

Despite pointing to numerous flaws and gaps between theory and practice in the enforcement of international law, Gross and Ní Aoláin concluded by voicing confidence in international law. It had the capacity to provide oversight 'with an eye to the primacy of certain human rights law norms' and send 'a normative signal to states' that responses to terrorism 'should be contained within a pre-agreed legal framework' (Gross and Ní Aoláin 2006: 420).

At the same time, the co-authors insisted on a 'fluid' approach, 'where state legal responses can move between the various models set out in this work'. This 'fluidity', they maintained, was essential to 'both retain the applicability of law to crisis and to acknowledge that the law applied in times of crisis may vary in substance and content, a quality dependent on the nature and intensity of the crisis itself at any particular point' (Gross and Ní Aoláin 2006: 421). This amounts to an argument that the law, in the name of preserving its own 'applicability', must permit governments to impose extreme measures, and eviscerate core legal and democratic rights, whenever the 'nature and intensity of the crisis' demands it.

The role of international law is also affected by issues that go beyond the scope of this book. They include defences such as self-preservation, necessity and self-defence. Further issues are posed by non-enforcement or selective enforcement, usually favouring the major global powers. Likewise, this book cannot cover the international law issues relating to the declaration or conduct of wars, formal or informal, or examine domestic powers to declare or conduct war. These decisive questions require a book of their own.

US Torture and Political and Judicial Coverup: A Case Study in Immunity from International Law

The Senate Torture Report

An unclassified executive summary of a UN Senate Select Intelligence Committee report on Central Intelligence Agency (CIA) interrogation, released in December 2014, revealed a brutal programme of torture and abuse, implicating the US government in crimes more extensive than previously acknowledged. The 500-page report of CIA torture under the George W. Bush administration was a summary of a still classified, 6,700-page document compiled by Senate staff from 6 million pages of documents.

Though the Intelligence Committee report was completed in 2012, the CIA, with the collaboration of the Obama administration, sought to obstruct its release. The summary, though redacted, painted a picture of an intelligence agency that operates outside of all legal restraint, conducting grotesque experiments to test methods aimed at reducing prisoners to a state of absolute submission (Senate Select Committee 2014). According to the summary:

> **The interrogations of CIA detainees were brutal and far worse than the CIA represented to policymakers and others.**
>
> Beginning with the CIA's first detainee, Abu Zubaydah, and continuing with numerous others, the CIA applied its enhanced interrogation techniques with significant repetition for days or weeks at a time. Interrogation techniques such as slaps and 'wallings' (slamming detainees against a wall) were used in combination, frequently concurrent with sleep deprivation and nudity. Records do not support CIA representations that the CIA initially used an 'an open, nonthreatening approach', or that interrogations began with the 'least coercive technique possible' and escalated to more coercive techniques only as necessary.
>
> The waterboarding technique was physically harmful, inducing convulsions and vomiting. Abu Zubaydah, for example, became 'completely unresponsive, with bubbles rising through his open, full mouth'. Internal CIA records describe the waterboarding of Khalid Shaykh Mohammad as evolving into a 'series of near drownings'.
>
> Sleep deprivation involved keeping detainees awake for up to 180 hours, usually standing or in stress positions, at times with their hands shackled above their heads. At least five detainees experienced disturbing hallucinations during prolonged sleep deprivation and, in at least two of those cases, the CIA nonetheless continued the sleep deprivation.
>
> Contrary to CIA representations to the Department of Justice, the CIA instructed personnel that the interrogation of Abu Zubaydah would take 'precedence' over his medical care, resulting in the deterioration of a bullet wound Abu Zubaydah incurred during his capture. In at least two other cases, the CIA used its enhanced interrogation techniques despite warnings from CIA medical personnel that the techniques could exacerbate physical

> injuries. CIA medical personnel treated at least one detainee for swelling in order to allow the continued use of standing sleep deprivation.
>
> At least five CIA detainees were subjected to 'rectal rehydration' or rectal feeding without documented medical necessity. The CIA placed detainees in ice water 'baths'. The CIA led several detainees to believe they would never be allowed to leave CIA custody alive, suggesting to one detainee that he would only leave in a coffin-shaped box. One interrogator told another detainee that he would never go to court, because 'we can never let the world know what I have done to you'. CIA officers also threatened at least three detainees with harm to their families – to include threats to harm the children of a detainee, threats to sexually abuse the mother of a detainee, and a threat to 'cut [a detainee's] mother's throat'. (Senate Select Committee 2014: 3–4)

The summary also reported inhuman detention conditions that mounted to torture:

> **The conditions of confinement for CIA detainees were harsher than the CIA had represented to policymakers and others.**
>
> Conditions at CIA detention sites were poor, and were especially bleak early in the program. CIA detainees at the COBALT detention facility were kept in complete darkness and constantly shackled in isolated cells with loud noise or music and only a bucket to use for human waste. Lack of heat at the facility likely contributed to the death of a detainee. The chief of interrogations described COBALT as a 'dungeon'. Another senior CIA officer stated that COBALT was itself an enhanced interrogation technique.
>
> At times, the detainees at COBALT were walked around naked or were shackled with their hands above their heads for extended periods of time. Other times, the detainees at COBALT were subjected to what was described as a 'rough takedown', in which approximately five CIA officers would scream at a detainee, drag him outside of his cell, cut his clothes off, and secure him with Mylar tape. The detainee would then be hooded and dragged up and down a long corridor while being slapped and punched.
>
> Even after the conditions of confinement improved with the construction of new detention facilities, detainees were held in total isolation except when being interrogated or debriefed by CIA personnel.
>
> Throughout the program, multiple CIA detainees who were subjected to the CIA's enhanced interrogation techniques and extended isolation exhibited psychological and behavioral issues, including hallucinations, paranoia, insomnia, and attempts at self-harm and self-mutilation. Multiple psychologists identified the lack of human contact experienced by detainees as a cause of psychiatric problems. (Senate Select Committee 2014: 4)

Thus, beyond 'waterboarding' (a euphemism for repeatedly submerging a prisoner in water to the point of death), the torture methods approved by the CIA included 'rectal rehydration', by which prisoners were fed rectally 'without documented medical necessity'. This was done as part of efforts to exert 'total control over the detainee', according to the CIA's chief of interrogations.

Other detainees were subjected to 'mock burials', and were kept in small boxes in which they were unable to move for hours at a time. One prisoner, Gul Rahman, was forced to take 'ice water baths' and was then 'held partially nude and chained to a concrete floor' until he died of hypothermia. One of the officers responsible for Rahman's death was then given a 'cash award' of $2,500 by the CIA for his 'constantly superior work'.

A CIA employee noted that prisoners in the COBALT detention facility (described by the chief of interrogations as 'the dungeon') 'literally looked like a dog that had been kenneled', and that when the doors to their cells were opened, 'they cowered'.

The torture tactics were such that many prisoners attempted suicide and self-mutilation. The report summary noted that:

> Majid Khan engaged in acts of self-harm that included attempting to cut his wrist on two occasions, an attempt to chew into his arm at the inner elbow, an attempt to cut a vein in the top of his foot, and an attempt to cut into his skin at the elbow joint using a filed toothbrush. (Senate Select Committee 2014: 115)

The report summary detailed how the CIA hired two doctors, identified in the report by the pseudonyms Grayson Swigert and Hammond Dunbar, to develop a method of torture whereby prisoners could be reduced to a state of physical and mental devastation. The doctors based their recommendations on the theory of 'learned helplessness', in which individuals 'might become passive and depressed in response to adverse or uncontrollable events'.

According to the report summary, the two doctors 'received $81 million' from the CIA for their services. These methods were known to be unlawful: 'In 2007, the CIA provided a multi-year indemnification agreement to protect [the doctors' company] and its employees from legal liability arising out of the program' (Senate Select Committee 2014: 11).

At least 26 prisoners are acknowledged to have been held without any basis whatsoever. One of these prisoners was an 'intellectually challenged' person 'whose CIA detention was used solely as leverage to get a family member to provide information'.

The report summary enumerated dozens of occasions when high-ranking CIA officials lied to the US Congress and the public. In the course of a single hearing to the Senate Intelligence Committee on 12 April 2007, then CIA Director Michael Hayden lied about a total of 17 subjects related to the torture programmes (Senate Select Committee 2014: 2–17).

The report summary also contained revealing information about the relationship between the CIA and the corporate media. The report detailed how, 'in seeking to shape press reporting on the CIA's Detention and Interrogation Program, CIA officers … provided unattributed background information on the program to journalists for books, articles, and broadcasts'.

CIA Senior Deputy General Counsel John Rizzo noted on one occasion that the CIA Director had 'blessed' a journalist who was friendly to the torture programmes. These efforts were made as part of a 'public campaign' which included a strategy to provide journalists with inaccurate information on the torture programmes.

The document noted that the CIA developed a particularly cooperative relationship with the *New York Times*, and that *NY Times* journalist Douglas Jehl had 'informed the CIA that he would emphasize that the CIA's enhanced interrogation techniques worked, that they were approved through an inter-agency process, and that the CIA went to great lengths to ensure that the interrogation program was authorized by the White House and the Department of Justice' (Senate Select Committee 2014: 401, 405).

The Political Response

Upon the report's publication, President Obama, who had sought to obstruct its release, issued a statement praising the CIA and even portraying its activities as essential to uphold freedom, democracy and human rights:

> Throughout our history, the United States of America has done more than any other nation to stand up for freedom, democracy, and the inherent dignity and human rights of people around the world. As Americans, we owe a profound debt of gratitude to our fellow citizens who serve to keep us safe, among them the dedicated men and women of our intelligence community, including the Central Intelligence Agency. Since the horrific attacks of 9/11, these public servants have worked tirelessly to devastate core al Qaeda, deliver justice to Osama bin Laden, disrupt terrorist operations and thwart terrorist attacks. (Obama 2014c)

The president reiterated his administration's decision to formally end the torture programme because 'these harsh methods were not only inconsistent with our values as a nation, they did not serve our broader counterterrorism efforts or our national security interests'. However, he insisted that there would be no accountability for the crimes carried out under the Bush administration. He sought to exonerate those responsible, stating:

> In the years after 9/11, with legitimate fears of further attacks and with the responsibility to prevent more catastrophic loss of life, the previous administration faced agonizing choices ... Rather than another reason to refight old arguments, I hope that today's report can help us leave these techniques where they belong – in the past. (Obama 2014c)

By justifying abuses in the name of 'legitimate fears' and upholding human 'dignity', such statements effectively give a green light for further abuses in future alleged crises. As another indication of that reality, former Bush administration officials, led by former Vice President Dick Cheney, defended the CIA programme and denounced the release of the committee report. In doing so, they were given prominent platforms throughout the American mass media.

Speaking on the US television programme *Meet the Press*, Cheney defended the torture of innocent people ('I have no problem as long as we achieve our objective'); proclaimed the technique of 'rectal rehydration' necessary for medical reasons; and declared that the prolonged confinement of a prisoner in a coffin-sized box to be one of the 'approved techniques'. He declared: 'I'd do it again in a minute' (Meet the Press 2014).

The domestic and international law was unambiguous. According to the Federal Torture Act, anyone who 'commits or attempts to commit torture [defined as an 'act intended to inflict severe physical or mental pain or suffering'] shall be fined … or imprisoned not more than 20 years'; and, 'if death results to any person' – as was the case for at least one of those tortured by the CIA – the guilty party 'shall be punished by death or imprisoned for any term of years or for life'.

Under international law, torture was prohibited by the Geneva Conventions (where it is categorised as a war crime) and the Convention against Torture, which required signatories (including the United States) to prosecute violations of the convention. The UN special rapporteur on counter-terrorism and human rights, Ben Emmerson, stated in response to the Senate report:

> The identities of the perpetrators, and many other details, have been redacted in the published summary report but are known to the Select Committee and to those who provided the Committee with information on the programme.
>
> It is now time to take action. The individuals responsible for the criminal conspiracy revealed in today's report must be brought to justice, and must face criminal penalties commensurate with the gravity of their crimes.
>
> The fact that the policies revealed in this report were authorised at a high level within the US Government provides no excuse whatsoever. Indeed, it reinforces the need for criminal accountability.
>
> International law prohibits the granting of immunities to public officials who have engaged in acts of torture. This applies not only to the actual perpetrators but also to those senior officials within the US Government who devised, planned and authorised these crimes.
>
> As a matter of international law, the US is legally obliged to bring those responsible to justice. The UN Convention Against Torture and the UN Convention on Enforced Disappearances require States to prosecute acts of torture and enforced disappearance where there is sufficient evidence to provide a reasonable prospect of conviction. States are not free to maintain or permit impunity for these grave crimes.
>
> It is no defence for a public official to claim that they were acting on superior orders. CIA officers who physically committed acts of torture therefore bear individual criminal responsibility for their conduct, and cannot hide behind the authorisation they were given by their superiors.
>
> However, the heaviest penalties should be reserved for those most seriously implicated in the planning and purported authorisation of these crimes. Former Bush Administration

> officials who have admitted their involvement in the programme should also face criminal prosecution for their acts.
>
> President Obama made it clear more than five years ago that the US Government recognises the use of waterboarding as torture. There is therefore no excuse for shielding the perpetrators from justice any longer. The US Attorney General is under a legal duty to bring criminal charges against those responsible.
>
> Torture is a crime of universal jurisdiction. The perpetrators may be prosecuted by any other country they may travel to. However, the primary responsibility for bringing them to justice rests with the US Department of Justice and the Attorney General. (Emmerson 2014)

Yet, President Obama had already made it clear that no such prosecutions would occur. No steps were taken by the UN High Commissioner for Human Rights, or any other UN agency, to hold to account any of those implicated. The defendants would have to include former President George W. Bush and former Vice President Dick Cheney, who oversaw the torture; former CIA Director George Tenet, who officially approved it; subsequent CIA Director John Brennan, who was Tenet's executive assistant; and John Yoo and Jay Bybee, the Justice Department lawyers who authored the infamous torture memos.

The response of the Obama administration gave the lie to the president's claim to have halted the illegal practices. To the extent that the specific CIA torture programme no longer existed, it was replaced by equally criminal policies – above all, drone assassinations (see Introduction).

Among the commentators defending the CIA interrogation programme was US Supreme Court Justice Antonin Scalia, then the longest-serving justice on the country's highest judicial body. He proclaimed torture legitimate and in accordance with the US Constitution. 'The Constitution says nothing whatever about torture', Scalia said in an interview with Swiss radio network RTS. 'It speaks of punishment; "cruel and unusual" punishments are forbidden' (Ford 2014).

According to Scalia's legal reasoning, the Eighth Amendment to the US Constitution ('Excessive bail shall not be required, nor excessive fines imposed, nor cruel and unusual punishments inflicted') was relevant only 'if you condemn someone who has committed a crime to be tortured'. In other words, torture was constitutional if the person tortured had not been charged or convicted of any crime. Regarding torture during interrogations, Scalia said: 'We have never held that that's contrary to the Constitution. I don't know what provision of the Constitution that would contravene.'

This interpretation would give the government unlimited powers, so long as prisoners were not charged with anything. It rendered the Eighth Amendment meaningless, since on this basis the state could simply forgo all legal processes to make its actions – torture or anything else – constitutional. Torture is also barred by the Fifth Amendment protection against compulsory self-incrimination, which is inextricably linked to protection against forced confessions. Both the Fifth and Fourteenth Amendments, moreover, guarantee 'due process of law'.

Scalia accompanied his pseudo-legal sophistry with the standard 'ticking time bomb' arguments for torture. 'It is facile for people to say, "Oh, torture is terrible", he said in his interview with RTS:

> You posit the situation where a person that you know for sure knows the location of a nuclear bomb that has been planted in Los Angeles and will kill millions of people. You think it's an easy question? You think it's clear that you cannot use extreme measures to get that information out of that person? I don't think that's so clear at all.

Such fantastical scenarios are the standard arguments for every dictatorship. Previously, Scalia had publicly stated that mass internments, such as that of Japanese-Americans during World War II, would happen again.

The Judicial Coverup

In 2015 a US District Court judge in Washington DC dismissed a lawsuit brought by the American Civil Liberties Union (ACLU) that sought the release of the full Senate Select Committee on Intelligence (SSCI) report on CIA torture, as well as an internal CIA report commonly referred to as the 'Panetta Review', which consisted of summaries of material on CIA torture activities to agency leaders to assist them in avoiding legal repercussions.

In *ACLU v CIA* [Civil Action No. 13-1870 (JEB)] the ACLU originally requested the full SSCI torture report in early 2013 through a Freedom of Information Act (FOIA) filing with the CIA. The latter denied the FOIA request, stating that the full report was generated and controlled by Congress, making it exempt from the FOIA (only agencies of the federal executive are subject to US FOIA requests, unlike the legislative and judicial branches of the government).

Later in 2013, the ACLU filed another FOIA request for the document known as the Panetta Review, whose existence had just become known a few days earlier in a speech by then senator Mark Udall. The CIA denied this request as well, claiming that the Panetta Review fell under the deliberative-process privilege, a legal doctrine that protects documents that are part of an agency's decision-making process. In this context, the invocation of the deliberative-process privilege amounted to exempting from scrutiny every stage in a criminal conspiracy – to cover up torture – except the final overt act.

In the case of both the full SSCI torture report and the Panetta Review, the court refused to order the release of the documents in any form. The 24-page memorandum opinion by Judge James E. Boasberg (USDC 2015) offered a potted history of the internecine war between the CIA and Congress over the torture revelations, which reached boiling point during 2014 when Senator Dianne Feinstein publicly accused the agency of spying on congressional aides in violation of the separation of powers principle of the US Constitution.

The Senate Select Committee on Intelligence first announced its investigation into the CIA's torture, rendition and detention programme in March 2009. Feinstein headed the SSCI at that time. She and the CIA leadership agreed to have SSCI personnel review relevant documents at a CIA facility, where they would store their work on a CIA computer server. The SSCI vetted its 6,400-page full report and executive summary with CIA officials and the White House, and after final changes were made, approved both documents and released a heavily redacted version of the executive summary in December 2014.

During 2014, a crisis erupted over the CIA's spying on SSCI personnel using the CIA server to prepare the torture report. Feinstein made an hour-long speech on the floor of the Senate to denounce the unconstitutional CIA action against the committee, which was legally mandated to conduct oversight on the agency. Judge Boasberg referred obliquely to 'further discussions' and 'much negotiation' (USDC 2015: 4).

In considering whether the legislative exception to the FOIA applied to the full SSCI torture report, the relevant legal question was which branch of government possessed and controlled the document. The judge maintained that Senator Feinstein's sending of the full report to President Obama and the CIA, with a covering letter, gave the executive branch, including the CIA, ownership of the report. In her letter, dated 10 December 2014, Feinstein wrote:

> As you [Obama] said publicly on August 1, 2014, the CIA's coercive interrogation techniques were techniques that 'any fair-minded person would believe were torture' … I strongly share your goal to ensure that such a program will not be contemplated by the United States ever again … Therefore, the full report should be made available within the CIA and other components of the Executive Branch for use as broadly as appropriate to help make sure this experience is never repeated … I hope you will encourage use of the full report in the future development of CIA training programs, as well as future guidelines and procedures for all Executive Branch employees, as you see fit.

The letter clearly indicated that while Congress created the report, it entrusted the document to the executive branch, making it subject to public access under the Freedom of Information Act. Judge Boasberg, however, claimed to find in this quotation no relinquishing of ownership, instead saying that it 'does bestow a certain amount of discretion'. He concluded that the Feinstein letter 'should not be readily interpreted to suggest a wholesale abdication of control' (USDC 2015: 18).

A similar twisting of the applicable law occurred in the court's analysis of the Panetta Review. This review began in 2009 in response to the SSCI's investigation into the CIA torture programme. Initially known as Special Review Teams (SRT), the project had the character of a damage-control operation, designed to keep the CIA leadership 'apprised of 'the most noteworthy information contained in the millions of pages of documents being made available to SSCI' so as to 'inform other policy decisions related to the [Senate Intelligence] Committee's study'.

According to Senator Mark Udall, who had read it, the Panetta Review made admissions about the use of torture that contradicted what the CIA was saying publicly. While the Panetta Review was certainly not protected by the legislative exception to the FOIA, the court found that it was part of 'the give-and-take of the consultative process' (USDC 2015: 22), even though attorneys for the CIA could point to no specific decisions that the SRTs influenced. Perversely, the judge then ruled that Udall's accusation, made on the floor of the Senate, that the CIA was lying about the torture evidence, demonstrated the privileged character of the Panetta Review: 'If Senator Udall's statements are correct, they serve to *confirm*, rather than undermine, the Panetta Review's privileged status' (USDC 2015: 24).

The ruling in *ACLU v CIA* epitomised the extent to which the judiciary will shield the executive, notably the presidency and the military-intelligence apparatus from public scrutiny. Judge Boasberg declared:

> At the end of the day, the ACLU asks the Court to interject itself into a high-profile conversation that has been carried out in a thoughtful and careful way by the other two branches of government. As this is no trivial invitation, it should not be blithely accepted. (USDC 2015: 20)

Rather than a 'thoughtful and careful' conversation, what took place between the three branches of government – the executive, legislature and judiciary – was a conspiracy to suppress damning evidence of torture and the coverup of torture in the highest levels of the state, in order to keep the American people in the dark about what took place, supposedly in their name.

Chapter 11
Conclusions

Critical conclusions need to be drawn from this review of the theory and practice of emergency powers. Some of the most important are:

Emergency Powers Are on the Rise

1. The early years of the twenty-first century have seen increasing resort to emergency-type powers or claims of supra-legal executive authority, including by the Western countries regarded as the world's leading democracies, notably the United States.
2. These trends point to an underlying shift towards more totalitarian methods of rule, bound up with preparations for war, further economic crises, deepening austerity programmes and political disaffection.
3. One prominent aspect of this creeping authoritarianism is that, both globally and domestically, the indefinite supposed 'war on terrorism' declared by the US government in 2001 has set far-reaching precedents which have already been used to justify overturning legal and constitutional proscriptions against torture, detention without trial and extra-judicial executions.
4. Largely also on the pretext of protecting ordinary people against terrorism, mass electronic surveillance – directed against millions of ordinary people – has been instituted, notably by the US National Security Agency (NSA) and its global 'Five Eyes' partners in the UK, Canada, Australia and New Zealand.
5. Eruptions of social unrest, including protests against police killings and violence, have already triggered declarations of states of emergency in the name of protecting public safety and welfare, such as those imposed in Ferguson, Missouri, in 2014 and Baltimore, Maryland, in 2015.
6. Emergency financial powers have also been asserted to justify exceptional measures to rescue the economic system from financial breakdown, inflict social spending cuts or demand the elimination of previous entitlements, such as public sector job security or retirement benefits.

Underlying Emergency Powers Have Been Consciously Preserved

7. In the three such countries examined in most detail – the US, the UK and Australia – in addition to far-reaching emergency legislation of various kinds, great care has been taken within the political and judicial establishment to preserve potential recourse to authoritarian forms of rule from earlier periods, such as executive orders, royal prerogative powers and martial law.

8. Emergency is an inherently 'elastic' concept, open-ended and politically manipulable. From the 1933 Reichstag Fire, seized upon by Hitler to justify decree-making power, to the false claims of 'weapons of mass destruction' utilised by the US and its allies to invade Iraq in 2003, governments have inflated or fabricated pretexts for supposedly pre-emptive emergency measures.
9. The English-derived common law provides considerable scope for dictatorial measures.
10. The common law has been prepared to support the imposition of martial law, which is, in essence, the suspension of law altogether. Martial law declarations can pave the way for extensive military powers, including the right to summarily try and execute individuals, in order to put down civil unrest.
11. Over the past few centuries, the courts have also developed the doctrines of revolutionary legality and necessity to justify draconian government actions or 'successful' revolutions that become new legal orders.
12. Likewise, the courts have recognised indemnities, immunities from prosecution and defences such as self-defence and 'reasonable use of force' to condone brutality and repression.
13. Courts have repeatedly protected governments against punishment for official lawlessness – acts of surveillance, harassment, violence or intimidation undertaken in the name of defending the state.

Carl Schmitt is Being Revived for a Reason

14. A striking feature of the opening years of the twenty-first century has been the revival of references – in academic literature, governmental documents and judicial utterances – to conceptions of 'exception' that mirror those of Carl Schmitt.
15. Under doctrines developed by Schmitt – a legal academic who ultimately served the Nazi regime in Germany – urgency can justify a 'state of exception' under which basic legal and democratic rights can be abrogated, the rule of law suspended and the executive branch granted exceptional powers.
16. Within the academic realm, efforts have been made to rehabilitate Schmitt. There have been attempts to either justify his views, or at least relativise them – that is, to suggest that they deserve reconsideration as a legitimate response to the political instability of the Weimar Republic and the allegedly twin dangers of fascism and communism.
17. Schmitt is often cited for his association with Nazism, as the 'crown jurist of the Third Reich'. However, his doctrine developed more than a decade before the fascist seizure of power in 1933. Moreover, Schmitt's conceptions – fashioned during the formally democratic period of Germany's Weimar republic – helped clear the path for Hitler, both theoretically and practically.
18. Under fascism, the political logic of the conceptions advanced by Schmitt, a virulent anti-communist, became clearer. Having asserted that rapid changes in the political situation rendered any legal system built on fixed legal codes unstable, he justified permanently in-built emergency powers. Schmitt supported Hitler's continual suspension of the legal constitutional order during the Third Reich – first with the February 28, 1933 decree on the Reichstag fire, which was falsely attributed to communists, then the suspension being renewed every four years.

19. Schmitt saw his theories as essential to maintaining the German state against the danger of either a communist-led working-class revolution or a Nazi-led seizure of power. Ultimately, the inherent logic of his views saw him accommodate himself to the fascist regime as a means of ensuring the strength of the state against its domestic left-wing opponents and foreign rivals – particularly Britain, the United States and the Soviet Union. The Nazis, in turn, found his theories useful as a means of seeking to justify and sanctify their violence and tyranny.
20. Despite the Weimar Republic's formal adherence to democracy and civil rights, there was an underlying political continuity between it and the Nazi regime, which were both directed against the working class and the prospect of socialist revolution.
21. The historical record demonstrates that Schmitt was not simply a legal theorist, but a direct participant in the anti-democratic acts, political plots and counter-plots that led to Hitler's appointment as chancellor in January 1933.
22. During Nazi rule, Schmitt became an even more active advocate for the fascists than he had been for the authoritarian measures of the Weimar period. Schmitt's supposed theoretising provided a jurisprudential cloak for lawless Nazi repression, directed first against the workers' movement, then against the Jews.
23. Post-modernist responses to Schmitt present the wholesale adoption of emergency and dictatorial powers abstractly and ahistorically as a universal phenomenon, stripping it of any socio-economic and class content.
24. In Agamben's *State of Exception* the turn to totalitarian methods is portrayed as a continuous characteristic of modern society, particularly since the French Revolution of 1789–99, suggesting that the fault lies with humanity in general, or with those, such as Marxists, who fight for human progress, rather than with current socio-economic order based on corporate profit and rival capitalist nation-states.

History Points to the Use of Emergency Powers to Suppress Discontent

25. Three oft-cited and uncritically praised historical episodes of emergency provisions – the Roman dictatorship, the French 'state of siege' and Article 48 of the German Weimar Republic – offer instructive lessons.
26. Rather than providing a model for a constrained and delineated recourse to emergency powers, the Roman Republic's descent into dictatorial rule points to the increasing resort to authoritarian forms of rule to suppress the upheavals produced by the creation and threatening rise of an exploited class.
27. A similar conclusion can be drawn from another classical model of constitutional accommodation of emergency powers – the civil law 'state of siege'. The doctrine originated in the pre-French Revolution *ancien régime* of the absolutist monarchy. It was adopted for violently repressive purposes during the suppression of the 1848 revolution in France, which was part of a wave of popular revolutions in Europe in which, for the first time, leading roles were played by the emerging working class.
28. The record of the post-World War I German Weimar Republic provides an object lesson in the worthlessness of any formal constitutional constraint on emergency powers under capitalism, and how such constitutions prove to be antechambers of authoritarianism

whenever the ruling elite feels fundamentally threatened by discontent erupting from below. This constitution, with its Article 48 providing for presidential emergency powers, both facilitated the spiral into fascist rule and provided the initial legal justifications for Hitler's dictatorial measures.

29. Britain has been portrayed as a bulwark of the 'rule of law', most notably by Dicey. But its history, including that of the twentieth and twenty-first centuries, has been characterised by the repeated adoption of emergency powers. These measures were implemented not only during both World War I and World War II but also in peacetime, particularly against industrial action by the working class and left-wing political activity, as well as in Ireland.
30. Since the American Revolution, the ruling elite in the US has increasingly adopted measures designed to suppress any further or future social revolutions. In particular, the emergence of the industrial working class and its struggles for political and social emancipation produced laws and powers designed to answer the perceived threat from below. These measures have been especially directed against socialists, above all revolutionary Marxists who strive for another social revolution.
31. The post-9/11 practices in the US were not simply the product of the Bush administration or the Republican Party. The lawlessness, assertions of executive powers and blockages of judicial review went further under Obama, who claimed the right to assassinate people, including US citizens, via drone attacks.
32. The US Senate Select Committee report on CIA torture, released in a heavily redacted and truncated form in 2014, laid bare just some of the degrading horrors perpetrated by the United States, authorised at the highest levels of the government and the state apparatus.
33. President Obama had already made it clear that no prosecutions would occur over the torture programme. No steps have been taken by the UN High Commissioner for Human Rights, or any other UN agency, to hold to account any of those implicated.
34. What took place between the three branches of government – the executive, legislature and judiciary – was a conspiracy to suppress damning evidence of torture and the coverup of torture in the highest levels of the state in order to keep the American people in the dark about what took place, supposedly in their name.
35. During wars, major industrial struggles and political crises, extraordinary measures have also been imposed in other so-called advanced democracies with British-derived legal systems, notably in Australia, Canada and New Zealand, with the willing assistance of the courts.

Legislatures and Courts Complicit

36. Far from providing any protection against the expansion of arbitrary executive power, legislatures and courts have consistently embraced or rubberstamped executive assertions that crises exist and necessitate exceptional measures.
37. In repeated instances, courts have dismissed applications by victims, or their families, to challenge these practices, or seek redress. Despite paying lip service to the 'rule of law', the judiciary has substantially facilitated, and blocked scrutiny of, the adoption of unlawful or lawless measures – such as secret 'renditions' of detainees to be tortured and assassinations by remote control, via drones, without any trial or due process.

38. The complicity of the legislators and judges is rooted in underlying class and material interests, with legislatures and courts invariably dominated by members of the ruling elites.

'Rule of Law' Frauds

39. This volume exposes the frauds and flaws in efforts by legal and academic theorists to relativise, rationalise, legitimise or propose supposedly safe limits to the use of emergency powers, particularly in the wake of the September 2001 terrorist attacks and subsequent terrorist-linked incidents.
40. A common problem with these works is that they take as their starting point the continuation or re-establishment of the existing political and legal order, and discuss how to accommodate the resort to emergency rule. There is also little examination of the actual, often violent, measures adopted to restore order, why these extraordinary practices were employed or the underlying implications for democracy. In particular, they lack an examination of the socio-economic foundations and class character of the relevant ruling elites.
41. As a rule, these works also accept the 9/11 framework – that is, the claim that the terrorist attacks in New York and Washington on September 11, 2001 represented a genuinely new political and security paradigm that required a fundamental adjustment to the legal system.
42. The theoretical models offered by legal theorists are generally based on the assumption that emergency or exceptional powers, including anti-terrorism measures, are exercised temporarily or are temporary departures from the norm. Supposedly, the public can be expected to tolerate extraordinary or dictatorial provisions because these will facilitate a return to normalcy, or at least they will ultimately be replaced by a return to ordinary legal rules and norms.
43. The assumed paradigm of a stable politico-legal system in a 'liberal-democratic state' is a false one. Capitalism globally is increasingly beset by economic breakdown, growing social inequality and escalating geo-strategic conflicts between the major powers that threaten to lead to another world war. Under these conditions, even the most seemingly stable corporate, military and legal elites will confront the mounting likelihood of popular unrest, uprisings and war.
44. It is false to assume that the recourse to emergency or extra-legal powers is a temporary response to a particular perceived threat to the established order, rather than a more long-term and systemic tendency to turn to more authoritarian forms of rule.
45. It is false to assume that the existing Western states are democratic, and ultimately subject to the will of ordinary people, rather than increasingly plutocratic states scarred by a widening gulf between the rich and poor, and ultimately dominated by the interests and power of a wealthy corporate elite.
46. It is false to assume that the state itself, and its apparatus of enforcement – police, intelligence, military and judicial agencies – is a neutral institution dedicated to serving the needs of society as a whole, rather than an instrument of rule serving the interests of the most powerful class: the capitalist class.
47. It is false to assume that 'national security' is a concept that, although subject to misuse, is likewise an expression of the needs and interests of society as a whole, rather than those of the prevailing economic powers that be.

48. It is false to assume that the 'rule of law' is similarly a neutral phenomenon, rather than one that can not only accommodate and legitimise dictatorial measures but also mask and magnify social inequality and the imbalance in power between those at the top and bottom of society.

'Democracies' Have Long Backed Dictatorships Internationally

49. Dicey, the lauded champion of the 'rule of law', backed and put a gloss on the British ruling elite's protracted record of brutality – from Jamaica to South Africa, Ireland and the United Kingdom itself.
50. The world's leading 'democracies' have a record of supporting, and helping to impose, dictatorships in colonial and former colonial countries in order to further their own geo-strategic and economic interests. This makes it doubly artificial to separate the 'democratic' regimes from the 'authoritarian' ones, ignoring the connections between them.
51. The US government's resumption of multi-billion dollar aid and arms supplies to the military regime in Egypt must be added to a long list of countries in which Washington has backed despotic and violent regimes – from the Shah of Iran to General Suharto in Indonesia, General Pinochet in Chile, Presidents Sadat and Mubarak in Egypt and the Saudi royal dynasty.

International Law Provides No Protection

52. International law reserves to the national state the power to override fundamental legal and democratic rights in alleged 'public emergencies' that challenge the stability of the state. These emergency circumstances are often not defined, however, or defined only in open-ended and politically subjective terms.
53. In the Universal Declaration of Human Rights, the International Covenant on Civil and Political Rights, and other related instruments – such as the European Convention on Human Rights and Fundamental Freedoms and the UK Human Rights Act – the listed civil and legal rights are mostly subject to far-reaching 'emergency' exemptions.
54. The Genocide Convention and the Convention Against Torture permit no exceptions or derogations. However, the latter has certainly not stopped governments, notably that of the United States, resorting to torture or secretly 'rendering' detainees to be tortured in other countries.

The Capitalist State Cannot Be Reformed

55. The growing resort to emergency powers and other authoritarian measures, at the cost of core legal and democratic rights and principles, points to the fact that the capitalist state is an instrument of class rule. Its powers and massive resources are employed to defend the material interests of a relatively small wealthy elite, amid mounting militarism and social polarisation.

56. As the mass surveillance disclosed by intelligence agency dissidents such as Edward Snowden demonstrates, the preoccupation of this apparatus is not with handfuls of terrorists but with the danger of social unrest and an uprising from below.
57. Lenin accurately observed: 'There is not a single state, however democratic, which has no loopholes or reservations in its constitution guaranteeing the bourgeois the possibility of dispatching troops against the workers, of proclaiming martial law, and so forth, in case of a "violation of public order" and actually in case the exploited class "violates" its position of slavery and tries to behave in a non-slavish manner.'
58. The inability to hold anyone accountable for the US torture is a damning indictment. Crimes have been committed, exposed before the world; and, within the framework of official political channels, absolutely nothing can or will be done about it.
59. It is politically futile and delusional to believe that democratic rights can be secured through an appeal to any section of the state. By all its actions, the ruling class demonstrates again and again not only its indifference but also its hostility to democratic forms of rule.
60. This means the defence of democracy is a revolutionary question. The police-state methods of the ruling capitalist class must be countered by the independent mobilisation of the working class – that is, the vast majority of people, in opposition to the corporate and financial aristocracy and its state institutions.
61. The right to revolution proclaimed by the American Declaration of Independence to secure the 'inalienable' rights to life, liberty and the pursuit of happiness must be resumed. That declaration stated that revolution can become the *duty* of the people, insisting that 'when a long train of abuses and usurpations, pursuing invariably the same Object evinces a design to reduce them under absolute Despotism, it is their right, it is their duty, to throw off such Government'.
62. The establishment of workers' power cannot be achieved through the election of socialist candidates to the existing institutions of the bourgeois state. New forms and structures of genuine participatory democracy – arising in the course of revolutionary mass struggles and representative of the working-class majority of the population – must be developed as the foundations of a workers' government: that is, a government of, for and by the workers.

Bibliography

Abraham, D. 2007. The Bush Regime from Elections to Detentions: A Moral Economy of Carl Schmitt and Human Rights. *University of Miami Legal Studies Research Paper* No. 2007-20, May.

Acheson, D. 1963. The Cuban Quarantine: Remarks. *American Society of International Law Proceedings*, 57, 13.

Ackerman, B. 2004. The Emergency Constitution. *Yale Law Journal*, 113, 1029.

ACLU. 2008. ACLU v. NSA: The Challenge to Illegal Spying. [Online]. Available at: http://www.aclu.org/national-security/aclu-v-nsa-challenge-illegal-spying [accessed 11 May 2010].

Adelaide, D. 2002. G-8 Security Operation: The Stifling and Criminalizing of Dissent, *World Socialist Web Site*, 27 June. [Online]. Available at: https://www.wsws.org/en/articles/2002/06/g8-j27.html.

Agamben, G. 2005. *State of Exception* (trans. K. Attell). Chicago: University Of Chicago Press.

Amnesty 2014. *The Streets of America: Human Rights Abuses in Ferguson*. [Online]. Available at: http://www.amnestyusa.org/sites/default/files/onthestreetsofamerica amnestyinternational.pdf [accessed 20 December 2014].

Australian Government. 2010. *NATCATDISPLAN: National Catastrophic Natural Disaster Plan*. Canberra: Attorney-General's Department.

——. 2014. *COMDISPLAN 2014: Australian Government Disaster Response Plan*. Canberra: Attorney-General's Department.

Australian War Memorial. Egyptian Uprising 1919. [Online]. Available at: https://www.awm.gov.au/military-event/E26/ [accessed 24 May 2015].

Avilés, W. 2009. Policy Coalitions, Economic Reform and Military Power in Ecuador and Venezuela. *Third World Quarterly*, 30:8, 1549–64.

Babington, A. 1990. *Military Intervention in Britain: From the Gordon Riots to the Gibraltar Incident*. London: Routledge.

Bacevich, A. 2002. *American Empire: The Realities and Consequences of US Diplomacy*. Cambridge, MA: Harvard University Press.

Bandt, A. 2009. Had We But World Enough and Time (Reconsidering 'Emergency'). *Australian Feminist Law Journal*, 31, 15–32.

Barwick, G. 1985. The Economics of the 1975 Constitutional Crisis. *Quadrant*, March 1985, 37.

BBC. 2014. US Unlocks Military Aid to Egypt, Backing President Sisi. [Online]. Available at: http://www.bbc.com/news/world-middle-east-27961933 [accessed 18 March 2015].

Beddie, B and Moss, S. 1982. *Some Aspects of Aid to the Civil Power in Australia*. Sydney: University of New South Wales, Department of Government.

Beirne, P. and Hunt, A. 1990. Law and the Constitution of Soviet Society: The Case of Comrade Lenin, in *Revolution in Law: Contributions to the Development of Soviet Legal Theory* (Beirne, P. and Hunt, A. eds). Armonk, NY: Sharpe.

Bell, J. 1992. *French Constitutional Law*. New York: Oxford University Press.
Bendersky, J. 2014. *Carl Schmitt: Theorist for the Reich*. Princeton, NJ: Princeton University Press.
Bills, S. 1998. *Kent State/May 4: Echoes through a Decade*. Kent, OH: Kent State University Press.
Blackshield, A. 1978. The Siege of Bowral: The Legal Issues. *Pacific Defence Reporter*, 4, 6.
—— and Williams, G. 2006. *Australian Constitutional Law and Theory: Commentary and Materials*. 4th edn. Annandale: Federation.
Blackstone, W. 2001. *Commentaries on the Laws of England*. London: Routledge-Cavendish.
Blick, A. 2014. Emergency Powers and the Withering of the Royal Prerogative. *International Journal of Human Rights*, 18:2, 195–210.
Bloomberg. 2014. Injustice in Ferguson, Long Before Michael Brown. *BloombergBusinessweek*, 21 August 2014. [Online]. Available at: http://www.businessweek.com/articles/2014-08-21/ferguson-economic-political-conditions-fuel-protest-fury [accessed 20 October 2014].
Blum, W. 2002. *Rogue State: A Guide to the World's Only Superpower*. London: Zed.
Bobbitt, P. 2008. *Terror and Consent: The Wars for the Twenty-First Century*. New York: Anchor.
Bogdanor, V. 1995. *The Monarchy and the Constitution*. Oxford: Oxford University Press.
Boliek, B. 2013. Agencies in Crisis? An Examination of State and Federal Agency Emergency Powers. *Fordham Law Review*, 81, 3339–87.
Boulden, J. and Weiss, T. 2004. Whither Terrorism and the United Nations? In Boulden and Weiss. *Terrorism and the UN: Before and After September 11*. Bloomington: Indiana University Press.
Bradley, A. and Ewing, K. 2010. *Constitutional and Administrative Law*. 15th edn. London: Longman.
Bronitt, S. and Stephens, D. 2007. 'Flying Under the Radar': The Use of Lethal Force Against Hijacked Aircraft: Recent Australian Developments. *Oxford University Commonwealth Law Journal*, 7, 265.
Brook, D and King C. 2007. Civil Service Reform as National Security: The Homeland Security Act of 2002. *Public Administration Review*, 67:3, 399–407.
Broué, P. 2006. *The German Revolution 1917–1923*. Chicago: Haymarket.
Brown, H. 2007. *Ending the French Revolution: Violence, Justice, and Repression from the Terror to Napoleon*. Charlottesville: University of Virginia Press.
Brown, L. 2006. *Plan B 2.0: Rescuing a Planet under Stress and a Civilization in Trouble*. New York: Norton.
Cabinet Office. 2003. *Draft Civil Contingencies Bill*, June 2003 Cm5843. London: Cabinet Office.
——. 2009. *The Governance of Britain: Review of the Executive Royal Prerogative Powers – Final Report*. London: Cabinet Office.
Calder, G. 2008. Routing a Rebellion or Crushing a Crime Wave? Proclaiming Martial Law and a Call-to-Arms in Van Diemen's Land. *Legal History*, 12, 127.
Caldwell, P. 2005. Controversies over Carl Schmitt: A Review of Recent Literature. *Journal of Modern History*, 77, 357–87.
Campbell, C. 1994. *Emergency Law in Ireland, 1918–1925*. Oxford: Clarendon.
——. 2008. Law, Terror and Social Movements: The Repression-Mobilisation Nexus, in *Emergencies and the Limits of Legality* (Ramraj, V. ed.). Cambridge: Cambridge University Press.

Campbell, T. 2008. Emergency Strategies For Prescriptive Legal Positivists: Anti-Terrorist Law and Legal Theory, in *Emergencies and the Limits of Legality* (Ramraj, V. ed.). Cambridge: Cambridge University Press.

Capua, J. 1977. The Early History of Martial Law in England from the Fourteenth Century to the Petition of Right. *Cambridge Law Journal*, 1977, 152.

Caputo, P. 2005. *13 Seconds: A Look Back at the Kent State Shootings*. New York: Chamberlain.

Carlyle, T. 1867. Shooting Niagara: and After? *Macmillan's Magazine*, 16, 319.

Carsten, F. 1995. *The German Workers and the Nazis*. Aldershot: Scolar.

Cary, M and Scullard, H. 1975. *A History of Rome Down to the Reign of Constantine*. 3rd edn. New York: St. Martin's.

Center for Responsive Politics. 2014. Millionaires' Club: For First Time, Most Lawmakers are Worth $1 Million-Plus. [Online]. Available at: https://www.opensecrets org/news/2014/01/millionaires-club-for-first-time-most-lawmakers-are-worth-1-million-plus/ [accessed 8 May 2015].

Centers for Disease Control and Prevention. 2009. Surveillance for Violent Deaths: National Violent Death Reporting System, 16 States, 2009. [Online]. Available at: http://www.cdc.gov/mmwr/pdf/ss/ss6106.pdf [accessed 20 December 2014].

Cheney, R. 2001. Remarks to the Republican Governors Association, October 25, 2001. [Online]. Available at: http://www.whitehouse.gov/vicepresident/news-speeches/vp20011025.html [accessed 15 June 2014].

Chesterman, S. 2008. Deny Everything: Intelligence Activities and the Rule of Law, in *Emergencies and the Limits of Legality* (Ramraj, V. ed.). Cambridge: Cambridge University Press.

Church, F. 1977. Ending Emergency Government. *American Bar Association Journal*, 63, 197.

Clark, D. 2007. *Principles of Australian Public Law*. 2nd edn. Sydney: LexisNexis Butterworths.

Coady, T. and O'Keefe, M. (eds). 2002. *Terrorism and Justice: Moral Argument in a Threatened World*. Carlton: Melbourne University.

COAG. 2011. *National Strategy for Disaster Resilience*. Canberra: Commonwealth of Australia.

Cockburn, F. (ed). 1867. *Charge of the Lord Chief Justice of England to the Grand Jury at the Central Criminal Court, in the Case of The Queen Against Nelson and Brand*. London: William Ridgway.

Cockburn, P. 2013. Bombs May Rouse a Monster. *The Independent* [Online]. Available at: http://www.theage.com.au/comment/bombs-may-rouse-a-monster-20130421-2i8le.html#ixzz2RLCC3taf [accessed: 20 October 2012].

Congressional Research Service. 2001. *National Emergency Powers*. Washington. [Online]. Available at: http://fpc.state.gov/documents/organization/6216.pdf [accessed 27 May 2015].

Consider the Source. 2013. Majority of Supreme Court Members Millionaires. [Online]. Available at: http://www.publicintegrity.org/2013/06/14/12827/majority-supreme-court-members-millionaires [accessed 8 May 2015]

Cosgrove, R. 1980. *The Rule of Law: Albert Venn Dicey, Victorian Jurist*. Chapel Hill: University of North Carolina Press.

Cowen, Z. 2001. Understanding the Office of the Governor-General of Australia. *Australian Defence Force Journal*, 148, 21.

Coxsedge, J. Coldicutt, K and Harant, G. 1982. *Rooted in Secrecy: The Clandestine Involvement in Australian Politics*. Melbourne: Committee for the Abolition of Political Police.

Croce, M. and Salvatore, A. 2013. *The Legal Theory of Carl Schmitt*. Hoboken: Taylor & Francis.

Daly, M. 1988. *The British Occupation, 1882–1922*. Cambridge Histories Online: Cambridge University Press.

Damon, A. 2014. Attorney General Holder Backs Police-Military Siege in Visit to Ferguson, Missouri. *World Socialist Web Site*. [Online]. Available at: http://www.wsws.org/en/articles/2014/08/21/ferg-a21.html [accessed 20 December 2014].

Daniels, R. 1993. *Concentration Camps: North America Japanese in the United States and Canada during World War II*. Malabar, FL: Krieger.

DeConde, A. et al. (eds). 2001. 'Dictatorships'. *Encyclopedia of American Foreign Policy, Volume 1*. New York: Simon & Schuster.

de Smith, S. 1981. *Constitutional and Administrative Law*. 4th edn. London: Penguin/ Longmans.

Dicey, A. 1962. *Lectures on the Relation between Law and Public Opinion in England during the Nineteenth Century*. London: Macmillan.

——. 2005. *Introduction to the Study of the Law of the Constitution*. Boston: Adamant Media.

Douglas, R. 2003. Law, War and Liberty: The World War II Subversion Prosecutions. *Melbourne University Law Review*, 27, 65–116.

Douzinas, C. 2009. Polis, State, Cosmopolis, *Bedeutung*, 3*: Life and Death*.

du Bois-Pedain, A. 2007. *Transitional Amnesty in South Africa*. Cambridge: Cambridge University Press.

Dyzenhaus, D. 1997. Holmes and Carl Schmitt: An Unlikely Pair? *Brooklyn Law Review*, 63, 165.

Dyzenhaus, D. 2006. *The Constitution of Law: Legality in a Time of Emergency*. Cambridge: Cambridge University Press.

——. 2008. The Compulsion of Legality, in *Emergencies and the Limits of Legality* (Ramraj, V. ed.). Cambridge: Cambridge University Press.

Eburn, M. 2013. *Emergency Law*. 4th edn. Sydney: Federation Press.

——. 2014. Managing 'Civil Contingencies' in Australia. *International Journal of Human Rights*, 18:2, 143–58.

Edelson, C. 2013. *Emergency Presidential Power: From the Drafting of the Constitution to the War on Terror*. Madison: University of Wisconsin Press.

Edelstein, J. 2002. The Prasad Affidavits: Proof of Facts in Revolutionary Legitimacy Cases. *Sydney Law Review*, 29, 43.

Emmerson, B. 2014. Feinstein Report: UN Expert Calls for Prosecution of CIA Officers and Other US Government OFFICIALS. [Online]. Available at: http://www.ohchr.org/EN/NewsEvents/Pages/DisplayNews.aspx?NewsID=15397&LangID=E [accessed 29 May 2015].

Engels, F. 1942. *The Origin of the Family, Private Property and the State*. New York: International.

——. 1959. *Anti-Dühring*. Moscow: Progress.

——. 1975. Marx and Engels, *Selected Correspondence*. Moscow: Progress.

——. 1976. *The Condition of the Working Class in England*, vol 4, *Marx and Engels Collected Works*. London: Lawrence and Wishart.

Ewing, K and Gearty, C. 2000. *The Struggle for Civil Liberties: Political Freedom and the Rule of Law in Britain 1914–1945*. Oxford: Oxford University Press.

FEMA. 2006. *Select Bipartisan Committee to Investigate the Preparation for and response to Hurricane Katrina*, 15 February 2006. Washington: US Government Printing Office. [Online]. Available at: http://www.katrina.house.gov/ [accessed 15 January 2015].

Ferguson, N. 2004. *Empire: The Rise and Demise of the British World Order and the Lessons for Global Power*. New York: Basic.

Feuchtwanger, E. 1993. *From Weimar to Hitler: Germany, 1918-33*. London: Macmillan.

Finlason, W. ed. 1869. *Report of the Case of The Queen v. Edward John Eyre, on his Prosecution in the Court of Queen's Bench, For High Crimes and Misdemeanours Alleged to have been committed by him in his office of GOVERNOR OF JAMAICA; CONTAINING THE Evidence (Taken from the Depositions), the Indictment, and the Charge of Mr. Justice Blackburn*. London: Chapman and Hall.

Fisher, L. 2010. Abraham Lincoln: Preserving the Union and the Constitution. *Albany Government Law Review*, 3, 503.

Forbes. 2015. The World's Billionaires. *Forbes*, 3 March 2015. [Online]. Available at: http://www.forbes.com/billionaires/ [accessed 6 March 2015].

Forcese, C. 2008. *National Security Law, Canadian Practice in International Perspective*. Toronto: Irwin Law.

Ford, T. 1985. *Albert Venn Dicey: The Man and his Times*. Chichester: Rose.

Ford, M. 2014. Antonin Scalia's Case for Torture. *The Atlantic*, 13 December 2014. [Online]. Available at: http://www.theatlantic.com/politics/archive/2014/12/antonin-scalias-case-for-torture/383730/ [accessed 29 May 2015].

Friedrich, C. 1957. *Constitutional Reason of State: The Survival of the Constitutional Order*. Providence, RI: Brown University Press.

Frye, C. 1966. Carl Schmitt's Concept of the Political. *Journal of Politics*, 28, 818–30.

Fudge, J. and Tucker, E. 2004. *Labour Before the Law: The Regulation of Workers' Collective Action in Canada, 1900–1948*. Toronto: University of Toronto Press.

Fuller, L. 1964. *The Morality of Law*. New Haven, CT: Yale University Press.

Gillerman, M. 2014. Judge Denies ACLU Motion for an Order to Stop Police Tactics. *St. Louis Post-Dispatch*, 18 August 2014. [Online]. Available at: http://www.stltoday.com/news/local/metro/judge-denies-aclu-motion-for-an-order-to-stop-police/article_fb22afea-3720-5b45-8d4a-2d923e793925.html [accessed 20 December 2014].

Greenberg, U. 2015. *The Weimar Century: German Émigrés and the Ideological Foundations of the Cold War*. Princeton, NJ: Princeton University Press.

Greenland, H. 1998. *Red Hot: The Life and Times of Nick Origlass*. Sydney: Wellington Lane.

Greenwald, G. 2014. *No Place to Hide: Edward Snowden, the NSA, and the U.S. Surveillance State*. London: Hamish Hamilton.

Greer. 1983. Military Intervention in Civil Disturbances: The Legal Basis Reconsidered. *Public Law*, 1983, 573.

Gross, O. 2003. Chaos and Rules: Should Responses to Violent Crises Always be Constitutional? *Yale Law Journal*, 112, 1011.

——. 2008. Extra-Legality and the Ethic of Political Responsibility, in *Emergencies and the Limits of Legality* (Ramraj, V. ed). Cambridge, Cambridge University Press.

—— and Ní Aoláin, F. 2006. *Law in Times of Crisis: Emergency Powers in Theory and Practice.* Cambridge: Cambridge University Press.

Hagerty, C and Ramseur, J. 2010. *Deepwater Horizon Oil Spill: Selected Issues for Congress.* Washington: Congressional Research Service.

Hailsham, L. 1973. *Halsbury's Laws of England.* 4th edn. London: LexisNexis Butterworths.

Hammond, M. 1997. The Posse Comitatus Act: A Principle in Need of Renewal. *Washington University Law Quarterly*, 75, 953.

Hancock, N. 2002. *Terrorism and the Law in Australia: Supporting Materials.* Canberra: Parliament of Australia (Department of Parliamentary Library, Research Paper No. 13).

Hartnell, G. 1983. *The Problem of Command in the Australian Defence Force Environment: Canberra Papers on Strategy and Defence No 27.* Canberra: Australian National University.

Haslip, S. 2002. 'A Critical Consideration of the Use of the Aid to Civil Power Provision Against Aboriginal Peoples in the Light of the Promises of Protection Made to Aboriginal Peoples in Canada', CDA-CDAI Symposium. [Online]. Available at: http://www.cda-cdai.ca/symposia/2002/haslip.htm [accessed 15 August 2008].

Head, M. 2001a. The Military Call-Out Legislation: Some Legal and Constitutional Questions. *Federal Law Review*, 29:2, 273–94.

——. 2001b. A Victory for Democracy? An Alternative Assessment of *Republic of Fiji v Prasad. Melbourne Journal of International Law*, 2, 535–49.

——. 2002a. The High Court and the *Tampa* Refugees. *Griffith Law Review* 11, 23–33.

——. 2002b. Counter Terrorism Laws: A Threat to Political Freedom, Civil Liberties and Constitutional Rights. *Melbourne University Law Review* 26, 666.

——. 2004. Another Threat to Democratic Rights: ASIO Detentions Cloaked in Secrecy. *Alternative Law Journal* 29, 127.

——. 2005. A Disturbing Convergence? Civil Liberties and the 'War on Terror'. *Asia-Pacific Yearbook of International Humanitarian Law* 1, 63.

——. 2007. *Evgeny Pashukanis: A Critical Reappraisal.* London: Routledge-Cavendish.

——. 2009. *Calling Out the Troops: The Australian Military and Civil Unrest.* Sydney: Federation Press.

——. 2011. *Crimes Against the State: From Treason to Terrorism.* Farnham: Ashgate.

——. 2012. Global Governance Implications of Terrorism: Using UN Resolutions to Justify Abuse of Basic Rights, in *Transnational Governance: Emerging Models of Global Legal Regulation* (Head, M, Mann, S and Kozlina, S. eds). Farnham: Ashgate.

——. 2014a. Australian Paramilitary Police Kill Man in Brisbane Siege. *World Socialist Web Site*, 30 September. [Online]. Available at: https://www.wsws.org/en/articles/2014/09/30/kill-s30.html [accessed 2 September 2015].

——. 2014b. G20 Summit Held under Police-State Conditions. *World Socialist Web Site*, 17 November. [Online]. Available at: https://www.wsws.org/en/articles/2014/11/17/poli-n17.html [accessed 2 September 2015].

Heard, A. 2009. The Governor-General's Decision to Prorogue Parliament: A Chronology and Assessment. *Constitutional Forum* 18, 1–11.

Heiden, K. 1969. *Der Fuehrer: Hitler's Rise to Power.* Boston, MA: Beacon.

Heron, C. 1998. *The Workers' Revolts in Canada, 1917–1925.* Toronto: Toronto University Press.

Heuston, R. 1964. *Essays in Constitutional Law.* 2nd edn. London: Stevens.

Hill, C. 1940. *The English Revolution 1640*. London: Lawrence and Wishart.

Hoffrogge, R. 2014. Working-Class Politics in the German Revolution, in *The Revolutionary Shop Stewards and the Origins of the Council Movement* (Müller, R. ed.). Leiden: Brill.

Hogan, L. 2015. Executive Order 01.01.2015.14: Declaration of Emergency. [Online]. Available at: https://governor.maryland.gov/wp-content/uploads/2015/04/EO-4-27-2015.pdf [accessed 29 May 2015].

Holder, E. 2012. *Attorney General Eric Holder Speaks at Northwestern University School of Law*. Chicago, 5 March 2012. [Online]. Available at: http://www.justice.gov/iso/opa/ag/speeches/2012/ag-speech-1203051.html [accessed 8 May 2013].

Holdsworth, W. 1902. Martial Law Historically Considered. *Law Quarterly Review*, 18, 117.

Honig, B. 2014. Three Models of Emergency Politics. *boundary 2*, 41, 45–70.

Hooper, C. 2009. *The Tall Man: Death and Life on Palm Island*. Sydney: Penguin.

Horner, D. 2014. *The Spy Catchers: The Official History of ASIO, 1949–1963*. Sydney: Allen & Unwin.

Horton, S. 2005. The Return of Carl Schmitt. *Balkinization*, 7 November.

House of Representatives. 2006. *A Failure of Initiative: The Final Report of the Select Bipartisan Committee to Investigate the Preparation for and Response to Hurricane Katrina*. H. Rept. 109–377. [Online]. Available at http://www.katrina.house.gov/ [accessed 15 January 2015]

Jankowski, J. 2000. *Egypt: A Short History*. Oxford: Oneworld.

Johnston, P. 1990. *Re Tracey*: Some Implications for the Military–Civil Authority Relationship. *University of Western Australia Law Review*, 20, 73.

Joint Committee 2003. Joint Committee on the Draft Civil Contingencies Bill. London: Stationery Office.

Jones K. 2003. The Effect of the Homeland Security Act on Online Privacy and the Freedom of Information Act. *University of Cincinnati Law Review*, 72, 787.

Jones, K. 2012. Quebec Law Criminalizing Student Strike Threatens Basic Rights of All. *World Socialist Web Site* [Online]. Available at: http://www.wsws.org/en/articles/2012/05/queb-m19.html [accessed 13 January 2014].

Kelsen, H. 1946. *General Theory of Law and State*. Cambridge, MA: Harvard University Press.

Kershaw, I. 1998. *Hitler, 1889–1936: Hubris*. London: Penguin.

Kerr, D. 2011. Executive Power and the Theory of Its Limits: Still Evolving or Finally Settled? *Constitutional Law and Policy Review*, 13:2, 22–6.

Kolb, E. 2005. *The Weimar Republic*. London: Routledge.

Kostal, R. 2005. *A Jurisprudence of Power: Victorian Empire and the Rule of Law*. Oxford: Oxford University Press.

Kutz, C. 2005. Torture, Necessity and Existential Politics. *University of California Berkeley Public Law Research Paper* No. 870602, December.

Lackerstein, D. 2012. *National Regeneration in Vichy France: Ideas and Policies, 1930–1944*. Farnham: Ashgate.

Lane, P. 1974. *An Introduction to the Australian Constitution*. Sydney: Law Book.

Laybourn, K. 1993. *The General Strike of 1926*. Manchester: Manchester University Press.

Lazar, N. 2008. A Topography of Emergency Power, in *Emergencies and the Limits of Legality* (Ramraj, V. ed.). Cambridge: Cambridge University Press.

——. 2009. *States of Emergency in Liberal Democracies*. Cambridge: Cambridge University Press.

Lee, H.P. 1984. *Emergency Powers*. Sydney: Law Book.
Lefebvre, G. 1969. *Napoleon from 18 Brumaire to Tilsit 1799–1807*. New York: Columbia University Press.
Legras, F. 2001. 'Rubber Bullets, Tear Gas and Mass Arrests at the Summit of the Americas in Quebec City', *World Socialist Web Site*, 2 May. [Online]. https://www.wsws.org/en/articles/2001/05/queb-m02.html.
Lendrum, S. 1977. The 'Coorong Massacre': Martial Law and the Aborigines at First Settlement. *Adelaide Law Review*, 6, 26.
Lenin, V. 1964. *The State and Revolution: Collected Works*, vol. 33. London: Lawrence and Wishart.
——. 1970a. *The Proletarian Revolution and the Renegade Kautsky*. Moscow: Progress.
——. 1970b. *The State and Revolution*. Moscow: Progress.
——. 1972. *Collected Works*, vol. 20. Moscow: Progress.
——. 1977. 'Two Worlds'. *Collected Works*, vol. 16. Moscow: Progress.
——. 1987. Theses on Bourgeois Democracy and the Dictatorship of the Proletariat. *Founding the Communist International*. New York: Pathfinder.
Lerhe, E. 2004. Civil Military Relations and Aid to the Civil Power in Canada: Implications for the War on Terror. CDAI-CDFAI 7th Annual Graduate Students Symposium, RMC, 29–30 October. [Online]. Available at: http://www.cda-cdai.ca/symposia/2004 [accessed 15 August 2008].
Levinson, S. 2008. Thinking Out Loud about John Yoo (and about Carl Schmitt). *Balkinization*, 12 April.
Liberty. 2004. *Liberty's Second Reading Briefing on the Civil Contingencies Bill in the House of Lords*.
Lindsay, B. 2010. Climate of Exception: What Might a 'Climate Emergency' Mean in Law? *Federal Law Review*, 38, 255–81.
Lindsay, J. 2014. The Power to React: Review and Discussion of Canada's Emergency Measures Legislation. *International Journal of Human Rights*, 18:2, 159–77.
Lissagaray, P. 2007. *History of the Paris Commune of 1871*. St Petersburg, FL: Red and Black.
Loewenstein, K. 1937. Militant Democracy and Fundamental Rights. *American Political Science Review*, 31, 417 and 638.
——. 1938. Legislative Control of Political Extremism in European Democracies. *Columbia Law Review*, 38, 591 and 725.
Luban, D. 2011. Carl Schmitt and the Critique of Lawfare. *Case Western Reserve Journal of International Law*, 43:1/2, 457.
McBain, G. 2011. Abolishing Obsolete Crown Prerogatives Relating to the Military. *Nottingham Law Journal*, 20, 14–37.
——. 2012. Abolishing Obsolete Crown Prerogatives Relating to Martial Law, Conscription and Billeting. *International Law Research*, 1, 13–62.
McCormick, J. 1997. *Carl Schmitt's Critique of Liberalism: Against Politics as Technology*. Cambridge: Cambridge University Press.
McCulloch, J, 2001. *Blue Army, Paramilitary Policing in Australia*. Carlton South: Melbourne University Press.
McKinlay, B. 1979. *A Documentary History of the Australian Labor Movement, 1850–1975*. Melbourne: Drummond.

McPherson, J. 1990. *Abraham Lincoln and the Second American Revolution.* New York: Oxford University Press.

Maloney, S. 1997. Domestic Operations: The Canadian Approach. *Parameters*, 27:3, 135–52.

Marx, K. 1865. Address of the International Working Men's Association to Abraham Lincoln, President of the United States of America. *The Bee-Hive Newspaper* (London), No. 169, 7 November.

——. 1948. *The Civil War in France.* Moscow: Progress.

——. 1952. *The Communist Manifesto.* Moscow: Progress.

——. 1964. Provisional Rules of the Association. *The General Council of the First International, Minutes, 1864–66.* Moscow: Foreign Languages.

——. 1969a. *The 18th Brumaire of Louis Napoleon.* New York: International.

——. 1969b. Preface to *A Contribution to the Critique of Political Economy.* Marx and Engels, *Selected Works*, vol. 1. Moscow: Progress.

——. 1970a. *Critique of Hegel's Philosophy of Right.* Cambridge: Cambridge University Press.

——. 1970b. *Capital: A Critique of Political Economy*, vol 1. London: Lawrence and Wishart.

——. 1970c. *Critique of the Gotha Program.* New York: International.

——. 1976. *Capital: A Critique of Political Economy*, vol 1. London: Penguin.

——. 1993. *Grundrisse.* London: Penguin.

——. and Engels, F. 1971. *On the Paris Commune.* Moscow: Progress.

——. 1973. *The Communist Manifesto*, in *Selected Works*, vol. 1. Moscow: Progress.

——. 1975. *Selected Correspondence, 1846–1895.* Westport, CT: Greenwood.

——. 1977. *A Contribution to the Critique of Political Economy.* Moscow: Progress.

——. 1990. *Collected Works*, vol. 27. London: Lawrence and Wishart.

May, P. 1985. FEMA's Role in Emergency Management: Examining Recent Experience. *Public Administration Review*, 45, 40–48.

Meet the Press. 2014. Meet the Press Transcript – 14 December 2014. [Online]. Available at: http://www.nbcnews.com/meet-the-press/meet-press-transcript-december-14-2014-n268181 [accessed 29 May 2015].

Meier, H. 1988. *The Lesson of Carl Schmitt.* Chicago: University of Chicago.

Memorandum for the Attorney General. 2004. [Online]. Available at: http://apps.washingtonpost.com/g/documents/national/a-memo-for-the-attorney-general-may-2004/1226/ [accessed 20 December 2014].

Michigan 2012. Official Michigan General Election Results. State Proposal – 12-1: Referendum: The Emergency Manager Law. [Online]. Available at: http://miboecfr.nictusa.com/election/results/12GEN/90000001.html [accessed 24 March 2014].

Miller, G. 2014. Legal Memo Backing Drone Strike that Killed American Anwar al-Awlaki is Released. *Washington Post*, 23 June 2014.

Ministry of Defence. 2005. *Operations in the UK: The Defence Contribution to Resilience.* Joint Doctrine Publication 02.

Mommsen, H. 1998. *The Rise and Fall of Weimar Democracy.* Chapel Hill: University of North Carolina Press.

Moran, M. 2003. *The British Regulatory State: High Modernism and Hyper Innovation.* Oxford: Oxford University Press.

Muller, J. 2003. *A Dangerous Mind; Carl Schmitt in Post War European Thought.* New Haven, CT: Yale University Press.
Neumann, F. 1942. *Behemoth: The Structure and Practice of National Socialism.* London: Gollancz.
Nicholls, A. 2000. *Weimar and the Rise of Hitler.* New York: St. Martin's.
Nixon, J. 2014a. Governor Nixon Declares State of Emergency and Puts Curfew in Place to Protect Public Safety and Security. [Online]. Available at: https://governor.mo.gov/news/archive/gov-nixon-declares-state-emergency-puts-curfew-place-protect-public-safety-and-security [accessed 20 December 2014].
——. 2014b. Executive Order 14-08. [Online]. Available at: http://governor.mo.gov/news/executive-orders/executive-order-14-08 [accessed 20 December 2014].
——. 2014c. Executive Order 14-09. [Online]. Available at: http://governor.mo.gov/news/executive-orders/executive-order-14-09 [accessed 20 December 2014].
——. 2014d. Missouri National Guard to Support Law Enforcement Efforts in the Event of Unrest in the St. Louis Region, Gov. Nixon Announces. [Online]. Available at: https://governor.mo.gov/news/archive/missouri-national-guard-support-law-enforcement-efforts-event-unrest-st-louis-region [accessed 20 December 2014].
——. 2014e. Executive Order 14-14. [Online]. Available at: http://governor.mo.gov/news/executive-orders/executive-order-14-14 [accessed 20 December 2014].
——. 2014f. Gov. Nixon to Call Special Legislative Session to Provide Critical Funding for Ongoing Ferguson-Related Security Measures. [Online]. Available at: https://governor.mo.gov/news/archive/gov-nixon-call-special-legislative-session-provide-critical-funding-ongoing-ferguson [accessed 20 December 2014].
——. 2014g. Improving Conditions Allow Missouri National Guard to Begin Scaling Back Operations in St. Louis Region, Gov. Nixon Announces. [Online]. Available at: http://governor.mo.gov/news/archive/improving-conditions-allow-missouri-national-guard-begin-scaling-back-operations-st [accessed 20 December 2014].
Obama, B. 2013a. President Obama Signs Massachusetts Emergency Declaration. [Online]. Available at: http://www.whitehouse.gov/the-press-office/2013/04/17/president-obama-signs-massachusetts-emergency-declaration [accessed 20 October 2013].
——. 2013b. Statement by the President. [Online]. Available at: http://www.whitehouse.gov/the-press-office/2013/04/19/statement-president [accessed 20 October 2013].
——. 2014a. Statement by the President. [Online]. Available at: http://www.whitehouse.gov/the-press-office/2014/08/14/statement-president [accessed 20 December 2014].
——. 2014b. Statement by the President. [Online]. Available at: http://www.whitehouse.gov/the-press-office/2014/08/18/statement-president [accessed 20 December 2014].
——. 2014c. Statement by the President: Report of the Senate Select Committee on Intelligence. [Online]. Available at: https://www.whitehouse.gov/the-press-office/2014/12/09/statement-president-report-senate-select-committee-intelligence [accessed 29 May 2015].
——. 2015a. Executive Order: Blocking Property and Suspending Entry of Certain Persons Contributing to the Situation in Venezuela. [Online]. Available at: https://www.whitehouse.gov/the-press-office/2015/03/09/executive-order-blocking-property-and-suspending-entry-certain-persons-c [accessed 13 March 2015].

——. 2015b. Executive Order: Blocking the Property of Certain Persons Engaging in Significant Malicious Cyber-Enabled Activities. [Online]. Available at: https://www.whitehouse.gov/the-press-office/2015/04/01/executive-order-blocking-property-certain-persons-engaging-significant-m [accessed 6 April 2015].

O'Neill, W. 2003. Conference Report. In International Peace Academy. *Responding to Terrorism: What Role for the United Nations?* New York: International Peace Academy.

Orwell, G. 2003. *Nineteen Eighty-Four*. London: Penguin.

Oudraat, C. 2004. The Role of the Security Council, In *Terrorism and the UN: Before and After September 11* (Boulden, J. and Weiss, T. eds). Bloomington: Indiana University Press.

Oxfam. 2015. *Wealth: Having It All and Wanting More*. Oxfam Media Briefing. [Online]. Available at: http://www.oxfam.org/sites/www.oxfam.org/files/file_attachments/ib-wealth-having-all-wanting-more-190115-en.pdf [accessed 6 March 2015].

Pashukanis, E. 1978. *Law and Marxism: A General Theory*. London: Inks Links.

Paust, J. 2007. *Beyond the Law: The Bush Administration's Unlawful Responses in the 'War' on Terror*. Cambridge: Cambridge University Press.

Piccone, P. and Ulmen, G. 1987. Introduction to Carl Schmitt. *Telos*, 72.

Pierre, J. and Stephenson, G. 2008. After Katrina: A Critical Look at FEMA's Failure to Provide Housing for Victims of National Disasters. *Louisiana Law Review*, 68, 443–95.

Pollock, F. 1902. What is Martial Law? *Law Quarterly Review*, 70, 152.

Priest, D. and Arkin, W. 2010. Monitoring America. *Washington Post*. [Online]. Available at: http://projects.washingtonpost.com/top-secret-america/articles/monitoring-america/ [accessed 22 December 2010].

Radin, M. 1942. Martial Law and the State of Siege. *California Law Review*, 30, 634–47.

Ramraj, V. (ed.). 2008. *Emergencies and the Limits of Legality*. Cambridge: Cambridge University Press.

Reed, P. 2007. From the Freedmen's Bureau to FEMA: A Post-Katrina Historical, Journalistic and Literary analysis. *Journal of Black Studies*, 37:4, 555–67.

Reid, R. 1989. *The Peterloo Massacre*. London: Heinemann.

Relyea, H. 1974. *A Brief History of Emergency Powers in the United States*. Washington, DC: Government Printing Office.

Renfree, H. 1984. *The Executive Power of the Commonwealth of Australia*. Sydney: Legal Books.

Reza, S. 2006. Endless Emergency: The Case of Egypt. *New Criminal Law Review*, 10, 532–53.

Roach, K. 2008. Ordinary Laws for Emergencies and Democratic Derogation from Rights, in *Emergencies and the Limits of Legality* (Ramraj, V. ed.). Cambridge: Cambridge University Press.

Robertson, H. 1999. Darwin's Churchill: The Role of Major-General Alan Stretton in the Days Following Cyclone Tracy. *Journal of Northern Territory History*, 10, 55–8.

Roots, R. 2000. Government by Permanent Emergency: The Forgotten History of the New Deal Constitution. *Suffolk University Law Review*, 21, 259.

Rossiter, C. 1948. *Constitutional Dictatorship: Crisis Government in Modern Democracies*. Princeton, NJ: Princeton University Press.

—— and Longaker, R. 1976. *The Supreme Court and the Commander in Chief*. Ithaca, NY: Cornell University Press.

Rowe, P. and Whelan, C. (eds). 1985. *Military Intervention in Democratic Societies*. London: Croom Helm.

Rowland, L. 2014. There Is No 5-Second Rule for the First Amendment, Ferguson. *Politico*, 20 August 2014. [Online]. Available at: http://www.politico.com/magazine/story/2014/08/ferguson-first-amendment-5-second-rule-110208.html#ixzz3BmD0huNg [accessed 20 December 2014].

Rudé, G. 2005. *The Crowd in History*. London: Serif.

Salter, M. 2012. *Carl Schmitt: Law as Politics, Ideology and Strategic Myth*. Hoboken, NJ: Taylor & Francis.

Sands, P. 2006. *Lawless World*. New York: Viking.

Santosuosso, A. 2003. *Storming the Heavens: Soldiers, Emperors, and Civilians in the Roman Empire*. Boulder, CO: Westview.

Saul, B. 2006. *Defining Terrorism in International Law*. Oxford: Oxford University Press.

Savage, C. 2010. Court Dismisses a Case Asserting Torture by CIA. *New York Times*, 8 September.

Scheuerman, W. 1997. After Legal Indeterminancy: Carl Schmitt and the National Socialist Legal Order, 1933–1936. *Cardozo Law Review*, 19, 1743.

——. 2000. The Economic State of Emergency. *Cardozo Law Review*, 21, 1869.

——. 2006a. Emergency Powers and the Rule of Law after 9/11. *Journal of Political Philosophy*, 14:1, 61–84.

——. 2006a. Carl Schmitt and the Road to Abu Ghraib. *Constellations*, 13, 108–24.

Schlesinger, A. 1973. *The Imperial Presidency*. Boston, MA: Houghton Mifflin.

Schmitt, C. 1929. *Parliamentarianism and Mass Democracy*. n.p.

——. 1976. *The Concept of the Political*. New Brunswick, NJ: Rutgers University Press.

——. 1985a. *Political Theology: Four Chapters on the Concept of Sovereignty*. Cambridge, MA: MIT Press.

——. 1985b. *The Crisis of Parliamentary Democracy* (trans. Ellen Kennedy). Cambridge, MA: MIT Press.

——. 2005. *Frieden oder Pazifismus? Arbeiten zum Völkerrecht und zur internationalen Politik, 1924–1978*. Berlin: Duncker & Humblot.

Schwab, G. 1992. *Carl Schmitt Hysteria in the US: The Case of Bill Scheuerman*. Telos 91, 99–107.

Secretary of State for Justice and Lord Chancellor. 2007. *The Governance of Britain*. Cm 7170. London: Stationery Office.

Secunda, Paul M. 2011. Constitutional Contracts Clause Challenges in Public Pension Litigation. *Hofstra Labor and Employment Law Journal*, 29.

Séguin, P. 1990. *Louis Napoléon le Grand*. Paris: Bernard Grasset.

Senate Select Committee. 2014. Committee Study of the Central Intelligence Agency's Detention and Interrogation Program. [Online]. Available at: http://fas.org/irp/congress/2014_rpt/ssci-rdi.pdf [accessed 29 May 2015].

Shalom, S. 1993. Imperial Alibis: Rationalizing US Intervention after the Cold War. Boston, MA: South End.

Shirer, W. 1960. *The Rise and Fall of the Third Reich: A History of Nazi Germany*. New York: Simon and Schuster.

Simpson, A. 2004. *Human Rights and the End of Empire: Britain and the Genesis of the European Convention*. Oxford: Oxford University Press.

Socialist Equality Party. 2010. *Statement of Principles*. [Online]. Available at: http://www.wsws.org/en/articles/2010/03/sepp-m12.html [accessed 29 May 2015].

Spratt, D. and Sutton, P. 2008. *Climate Code Red: The Case for Emergency Action*. Melbourne: Scribe.

Stern, J. 2013. Egypt's New Constitution Legitimizes Coup, Enshrines Military Dictatorship. *World Socialist Web Site* [Online]. Available at: http://www.wsws.org/en/articles/2013/12/19/egyp-d19.html [accessed 13 January 2014].

Stone, G. 2004. *Perilous Times: Free Speech in Wartime*. New York: Norton.

Templeman, D. and Bergin, A. 2008. *Taking a Punch: Building a More Resilient Australia*. Barton, ACT: Australian Strategic Policy Institute.

Teschke, B. 2011. Decisions and Indecisions: Political and Intellectual Receptions of Carl Schmitt. *New Left Review*, 67, 61–95.

The 9/11 Commission. 2004. *The 9/11 Commission Report*. Washington, DC: Government Printing Office.

Thompson, G. 2010. Guantanamo and the Struggle for Due Process of Law. *Rutgers Law Review*, 63, 1195–213.

Thronson, P. 2013. Toward Comprehensive Reform of America's Emergency Law Regime. *University of Michigan Journal of Law Reform*, 46, 737–78.

Tigar, M. 2007. *Thinking About Terrorism: The Threat to Civil Liberties in Times of National Emergency*. Chicago: American Bar Association.

Travis, A. 2014. Thatcher Had Secret Plan to Use Army at Height of Miners' Strike. *The Guardian* [Online]. Available at: http://www.theguardian.com/politics/2014/jan/03/margaret-thatcher-secret-plan-army-miners-strike [accessed 13 January 2014].

Trotsky, L. 1968. *Their Morals and Ours: The Moralists and Sycophants against Marxism*. London: New Park.

——. 1969. *Writings 1932–33*. New York: Pathfinder.

——. 1970. *Germany 1931–32*. London: New Park.

——. 1971. *The Lessons of October*. London: New Park.

——. 1975. *Terrorism and Communism: A Reply to Karl Kautsky*. London: New Park.

——. 1991. *The Revolution Betrayed: What Is the Soviet Union and Where Is It Going?* Detroit: Labor.

——. 1997. *Writings of Leon Trotsky, 1929*. New York: Pathfinder.

Turner, H. 1996. *Hitler's Thirty Days to Power*. New York: Addison-Wesley.

Turner, I. 1969. *Sydney's Burning (An Australian Political Conspiracy)*. Melbourne: Heinemann.

Tushnet, M. 2005. Controlling Executive Power in the War on Terrorism. *Harvard Law Review*, 118, 2673.

Twomey, A. 2010. Pushing the Boundaries of Executive Power: *Pape*, the Prerogative and Nationhood Powers. *Melbourne University Law Review*, 34, 313–43.

United Kingdom. 1951. House of Commons. *Parliamentary Debates*, 21 March, 2410.

United Kingdom. 1983–84. *Parliamentary Papers*, 17.

USDC. 2015. *American Civil Liberties v. Central Intelligence Agency*. [Online]. Available at: http://pdfserver.amlaw.com/nlj/cia_report_20150520.pdf [accessed 29 May 2015].

Vad, E. 2003. Freund oder Feind: Zur Aktualität Carl Schmitts. *Sezession*, 1 (April). [Online]. Available at: http://www.sezession.de.

Vatikiotis, P. 1992. *The History of Modern Egypt: From Muhammad Ali to Mubarak*. 4th edn. Baltimore, MA: Johns Hopkins University Press.

Vinx, L. 2015. *The Guardian of the Constitution: Hans Kelsen and Carl Schmitt on the Limits of Constitutional Law*. Cambridge: Cambridge University Press.

Wade, E. and Phillips, G. 1970. *Constitutional Law*. 8th edn. London: Longmans.

Walker, C. 2014a. Legal Perspectives on Contingencies and Resilience in an Environment of Constitutionalism: An Overview. *International Journal of Human Rights*, 18:2, 119–26.

——. 2014b. The Governance of Emergency Arrangements. *International Journal of Human Rights*, 18:2, 211–27.

—— and Broderick, J. 2006. *The Civil Contingencies Act 2004: Risk, Resilience, and the Law in the United Kingdom*. Oxford: Oxford University Press.

Wall Street Journal. 2014. Hundreds of Police Killings Are Uncounted in Federal Stats. *Wall Street Journal*, 3 December. [Online]. Available at: http://online.wsj.com/articles/hundreds-of-police-killings-are-uncounted-in-federal-statistics-1417577504 [accessed 20 December 2014].

Weekend Australian. 1995. Looking Back at the Dismissal. *Weekend Australian*, 11–12 November.

Wheeler-Bennett, J. 1967. *The Nemesis of Power*. London: Macmillan.

Whelan, C. 1985. Military Intervention in Democratic Societies: The Role of Law, in *Military Intervention in Democratic Societies* (Rowe, P. and Whelan, C. eds). London: Croom Helm.

White, J. 2013. Detroit Bankruptcy Ruling Triggers Calls for Pension Cuts across the US. *World Socialist Web Site*. [Online]. Available at: https://www.wsws.org/en/articles/2013/12/06/detr-d06.html [accessed 24 March 2014].

White House. 2001. Address to a Joint Session of Congress and the American People. [Online]. Available at: http://georgewbush-whitehouse.archives.gov/news/releases/2001/09/20010920-8.html [accessed 14 June 2011].

Williams, G. 2001. *Republic of Fiji v Prasad*: Introduction. *Melbourne Journal of International Law*, 2, 144.

Wills, G. 1984. *Cincinnatus: George Washington and the Enlightenment*. Garden City, NY: Doubleday.

Windeyer, V. 1979. Opinion. Appendix 9 of Hope, R. *Protective Security Review Report*. Canberra: Australian Government Publishing Service (AGPS).

Winterton, G. 1998. The 1998 Convention: A Reprise of 1898? *University of New South Wales Law Journal*, 21:3, 856–67.

——. 2003. 1975: The Dismissal of the Whitlam Government, in *Australian Constitutional Landmarks* (Lee, H. ed.). Cambridge: Cambridge University Press.

Wolfowitz, P. 2004. *Memorandum for the Secretary of the Navy: Order establishing Combatant Status Review Tribunal*. 7 July 2004. [Online]. Available at http://www.defense.gov/news/Jul2004/d20040707review.pdf [accessed 15 January 2015].

Wolin, R. 1990. Carl Schmitt, Political Existentialism and the Total State. *Theory and Society*, 19, 389–416.

Workers News. 1975. *The Canberra Coup*. Sydney: Labor Press.

World Socialist Web Site. 2005. *Hurricane Katrina: Social Consequences and Political Lessons*. Detroit: Mehring.

Yoo, J. 2001. *The President's Constitutional Authority to Conduct Military Operations against Terrorists and Nations Supporting Them.* Office of Legal Counsel Memorandum Opinion, 25 September. [Online]. Available at: http://www.fas.org/irp/agency/doj/olc092501.html [accessed 11 February 2015].
—— and Bybee, J. 2002. Memorandum for John Rizzo. [Online]. Available at: http://www.fas.org/irp/agency/doj/olc/zubaydah.pdf [accessed 11 February 2015].
Young, T. 1976. *Incitement to Disaffection.* London: Cobden Trust.

Index